Therapeutic Residential Care
For Children and Youth

Child Welfare Outcomes
Series Editor: Harriet Ward, Centre for Child and Family Research, Loughborough University, UK
This authoritative series draws from original research and current policy debates to help social work managers, policy makers and researchers to understand and improve the outcomes of services for children and young people in need. Taking an evidence-based approach, these books include children's experiences and analysis of costs and effectiveness in their assessment of interventions, and provide guidance on how to develop more effective policy, practice, and training.

other books in the series

Therapeutic Residential Care
For Children and Youth

Developing Evidence-Based International Practice

Edited by James K. Whittaker,
Jorge F. del Valle and Lisa Holmes

Foreword by Robbie Gilligan

Jessica Kingsley *Publishers*
London and Philadelphia

First published in 2015
by Jessica Kingsley Publishers
73 Collier Street
London N1 9BE, UK
and
400 Market Street, Suite 400
Philadelphia, PA 19106, USA

www.jkp.com

Library of Congress Cataloging in Publication Data
Therapeutic residential care for children and youth : developing
evidence-based international practice /
edited by James K. Whittaker, Jorge F. Valle and Lisa Holmes ; foreword by Robbie Gilligan.
pages cm
Includes index.
ISBN 978-1-84905-963-3 (alk. paper)
1. Child psychotherapy--Residential treatment. 2. Adolescent
psychotherapy--Residential treatment. 3.
Child mental health services. 4. Problem children--Institutional
care. I. Whittaker, James K. II. Fernandez
del Valle, Jorge. III. Holmes, Lisa.
RJ504.5.T48 2014
616.89'140835--dc23
2014008691

British Library Cataloguing in Publication Data
A CIP catalogue record for this book is available from the British Library

ISBN 978 1 84905 792 9
eISBN 978 0 85700 833 6

Printed and bound in Great Britain

Contents

List of Tables

List of Boxes

List of Figures

Foreword

Robbie Gilligan

This book makes an important contribution to one of the critical issues in the field of child welfare. It engages with many of the challenges of caring for very troubled young people who require resource-intensive support. It grapples with concerns that will be instantly recognisable to people working in relevant child welfare services. Indeed, many of the topics will also resonate with the experience of people working with high-need young people – and adults – in related fields such as juvenile justice, mental health, disability and beyond.

Troubled young people demand attention on the grounds of their manifest needs, but also because of the impact that their challenging behaviours frequently have on families, communities and wider society. The very troubled young people who are the focus of this book have high-intensity special needs. Typically, they require a response after families and community services have admitted defeat in meeting these needs. The young person often emerges into view in the midst of a crisis that calls for urgent attention. What form should that attention take? What is likely to be most effective in responding? This book enters this territory. The editors – James Whittaker, Jorge F. del Valle and Lisa Holmes – have done a wonderful job in gathering together a set of international experts who bring different perspectives to bear on addressing such questions. They look at the issues through a range of geographical, cultural and disciplinary lenses. They also approach the issues from the vantage point of different experiences of researching – and working in – systems and institutions serving troubled young people. This makes for a very rich (and rare) *mix* of evidence, insights and (informed) opinions. It also offers a very distinctive immersion in the issues – where else will one find such a diverse and informed briefing on critical issues in serving high-need troubled young people? Too often, thinking and debate in relation to troubled young people occur in 'silos' of isolated thinking; people in different disciplines, systems and national contexts fail to talk with, and listen to, each other. This book tries to break down such silos and open up to the reader shared discussion and reflection. It should also be noted that the book draws on expertise from many countries beyond the English-speaking world, again, a rare treat.

The editors have a number of motives for embarking on this book project. They want to identify and promote good practice in serving high-need young people. They want to harvest international expertise to learn lessons from different cultural and institutional systems in a range of countries. But they also want to assert the importance of taking residential care seriously as a potentially key resource in the range of responses to troubled young people. The broad field of residential child care has taken a battering, reputationally, in many countries because of a succession of scandals and failings – historical and current – that have commanded huge media coverage and caused great public concern. There is no question that there have been terrible scandals and failings. There have been strident critics of residential care. A striking example of such criticism is reflected in the Stockholm Declaration on Children and Residential Care (2003) that argues for, at best, a residual role for residential provision. But while accepting that there are real grounds for concern, it seems important not to end up throwing the baby out with the bathwater.

Courageously, and correctly, the editors are asserting the need for a more nuanced approach. They suggest that *residential child care* is such a blanket and catch-all term that it is almost meaningless. There is, in their view, a need to unpack the term and see what elements in the residential care 'offering' may be positive and sustainable, for what purposes they remain so and under what conditions. This book represents an important and sophisticated contribution to this effort of reclaiming the potentially positive elements of residential care. The editors seek to take the ambition of residential child care beyond the concept of a tainted and slightly embarrassing fallback response. Therapeutic Residential Care (TRC), as they term it, deserves serious consideration and debate – as an option of positive choice in certain circumstances. It does so not only because of evidence assembled here and elsewhere, but also because the repertoire of service responses to troubled young people urgently needs development. We are not so awash with viable prospects that we can discount any form of possible provision with serious potential. We cannot afford to discard any reasonable option in service provision and development. TRC has a strong claim to being taken seriously as one element in a suite of responses to high-need troubled young people. This book does not claim to prove the case, but it certainly proves that there is a case that deserves to be seriously considered.

The editors and many of the contributors have strong ties to the residential child care tradition. But they are not uncritical. They bring a reassuring rigour to their description and analysis. They are critical friends of the cause of TRC. They appreciate that it is in the best interests of the young people, their families and those who devote their lives to the practice and study of TRC that hard questions are valued and addressed. This book marks a very considerable step forward in that process of recognising and addressing some of the hard questions. Tackling those questions is a major project, well beyond the scope of one book. But this book represents a hugely valuable starting point. It helps to assemble many of the key elements of an agenda for future work. It makes progress in developing a more robust base for developing therapeutic and evaluative capacity in the field of TRC for children and young people.

Whether a novice or a veteran in the field, the reader will find much within these pages to stimulate thinking and understanding. They may find provocation – and reassurance – at various points. What is certain is that they will look differently on many issues because they have read these chapters. I would also be confident that copies of this book will become well-thumbed as loyal readers return for refreshment and stimulation in the face of the challenging issues posed by understanding and serving the needs of troubled young people day in, day out. Researcher, policy maker and practitioner will find food for thought here.

In writing this foreword, I salute the approach and the achievement of the book. The critical friends have honoured the positive aspects of the tradition of residential child care. They have also done justice to their claim that the potential of TRC deserves attention. I see myself as a critical friend of the critical friends. My task is to invite the reader to engage, to sell the case for what the book has to offer, to tempt the reader to read and reread. I also see myself as having a quiet word in the reader's ear – flagging what is in the book – and celebrating that. But I also go on to point out issues that may need attention – that have proved beyond the scope of an already ambitious book or have received necessarily limited coverage. This is to ensure the reader feels they have had some kind of briefing before engaging with the case the book is making and the evidence it is producing. What does the reader need to take into account in assessing what the editors and authors are saying?

TRC aims to make a real difference. It will be labour intensive; it will require an investment of skilled people. Such an investment will not come cheap. The advocates of TRC may have faith in its potential, but those who provide the money (taxpayers, insurance companies, philanthropists etc.) will want *evidence* that it works, not just heartfelt claims. Does TRC do what it says? Does it achieve what its proponents assert? Answering these questions is no simple matter. For one moment, let's assume that we have a programme that has been rigorously examined and found to be effective with young people with certain profiles according to widely agreed criteria. Success draws attention and funders come knocking on the door, anxious to share in the glow of that success and glad to spend their money on something useful. They are saying that the money is available to run the successful programme many times over in a whole range of different locations. Again, to take up this opportunity is no simple matter. It may not be easy to reproduce the right mix of ingredients every time, for example the key qualities of leadership and staff skill and commitment that underpinned the first success. To use an example from the world of restaurants, it is a big challenge to build the reputation of a high-quality restaurant, but an even bigger one to repeat the same successful formula in many different places. It can be done, but there is no guarantee of success. The level of skill and commitment and that 'X factor' of success may not be easy to repeat in many different places, each of which will inevitably bring different conditions and exert subtly different pressures. Restaurants and human service programmes are not like laboratories working under highly controlled conditions. They have to perform in the real world, challenging and exciting as that is. They have to be able to operate in and adapt to a rapidly evolving scene.

Running a therapeutic residential programme requires a considerable investment of knowhow and therefore money. The money and knowhow to deliver on the potential of TRC do not walk through the door. People have to be persuaded; people have to be trained. A case has to be made. Let's look now at some of the issues that case has to address. These issues include (hard) questions of effectiveness, cost and replicability. Does TRC deliver? What does it cost and does that represent value? Where it looks good, can it be rolled out to many places beyond the original site? There is also the considerable matter of clarifying whether we are actually talking about the same thing when we use the phrase *Therapeutic Residential Care.*

Does Therapeutic Residential Care work?

Arguably, there has been one great historic error by the proponents of residential child care generally (and, by extension, proponents of TRC specifically). This has been to *over*estimate (or overstate) the influence of the residential episode in the child's life and to *under*estimate the influence of the world outside the setting, before, during and after the residential episode. It is a challenge to achieve change in one or more key aspects of the child's profile between T1 (time of entry to residential setting and programme of care) and T2 (time of exit from same). It is an even greater challenge to achieve *enduring* change – change that persists over time well after the young person's exit when measured later at long intervals at T3, T4 and so on. And in thinking of change, the focus needs not only to be on change in the profile of the child or young person in isolation, but also on change in the surrounding circumstances or ecology of the child. This is highly relevant since it is this ecology that may have cultivated and sustained the difficulties behind the young person's placement and may threaten to compromise or undermine subsequent change efforts. Family-systems thinking underlines for us that change in the child is unlikely to 'take' or endure, if the circumstances triggering difficulties are not themselves also subject to change. This point about the historic 'error' of residential care is especially relevant for residential care that lays claim to being 'therapeutic', since efforts at therapy beg questions about outcomes, focus of attention, theory of change, intended and actual impact and so on.

These questions in turn raise complex issues about the extent and nature of such change – how it is to be assessed/measured and how often etc. A further point is that knowing that something works is not the same as knowing *why* it works – a point to which we return below. There is also another important – and challenging – point to bear in mind. Where intervention has indeed been shown to have positive effects, these gains may not always become evident in the short term. It may sometimes be the case that there may be longer-term 'sleeper' effects involved that may be hard to identify, since they only emerge or are only observable after a certain – possibly long – period of time has elapsed. A related point is that such gains may only come to be activated under certain relevant conditions in the future, and it may be quite difficult to identify those trigger conditions. These are all issues with which many of the chapters in the book are grappling – offering useful evidence and insights that can help increase our understanding.

If it works, why does it work?

One of the abiding motivations for forming the residential world in the care setting has been to separate and insulate the child from the 'real world'. Protected from the malign influences of the real world, the child could be helped to thrive. Without competition from malign influences, residential care could weave its magic. All very good, if this indeed proved to be the case. But even where it did, there was the under-recognised reality that the child had to go back at some point to the 'big bad world'. In the long run, insulation risked becoming self-defeating. The 'big lie' or big fib of residential care was that such massive 'inoculation' of the child could occur in the care setting, that the child or young person would thereby be rendered strong enough to resist any harm that would fall their way once out again in, and exposed to, 'the world outside'. Yet, as in inoculation in medicine, the inoculation would have to remain effective for a decent and often quite long period of time. But the evidence generally was that such dreams of inoculation were frequently dashed. The effect of successful 'treatment' gradually wore off and the 'symptoms' that precipitated placement would gradually reassert themselves.

While the term inoculation may not be explicitly used in residential care, the underlying concept emerges implicitly in many practices and debates. If we return to the home turf of inoculation – medicine – we know that inoculation, in practice, requires, an element of controlled *exposure* to the relevant toxin as part of the treatment. Yet, traditionally, residential care has had more of an instinct for insulation rather than inoculation. Residential staff could exert influence in the inner world of the care setting, whereas they seemed less 'at home', less engaged, less equipped and less influential in the outer world – in the world outside.

While separation and insulation might historically have been understood to be the key mechanisms of enduring change, there is a gradually growing understanding that any recipe for successful change in a young person requires a more complex set of efforts. What may comprise the basis for successful intervention is beginning to emerge from specific well-designed and evaluated programmes or projects, some of which are reported in this book. The future lies in models of TRC that embrace serious work not just with the child in the care setting, but also with key players – family members and others – in the social ecology from which the young person came, and crucially to which they will return.

Yet, even if we seem close to knowing some of the key ingredients for success, how important is it that we follow the recipe very strictly? In the world of television chefs, viewers may become deeply frustrated by the chefs who seem so carefree (or careless) about the precise mix of ingredients and processes in their given recipe. The frustration for the viewer is that these same 'careless' chefs still seem able to deliver a magnificent result. If we know the recipe in TRC, must we follow that recipe slavishly or can we afford to be more relaxed and follow the spirit rather than the letter of the 'dish' as in the case of the 'careless' (but extraordinarily gifted and confident) celebrity chefs?

To move our analogies from the world of cooking to the world of sport, must TRC offer something beyond well-intentioned and possibly well-trained staff 'playing it as they see it' as they deal with the challenges and contingencies of the care environment day in, day out? Can TRC flow from a well-intentioned (and well-informed) care that is pragmatic and benign, that is principled rather than programmed? Or must TRC operate more like a very well-drilled sports team playing to an extremely formulaic pattern, responding in well-rehearsed and stylised moves to the 'plays' unfolding before them? To continue this analogy, different teams and coaches may emphasise different styles while still adhering closely to a preordained and pre-structured approach. Is this highly prescribed approach the hallmark of TRC in its different variations, or is there room in the TRC space for the well-informed intuition as well as highly guided practice?

There are no easy answers to some of these very real questions. The content of the book reflects different views. Some authors describe carefully developed models, many of which have been impressively tested. But there has also been caution advised on two counts: first, how difficult it is to stick to the 'programme', how demanding it is to adhere consistently to all the conditions of the programme and to do so over the long term. Second, there is the issue of how close the adherence should be – back to this issue of the interpretation of recipes. While clearly some authors argue for conformity, the case is also argued for a more expansive view. In this alternative view, the actual practice in work with young people needs to be *systematic* (true to well-informed principles) rather than *programmatic* (meticulously implementing the detail of a care curriculum).

If we know how and why it works, can we afford it?

In French travel guides a phrase is used frequently to signal approval – *bon rapport prix-qualité*. Translated, the phrase means a good rapport or balance between price and quality. In reality, that is an important principle to guide business endeavour or consumer behaviour in any field. And so it also applies in TRC. Part of sustainability is achieving a good balance between cost and quality. Necessarily labour-intensive, TRC will be vulnerable to cost pressures.

Costs are an important constraint. Otherwise, well-developed (and therefore likely to be resource-intensive and costly) models of TRC are set to remain an exclusive concept accessible, in practice, to very few.

Those few are able to access a place directly thanks to their own resources, indirectly via insurance or with the support of an unusually wealthy and generous public authority. In some jurisdictions, the public authorities may ensure accessibility for those in need; in others, insurance or philanthropy may offer access for some. But the cost of TRC is likely to remain a real barrier to provision and access in many contexts.

In terms of costs, it is important not only to know aggregate annual costs of a centre or a programme, but also to have a good sense of the costs of different elements of a programme. Traditionally, this has been a weakness in social care – and child welfare. It has not always been possible to calculate accurately the relative cost of different choices or elements in the care mix. In this collection, one of the leading scholars in this area in social care and a co-editor, Lisa Holmes, contributes a valuable chapter ensuring an angle that is often missing from discussions of care provision is properly represented.

What are some of the challenges facing Therapeutic Residential Care?

The impact of an increasingly demanding regulatory framework

As a consequence of more rigorous regulation, monitoring and scholarship, TRC centres or programmes are no longer shaped by the values of a charismatic leader, or their imagination, experience or ambition. Just as baking a cake and selling it on in any quantity is no longer a simple process in many countries because of regulation, there is also less room for the energetic pioneer who previously might have spontaneously launched into a venture to found a new centre. Residential centres now operate in an ever-more heavily regulated environment. In many ways, inspirational, charismatic leaders have been replaced by representatives of regulators (and funders), who lay out parameters for practice and self-monitoring. Management teams at centres, in many contexts, must spend a lot of time worshipping before the god of compliance. This may make sense, but it is important never to lose a critical perspective in appraisal of systems. Compliance is a close relative of caution, so it may be difficult for innovation and imagination to gain access in a house where compliance has charge. The regulators who stipulate the requirements, and their staff who interpret levels of compliance and performance, may not always have the 'hours on the clock' to support fully informed, nuanced and appreciative judgements, which can so often be important.

Responding to the lived experience of children and young people

What is the lived experience of care for the children and young people receiving TRC? This is not a question that traditionally has received a lot of attention in the field. Yet the lived experience of young people receiving care is an important source of evidence for regulators, researchers and those seeking to improve the theory and practice of TRC. Attention to the children's world in care settings is an essential way of protecting the interests and rights of the children involved, protecting them from abuses of informal power by peers and of formal power by staff. Accessing the children's world is not a simple matter for adults, since it is in so many ways beneath the gaze of adults. But the first step to access is a strong commitment to the value of the child's perspective on the care experience.

How to avoid history repeating itself

The evidence base for TRC is a work in progress. While it is hardly a fatal charge against TRC to state this, it is important to assess how the field of TRC responds to this reality. Medicine has built what might be termed an extensive 'architecture of scepticism' to defend itself and its patients against too many blind leaps of faith. This architecture of scepticism – when functioning properly – builds in layers of questioning of new and established practices. Is the field of TRC developing credible equivalents? Given the longer history of the broad residential child care field, it seems vital that such questioning becomes deeply embedded in the culture of TRC. This book can help to resource the kind of professional curiosity and openness that such a new culture requires.

How to cope with the 'competition'

TRC may sometimes seem a little like part of a longstanding business with an established business model that finds it hard to cope with new competition – with new kids on the block who operate with a quite different model. The airline industry may be a useful analogy. The old-style airlines found it hard to cope with the new, low-cost carriers. Will TRC be able to cope with the competition from Multi-Dimensional Treatment Foster Care (MTFC) and related initiatives? In many ways, this remains to be seen. TRC may have to mimic key aspects of MTFC – especially by becoming more multi-dimensional in its own approach. Doing this will have cost implications, which raises big questions. TRC will face big challenges to demonstrate effectiveness within feasible cost levels.

Conclusion

While residential care has had a bad press, the contributors to this book underline that there are a number of reasons why we must continue to explore the potential of a specialist residential care that is well conceived and delivered. There are many reasons for such a view – the considerable needs of troubled young people who need successful placements, the challenges of finding a sufficient range of responsive and effective service models and slivers of evidence that suggest that under the right conditions TRC may be able to offer valuable help to troubled young people.

If it is to 'sell' its role – its potential – it has to recognise and address certain key challenges – challenges arising from history and current practices and challenges arising from the emerging policy environment. It has to develop evidence that answers certain challenges. My task in this foreword has been to suggest some of the challenges that the proponents of the case have to address. This book represents an important and exciting engagement with these challenges.

Robbie Gilligan
Professor of Social Work and Social Policy,
Trinity College, Dublin

Acknowledgments

Together we would like to thank Professor Harriet Ward of Loughborough University, Editor of the *Child Welfare Outcomes Series* for her encouragement of this current project and for providing enduring support, keen insight and friendship over many years. Steve Jones, Commissioning Editor, Sarah Hull and Kitty Walker of Jessica Kingsley Publishers offered useful suggestions and help throughout the entire editorial process. We are in debt to Robbie Gilligan of Trinity College, Dublin, both for his insightful Foreword and his leadership contributions to international child and youth care over several decades. Laura Dale and Harriet Lowe, and other team members of the Centre for Child and Family Research at Loughborough University, worked wonders in transforming the contributions of our many authors into an integrated manuscript. Given the collective nature of this present effort, we wish to acknowledge at the outset the patience, good humor and commitment of our distinguished international contributors in meeting deadlines, revising their chapters and providing thoughtful critical commentary on the work of colleagues. We are in their debt.

James Whittaker wishes to thank Richard Small for his multiple contributions to this volume, as well as for providing valuable insights and critical reviews of all phases of our collective project. His unique blend of clinical, administrative and research expertise for nearly 30 years as Executive Director of the Walker School, in Needham, Massachusetts—a sentinel agency in Therapeutic Residential Care (TRC) where I began my own career many years ago—has been an enduring source of support and critical insight to me for decades. I wish also to thank my colleagues in IAOBER—the International Association of Outcome-Based Evaluation and Research in Family and Children's Services—under the leadership of Tiziano Vecchiato, Cinzia Canali and Anthony Maluccio, for creating multiple opportunities over the years for cross-national dialogue and international exchange on matters relating to child welfare services outcome research. In particular, I wish to recognize the valuable insights gained from members of IAOBER's residential services work group including Colette McAuley, Nina Biehal, Laura Palareti, Chiara Berti, June Thoburn, Frank Ainsworth, Trish McNamara, Pat Hansen and Anat Zeira. Peter Pecora—IAOBER as well as University of Washington colleague—has contributed much to my vision for child and family services and outcome research for nearly 35 years. I am also in debt to my many colleagues on the past and present EUSARF board—*European Scientific Association for Research on Residential and Family Care*—for their many insights on TRC and on child and family services research. These include Walter Hellinckx, Paul Durning, Hans Grietens, Erik Knorth, David Quinton, Robbie Gilligan, Harriet Ward, Jim Anglin, Jorge Fernández del Valle, Andy Kendrick and others. Finally, I wish to thank the many colleagues from the worlds of practice and academic research who have stimulated and shaped my vision of TRC over many years. These include the singular pioneering contributors such as Al Trieschman, Fritz Redl, David Wineman, Nicholas Hobbs and Martin Wolins along with other colleagues such as Edward "Ted" Teather, Jim Mann, Edward Overstreet, Lonnie Phillips, Larry Brendtro, Jerome Beker and Sue Ann Savas whose passion for high-quality TRC stimulated, shaped and sustained my own.

Jorge Fernández del Valle wishes to thank all colleagues of the Child and Family Research Group (GIFI in Spanish) at the University of Oviedo for all their commitment and excellent research work carried out during the last 15 years in the field of residential and foster care, because this is the source of experience and knowledge that allows us to be involved in this book. Indeed, this work wouldn't be possible without the support, funding and close collaboration of many regional and local governments in Spain such as the Principality of Asturias, Castilla y León, Tenerife, Guipúzcoa, Extremadura, Mallorca, Cantabria and Murcia. Finally, I also thank my colleagues of EUSARF and INTRAC (International Research Network on Transitions to Adulthood from Care) for giving me the chance to share international experiences and enlarge my views on childcare.

Lisa Holmes wishes to thank all colleagues at the Centre for Child and Family Research, Loughborough University. In particular thanks to Harriet Ward and Jean Soper who were involved in the initial development of the Cost Calculator research. Thanks also to her close colleagues currently working on the Costs and Outcomes research programme (Samantha McDermid and Helen Trivedi) for graciously supporting her desire to be involved in this project. Lisa also wishes to thank all the research participants—both practitioners and service users—who have given their time and commitment to research reported in this book.

CHAPTER 1

Introduction
The Current Landscape of
Therapeutic Residential Care

James K. Whittaker, Jorge F. del Valle and Lisa Holmes

Why a book about Therapeutic
Residential Care? Why now?

In their closing essay to a recent insightful and cogent volume on residential care in international perspective, three of the contributors—Mark Courtney (US), Talal Dolev (Israel) and Robbie Gilligan (Ireland)—set the direction for the work that lies ahead:

> As the role of residential care within the child welfare systems in each country continues to evolve, the authors raise a number of questions about the efficacy both of residential care and its alternatives... As we search internationally for models of care appropriate to meeting the needs of at-risk children, this volume tells us that many of the dilemmas we confront and the solutions we imagine are shared across cultural and geographic boundaries, and across time. It highlights the importance of developing a body of evidence to support our care choices. (Courtney and Iwaniec 2009, p.208)

We agree. In fact, this present volume is in no small measure inspired by Courtney and Iwaniec and their distinguished international contributors, several of whom including Mark Courtney, Robbie Gilligan and Frank Ainsworth are contributors to this book. Among the many topics of vital concern in their volume are the potential effects of sweeping reform statements, like the 2003 Stockholm Declaration, which cites "indisputable evidence that institutional care has negative consequences for individual children and for society at large" (quoted in Courtney and Iwaniec 2009, p.xi). Even if one clarifies that the major focus of the conference that produced this declaration was long-term institutional care, as opposed to, say, purposeful, short-term Therapeutic Residential Care (TRC), the declaration also speaks authoritatively about using residential provision solely as a "last resort." We believe the presumption that the only pathway for children and youth with high-resource needs and their families to access intensive therapeutic residential service is through repeated failure at other points on the service spectrum is one that needs to be critically examined. We hope that fresh insights garnered from empirical research and careful analyses of TRC viewed in cross-national perspectives will help to build that "body of evidence" and thus inform future policy, practice and research priorities in this vital, yet ever-more contested area of service.

What we mean by "Therapeutic Residential Care"

For the purposes of this international review volume and building on Whittaker (2005), we offer the following nominal definition for "Therapeutic Residential Care":

> Therapeutic Residential Care involves the planful use of a purposefully constructed, multi-dimensional living environment designed to enhance or provide treatment, education, socialization, support and protection to children and youth with identified mental health or behavioral needs in partnership with their families and in collaboration with a full spectrum of community-based formal and informal helping resources.

TRC is typically delivered through community-based group homes utilizing community schools or through campus-based residential treatment centers that provide on-site school programs. We view TRC in either form as a specialized segment of residential or group care services for children. While sharing certain common setting characteristics, these services vary greatly in treatment philosophies and practices, including their purposes and the intensity and duration of interventions provided. We are well aware that discussions of "residential care" often lump together many of these services in ways that blur and confuse key distinctions. Hence, while there are a wide variety of group care arrangements in the international service arena, our specific focus here will be on those purposefully designed as complex interventions to meet the needs of high-resource using children and youth.

Our book proceeds from the assumption that TRC as an intervention has suffered from a kind of benign neglect in model and theory development, including demonstration research and development of protocols for practice and training. The resultant imprecision of the "therapeutic residential approach," coupled with a reflexive aversion to anything perceived as "institutional" and heightened by often legitimate concerns about the potential for child maltreatment and iatrogenic effects in group settings, along with cost disparities when compared with other forms of intervention, have called into serious question the uses of TRC as anything but a last-resort alternative. This has been particularly the case in the US, but it is a theme that resonates in other developed countries with complex social service systems as well. As an example, as the critical mental health needs of children presenting for out-of-home care services are better understood, there is an increasing urgency to determine the full spectrum of intensive services available to meet their needs.

In international scientific literature there has long been evidence of the higher frequency with which children on child welfare programs present mental health disorders, by comparison with the rest of the population (Burns *et al.* 2004; Clausen *et al.* 1998; Farmer *et al.* 2001; Garland, Landsverk and Lau 2003; Heflinger, Simpkins and Combs-Orme 2000; Landsverk *et al.* 2006; Pecora *et al.* 2009a; Tarren-Sweeney and Hazell 2006). In the case of Europe, recent French data indicate that 48 percent of children in residential care present some type of disorder (Bronsard *et al.* 2011). In the UK research data have yielded similar results indicating ratios of four to one for children with disorders with respect to the general population (Ford *et al.* 2007; Nicholas, Roberts and Wurr 2003; Sempik, Ward and Darker 2008). In Spain, Sainero, Bravo and del Valle (2014) have found that 26 percent of children in residential care in an autonomous community of Spain were receiving mental health services. Similar conclusions have been reached by studies carried out in other European countries (EUROARC 1998; Holtan *et al.* 2005; Hukkanen *et al.* 2005).

In the light of these data, better understanding of the essential elements and the utilization of therapeutic services should be a priority. Nevertheless, international research shows that many children with substantial behavioral and emotional problems are not receiving the necessary attention (Burns *et al.* 2004; Farmer *et al.* 2001; Pecora *et al.* 2009a; Tarren-Sweeney 2010), and that there is commonly a lack of clear criteria for referral to therapeutic services and a failure to use rigorous detection instruments.

We believe that properly designed and monitored TRC represents *one* critical form of specialized mental health treatment. Due to the high prevalence of mental health disorders in children in need, the problem of defining *who* is going to be referred to those specialized resources becomes a key question for future research. As but one example, recent research from Spain highlights the importance of intellectual disability as a co-occurring condition among the population of children presently receiving TRC (Sainero *et al.* 2013): see also del Valle *et al.* in Chapter 2, Section 1 of this volume.

As noted, we believe that a well-specified, evidence-informed and closely evaluated TRC alternative can and should have a place among the array of family- and community-centered intensive interventions that are available to high-resource using children, youth and their families. Our aim is to point the way forward—in understanding key child needs, model programs and practices, training, evaluation and organizational support structures, successful pathways for engaging families as partners, preparing for transitions from the residential experience and accurately forecasting and monitoring service costs. We believe, finally, that through analysis of carefully selected cross-national examples and critical commentaries, we can begin to shed some light on what an effective, humane and replicable TRC intervention should consist of. Where lacunae persist in the present knowledge base, we hope that the critical questions raised in each chapter can be formulated into a future cross-national research agenda for TRC, something that is sorely needed if we are to substitute evidence for ideology in service planning. Ultimately, we hope this present volume brings us some small measure closer to a more precise understanding of the critical components of TRC, and that these can then be rigorously evaluated and compared empirically with other evidence-based intervention alternatives. Let the data lead us where it will.

Our aims for this volume

Through carefully selected cross-national examples, this volume seeks to identify and critically examine promising programs and practices that will enhance a wide range of therapeutic residential services for troubled children, youth and their families. Our goal is to advance the search for the critical elements in an empirically based, effective and humane TRC service. We seek to point the way forward to a TRC sector, which is, at once, firmly embedded in the values, and principles of family support, cultural relevancy and community-centered intervention. We anticipate that such a service will be used sparingly and judiciously and only for high-need children and youth with multiple challenges in active collaboration with the full suite of empirically based family-

and community-centered programs that have recently enriched our contemporary practice response.

Locating Therapeutic Residential Care in the broader array of child and family services[1]

Group residential care for children remains a service in flux. Echoes of the century-old debate about the relative merits of foster-family care and group care captured in the classic monograph by Wolins and Piliavin (1964) find current expression in the previously noted volume by Mark Courtney, Derota Iwaniec and their contributors (2009) on the current state of group child care viewed in cross-national perspective. Concerns about effectiveness, child safety and costs continue within the services research community, as well as in discussions of best practices and policies for children and families (Whittaker 2011). For example, recently expressed concerns about "deviancy training"—the subtle and unintended consequence of reinforcing anti-social behavior through the congregation of acting-out (delinquent) youth in group treatment conditions of all kinds—continue to surface, though recent rigorous analyses by Weiss *et al.* (2005) cast doubt on such claims (Dishion, McCord and Poulin 1999; Poulin, Dishion and Burraston 2001). Deviancy training provides but one example of a critical question concerning therapeutic group care deserving of further carefully designed empirical research.

While it is difficult to summarize current trends in TRC viewed cross-nationally, a general trajectory seems to be away from residential services and towards community and family-centered alternatives for those children and youth in need of intensive services.

While many factors explain this preference, a central issue is the lack of empirical support for residential treatment. The US experience offers some useful points of reference. For example, a research review prepared for the last US Surgeon General's Report on Child Mental Health observing the limitations of current research concludes that it is risky to reach any strong conclusions about the effectiveness of residential treatment for adolescents (Burns, Hoagwood and Mrazek 1999, p.309). A more recent, systematic, thoughtful and detailed review by Lee *et al.* (2011) found that in studies where residential treatment was compared with a carefully designed non-residential alternative, more desirable outcomes tended to favor the alternative. Nonetheless, these authors point to model

---

1 Portions of this section draw on an earlier review of primarily US-based TRC by the first author (Whittaker 2011).

characteristics for certain types of therapeutic group care, for example, those designed to utilize a family-like environment, which appear to be associated with positive outcomes and are deserving of further research (Lee and Thompson 2008).

In the US, a general wariness concerning residential provision echoes those sentiments expressed earlier by others in the child mental health sector including the previously cited concerns about the dangers of "deviancy training," institutional abuse and a lack of effectiveness data in the corpus of residential care outcome research (English 2002; Kutash and Robbins Rivera 1996).

To be sure, concerns about continued use of TRC for children are not exclusively a US preoccupation as the previously cited volume by Courtney and Iwaniec (2009) illustrates. For example, Kornerup (2009) describes a sweeping municipal reform effort in Denmark, which alters administrative responsibility for residential treatment homes and suggests that the new policy environment will require "a 'researched anchoring' of the therapeutic milieu with the continued aim of getting to know more of what helps whom and under what circumstances" (p.40). In the UK, Ian Sinclair, a leading children's services researcher, offers an unvarnished view of the challenge facing those who argue that therapeutic group care remains a valued service option: "The context of the attack on residential homes is that many people no longer believe in them" (Sinclair 2006, p.207).

Considering the weight of what could only be called an increasingly skeptical consensus about the continued reliance on therapeutic group care as a major child mental health service, or as an alternative to therapeutic foster care, or, largely for reasons having to do with the potential for institutional abuse, child and family services researchers and practitioners need to direct serious attention including both theoretical and empirical analysis to the purposes, change theories, treatment protocols, expected outcomes, comparative advantages and organizational requisites for TRC if it is to retain its legitimacy as a viable service option for troubled children and their families in the US context.

What are the specific concerns about Therapeutic Residential Care?

Multiple reasons have been offered as at least partial explanations for concern about TRC. Looking at the US context, Whittaker (2013) identifies several major problem areas:

- Absence of clear-cut diagnostic indicators for therapeutic residential placement.

- Concerns about attachment in particular for young children placed in residential care.

- Fear of abuse and neglect within residential settings.

- Questionable effectiveness of TRC.

- Lack of consensus on critical intervention components.

- Atrophy of TRC theory and model development.

- Rising costs of TRC.

- A growing preference for family-based treatment alternatives.

Since at least the first decade of the 20th century, there has existed a presumption that residential care if used at all ought to be seen as a "last resort." This is particularly so when child dependency is the primary issue. As Courtney, Dolev and Gilligan (2009) point out, the previously cited 2003 Stockholm Resolution is quite similar to the sentiments expressed by the First White House Conference on Children (1909) that "home life is the highest and finest product of civilization" (2009, p.197). Where placement is indicated, preference should go to foster family care, adoption, guardianship or other alternatives. In child mental health, this translates to viewing treatment foster care as a more desirable alternative to residential treatment.

For out-of-home placement as a whole in the US, the single most stable trend line in child welfare for much of the 20th century was the shifting ratio of children in foster family vs. residential care as a proportion of the total number of children in out-of-home care. As Kadushin (1980) notes, from approximately the early 1930s to the mid-1970s, the percentage of children in residential care declined from 57 percent to 15 percent, while the percentage in family foster care increased from 43 percent to 85 percent for the total population of children served in out-of-home care. A recent survey by the US Department of Health and Human Services (2013) on the Adoption and Foster Care Analysis and Reporting System (AFCARS) reports that for 2011 the numbers of US children in all forms of out-of-home care yielded a single night count of approximately 15 percent of the 400,000+ children residing in residential settings, whereas nearly five times that number were placed in kinship or non-relative foster family care.

Limited evidence of effectiveness and recent service innovations

As noted, recent reviews of extant research on TRC are not encouraging. While space limits what can be included here, the interested reader is directed to Curry (1991) and Pecora *et al.* (2009b). More recently as noted, Lee *et al.* (2011) provide a carefully executed, detailed and thorough analysis of residential care research in a US context. Focusing their review on studies where group care was contrasted with a non-residential treatment alternative such as Multi-Systemic Therapy (MST), therapeutic foster family treatment such as Multi-Dimensional Treatment Foster Care (MTFC) or some variant of group care treatment, the authors found little in the research base favoring therapeutic residential services over these alternatives, with the exception of some family-oriented group care models, which appear to outperform the treatment foster care condition with which they were compared (Lee and Thompson 2008). The authors note the extremely variegated nature of group care treatment theory and suggest some tantalizing pathways for future study of family-oriented therapeutic group care. To fill out this picture, Courtney and Hughes-Heuring (2009) provide an excellent broader contextual overview of the state of residential care in the US For European perspectives, see Hellinckx *et al.* (1991), the excellent UK review authored by Roger Bullock, Michael Little and Spencer Millham for the Dartington group (1993), a recent meta-analysis of European residential research by Knorth *et al.* (2007a) and a recent research review on Spanish residential services by Bravo and del Valle (2009).

In contrast, much interest has been generated in recent years through successful randomized control trials involving several promising non-residential alternatives such as MST, MTFC and "Wraparound Services" (Burns and Hoagwood 2002). Thus, increasingly in the US, service agencies once wholly residential in their service now reflect a range of service options to meet differential needs of children in need of intensive services. Sigrid James's recent review (James, Alemi and Zepeda 2013), as well as her contribution to this present volume, suggests the increasing integration of these "evidence-based practice" models in existing child and family service agencies will encourage cross-fertilization and the development of new and empirically tested intensive treatment services that include a TRC component. See also Whittaker *et al.* (2006) for an earlier illustration of agency integration of evidence-based practices.

In other domains, a recent US government initiative championed by the Center for Mental Health Services (SAMSHA 2006) seeks to "Build

Bridges" between residential provision and other services within what is known as the "systems of care" framework. This framework, developed originally by Stroul and Friedman (1986), has evolved into the template for children's mental health services efforts in the US and has been in the forefront in providing effective strategies and solutions to improve services and outcomes. The system of care approach emphasizes home- and community-based care, comprehensive and individualized services and support, family-driven and youth-guided care, cultural and linguistic competence, services provided within the least restrictive environment and co-ordination across child-serving systems (Pecora *et al.* 2009b). To succeed, any serious attempt at reformulation of TRC, at least in the US, must conform to the values and principles of systems of care. A closely related critical question for practice and practice research in child and family services will be aligning and integrating what is known as "culturally competent" practice with "evidence-based practice" (Miranda *et al.* 2005).

Thus, as this brief and primarily US-based overview of TRC indicates, increasingly residential providers are encouraged to adopt evidence- based alternative family- and community-centered interventions in lieu of residential services. Moreover, concerns continue about institutional abuse and neglect as well as the potential for deviancy training, and cost disparities between residential and non-residential options loom larger in policy discussions as service budgets are tightened. All of this is playing out in a state-by-state context where legal challenges brought by child and family advocates and initiatives from philanthropic foundations such as the Annie E. Casey Foundation's "Rightsizing Congregate Care Initiative" (2010) have challenged the quality of care and treatment for children placed out of home as well as altered the direction of traditional placement patterns: e.g. away from group ("congregate") care settings and towards community and family-centered placements. As a recent review by Alpert and Meezan (2012) documents, such initiatives often serve as catalysts for a range of administrative actions (moving to needs-based as opposed to setting-based funding; performance-based contracting; winnowing the pool of service providers; introducing a continuum-based model of service) which, notwithstanding their positive effects, such as reducing inappropriate residential placement, do little to improve our understanding of the critical ingredients of high-quality TRC or clarify its place in the suite of available service alternatives. As will be seen in the chapters to follow, ripples from these and other currents are being felt as well in many other developed countries with complex social service systems.

How we have organized the volume

In the chapters to follow, we will expand and explore a number of important thematic areas affecting TRC through carefully selected, cross-national examples of relevant research, policy, administrative innovations and promising practices. We will link these exemplars with a series of critical commentaries throughout the volume from the editors, as well as from our international contributors.

The invited foreword by Professor Robbie Gilligan and this introduction will locate TRC in the spectrum of child, youth and family services, provide a working definition of its critical elements and briefly summarizing some of the key issues and challenges that confront policy, research and practice around its use.

Notwithstanding the fact that our distinguished contributors represent 11 countries: Spain, England, Denmark, Norway, the Netherlands, Italy, Australia, Israel, Canada, Scotland and the US, we opted not to organize the material on a country or regional basis. Rather, we chose to follow a series of six critical dimensions that would allow authors to pursue in-depth issues and themes which, taken together, will serve to illuminate the current state of TRC:

- Pathways to Therapeutic Residential Care.

- Promising Program Models and Innovative Practices.

- Preparing Youth for Successful Transitions from Therapeutic Residential Care.

- Critically Examining the Current Research Base for Therapeutic Residential Care.

- Calculating Costs for Therapeutic Residential Care: Regional and National Perspectives.

- Linking Focused Training and Critical Evaluation in Therapeutic Residential Care: A Foundation for Staff Support.

We believe that this thematic organization will allow authors to focus on areas where they possess deep expertise. Our hope is that country- and region-specific variations will emerge through specific examples. We chose to continue the practice utilized by Elizabeth Fernandez and Richard Barth (2010) in their exemplary recent review of foster care by following each selection with a brief critical commentary to highlight both regional variation and potential arenas for future research. Introductory and concluding sections by the editors will help set the context for the volume and point the way forward for next steps in policy, research and practice critical for TRC.

In the book's initial section, a contribution by June Thoburn (UK) and Frank Ainsworth (Australia) will explore the policy implications of differential placement rates for residential and family fostering across a series of developed countries through original research. This will be followed by contributions that explore research and clinical observations on needs and characteristics of high-resource using children and youth in three different contexts by Jorge F. del Valle and colleagues (Spain), Ana Sainero (Spain) and Amaia Bravo (Spain), John Lyons (North America), and Mette Lausten (Denmark). In Section 2, a variety of promising program models and innovative practices will be offered by Turf Jakobsen (Denmark), Tore Andreassen (Norway), Ron Thompson and Dan Daly (US), Patricia McNamara (Australia), Sigrid James (US), Richard Small, Christopher Bellonci and Susan Ramsey (US). In Section 3, Nathanael Okpych (US) and Mark Courtney (US) will examine original research for implications relevant to preparing for successful transitions from TRC, Mike Stein (UK) will share lessons learned from four decades of research on building supportive pathways for young people leaving care and Anat Zeira (Israel) will share original research on listening to young people leaving care in Israel. In Section 4, Annemiek Harder (Netherlands) and Erik Knorth (Netherlands) will explore original research on what is inside the "Black Box" of effective TRC, and Bethany Lee (US) and Richard Barth (US) will examine ways of improving the research base for TRC methodological innovations and logistical and analytic challenges. Section 5 consists of a single chapter on an innovative method for calculating service costs with potential implications for TRC authored by Lisa Holmes (UK). This will be followed by four extended regional commentaries by Richard Small and Chris Bellonci (US), Laura Palareti and Chiara Berti (Italy), Andrew Kendrick (Scotland), and Frank Ainsworth and Deirdre Cheers (Australia). Section 6 includes a chapter by by Amaia Bravo, Jorge F. del Valle and Iriana Santos reporting on original research on an innovative model for helping staff connect quality, practice and evaluation in TRC in Spain; Hans Grietens (the Netherlands) offers a European perspective on content and context for social pedagogy; Martha Holden (US), Michael Nunno (US) and James Anglin (Canada) and Charles Izzo (US) offer research and practice experience from the CARE Model—a quality improvement program widely used in North America, Europe and Australia. Finally, John Lyons and Lauren Schmidt (Canada) will present research and implementation insights from the widely used CANS Model—a strengths-based information system designed to improve outcomes in TRC.

SECTION 1

Pathways to Therapeutic Residential Care

CHAPTER 2

Making Sense of Differential Cross-National Placement Rates for Therapeutic Residential Care
Some Takeaway Messages for Policy

June Thoburn and Frank Ainsworth

Introduction: the history and language of residential child care across continents

Before we can get to grips with the differential use made of residential child care (and more specifically, Therapeutic Residential Care (TRC)) in different countries, it is important to understand the impact of language and terminology on the available data, analyses and debates. There is a term for 'orphanage' in most languages (still in use in many countries even though most of those cared for in them are not orphans in the sense of having no parents). However, whilst in the English language 'institution', 'children's home', 'group care facility' or 'residential treatment unit' may all be in use (sometimes synonymously but more often to denote different types of care regime), in many languages there is only one term to cover all of these. Most often this is translated into English as 'institution', which can lead to difficulties in interpreting the UN and EU exhortations to 'de-institutionalise' (Stockholm Declaration 2003). There is a lack of clarity as to whether this means that all group care facilities should be closed down or refers only to large institutionalised settings, especially those caring for young children.

As we discuss below, many Eastern European and some Western European countries still make use of larger-scale facilities for children of all ages, which, depending on the approach to the provision of care, may be characterised as 'institutions', 'orphanages' or 'children's homes'. Both UNICEF and the EU support 'de-institutionalisation' programmes (with grant aid often dependent on evidence of closure of large institutions), which have resulted in a move towards smaller units (usually for between 8 and 15 children) within urban environments. However, the dominant model is still either small family group-type units, within a campus that may be far from the children's family homes, or a large institution characterised by dormitory living. They may provide predominantly short or intermediate length care as part of a family support or family strengthening measure; (more often) care and upbringing to children who may or may not retain meaningful links with birth parents; or a combination of these.

In richer countries, and especially in Anglophone jurisdictions, from the 1970s onwards the response to the messages on the negative consequences of institutional living, alongside the search to reduce costs, has been to develop foster family care and kinship care as the placements of choice. In these countries, residential facilities are now largely seen as 'last resorts', to which children (mostly teenagers) are moved when foster or adoptive placements have disrupted, often on several occasions.

The theoretical underpinnings of these changes, which went alongside a drive to cut costs, were taken from other service systems including mental health and developmental disability (therapeutic communities, de-institutionalisation, normalisation), education (mainstreaming, least restrictive environment) and youth justice (minimal intervention, diversion) (Ainsworth 1999). These were mostly derived from work undertaken in the USA (influenced in some measure by Scandinavian ideas) in the 1950s and 1960s.

Making sense of the numbers

This brief summary goes some way towards explaining the big differences in rates of children in residential care in different countries. Recent publications and government and international reports that provide comparative data include the work of Browne and colleagues (2006) (documenting the large numbers of children under the age of three still placed in institutions in Eastern Europe, but also in some Western European countries); the Eurochild (2010) survey of children in alternative care (providing background policy information and data on the balance between foster family care and residential care in 30 European jurisdictions); and Sherwin's (2011) report for SOS Children's Villages (discussing policy and providing data from seven rich and transition economies). In

2012, UNICEF's Central and Eastern Europe and Commonwealth of Independent States Office (as part of UNICEF's *State of the World's Children* report) published the 'TransMonEE' data on 16 of the 22 countries in its region. However, as the Eurochild report points out, discrepancies between the data presented in these sources illustrate the difficulty of identifying reliable data for cross-national comparisons.

A further reason for caution when making cross-national comparisons lies in the different national conventions for collecting data. Data may be presented as the percentage of all those entering care over a 12-month period who are placed in residential care ('flow' data); as the number and percentage of all those in care on a given date who are living in a group care setting ('stock' data); or (less frequently but leading to more reliable cross-national comparisons) the rate in residential care per 10,000 children in the population (see Thoburn 2010 for a discussion of different reporting conventions). Another question to be asked concerns the criteria for inclusion in 'in care' statistics. For example, in some jurisdictions substantial numbers of children with kin are formally 'in-care', whilst in others, kinship care is mainly provided and supported via informal arrangements without the need for formal care. In the former, the percentage of those in care who are in group care is likely to be lower than in countries in which similar children will be cared for by relatives outside the care system. A further area of difference is around youth justice services. In Australia, the UK and the USA most young offenders placed away from home are in criminal justice establishments and not included in the 'in-care' statistics. In contrast, in the Nordic countries, most young offenders are placed within the out-of-home care system, and since these are more often placed in group care settings, this will increase the percentage of all those in care who are in a group care setting. In some countries (France, for example) disabled children assessed as needing residential care are in facilities provided by the health service (and not included in the 'in care' statistics). Of particular relevance to this book, in the USA the numbers in residential care are lower than they might be because some children and youth with challenging behaviour are placed in residential treatment facilities provided by mental health services. Similarly, boarding school provision for children with special educational needs (often because of challenging behaviour) may or may not be included in public care statistics (see the report by Berridge *et al.* 2003 on the characteristics of and outcomes for adolescents in local authority children's homes and foster care, and in boarding schools).

Despite these differences in reporting conventions, the data from the above sources give a broadly consistent picture of the numbers and proportions of children in formal care who are placed in a group care setting. Table 2.1 is compiled from a data-based study of children in out-of-home care in 28 rich nation jurisdictions (Thoburn 2010), with additional information from the reports cited above.

TABLE 2.1: Percentages and rates in residential care in a sample of 'developed' and 'transitional' economies (in some countries without child as unit of return data, these are estimates)

COUNTRY	RATE IN CARE PER 10,000 AGED 0–17	APPROX. NO. IN GROUP CARE	RATE IN GROUP CARE PER 10,000 AGED 0–17	% OF CHILDREN IN CARE IN A GROUP CARE PLACEMENT	APPROX. % IN CARE AGED 10–17
Armenia (2009)**	66	4936	65	<95%	
Australia (2011)	73	1628	5	6%	45%
Czech Republic (2009)*	175	23,384	127	72%	
Denmark (2007)	120	5087	59	47%	74%
France (2008)	105	53,077	40	37%	64%
Germany (2005)	76	60,571	41	54%	64%
Hungary (2009)*	146	6856	37	25%	
Ireland (2005)	51	401	4	8%	50%
Israel (2007)***	42	8300	34	80%	
Italy (2007)***	38	15,600	15	48%	
Japan (2005)	17	35,146	15	92%	
Lithuania (2009)*	246	8715	137	56%	
Poland (2009)*	147	52,293	72	49%	
Russian Federation (2009)**	305	345,630	133	43%	

Romania (2009)**	169	23,817	60	35%	
Spain (2007)	52	14,948	19	38%	
Sweden (2008)	63	4000	21	27%	74%
UK— England (2010)	58	8170	7	14%	62%
UK— Scotland (2009)	76	1611	15	23%	59%
Ukraine (2009)**	194	8821	109	57%	
USA (2009)	57	424,000	9	15%	50%

* Data from Eurochild (2010)
**Data from UNICEF (2012)
***Data from IAOBER (2011)
Source: Ainsworth and Thoburn (2013)[1]

The table demonstrates that, in a given country, the likelihood of a child being placed in residential care at a given point in time depends on the use made of residential care as a placement of choice, but also on the likelihood of being placed in care at all, and the average duration of care episodes (which can differ considerably, even in apparently similar countries).

In summary, the data show that, whether measured in percentage terms or rates per 10,000 children, the Anglophone nations are the lowest users of group care (Australia, England, New Zealand, Ireland and the USA all having a rate of less than 10 per 10,000 children aged 0–17 in a publicly provided or funded group care setting on a given date). At the other end of the continuum in terms of percentages (with around 90% of the in-care population in a group care setting) is Japan, a rich country that has traditionally placed children in all age groups in professionally staffed small units, mainly within the voluntary sector-provided children's homes. But because of low rates in care, the likelihood of a Japanese child entering a group care setting is comparatively low (along with Italy, Scotland, Spain and Sweden, with rates of between 11 and

---

1   We are grateful for the permission of the editors of the *International Journal of Social Welfare* and Blackwell Publishers for permission to include Table 2.1, first published in Ainsworth and Thoburn (2013).

21 per 10,000 children in the population). The traditionally high use of residential care in Eastern Europe, together with increasing levels of poverty and lower levels of expenditure on public services following the collapse of Communist regimes, have contributed to the high rates in care and, specifically, in residential care (over 100 per 10,000 children in the Czech Republic, Lithuania, the Russian Federation and Ukraine), although 'de-institutionalisation' policies supported by EU funding are gradually reducing these very high rates, both in care, and in residential care. There are more nuanced explanations for the comparatively high rates in group care in Denmark, France and Germany, with over 40 per 10,000 children in group care (Ainsworth and Thoburn 2013).

Whilst complex historical, cultural, political and economic differences in part explain these differences, other explanations are to be found in the characteristics of the children entering care, which in turn are related to the availability of universal and targeted family support services and family strengthening measures including child mental health services. The availability of free or state-subsidised early years services in Nordic and some continental Western European countries helps to reduce the need for out-of-home care in the younger age groups, with the result that a larger percentage enter care as teenagers, for whom a residential care facility is more likely to be the placement of choice. Table 2.1 shows that 74 per cent of the children in care in Denmark in 2007 were aged ten or over compared with 50 per cent in the USA and 45 per cent in Australia.

It is harder to come by reliable data on reasons for entering care so age has to serve as a proxy for other child characteristics. Most of the minority countries that do provide data on reasons for entry have a 'main reason' category, and most often 'child maltreatment' masks other important contributory child or family characteristics. From Denmark's 'tick any that apply' data collection system, a more nuanced picture emerges. Whilst severe neglect was cited as a reason for care in 12 per cent of cases and violence or threats of violence against the child in 10 per cent of cases, in 56 per cent of cases 'general behaviour problems', in 38 per cent 'severe disharmony in the home' and in 35 per cent 'difficulties in school' were given as reasons for entry to care (Thoburn 2010, p.42).

The child's ethnicity and culture also impact on rates in care and placement choices. Tilbury and Thoburn (2009) show that in countries with substantial indigenous populations (Australia, Canada and the USA and New Zealand) these children are likely to be over-represented in care. Although adoption is used as a route out of care for non-indigenous children, first nation Canadian children are less likely to leave care via adoption and are more likely to be in group care settings. In several countries in Eastern Europe, Roma children are far more likely to be in an institution or special school than non-Roma children (UNICEF Regional Office for CEC/CIS 2007). In contrast, most aboriginal children in care in Australia are in (often unstable) kinship or (less often) non-kin foster family care.

Understanding therapeutic care across jurisdictions

It can be predicted that very different rates in residential care and different understandings of the purpose of residential care within child welfare services will have an impact on the characteristics of the children living there and on their length of stay. We would argue that, as a consequence, different approaches to service provision and different care regimes are likely to be (or should be) apparent in different jurisdictions. This leads to a consideration of how what we understand as 'residential treatment' fits within the broader concept of what is 'therapeutic' for the different groups of children in out-of-home care and their families. This requires us to start by unpicking the characteristics of residential care that are considered to be therapeutic – in the sense of contributing to enhanced well-being.

In very broad terms, explored in more detail in other chapters in this volume, children and young people need, in different combinations:

- stability and predictability (for long-stayers, 'a sense of permanence' and for short-stayers, confidence that they will not be moved unnecessarily and that their place is secure in the family they will return to)

- relationships with professionally qualified, skilled, available and well-supported carers they can trust

- the availability of a range of evidence-informed interventions or therapies that address their identified difficulties and are congruent with the aims of the group care setting and the needs of the children and young people in residence.

Lee *et al.* (2010, p.6) conclude from their study of residential care in the USA that the common elements of successful care regimes 'appear to include: family involvement, family type living, adult supervision and behaviour monitoring, positive reinforcement and social skills training'.

Broadly speaking, when residential care is used mainly as a 'care and upbringing' provision (as in Japan and Eastern Europe), the therapeutic emphasis will be on providing stability, a 'sense of permanence' and community membership, and trusting relationships with staff who care about them as well as for them and who are available to provide good quality parenting. Appropriate links with family members and support through the transition to adulthood, with access to therapy and specialist services when needed, will also be part of the care regime.

When group care is part of a support service to parents and/or children with disabilities or where relationships are under severe stress (mainly for teenagers and often as a first resort in preference to foster family care, as in Germany, France and Denmark), the balance will be different and more differentiated, with a more prominent place for defined therapeutic approaches, including work with parents and other birth family members. In some countries, including the USA, residential treatment facilities within the child mental health system, or for children with complex disabilities, may also fulfil this role.

Where residential care is used primarily as a 'last resort' when kinship and foster family or adoptive placements have failed, the service has to be more differentiated to meet the therapeutic needs of the young people. Most will have suffered trauma, and most will have suffered from instability and multiple losses. Although a majority will have entered care in their middle years or as teenagers, their relationships with birth family members are likely to have become distanced, especially if they reach their group care placements (often as their own preferred option) after previous attempts to be part of an adoptive or long-term foster family have not worked out. They are likely to need therapy and remedial education in the broadest sense of the word and help to rebuild tenuous relationships, but they also need stability and a sense of belonging, as most will remain until they transition out of care as young adults.

Does group care provision meet needs in different jurisdictions

Ainsworth and Hansen (2009) identify that in Western child welfare systems and transition economies the main programme emphasis is on care, education and/or treatment in various combinations. They note that, irrespective of the reason for a residential care placement, in most jurisdictions the majority of the residential care services have a care and accommodation rather than a treatment focus. In the UK and Australia, most residential child care workers have lower level vocational qualifications and are ill-equipped to provide the education and treatment services needed by the troubled young people who are placed in these 'last-resort' children's homes (Berridge, Biehal and Henry 2011). In continental

Western Europe and the Nordic countries, a high proportion of the staff of children's homes, which have a broader intake and may be a placement of first choice rather than last resort, have qualified at degree level as social pedagogues (*educateurs specialisés* in France and *educatore* in Italy) (Cameron and Moss 2011). These homes are often larger and the average stay tends to be longer. Education (in the broader sense of 'upbringing' rather than 'teaching') is a more major component of these child welfare regimes.

Across jurisdictions, a much smaller proportion of group care facilities are designated as residential treatment services. As noted above, they may be provided within mental health, youth justice and education, as well as child welfare systems, and they may focus specifically on children with cognitive impairment, physical disabilities and mental health problems or challenging behaviour (Ainsworth 1985). Most group care facilities, even in Anglophone countries where a large proportion of entrants are likely to be seriously disturbed after suffering trauma followed by a series of placement breakdowns, would not be described as offering 'residential treatment'. In 2011 the National Child Protection Clearinghouse (part of the Australian Institute of Family Studies) reviewed the extent of TRC in Australia and considered how this service might develop in the future (McLean, Price-Robertson and Robinson 2011). While the paper drew on international literature and described a number of USA residential care models, it found little evidence of Australian examples of these service models. The 2013 report of the Carmody Inquiry into child protection services in Queensland identified 105 generic residential care facilities and only four that the authors categorised as offering TRC (Carmody 2013). However, this definition appears to be based on the facilities being purpose-built by government, rather than because of their consistent use of a particular programme model. In Australia, the most clearly articulated model of TRC is that offered by the Lighthouse Foundation (Ainsworth 2012; Barton, Gonzales and Tomlinson 2012) that owes much to the Cotswold Community in the UK. A small number of other facilities describe themselves as following the USA-originated Sanctuary model (Clarke 2011; Esakl *et al.* 2013), though, to date, there is no independent descriptive or evaluative study of the service actually provided. There is one positive outcome evaluation of a Victorian pilot TRC programme (although the evaluation does not detail the programme model) (Verso Consulting 2011).

In England, apart from a small number of highly specialised residential units focusing on particular groups such as sexually traumatised or abusive children, most children's homes are not specific about the treatment regime they provide and will source therapy as needed from outside sources. Fourteen of the 16 homes in the Berridge, Biehal and Henry (2011) survey said they cared for children with emotional, behavioural and social difficulties, but only a small minority said they provided 'treatment' or 'therapy'. Only five of the homes reported that their work was underpinned by a specific theoretical approach.

In the USA, some group care facilities have responded to the high level of need of the young people typically placed with them following trauma and placement breakdown by employing psychologists and other therapists. However, Libby *et al.* (2005) surveyed residential treatment facilities in Colorado and concluded that there were few differences in the type of programme provided to young people with very different presenting symptoms and therapeutic needs.

Conclusion

All of the above confirm that residential 'services vary greatly in treatment philosophies and practices including their purpose and the intensity of intervention provided' (Whittaker, del Valle and Holmes, this volume, Chapter 1). It is the exception rather than the rule for the therapeutic philosophy and treatment methods to be specifically tailored around the needs of the young residents. A 'care' philosophy may have more relevance in countries where political and economic factors, especially poverty, make everyday physical survival the dominant issue, or where a place in a children's home is part of a package of support services in response to acute family stress or to support parents in meeting the needs of a disabled child (Ainsworth and Thoburn 2013). We would argue that it is more necessary to promote a model of TRC in communities that use residential placements when foster or adoptive placement has been tried and has failed. What emerges in these 'last-resort' regimes, caring predominantly for children and young people who display serious behavioural and mental health difficulties, is the need for a 24/7 clinically staffed care and treatment environment, although the 'stability' and 'belonging' needs of teenagers who are not part of any family have to be sensitively and imaginatively catered for within a treatment regime. Other than in the USA, where the availability of private health insurance has supported the growth of mental health services of this type for some children and young people, progress towards the creation of TRC programmes has been extremely slow. The lack of research and programme development initiatives to which this volume draws attention has significantly contributed to this slow progress.

Making Sense of Differential Cross-National Placement Rates for Therapeutic Residential Care: Some Takeaway Messages for Policy

June Thoburn and Frank Ainsworth

This chapter is particularly valuable because the authors introduce several important cautions and keys to understanding the complexity of international comparisons. Special caution must be taken when using concepts that seem similar but could have really different meanings depending on the country and the language. Even more important, there are also relevant differences about the system responsible for running services. Some residential care services can depend on the educative system (boarding schools), mental health services (therapeutic units), justice system (young offenders) or child protection (children's homes). This question is absolutely relevant to understanding differences in figures about the use of residential child care in some countries, as some of them can be included, or not, in statistics (children in care could be referred to mental health services as in the USA or young offenders could be included in child welfare facilities as in the Netherlands). Relationships between systems seem to be essential to analysing TRC because young people placed in these programmes are eligible to be attended by two services: child care because of abuse or neglect and mental health services due to behavioural and emotional disorders. Depending on the country, they can be in one or another system, or even in a mixture of services shared by child care and mental health departments.

This chapter establishes an interesting division between countries where residential care is mainly intended for substitute care on the one hand, the main characteristics of which are permanency, stability and a normalised and family-like environment. On the other hand, some countries use residential care as a last resort for extremely complex cases not suitable for other types of placement (family foster care), principally due to behavioural disorders. In this case, the main characteristics are usually related to a therapeutic change, and outcomes evaluation becomes essential.

Although this division represents rather well the two major trends in residential care, nowadays the evolution of this form of out-of-home care may be more complex. In some countries, such as Spain for example, during the last decade a great effort was made to design residential care as a network of specialised resources. Therefore, most regions developed a system of residential care consisting of: emergency care homes (see Chapter 3), asylum-seeking centres for unaccompanied young people, therapeutic or socialisation homes, supervised independent living homes and, of course, normalised children's homes for sibling groups or younger children. This network of specialised programmes, based on the high qualification of the socio-pedagogical model, facilitates addressing many different needs, which are extremely difficult to be treated when they are all together in the same place. As the authors of the chapter say, there are few residential programmes defined as therapeutic in an international perspective. However, I would suggest that perhaps in many countries there was not a comparable need for specialisation or a clear design of residential care resources with clear definition. In those cases, young people with severe disorders could be dispersed in different facilities (a practice that is very dangerous and ineffective) or concentrated in some last-resort centres, but without a definition of therapeutic programme (which usually results in inappropriate resources, lack of an intervention model and also ineffectiveness). This book tries to contribute models and experiences to help in properly designing therapeutic programmes and avoiding those risks.

CHAPTER 3

Needs and Characteristics of High-Resource Using Children and Youth
Spain

Jorge F. del Valle, Ana Sainero and Amaia Bravo

The historical context of Therapeutic Residential Care in Spain

Residential child care is a particularly important protection measure in Spain, because following the civil war (1936–1939), and during the almost 40 years of dictatorship that ended with the democratic constitution of 1978, child protection was managed by the Catholic Church and charitable organisations, which created an extensive network of residential institutions. Family foster care was not set out in Spanish legislation until the 1987 reform of the civil code. Consequently, family placement in Spain began very late compared with other countries, and even today residential care is very common (Bravo and del Valle 2009; del Valle *et al.* 2009).

At the same time as steps were being taken to implement foster care and reduce residential placement to a minimum, reforms were instituted to eliminate the large macroinstitutions where, even up to the end of the 1980s, hundreds of children were housed. The reforms consisted of the creation of small children's homes, flats/apartments or small houses where eight to ten children would be able to live a more family-like life.

The aim of this model, which we could call normalisation, is to create the kind of space and relationships most similar to those of a family, including essential aspects such as the use of community services (school, medical centres, leisure centres, etc.). In addition, the aim is to include children of all ages in the homes, again imitating a family and facilitating the placement of groups of siblings of different ages.

This situation changed rapidly in the 1990s as the reforms of 1987 led to a significant deinstitutionalisation movement of returning children to their families (with additional economic, social and other assistance), which allowed residential placement only in cases of serious mistreatment. From the 1990s onwards, small children's homes experienced a serious crisis because the residential workers (who, in Spain, are called social educators, and who have a university degree) were trained in normalising care, which was based on creating everyday life-spaces (according to the social pedagogy model) and which strongly emphasises community integration as the grand solution for children's socialisation. Nevertheless, they had to cope with adolescents who had serious behavioural problems, who were disobedient, very destructive to the premises, and aggressive to staff and especially to younger children.

In addition to this change in profile, the youngest children were benefiting from foster care. In Spain, kinship care represents almost 80 per cent of all family foster care and its use was expanded enormously in those years (del Valle *et al.* 2009). Consequently, residential care was increasingly used for adolescents with serious emotional or behavioural problems. Today, 80 per cent of children in residential care are over 13 (Bravo and del Valle 2009). The smaller children's homes were not prepared for groups of adolescents with such problems.

This mismatch between needs and resources precipitated a change of model in which the main principles of normalisation were to be preserved, while at the same time the residential units needed to be capable of dealing with the difficulties posed by those cases. Many challenges were posed by other, specific profiles, such as children with serious disabilities, children diagnosed with autism or psychoses, etc., as well as the arrival of unaccompanied asylum seekers.

The situation of adolescents with serious disruptive problems in family-like spaces with low ratios of educators (two adults per eight to ten children) and with younger vulnerable children became unsustainable and there was a demand for specialised homes that would be able to deal with the most difficult cases. This idea directly contradicted the ideals of the normalising model, as a specialised centre would function with a much more controlling model, capable of coping with serious behavioural problems. Added to that, it was common for some young people to regularly abscond, and thus programmes to deal with that issue were required, i.e. secure locations.

The authorities responsible for child protection responded to this challenge in diverse ways. It is important to bear in mind that in Spain there are 17 autonomous communities, each with its own parliament and government that, among other things, is responsible for social services. Each of them came up with different solutions. Some decided not to create any specialised programmes, thinking that the principle of normalisation should prevail and that segregation of the most problematic cases contradicted this (although this results in significant conflict in the homes and is a characteristic example of how rigid theoretical approaches can end up causing substandard care for children).

Nevertheless, most autonomous communities developed some kind of response, although with very different names and approaches. Thus, the first 'socialisation' residential programmes appeared in some communities towards the end of the 1990s (80% of this type of resource available today began after the year 2000). In other regions, various terms were in use, such as 'special regime', 'high intensity education', 'attention to youths in social difficulties or social conflict' etc. The term 'therapeutic' began to be used later (in very few communities) and was defined as measures directed towards adolescents with serious mental health diagnoses (autism, psychosis, antisocial disorder, etc.) who, in addition, had significant behavioural issues. However, in the majority of autonomous communities, the idea of a therapeutic centre was confused with the idea of centres dealing with serious behavioural problems, so an early conclusion we can make is that there is a lack of clarity in these concepts.

Once established, the enormous demand for these types of programmes, thanks to the significant increase in cases, led to the increase in private, non-profit organisations (there are hardly any for-profit organisations in this sector in Spain) who offered to provide these resources, since the cost is somewhere between double and triple the cost of a normal place, around €3000–5000 per month according to the Ombudsman's report (Defensor del Pueblo 2009). In this way, the most specialised care fell into the hands of the private sector, which in a large part was without previous experience in such demanding programmes and had very different working methods and approaches in different communities. This gave rise, as evidenced in the aforementioned report, to practices that failed to respect the basic rights of children, in which control and coercion were the primary psychological treatments. The report shed light on some administrations' lack of control over the development of these programmes, on which they had spent large amounts of money.

The therapeutic residential child care network in Spain

Spain has a serious problem when it comes to statistical data on social services because they are managed by each of the 17 autonomous communities individually and there is no unified statistical system. One of the data points that is not available is the number of residential resources, let alone the type, therefore any estimates must be based on specific research. The data below is from work carried out by our research group, although unpublished, in which information was requested from all of the autonomous communities about their network of residential child care, with the aim of collecting all of the current information.

As of 2012, throughout the 17 autonomous communities, there are four types of centres for children and young people with serious issues: 33 therapeutic homes (456 places); 58 socialisation homes (622 places); 39 homes for children with serious disabilities (377 places); and 4 for adolescents with substance abuse problems (19 places). In total there are 124 specialist resources with 1,424 places. The total child care network in Spain comprises 1146 centres and 14,962 places, thus the specialised resources represent 10.8 per cent of the resources in the network and 9.9 per cent of the total places.

The difference between therapeutic and socialisation programmes lies in the emphasis on the existence of a formal mental health diagnosis with which the case is referred to a therapeutic centre or the presence of serious emotional or behavioural problems that require a socialisation home. Nevertheless, there are communities that use only one of these two types or use other designations and, in the end, these types of care are not clearly differentiated. Ultimately, it is more useful to combine both types together, as serious emotional or behavioural problems, which is what we will do henceforth, while maintaining the term 'therapeutic' in line with the title of this book. Adding together therapeutic and socialisation centres gives us a total of 91 centres (7.9% of the network) and 1078 places (7% of the network). Homes for severely disabled children deal with a wide range of problems – mostly with significant developmental problems, but also with physical disability (which may or may not be associated with developmental disability) requiring special care (this mix of centres for children with disabilities is 3.4 per cent of the total homes and 2.5 per cent of the places). Finally, there are few centres (four) for adolescents suffering from substance abuse, which may be misleading as the majority of communities, not having this resource available, use the mental health drug-dependency network (for which there is also no data). In conclusion, we might say that high-resource using children in Spain represent between approximately 7 and 10 per cent of the total in the network.

Regrettably, this data is all that we know in Spain about these special programmes. There are no evaluative studies on the efficacy of the interventions in therapeutic programmes, despite the cost being three times higher than the rest of the children's homes and the severe criticism of the Ombudsman's report.

Profiles and needs of young people in therapeutic residential child care

There are no studies in Spain about the profile of children in these specialised homes, but it is possible to extract some indicative data from some recent studies. In one, looking at the mental health of children and young people in residential care (Sainero, Bravo and del Valle 2014), the prevalence of cases with mental health disorders was investigated in all children aged between 6 and 18 in residential care in one autonomous Spanish community (Extremadura), which found that 28 per cent were receiving treatment. In the community being investigated, there were no special or therapeutic programmes; instead, such cases were sent to other regions. Specifically, there were 14 cases, which was 4 per cent of the children in residential care in this region. Looking at the profile of these children, it is clear that we are dealing with disruptive disorders, with diagnoses of antisocial disorder or oppositional defiance disorder, in addition to intellectual disability in half of the cases. The addition of a behavioural disorder to intellectual disability makes these cases demandingly problematic and poses a high risk to the children and to their surroundings.

The problem of intellectual disability (mental retardation in terms of the DSM-IV-TR) is hugely significant because it affects a population commonly found in residential care about whom there has been very little study (Trout *et al.* 2009). One recent piece of work about this specific group of children (Sainero *et al.* 2013) found that these young people make up 17 per cent of the total in residential care, approximately half of whom had emotional or behavioural disorders for which they were receiving therapeutic care. We have also seen that 2.5 per cent of places in the national network are for children with very serious disabilities. This undoubtedly reflects a population with very special needs, which has, up to now, been scarcely visible in research on child care in the international scientific literature.

In this part of the chapter we present a preview of data gathered from a large study carried out in Spain to evaluate the mental health needs of children and young people in residential care. The sample was made up of all children and young people aged between 6 and 18 in residential care in five autonomous communities and eight SOS Villages. The key objectives of the study were: to gather data on the prevalence of mental health disorders in this population, including the diagnoses and the types of care being given; to use screening techniques to study and evaluate possible cases that present clinical indicators, which may not be receiving treatment (as demonstrated by some research: Burns *et al.* 2004; Sainero *et al.* 2014); and finally, to assess the progress of these cases over three years, in particular the results of the treatments for the group referred to therapeutic services.

The method consisted of data collection about family histories and the protection intervention (reasons for admission, length of stay, care plan, etc.) from a data sheet completed by the key social educators and social case workers. Second, information was requested about the cases with any type of treatment for mental health problems, such as the diagnosis and the type of care being given. Following that, cases were examined using the screening techniques of the CBCL and YSR (Achenbach and Rescorla 2001). The study had a longitudinal design of three years (2013–2015) whereby the tests would be performed once a year and follow-ups done on the cases under treatment to assess their progress every six months (admissions, discharges, changes of service, etc.).

At the time of writing, we have initial data from three autonomous communities in which there are therapeutic centres dealing with a total of 51 cases. We compared the profiles of this group with the rest of the young people in residential care in these communities (excluding cases of children under 13, as that is the minimum age in the therapeutic centres). In total, the sample was composed of 334 adolescents (51 in therapeutic centres and 283 in the remaining residential homes).

Table 3.1 shows comparative data (we used analyses based on Chi^2 for the percentages and on the student t-test for the averages) of sociodemographic variables and variables about the intervention. With respect to gender, there is a predominance of males in the general group (58%); however, it is more marked in the therapeutic group (68%), although not statistically significant. The age range is between 13 and 18 years with a mean of 15.5, which is very similar to the general group, but it can be seen that within the distribution, the ages 15–16 characterise the therapeutic group, making up more than half the cases.

TABLE 3.1: Child and family characteristics and differences

CHILD AND FAMILY CHARACTERISTICS	TOTAL SAMPLE (N =334) % OR M(SD)	THERAPEUTIC (N = 51) % OR M(SD)	GENERAL (N =283) % OR M(SD)
	100	15.3	84.7
Gender			
Female	40.1	31.4	41.7
Male	59.9	68.6	58.3
Age			
M (SD)	15.4 (1.4)	15.53 (1.2)	15.40 (1.4)
13–14	28.1	19.6	29.7
15–16	43.4	58.8	40.6*
17 y+	28.4	21.6	29.7
Unaccompanied asylum seeking	14.1	9.8	14.9
Immigrant family	10.8	7.8	11.4
Roma	11.4	15.7	10.7
Length of stay	29.3 (34.8)	12.0 (11.5)	32.4 (37)***
Length of stay in residential care	48.5 (46.4)	43.2 (40)	49.8 (48)
Number of transitions	1.82 (1.13)	2.4 (1.6)	1.68 (0.9)***
Reason for admission[a]			
Physical neglect	30.2	15.7	32.9**
Emotional neglect	29.6	21.6	31.1
Physical abuse	19.8	13.7	20.8
Emotional abuse	20.7	21.6	20.5
Sexual abuse	6.9	9.8	6.4
Out of parental control	40.8	68.6	35.7***
Violence against parents	6.1	11.8	5.0

[a] More than one category per case is possible. * $p \leq 0.05$; ** $p \leq 0.01$; *** $p \leq 0.001$ on Chi^2 for categorical variables and student t-test for quantitive variables.

What was significant was the time of stay in a residential facility, which was found to be in the region of a year in therapeutic care and two-and-a-half years in the general group. Intensive programmes do not normally involve more than one or two years of treatment. Nevertheless, the total time spent in residential care is similar in both groups – around four years, which is a long stay and a significant problem in the child care system (see the analysis by López and del Valle 2013). There were also differences in the mean number of changes of residential facility – 2.4 in the therapeutic group and 1.7 in the general one.

Although unaccompanied asylum seekers (largely from Morocco) are quite numerous in the general sample (15%), they account for 10 per cent of the therapeutic group. By contrast, the opposite applies to young Roma who account for 11 per cent of the general group and 16 per cent of the therapeutic group. Finally, 8 per cent of the young people in the therapeutic group are from immigrant families (11% in the general group).

Significant differences can also be seen in the reasons for admission when it comes to the out-of-parental-control cases, which are 68 per cent of the therapeutic group and a little over twice that of the general group. The problem of adolescents demonstrating rebellious behaviour against their parents – up to and including aggression – has been a serious and growing problem in Spain in recent years. In contrast, problems related to physical negligence are double in the general group (33%) compared with the therapeutic group (16%).

As expected, significant differences were found in those aspects related to mental health problems (Table 3.2). Intellectual disabilities were seen in 15.5 per cent of the sample, confirming the previous suggestion of this group's importance in residential care.

TABLE 3.2: Mental health characteristics

MENTAL HEALTH CHARACTERISTICS	TOTAL SAMPLE (N = 334) % OR M(SD) 100	THERAPEUTIC (N = 51) % OR M(SD) 15.3	GENERAL (N = 283) % OR M(SD) 84.7
Disabilities	16.1	14	16.5
Psychical	4.6	2.0	5.0
Sensorial	2.4	2.0	2.5
Intellectual	15.5	12.0	16.1
Mental health treatment	50	66	47.2*
Psychiatric	9	6	9.6
Psychological	29.2	18.0	31.2
Simultaneous treatment	11.7	42	6.4*
Psychotropic medication	20.2	45.7	16.0***
Psychiatric therapy			
Residential care	5.1	33.3	0.0*
Public service	15.3	15.7	15.2
Psychological therapy			
Residential care	40.3	65.6	32.7***
Public service	20.1	21.9	19.6
Private service	10.5	12.5	10.3
Suicidal behaviour			
Threaten	13.1	26.3	11.0
Intent	6.6	10.5	5.9
Substance abuse			
Alcohol	4.2	18	1.8***
Cannabis	15.3	37.3	1.2***
Cocaine (sporadic use)	5.5	22.4	2.5***

* $p \leq 0.05$; ** $p \leq 0.01$; *** $p \leq 0.001$ on Chi^2

Two thirds of young people (66%) in therapeutic care were found to be receiving psychotherapy, whereas in the general group it is 47 per cent (which is, incidentally, also rather high). There are differences in the types of treatment. In therapeutic care, 42 per cent are being treated by both psychiatrists and psychologists, something that only happens in 6 per cent of the general group. It is clear that those in the therapeutic group need pharmacological support and therefore a psychiatrist, and, in fact, 46 per cent were found to be receiving medication as opposed to 16 per cent in the general group. Although no significant difference was found between the two groups, it is worth drawing attention to behaviours related to suicide. In therapeutic care, 26 per cent of the adolescents had threatened suicide (11% in the general group) and 10.5 per cent had attempted suicide (double that found in the general group). The topic of suicidal behaviour is another that we believe should be investigated much more deeply in residential care.

One of the biggest differences between the groups was with respect to substance abuse. There were problems of abusive alcohol consumption in 18 per cent of the therapeutic group (1.8% in the general group); equally, there were problems of excessive cannabis consumption in more than a third of the therapeutic group as opposed to 11 per cent in the general group.

Psychiatric treatments are carried out in the centre itself in a third of the cases in the therapeutic group but not in any of the general group. Visits to the public health service psychiatrist were found to be 15 per cent in both groups. In contrast, psychological treatment in the centres themselves is much more common – 66 per cent of cases in the therapeutic group and 33 per cent of cases in the general group. The use of public health system psychologists was also very similar.

We end with a preview of data from the application of the Achenbach CBCL. As can be seen in Table 3.3, there are significant differences in sections about rule-breaking behaviour and aggressive behaviour. This is evident in the externalising broadband scale in which 80 per cent of the cases in therapeutic care are in the clinical range (56% in the general group). No differences are seen with internalising problems, but there is a slight tendency towards higher scores in the general group. The lack of difference in the thinking problems section, which refers to possible diagnoses of psychosis, indicates that this type of problem is not necessarily referred to therapeutic centres. Finally, it can be seen that 82 per cent of the therapeutic group have some clinical broadband scale as opposed to 64.5 per cent of the general group.

TABLE 3.3: Cases in clinical range in CBCL

	TOTAL SAMPLE (N = 326)	THERAPEUTIC (N=50)	GENERAL (N=276)
	CLINICAL RANGE N (%)	CLINICAL RANGE N (%)	CLINICAL RANGE N (%)
Anxious/depressed	43 (13.2)	6 (12)	37(13.4)
Withdrawn/ depressed	58 (17.8)	6 (12)	52 (18.8)
Somatic complaints	37 (11.3)	6 (12)	31 (11.2)
Social problems	62 (19.0)	10 (20.0)	52 (18.8)
Thought problems	33 (10.1)	5 (10.0)	28 (10.1)
Attention problems	63 (19.3)	13 (26)	50 (18.1)
Rule breaking behaviour	108 (33.1)	24 (48)	84 (30.4)*
Aggressive behaviour	111 (34.0)	25 (50)	86 (31.2)**
Internalising	102 (31.3)	14 (28)	88 (31.9)
Externalising	196 (60.1)	40 (80)	156 (56.5)**
Total behaviour problems	175 (53.7)	33 (66)	142 (51.4)
Any broadband	219 (67.2)	41 (82.0)	178 (64.5)*

* p ≤ 0.05; ** p ≤ 0.01; *** p ≤ 0.001 on *Chi²*

Conclusions

Unfortunately, Spain has not historically had a culture of programme evaluation, which would strengthen the residential resources that are most effective and efficient. In the area of therapeutic residential care this is even more serious because these evaluations could have avoided some cases in which it was later discovered that the rights of young people had not been respected. In Spain, unlike other countries, the idea of evidence-based programmes, of which there are excellent examples in child care, have not become widespread. The urgent need to respond to young people with serious behavioural problems has led to a boom in many different specialised programmes and in some cases has resulted in hurried and improvised solutions. Currently, the drive of the Ministry of Health and Social Services towards publishing quality standards for special residential programmes (del Valle *et al.* 2012) and certain control measures from the administrations seem to have corrected many of the irregularities. A significant piece of data is the relatively high percentage

(34%) of adolescents in therapeutic programmes not receiving mental health treatment, which begs the question, what are they doing there? There are resources of this type that rely on their own psychiatrists and psychologists, others that only have one and others that depend on referrals to external mental health services. It is obvious that there is an urgent need for criteria to define what is required to be a programme of TRC, together with the associated resources and possible methods of working.

The profiles of these young people in Spain show that more than half are between 15 and16 years old and the majority are male. In addition, the questions of cultural origin and ethnicity are important, particularly with adolescents from Roma families who are overrepresented in therapeutic programmes.

As expected, there is a higher incidence of externalising disorders, which hinder adaptation to the more family-like children's homes. The intellectual disability associated with these disorders commonly results in a particularly complicated profile. In general, children with intellectual disabilities represent around 15 per cent of the total in residential child care in Spain but nonetheless, as has been pointed out in the scientific literature, as a group they are scarcely visible.

Another worrying and little studied issue is suicidal behaviour, as 10 per cent of adolescents in therapeutic centres have attempted suicide (almost double the percentage of their peers in children's homes, although that number is by no means negligible). This issue might have more to do with internalising problems, in particular with depression, which often goes unnoticed by adults (parents as much as residential social educators) and calls for more attention, as well as mechanisms for its early detection and prevention.

The situation of therapeutic residential care in Spain is still confusing, despite the fact that significant errors of lack of control in these programmes have been corrected. Some quality standards have been published and there are some recent publications about the need for mental health care in this group, as well as a guide to help residential care staff detect and work with emotional and behavioural problems (del Valle, Sainero and Bravo 2011). All of this is creating a climate of increased awareness of these serious problems, which, together with the gradual introduction of the concept of evidenced-based programmes (although that is in the very early stages), could bring about very positive changes in the future.

Needs and Characteristics of High-Resource Using Children and Youth: Spain

JORGE F. DEL VALLE, ANA SAINERO AND AMAIA BRAVO

The chapter first locates therapeutic residential care in Spain in the context of the broader child welfare sector now and in the past. The Civil War in the 1930s, and the long period of dictatorship, resulted in large numbers of children living for long periods in large, mainly church-run institutions. Legislation paving the way for deinstitutionalisation came late to Spain – not until 1987. However, the pace of change since then has been comparatively rapid, with the development of reunification policies and foster care services, and especially of kinship placement. But comparatively large numbers of children are still in residential settings, mostly now in family group-style homes. As across much of Western Europe, the dominant theoretic approach is based on concepts of normalisation, and children's homes are largely staffed and managed by social pedagogues. The authors note that this was appropriate when the institutions were being closed, since many of the children to be moved into the smaller group homes were in care because of material deprivation (and more recently, those with unaccompanied child migrant status). As the authors describe it, policy in Spain has since become more like the Anglophone countries (see Chapter 2 by Thoburn and Ainsworth) in aiming to use residential care as a 'last resort' rather than a first placement of choice, with the consequent changes in the characteristics of the young residents.

The authors raise important questions around the place of the normalisation and social educative approaches in the present decade, given changes to the age range, characteristics and likely duration of stay of the young people now starting a residential care placement. Specifically, these now tend to be young people who have been maltreated (often coupled with instability in care) or who are in serious conflict with their parents or have mental health difficulties. An important minority have intellectual impairment alongside these other difficulties.

Spain has recognised this change by setting up specialist children's homes to provide therapy for those with a recognised mental health problem and 'socialisation homes' for those with challenging behaviour (though the authors question the usefulness of such a distinction). The chapter then uses early findings from a large and detailed cohort study conducted by the authors in six autonomous communities. A cohort of 51 young people in treatment centres is compared with 283 in 'general' residential care. Whilst more of those in the treatment centres had a diagnosed mental condition or addiction, this applied to many in the other settings and, importantly, those in general settings were just as likely to have 'internalising' problems. This gives further emphasis to the important question posed in the early sections as to the strength or otherwise of a 'model in which the main principles of normalisation were to be preserved while at the same time the residential units needed to be capable of dealing with the difficulties posed by [an intake of young people with more serious problems]'. Other studies have concluded that group care settings for young people with very different needs and fulfilling a range of purposes struggle to achieve good outcomes for all. The three-year follow-up period of this will provide valuable information.

I also found it interesting that length of stay in the treatment units is on average one year and in the general groups two-and-a-half years, whereas the length of stay in residential care is on average four years. This appears to point to a high degree of turbulence. A question that I would hope the researchers will explore is around long-term plans for those young people who cannot return to their birth families. How well does the system meet their needs for stability and 'a sense of belonging' whilst also meeting their needs for therapy?

Although starting late on the search to meet the needs of young people who can benefit from a group care setting that includes appropriate therapeutic input, there is evidence from this chapter that considerable attention is now being paid by policy makers and practitioners, supported by high quality research, on how best to meet the needs of some very troubled young people for whom a family setting is inappropriate.

CHAPTER 4

Needs and Characteristics of High-Resource Using Youth
North America

John S. Lyons, Nicole Obeid and Megan Cummings

Over the past several decades, residential treatment in North America, and particularly in the United States, has undergone significant change. Since the initiation of System of Care Philosophy (Stroul and Friedman 1986), the emphasis within the child-serving system has been on developing strategies to maintain youth in the community whenever possible. This philosophy has resulted in the development of intensive community treatment options, such as wraparound (Hodges *et al.* 2010) and pressure to restrict the use of residential treatment to serve only the highest need youth (Whittaker, del Valle and Holmes, this volume, Chapter 1). Use of residential treatment for children has become increasingly less common, and some even consider it to be counter-indicated (Courtney and Iwaniec 2009).

Commensurate with the increased pressure to reduce admissions into residential treatment, there has been rising interest in the outcomes of all interventions in the child-serving system to better inform approaches to systems change (Sternberg *et al.* 2013). Outcome-management strategies emphasize the simultaneous valuing of clinical outcomes with economic investments to assist decision making about the value of investing in different intervention (Lyons 2004). In our current environment, then, the question becomes whether it is possible to identify which youth benefit from this complex and expensive intervention sufficiently to justify the significant societal investment. Of course, given the rapidly changing policy environment, efforts to understand the needs of youth in residential treatment is a moving target. Therefore, the best way to review these needs is as they relate to the outcomes from residential treatment episodes of care. The present chapter reviews the emerging body of research on this topic.

A learning collaborative approach

A collaborative approach has developed over 18 years that is focused on developing, implementing, and utilizing outcomes data for managing personal change processes (Lyons and Weiner 2009; see also Lyons and Schmidt, Chapter 21, this volume). In this collaboration, the primary strategy for system evolution has been the Child and Adolescent Needs and Strengths (CANS) (Lyons 2009a). This theory-based approach has created large databases that are clinically informed to support re-visioning the system based on the needs and strengths of children and youth rather than on services or financing. Examples from this two-decade long collaboration will be used to inform the present chapter.

The Illinois experience

In 1995, Illinois' Department of Children and Family Services (IDCFS) initiated a system reinvestment strategy that attempted to identify which children and youth currently placed in residential treatment could return to the community (Lyons *et al.* 1998). The problem faced by IDCFS at that time was that they had more than 6000 children and youth in out-of-community care and these cases were consuming about 80 percent of all resources available to address the behavioral and emotional wellbeing of state wards. The idea was that by saving money on residential treatment, these savings could be reinvested in the community to begin to build an improved community infrastructure. The original process of identifying these "stepdown" candidates was to have residential treatment providers nominate specific children and youth. This approach was an unmitigated disaster. The trend was for residential providers to recommend that those who were thriving in residential treatment should stay (e.g. please don't disrupt their treatment) while those failing were nominated (e.g. we aren't helping them, maybe you can). This approach proved extremely ineffective and ended when one of these youth murdered his grandparents with whom he had been placed.

Following the deadly results of this "nomination" strategy, IDCFS reconsidered their strategy and decided to engage in a process whereby the needs of the youth drove the decision making rather than the perspective of the providers. As such, a process was initiated to define precisely what characteristics of children and youth should inform decisions about placement into residential treatment (Lyons *et al.* 1998). Focus groups were impaneled across Illinois to include representatives of all stakeholders in residential treatment, including families and youth. From these discussions, the first decision model for residential placement was identified. It was a simple one. First, there needed to be something to treat (e.g. an actionable behavioral or emotional need). Second, there had to be some level of risk (e.g. concern that if action wasn't taken someone would get hurt). The application of this simple decision model at both placement and during care (i.e. front door and back door) resulted in a nearly one third reduction in residential treatment admissions within an 18-month span. Unlike the previous approach, no child or youth died in the process.

Since that initial decision model was developed, the approach to decision support around identifying which youth are likely to benefit from an admission into residential treatment has evolved. Brian Chor and his colleagues have published a series of articles looking at the outcomes associated with a case complexity approach to decision support, again with the IDCFS population (Chor *et al.* 2012, 2013, 2014). The residential treatment level of the decision model studied in this series of articles is provided in Box 4.1. Review of this model reveals that residential treatment is suggested when a youth is presenting with significant multiple, actionable, behavioral-emotional needs and multiple dangerous behaviors—in other words, both complex and dangerous. Analyses of outcomes suggest that when the model is followed, improved outcomes are obtained from residential treatment. Youth who are admitted to residential treatment but fall below these thresholds do not get as much out of their residential treatment episode as those who fit the model. In the final article in this sequence (Chor *et al.* 2014) strengths were identified as a consideration for community-based treatment over residential treatment. The presence of some community-based strengths might potentiate better intervention in the community, regardless of a very high-need/high-risk presentation of the youth. Regardless, the conclusion from this body of research is that residential treatment works best for very complicated, high-need, and high-risk youth.

TABLE 4.1: Child and Adolescent Needs and Strengths (CANS)

Decision support for suggestion admission into residential treatment for Illinois' Department of Children and Family Services (IDCFS) as studied by Chor et al. 2012

CRITERION 4.1. AT LEAST TWO OR MORE "3" AMONG THE FOLLOWING NEEDS	
Psychosis	Adjustment to trauma
Attention deficit/impulse	Substance use
Depression	Anger control
Anxiety	Affect dysregulation
Oppositional behavior	Eating disturbance
Antisocial behavior	Behavioral regression
Attachment	Somatization

CRITERION 4.2 THREE OR MORE "2" AMONG THE FOLLOWING NEEDS	
Psychosis	Adjustment to trauma
Attention deficit/impulse	Substance use
Depression	Anger control
Anxiety	Affect dysregulation
Oppositional behavior	Eating disturbance
Antisocial behavior	Behavioral regression
Attachment	Somatization

CRITERION 4.3 A RATING OF "2" OR "3" ON DEVELOPMENTAL

CRITERION 4.4 AT LEAST ONE "3" AMONG THE FOLLOWING RISK BEHAVIORS	
Suicide risk	Sexual aggression
Self mutilation	Fire setting
Other self harm	Delinquency
Danger to others	

CRITERION 4.5 THREE OR MORE "2" AMONG THE FOLLOWING RISK BEHAVIORS	
Suicide risk	Fire setting
Self mutilation	Delinquency
Other self harm	Judgment
Danger to others	Social behavior
Runaway	Sexually reactive behavior
Sexual aggression	

To be suggested for Residential Treatment Care (RTC), a child should meet (*either* Criteria 4.1 *or* 4.2 *or* 4.3) *and* (Criteria 4.4 *or* 4.5)

If Criterion 4.3 is met, consider a specialty program

If "Sexual aggression" is rated a "2" or "3," consider a specialty program

If "Physical/medical" is rated a "2" or "3," consider a specialty program

If "delinquency" is rated a "2" or "3," consider a specialty program

The New Jersey experience

Lyons *et al.* (2009) published a study of youth in New Jersey's system of care, which compares the role and outcomes of youth in residential treatment to other types of interventions and levels of care. Figure 4.1 is taken from that study. This figure presents changes in overall symptoms, risks, and functioning on the CANS before and after admission into different programs. Residential treatment is the highest line. Review of this trajectory analysis reveals that in New Jersey, residential treatment serves the most challenging youth and is a step up (youth have escalating needs prior to admission). Improvement over the course of residential treatment takes about six months to prepare a youth for an intensive community intervention (i.e. Care Management Organizations, CMOs), while it takes about 15 months to prepare a youth for transition to supportive case management (i.e. Youth Case Management, YCM). During the period of this analysis, New Jersey used a residential placement decision model modified from the Illinois model presented in Table 4.1 (e.g. modified to fit the items included on New Jersey's version of the CANS).

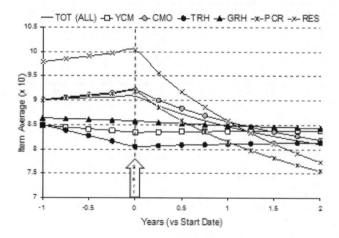

FIGURE 4.1: Hinge analysis of outcome trajectories prior to and after initiation across the system of care in New Jersey

Comprising Youth Case Management (YCM), Care Management Organization (CMO, wraparound), Treatment Home (TRH), Group Home (GRH), Psychiatric Community Residence (PCR), and Residential Treatment (RES) on the CANS overall score

Understanding differential need outcomes

An alternative way of understanding youth in residential treatment and how they change as a function of their presenting needs is displayed in Table 4.2 taken from a panel of 5268 youth treated in residential care in Illinois. One of the interesting features of the CANS is that it is reliable and valid at the item level (Anderson *et al.* 2002). In addition, items are scored based on action levels rather than severity or frequency per se. The action levels for needs on the CANS are as provided in Table 4.3.

TABLE 4.2: Outcomes on behavioral and emotional needs of 5248 youth over a residential treatment episode of care using items of the Child and Adolescent Needs and Strengths (CANS)

MENTAL HEALTH	% PRESENTING	% RESOLVED	% IMPROVED	% IDENTIFIED	% WORSENED	% TRANSITIONING	% NET GAIN
Anger control	60.2	47.1	56.1	25.6	14.0	42.0	30.2
Psychosis	10.9	70.5	74.7	5.0	10.8	7.6	30.2
Adjustment to trauma	48.5	50.1	60.1	22.2	15.2	35.0	27.8
Depression	48.0	52.0	55.9	24.5	5.3	35.8	25.4
Opposition	49.5	42.7	50.5	22.9	12.5	37.9	23.4
Conduct	29.6	59.3	66.1	16.7	14.6	23.8	19.6
Attention-impulse	49.7	46.7	55.1	20.0	9.1	40.1	19.3
Anxiety	29.5	50.9	54.1	19.0	6.0	25.1	14.9
Substance use	16.0	55.8	61.1	11.6	17.3	15.5	3.1
Dangerous behaviors							
Suicide	11.0	82.0	83.9	3.9	10.3	5.4	50.9
Sexual aggression	11.6	76.7	82.9	5.0	14.0	6.5	43.9
Self injury	9.2	80.2	83.0	3.7	20.3	5.2	43.4
Danger to others	37.6	66.1	69.8	27.2	8.6	23.3	38.0
Other self harm	17.1	78.4	80.7	9.0	5.2	11.2	34.5
Runaway	37.2	49.2	58.1	22.5	35.7	33.0	11.3

TABLE 4.3: Action levels for need items from the Child and Adolescent Needs and Strengths (CANS)

0	No evidence, no need for action
1	Watchful waiting/prevention/assessment
2	Action (the need is interfering with someone's functioning)
3	Immediate/intensive action (the need is dangerous or disabling)

Given the non-arbitrary measurement in the individual items of the CANS, outcomes analyses can be accomplished for individual items. These analyses can be quite interesting for program design considerations. Table 4.2 is a selection of CANS item ratings used prior to admission and at transition to study the following characteristics.

- % Presenting: This number is the percentage of admissions with an actionable level (i.e. rating of 2 or 3) on the indicated need.

- % Resolved: This number is the percentage of admissions presenting with an actionable need for whom, by the time they transition from residential treatment, that need is no longer actionable (i.e. rated a 0 or 1).

- % Improved: This number is the percentage of admissions presenting with an actionable need who, by the time they transition, have a lower level of need (e.g. includes moving from a 3 to a 2 rating).

- % Identified: This number is the percentage of admission who do not have an actionable need (i.e., ratings of 0 or 1) at admission but by the time they transition are identified as having an actionable need.

- % Worsened: This number is the percentage of youth who are rated a "2" at admission (they have an identified actionable need) but by the time they transition are rated as a "3."

- % Transitioning: This number is the percentage of youth who have an actionable need (ratings of 2 or 3) at transition from the residential episode.

- % Net Gain: This is the percentage improvement in the total number of admissions with an actionable need at admission to transition. It is calculated at % Transiton−% Presenting/% Presenting.

So, when looking at Table 4.2 you can see that anger control is the most common presenting mental health need with 60.2 percent of all admissions rated as actionable (2 or 3). Of these, fewer than half have their anger issues resolved (47.1%) but more than half are seen as improving (56.1%). There are quite a few youth who are not seen as having anger issues at admission who, by the time they leave residential treatment, have a clear need (25.6%). Additionally, anger needs tend to get worse in about one in seven youth admitted with a "2." While more than one third of youth transition from their residential treatment with ongoing anger treatment needs (42.0%), there is a substantial improvement in the overall percent of youth with this need.

Comparison across mental health needs reveals a common observation for a transformational analysis of outcomes (rather than a status analysis). The youth who get the most out of the experience in terms of change are among the most challenging—anger, psychosis, and adjustment to trauma. Perhaps not surprisingly, there is not much overall improvement in substance use during these episodes of care. It is also pretty clear from these analyses that residential treatment does a consistently good job of treating most needs that are recognized at admission. This table, however, also demonstrates the potential iatrogenic effects of residential treatment on some needs and, while not directly addressed in these analyses, the potential challenge of successfully intervening on needs not recognized at admission.

Comparison between mental health and dangerous behaviors is also telling. Residential treatment has a clear and consistent benefit to reducing these risky behaviors. With the exception of runaway, the % Net Gain associated with every dangerous behavior is better than all of the mental health needs. Runaway is likely not a clear indicator for use of a residential treatment admission unless it is complicating the ability to address other dangerous behaviors.

The challenge of institutionalization

Whittaker, del Valle and Holmes (this volume, Chapter 1) stress the importance of model development to help evolve residential treatment into a cogent and complete intervention strategy. Based on data from the United States, any model that is developed must be trauma-informed, simultaneously address multiple mental health needs, and focus on the reduction of high-risk behavior in both the present and future.

Since residential treatment is a combination of active treatment, a therapeutic milieu, and a place to live, it is often the placement of last resort for challenging youth who have no other placement options (Whittaker, del Valle and Holmes, this volume, Chapter 1). The multi-purpose nature of this intervention creates a complicated challenge. While it is an important contribution to the system to provide a place to live for otherwise hard-to-place youth, this strategy runs the risk of institutionalizing these same youth in out-of-community placements. It is clearly the case that it is easier to transition a youth from residential treatment to the community if there is a family willing and waiting for his/her return (Brown *et al.* 2010). If there is no one, the very fact that the youth has been placed out of community makes community return more difficult. Consideration of this risk of institutionalization should factor into decisions regarding the use of residential treatment as an options (Courtney and Iwaniec 2009).

Conclusion

In sum, the emerging evidence suggests that residential treatment, at least in the United States, is the optimal intervention for very high-risk, multi-need youth who have someone in the community who is willing to take them back. Lower-risk youth are in danger of the contagion effect of learning high-risk behaviors from peers. Youth with no one in the community are at risk of staying in congregate care until they age out—basically becoming institutionalized to this level of care. Efforts to develop effective models of residential treatment should focus on the complex needs of these youth in preparation for them to transition to intensive community care.

Needs and Characteristics of High-Resource
Using Youth: North America

JOHN S. LYONS, NICOLE OBEID AND MEGAN CUMMINGS

One of the many contributions of John Lyons' research is the spotlight it sheds on the benefits and challenges posed in attempting agency-based and system-wide research. To paraphrase what one senior state official related to a group of us academics many years ago: "You folks are always arguing for more research. Meanwhile, we're trying to change the fan belt while the motor's still running!" Lyons and his team are one of those rare cohorts who have attempted just that and some of the unanticipated consequences—positive and negative—of bringing research to the cauldron of contemporary youth services practice are detailed in this present contribution.

Lyons, Obeid and Cummings crystallize one of the paramount decisions faced in services planning: Who belongs in therapeutic residential care?

Since residential treatment is a combination of active treatment, a therapeutic milieu, and a place to live, it is often the placement of last resort for challenging youth who have no other placement options. While it is an important contribution to the system to provide a place to live for otherwise hard-to-place youth, this strategy runs the risk of institutionalizing these same youth in out-of-community placements. It is clearly the case that it is easier to transition a youth from residential treatment to the community if there is a family willing and waiting for his/her return (Brown *et al.* 2010). If there is no one, the very fact that the youth has been placed out of community makes community return more difficult. In sum, the emerging evidence suggests that residential treatment, at least in the United States, is the optimal intervention for very high-risk, multi-need youth who have someone in the community who is willing to take them back.

To me, this statement underlines the critical interface between different strands of needed research on therapeutic residential care including:

- research such as that of Lyons and colleagues, which improves our precision in measuring risk and acuity and helps to sort out the intake queue

- research on effective strategies for family engagement, including the important work of "family finding" such as that currently underway at the National Institute for Permanent Family Connectedness.[1]

• research on model development for which Lyons, Obeid and Cummings provide some tantalizing directions.

Whittaker, del Valle and Holmes (this volume, Chapter 1) stress the importance of model development to help evolve residential treatment into a cogent and complete intervention strategy. Based on data from the United States, any model that is developed must be trauma-informed, simultaneously address multiple mental health needs and focus on the reduction of high-risk behavior in both the present and the future.

One hopes that all three of these research strands move forward along with others. Key partnerships between academic researchers and service providers will be vital to insuring reliability and validity. John Lyons and his research team offer one snapshot of the many fruits of such alliances. One hopes for more.

---

1   This can be found at www.familyfinding.org/NIPFC/CPYP.html.

CHAPTER 5

Needs and Characteristics of High-Resource Using Children and Youth
Denmark

Mette Lausten

This chapter unveils the needs and characteristics of high-resource using children and youth in a Danish context by comparing children in Therapeutic Residential Care (TRC) and children in foster care. Residential care has always been used to take care of orphans or children abandoned by their parents (e.g. Boswell 1988). In conjunction, Denmark has always been defined as a child-welfare oriented country (Gilbert 1997) or "social democratic welfare state regime" (Esping-Andersen 1990), taking care of children in need with a range of interventions (Egelund and Lausten 2009). At any time across the year and over the last 100 years (Bryderup 2005), 1 percent of all children in Denmark aged 0–17 years, are in out-of-home care; data from the last three decades using data from Statistics Denmark is shown in Figure 5.1. In addition, a growing number of children receive preventive programs while staying at home, a figure that has been increasing since the introduction of this type of prevention in the legislation from 1993 (Bryderup 2005).

Although the share of children in care has not changed, the distribution within the care system has changed over time. Children in care are mainly placed in three types of care environments: foster care, residential care, and socio-pedagogical homes. Residential care is defined as a publicly owned housing institution employing 24-hour staff, whereas socio-pedagogical homes are privately owned homes, through publicly approved housing institutions, where the principals (often a married couple with socio-pedagogical experience) are living at the setting (e.g. an old farm being used as riding school for the locals too) and employing 24-hour staff. The socio-pedagogical homes are usually small but highly specialized to take care of children and youth with specific types of problems or psychiatric diagnoses. Residential care and socio-pedagogical homes are paid a fixed amount per child according to their total costs, whereas foster parents are given a fixed payment stated by the legislation, although it is flexible according to the needs of the child.

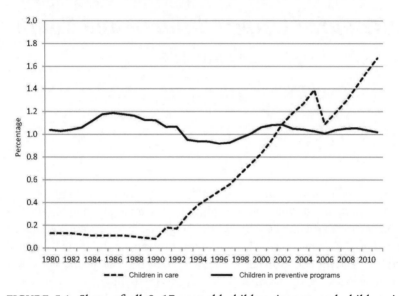

FIGURE 5.1: Share of all 0–17-year-old children in care and children in preventive programs, 1980–2010

Note: Due to structural changes in the number of municipalities from 271 to 98, data encloses a break from 2005 to 2006, mostly visible in the curve for preventive programs.

Source: Own calculations on register data, Statistics Denmark

Children in foster care make up 40–50 percent of all children in care (see Figure 5.2). This share has been growing over time, showing slow changes from TRC into less expensive foster care. The number of children in residential care changes from 35 percent in the early 1980s to 20–25 percent in recent years. At the same time, boarding schools have been declining steadily, mainly because of the changing status in the legislation of this type of out-of-home care. Interestingly, the number of children in socio-pedagogical homes has increased from not existing before 1982 to covering almost 20 percent of all children in care in recent years.

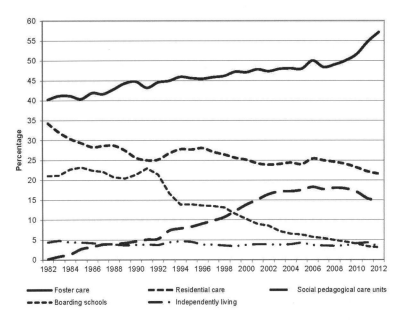

FIGURE 5.2: Children in care, distributed at the five main care environments, 1982–2011

Source: StatBank Denmark, Statistics Denmark

The three main types of care environments cover different types of children in care. The most visible difference is that of age, as shown in Figure 5.3. If a child is placed in care as an infant, almost all (90%) do go into foster care. Very few newborns are put in residential care for observation and further assessment. As the children get older, more and more of them are placed in residential care and socio-pedagogical homes. By the age of 17, the youngsters are almost evenly split across the three care environments: 37 percent in foster care, 35 percent in socio-pedagogical homes, and 28 percent in residential care.

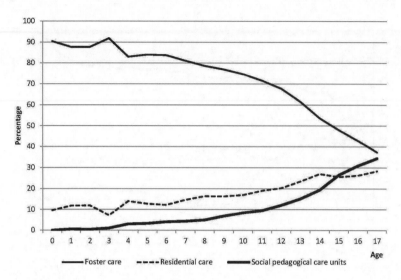

FIGURE 5.3: Children in care, distributed at the three main care environments by age, 2011
Source: StatBank Denmark, Statistics Denmark

Data on children in care

Detailed analysis of children in out-of-home care in Denmark is made possible by the existence of national administrative register data from Statistics Denmark that can be used for research purposes. First, the register data on all children can be linked by personal ID codes with information about their own and their parents' demographic, ethnic and socioeconomic backgrounds, diagnosed illnesses (including mental illness), substance abuse, delinquency, and placement outside the home. Second, SFI (The Danish National Centre for Social Research) has collected data on the Danish Longitudinal Study of children born in 1995 (DALSC), financed by the Danish Ministry of Social Affairs, where a subsample of the study is particularly focused on children in care (DALSC-CIC) (Egelund and Hestbæk 2007; Egelund and Lausten 2009). The aim of this longitudinal study is to map out the risk and resilience factors for children in Denmark in general and for those children in out-of-home care, and to analyze the relationship between patterns of risk and resilience factors and developmental outcomes. The study follows all children born in 1995 who are or have been in out-of-home care approximately every third year. The analyses in this chapter use data from the 2011 data collection period when the children were 15 years old, and contain face-to-face interviews with the children and postal questionnaires sent to the care units (foster carers, residential staff, etc.). Combining these two data sources of register and survey data provides a valuable opportunity to analyze the difference in needs and characteristics of high-resource using children and youth.

This chapter will focus on a study showing the fundamental differences between high-resource using children and low-resource using children. For this purpose, data can be used for both bivariate and multivariate analyses. First, bivariate analyses describe the characteristics of the children in care, comparing low-resource and high-resource using children. Second, multivariate analyses are used to explain the factors making high-resource children different from low-resource children by estimating a logistic regression on being placed in a residential or foster care setting.

Factors related to the parents

By using the register data, the parental background of children in care is better understood. The data gives a highly specified characteristic of the children's parental background and the opportunity to compare between groups. In Table 5.1, children not in care (represented by the DALSC data on children representative of the Danish population) are compared with children in foster care, children in socio-pedagogical homes, and children in residential care. The children not in care serve as the baseline for children in general, where most parents have some sort of education and earn their own living.

TABLE 5.1: Factors related to the mothers of 15-year-old children in care

PARENT-RELATED CHARACTERISTICS	CHILDREN NOT IN CARE	CHILDREN IN FOSTER CARE	CHILDREN IN SOCIO-PEDAGOGICAL HOMES		CHILDREN IN RESIDENTIAL CARE	
Teenage mothers (%)	1.3	8.0	9.0		5.2	
Single living (%)	21.7	51.6	54.8		49.3	
Without any education (%)	22.5	65.6	65.1		61.0	
Being employed (%)	85.8	16.4	24.7	a)	36.8	a)
On social benefit (%)	3.5	30.0	33.7		28.7	
On early retirement pension (%)	3.5	35.6	23.5	a)	18.4	a)
Number of psychiatric diagnosis (%)	0.2	2.4	1.4	a)	1.5	a)

cont.

PARENT-RELATED CHARACTERISTICS	CHILDREN NOT IN CARE	CHILDREN IN FOSTER CARE	CHILDREN IN SOCIO-PEDAGOGICAL HOMES		CHILDREN IN RESIDENTIAL CARE	
Number of somatic diagnoses (%)	13.4	25.8	23.1		22.2	a)
Have been in treatment for substance abuse (%)	0.4	14.0	9.0		7.4	a)
Previously convicted (%)	0.8	12.0	13.3		8.1	
Were in out-of-home care themselves as children (%)	5.8	37.6	28.9	a)	29.4	
Died before the child was 15 (%)	1.1	10.8	3.0	a)	3.7	a)
Total number of children	6,000	250	166		136	

Note: a) Indicates significant difference at 5% level between the group of children in foster care and the group of children in residential care or socio-pedagogical homes, respectively. *Source: Register data, Statistics Denmark, and survey data on DALSC-CIC, when the children are 15 years old*

Of all the children in care, 20 percent are not registered as having a father, despite Danish legislation requiring the name of the father on the birth certificate. The analyses on parents, therefore, are solely based on information about the mothers.

Mothers of children in care are a specific and vulnerable group. This is true from the beginning of the children's lives, and does not change over the years. Mothers of children in care are much more likely to be teenage mothers and single mothers, and to be living on social benefit or early retirement pension. About two-thirds of the mothers do not have any kind of education beyond primary school and less than a third is attached to the labor market. In comparison, only 22 percent of the mothers of 15-year-olds in general are without any kind of education, and 85 percent of them are working.

Looking at the three groups of children in care, the mothers of the children in foster care are socially worse off than the children in socio-pedagogical homes, who are worse off than children in residential care. This is also true when looking at the mother's health, treatment for substance abuse, and convictions. Mothers of children in care have at least one psychiatric diagnosis and a large proportion of them (7–14%) have been in treatment for substance abuse. However, treatment for substance abuse is not a representative figure for the number of mothers suffering with substance abuse, as only a tiny proportion of them go into treatment.

At the same time, treatment of substance abuse can be a way of "getting the child back"—an easier route to take than to gain education and employment. One additional factor in vulnerability is the fact that many mothers of children in care (29–38%) have been in out-of-home care themselves as children. This is only true for 6 percent of the mothers in general.

Finally, if the mother died before the child turned 15, the child is more likely to be in foster care. This fact is distinctive of children in foster care. The mothers of children in foster care are more vulnerable than mothers of children in residential care or socio-pedagogical homes. Combining these points with the fact that children in foster care are placed in care at an earlier age and that the reasons for putting them in care (not shown here) to a larger extent concern parental problems rather than problems with children, the children in foster care are low-resource children compared with the children in residential care and socio-pedagogical homes, who, as the next section shows, are high-resource children.

Factors related to the child

While factors related to the parents are taken from register data, factors related to the child come from both data sources (i.e. register data at Statistics Denmark and survey data from the specific Danish sample of children in out-of-home care from DALSC-CIC). In Table 5.2 the first half of the data is based on register data, showing that boys are more likely to be in socio-pedagogical homes (59%) or residential care (57%), compared with foster care, and that children in care are more likely to have low birth weight than children in general. Children in care do have fewer full siblings and more half siblings due to the instability of the mother's life. There is an overrepresentation of children with ethnic minority backgrounds in care, especially in socio-pedagogical homes, where almost 19 percent of children are from an ethnic minority background.

The second half of Table 5.2 contains subjective measures from survey data, based on the questionnaires sent to the care units. The questionnaire includes the SDQ scale (Strengths and Difficulties Questionnaire; Goodman 1999, 2001), the ADHD-RS (the ADHD Rating Scale teacher form for the people in charge of the child's care; Barkley, Edwards, and Robin 1999) split into subscales of inattention, hyperactivity-impulsivity, and oppositional defiant disorder, and two subscales from the DAWBA (Development and Well-Being Assessment), a recently developed package of questionnaires specifically using the eating disorder section (section P) and the section on depression (section H) (Ford *et al.* 2007; Foreman, Morton, and Ford, 2009).

TABLE 5.2: Factors related to 15-year-old children in care

CHILD-RELATED CHARACTERISTICS	CHILDREN NOT IN CARE	CHILDREN IN FOSTER CARE	CHILDREN IN SOCIO-PEDAGOGICAL HOMES		CHILDREN IN RESIDENTIAL CARE		
Register data							
Boys (%)	52.3	49.2	59.0	a)	57.3		
Birth weight lower than 2500 g (%)	5.0	14.0	9.6		15.4		
Number of full siblings	1.2	0.8	1.1	a)	1.1	a)	
Number of half-siblings, mother's side	0.2	0.9	0.8		0.8		
Number of half-siblings, father's side	0.2	0.7	0.6		0.6		
Ethnic minority (%)	4.5	11.2	18.7	a)	12.5		
Dummy for having a psychiatric diagnoses (%)	6.9	22.4	40.3	a)	54,4	a)	b)
Number of psychiatric diagnoses (%)	0.1	0.4	0.9	a)	1.4	a)	b)
Number of somatic diagnoses (%)	7.3	8.7	10.1	a)	14.1	a)	b)
First time in care before the age of 3 (%)	-	33.6	14.9	a)	8.8	a)	
Survey data							
SDQ category: outside normal area	5.3	5.4	20.6	a)	19.0	a)	
Subscale on inattention from ADHD-RS	n.a.	10.4	12.2	a)	12.3	a)	
Subscale on hyperactivity-impulsivity from ADHD-RS	n.a.	3.3	5.1	a)	5.3	a)	
Subscale on oppositional defiant disorder from ADHD-RS	n.a.	4.4	6.8	a)	7.4	a)	
DAWBA scale on depression (%)	4.5	1.6	9.7	a)	16.3	a)	
DAWBA scale on self-harming behavior (%)	1.3	4.5	4.3		4.9		
Number of observations	6,000	250	166		136		

Notes: a) Indicates significant difference at 5% level between the group of children in foster care and the group of children in residential care or socio-pedagogical homes, respectively. b) Indicates significant difference at 5% level between the group of children in residential care and the group of children in socio-pedagogical homes.

n.a. indicates that the subscale is not included in the questionnaire for children not in care, i.e. there is no value.

Source: Register data, Statistics Denmark, and survey data on DALSC-CIC

Using the SDQ scores split into categories, about 20 percent of all children in socio-pedagogical homes and residential care do score at a level outside the normal area of child wellbeing, whereas this is only true for 5 percent of children in foster care and children not in care. Additionally, children in socio-pedagogical homes and residential care are more exposed to experiencing depression than children in foster care and children not in care. Although there is a higher frequency of self-harming behavior at residential settings, there is no significant difference to children in foster care, as 4–5 percent of all children in care have self-harming behavior.

The probability of being in Therapeutic Residential Care

Multivariate regression are used to analyze what factors are associated with the probability of being in care in a residential care setting (Table 5.3, Model 1, adding residential care and socio-pedagogical homes into one) and what factors are associated with the probability of being in residential care compared with being in care at a socio-pedagogical home (Table 5.3, Model 2).

TABLE 5.3: Odds ratios on the probability of being in residential care

	MODEL 1	MODEL 2
CHILD-RELATED CHARACTERISTICS		
Boys (%)	1.86	-
Number of psychiatric diagnoses (%)	1.49	1.49
Number of somatic diagnoses (%)	1.03	1.04
First time in care before the age of 3	0.16	0.31
Subscale on hyperactivity-impulsivity from ADHD-RS	1.11	0.79
Subscale on oppositional defiant disorder from ADHD-RS	-1.10	1.10
DAWBA scale on self-harming behavior (%)	4.18	-
PARENT-RELATED CHARACTERISTICS		
Mother on early retirement pension (%)	0.47	-
Mothers who have died (%)	0.23	-

Note: All values in the table are statistically significant at a 5% level. All variables from Table 5.1 and 5.2 are included, but only the significant parameters from the logistic regression are shown here with an odds ratio.
Source: Register data, Statistics Denmark

Only a few of the factors show significant differences when analyzing what is different for the children in residential care settings (Model 1 pooling residential care and socio-pedagogical homes), and even fewer when analyzing the difference between children in socio-pedagogical homes and children in residential care (Model 2). It is characteristic that the worse off the child is in terms of mental health, negative impulsivity, hyperactivity, and self harm, the more likely the child is to be in care at a residential setting, as these are larger units specializing in high-resource needs. Children with several psychiatric diagnoses are most likely to be placed in the publicly owned residential care units, probably because the treatment is in house and can be given quicker.

Concluding remarks

This chapter shows some differences from high-resource using to low-resource using children in care. Danish data about children in care are divided into separate care environments. On the one hand, low-resource using children—children having the most vulnerable parents according to demographic and socioeconomic factors as well as mental and physical health issues—are cared for by foster parents, whereas on the other hand, high-resource using children—much more troubled children according to their mental and physical health, behavioral patterns, and other kinds of behavioral disorders—are cared for in socio-pedagogical homes and residential care. Furthermore, foster care is economically low cost and TRC is economically high cost. The staff in TRC are highly skilled (with three to five years of education at university college or university, depending on the topic) at specifically treating the high-resource using children in care. In comparison, foster parents only have a short and practical training (an approximately five-day course with an annual two-day follow-up) using their parental skills to treat the low-resource using children in care. The needs and characteristics of the high-resource children are therefore correctly met by the high-resource budgeting and highly skilled TRC environment.

Needs and Characteristics of High-Resource Using Children and Youth: Denmark

METTE LAUSTEN

Mette Lausten presents a succinct summary of children in out-of-home care in Denmark. Although the share of children in care has not changed, the distribution within the care system has changed over time. Children in care are mainly situated in three types of care environments: foster care, residential care, and socio-pedagogical homes. Residential care is defined as a publicly owned housing institution employing 24-hour staff, whereas socio-pedagogical homes are privately owned, through publicly approved housing institutions, where the principals (often a married couple with socio-pedagogical experience) are living at the institution (e.g. an old farm being used as riding school for the locals too) and employing 24-hour staff. The socio-pedagogical homes are usually small but highly specialized in taking care of children and youth with specific types of problems or psychiatric diagnoses. Residential care and socio-pedagogical homes are paid a fixed amount per child according to their total costs, whereas foster parents are paid a fixed payment stated by the legislation, though this is flexible according to the needs of the child.

To the North American observer, one obvious difference involves the variations in care settings across the population of children in out-of-home care. Particularly distinctive are the apparently increasing percentage of children—now approaching 20 per cent who now reside in *social pedagogical care units*. As Lausten notes, these are described as privately owned but publicly supported housing arrangements where the principals are often a married couple with social pedagogical experience. These units are further described as highly specialized in caring for children with specific types of problems or psychiatric diagnoses. Viewed through a North American lens, these settings seem to suggest something akin to treatment fostering—as in Chamberlain's innovative Multi-Dimensional Treatment Foster Care (MTFC), or possibly variations on the Teaching Family model described in Chapter 8 by Thompson and Daly later in this volume. As the chapter by Hans Grietens (Chapter 19, this volume) and commentary by del Valle make clear, however, the theoretical, epistemological and cultural underpinnings of *social pedagogy* represent something distinctly European and must be viewed in context. That said, Mette Lausten's brief introduction to the Danish service scene suggests to me that the value of a more intensive and systematic comparative review of the out-of-home care services array in both Denmark and the US would be well worth the effort, particularly at a time when many states and counties are struggling with the question of what constitutes a robust suite of services to replace institutional provision for high-resource using children and youth.

A second takeaway, particularly telling for the North American reader, is the care and attention given in Denmark to the on-going collection of high-quality information on children and families entering the intake stream, including risk and resilience factors. Systematic analyses of these data, combined with that of companion studies on the critical elements in a variety of service alternatives, will ultimately help us to discern the combination of factors associated with successful outcomes and make more efficient use of service resources. We have much to learn from each other.

Promising Program Models and Innovative Practices in Therapeutic Residential Care

CHAPTER 6

Varieties of Nordic Residential Care
A Way Forward for Institutionalized Therapeutic Interventions?[1]

Turf Böcker Jakobsen

As with other parts of the Western world, the residential care sector in the Nordic countries has been subject to increasing pressure throughout the last decade. The reasons are multiple but appear to revolve around the combination of a growing disbelief in residential services as an effective way to improve the living conditions of troubled children and a financial crisis that calls for more cost-effective interventions. The situation is a discomforting one for a residential sector providing some of the most costly services for socially disadvantaged children, while finding it difficult to deliver "hard" evidence of the outcomes of services rendered. In such a climate, alternatives are called for, which partly explains the advance of evidence-based family intervention programs such as Multi-Systemic Therapy (MST) and Multi-Dimensional Treatment Foster Care (MTFC).

While policymakers and the media tend to frame residential care as almost a phenomenon of the past, or at best a "last resort" for the children for whom other and more ready options have run out, the picture appears to be somewhat different if one takes a look at the actual landscape of out-of-home care in the Nordic countries. Interestingly, residential care unremittingly plays a key role in the total range of services, even if the picture differs between national settings. Also, one soon realizes that residential care comes in very different shapes, to the extent that one can

1   I would like to thank Senior Researcher Elisiv Bakketeig (Norway), Professor Tommy Lundström (Sweden) and Professor Tarja Pösö (Finland) for kind assistance in providing updated statistics from their respective countries.

discuss whether common labels across a magnitude of "institutional" care services makes sense at all. This diversity becomes particularly clear when one tries to contemplate the distinct role of Therapeutic Residential Care (TRC) in the collective landscape of out-of-home care. The variety of ways to organize residential services with a therapeutic approach, or within a therapeutic framework, is so extensive that lines between definite types of interventions quickly become blurred.

The aim of this chapter is not to set up clear demarcations between specific services or approaches across the Nordic country in order to conclude what TRC "is" in a Nordic context; my goals are more modest. First, I will shed some light on the varieties of residential care services in the Nordic countries, with a particular focus on the Danish context. Second, I wish to discuss the notion of TRC—what it may imply in a Nordic context and how it is turned into practice. My main argument will be that the essence of TRC in a Nordic context cannot be captured by specific theoretical models, therapeutic programs, or organizational structures. Rather, what we find is a common core of characteristics, or, in the words of the editors of this volume, a set of "active ingredients" pointing to the potentials of TRC. Some case examples will be offered from the Danish context.

Nordic residential care for children and young people: differences and similarities

The data presented in this section is based on a comparative study of residential care services in the Nordic countries that included Denmark, Finland, Norway and Sweden[2] (Bengtsson and Jakobsen 2009). Also, updated statistics have been collected specifically for the preparation of this chapter. The comparative study focused on a number of issues in each country, including historical background, legislative framework and organizing principles in connection to out-of-home placements. For the purposes of the present discussion, I will look only at the use of different out-of-home care services in the Nordic countries.

The Nordic countries are known to represent an extensive welfare state system, building on a high level of redistribution of wealth and extended services in the social and other areas (Esping-Andersen 1990). In terms of child protection work, the immediate expectation is correspondingly

---

2   Greenland and Iceland were also part of the study, but they are left out in this context due to difficulties of establishing comparative statistics.

that a fine-meshed safety net is held out for troubled children and their families. The structural similarities found across countries often lead to the conclusion that the notion of a specific "Nordic welfare state model" applies, suggesting that similarities are greater than differences. To some extent, this thesis is confirmed by our comparative study of Nordic child protection work. There are, however, some noticeable differences as well, particularly in terms of the out-of-home care services in use. From an international perspective, all Nordic countries are characterized by relatively high proportions of children in out-of-home care. Denmark in particular has been known to employ out-of-home care services for a large number of children, and for decades placement rates have steadily revolved around 1 percent of all children (aged 0–17 years) placed in care at any time. Our comparative study from 2009 (based on statistics from 2006) showed that while Finland had placement rates close to the Danish level, Norway and particularly Sweden used out-of-home care to a considerably lesser degree. However, the most recent statistics demonstrate that while the number of placements has decreased slightly in Denmark in the past five years, the opposite has been the case in the other Nordic countries. Thus, close to 1 percent of all children are now in care in both Norway and Sweden (per set date), bringing placement rates more or less on a level with Denmark. In fact, today, Finland appears to have the highest proportion of children in out-of-home care among the Nordic countries, placing more than 1.3 percent of all children in care at any time. However, these numbers include placements as after-care services for 19–20-year-olds. Thus, even if numbers are not directly comparable, it is clear that placement rates are high in all the Nordic countries when compared with most other countries in the Western world.

If we take a look at the out-of-home care services of preference in each of the Nordic countries, some noteworthy differences appear. For our current purposes, the most interesting feature is the use of residential care. Denmark and Finland stand out in the Nordic context (and more generally) as countries with remarkably high numbers of cared-for children and young people in residential settings. In Finland, close to 39 percent of all children are placed in some form of residential care. Until a few years ago, somewhat higher rates applied to Denmark, but the most recent statistics show that "only" 40 percent of all children are now found in institutionalized settings, still forming a Nordic record. Norway has the lowest share of institutional placements (approximately 30%), while in Sweden, 37 percent of all children are placed in residential care.

Obviously, statistics never tell the whole story; the administrative categories and the interventions they denote may not always be directly comparable, neither across countries nor in time. For example, public care for children with physical disabilities is included in the statistics in some countries (such as Denmark) and not in others. Similarly, from 2006 the Swedish statistics on out-of-home care include refugee children without parents or other relatives, contributing to the increase in the total number of placements described above. More fundamentally, categorizations of troubled children can be expected to differ across national settings, meaning that children with similar needs or difficulties may appear equally well within, for example, "social," "psychiatric" and "criminal" services. Besides from being a hugely understudied matter, differences in such classificatory practices obviously form a massive challenge for comparative work on child welfare services.

However, the most important statistical finding in this context concerns the inevitable fact that residential care continues to play a vital role in the child protection landscape in all of the Nordic countries. This result raises questions about the content of such services: what characterizes the kind of services that we dub "residential" and to what degree are we talking about a coherent and homogenous phenomenon? Below, these questions are discussed specifically from a Danish angle.

Residential care in Denmark: types of interventions and key features

It is well known that residential care is a common denominator for a mixed and diversified array of interventions that are by some definition "institutional" by nature. This situation is perhaps more obvious in Denmark than in most places. First, Danish social work has had a long tradition for experimental practices, often described as "letting the thousand flowers blossom" (Heglund 1994), and this tradition has had its stronghold in social pedagogy as well, paving the way for a variety of practices in the residential care sector.[3]

Second, even if Danish social work went through an "anti-institutionalist" era in the 1960s and 1970s—a more general, societal

---

3   In recent years, this principle of methodological freedom in social work and social pedagogy has started to be criticized heavily by politicians and policymakers arguing for a turn towards a more evidence-based practice to the detriment of the traditionally more experience-based practice. Currently, it is unclear where this strong push will take child protection work and how great the impact will be on the services in use.

critique of the incarceration policy of deviant citizens in large-scale hierarchically organized institutions—the response was not the abolishment of residential care as such. Rather, a gradual *transformation* of the institutional landscape began to take place (Egelund and Jakobsen 2009a, 2011). A plethora of alternatives arose, from smaller but relatively traditional public institutions with reduced numbers of residents and less hierarchical principles of organization, to the apparently self-contradictory notion of "anti-institutionalist" residential settings: communes based on "working solidarity" where staff would live at the care premises along with their own families (Heglund 1983, 1988). Few of the communes exist today, but their predecessors have seen the light in the shape of a growing number of "socio-pedagogical homes." These are privately owned residential settings, typically based on what may look like a foster home writ large—a family living at the care premises along with a number of children in care—but professionalized and institutionalized in the sense that pedagogical staff are hired to work there, internal schools may be established in connection to the residential setting, etc.

In numbers, we can see that approximately 40 percent of all Danish children and young people in care were placed in residential settings. But what does "residential" more specifically entail? If we look more closely at the statistics, 22 percent of all children in care (or slightly more than half of all children in residential care) are placed in various types of public institutional care, including children's homes, treatment homes (expected to provide "treatment" or "therapeutic" care), respite care facilities and secure accommodation for young people. Further, a substantial group of children are placed in socio-pedagogical homes (15% of all children in care) while three percent of all children are placed in "boarding schools"[4] (National Social Appeals Board 2012).

In an ethnographic study of residential services in Denmark—which included an array of settings from children's homes and socio-pedagogical homes to therapeutic residential settings and secure accommodation—we found that while great differences in social practices could be observed, variations did *not* follow the official labels of institutional types in any

---

4   Placement in "boarding schools" is arguably a unique Danish phenomenon. A large proportion of children choose to attend a certain type of boarding schools, typically for one year in succession after their primary school exam at age 15–16. For many, this is a way to try to live away from home in a rather tightly organized and protected environment. Some of these boarding schools also receive young people going into care. It has been argued that this arrangement provides a promising model for integrating children and young people who are "on the edge" of more serious difficulties. Such potential, however, has not been studied systematically.

straightforward sense (Egelund and Jakobsen 2009a, 2011). Rather, one might argue that demarcation lines between different forms of residential care mainly serve administrative purposes, and that the more interesting question concerns the kind of care environment they permit. In particular, the great variety in practices provokes the question of *how* we should view and understand the "therapeutic" quality of certain types of residential services.

"Therapeutic" residential care: where to draw the line

In the introduction to this book, the editors set the broader frame for understanding TRC, emphasizing that it:

> ...involves the planful use of purposefully constructed, multi-dimensional living environment designed to enhance or provide treatment, education, socialization, support and protection to children and youth with identified mental health or behavioral needs in partnership with their families and in collaboration with a full spectrum of community-based formal and informal helping resources. (p.24)

In a Danish context, "therapeutic" residential care relates most directly to the type of institutional settings officially coined *behandlingshjem*, which literally translates as "treatment homes." These are specialized and professionalized care environments, typically based on theoretically informed understandings of the nature of traumas suffered by children at an early age. Such understandings result in care settings meticulously designed to deal with those traumas in an all-encompassing way (Egelund and Jakobsen 2009b, Jakobsen 2010).

In Denmark, as in other Nordic countries, there is a lengthy tradition for this type of TRC, which, in theoretical terms, is often cast within the context of "milieu-therapy" or "planned environmental therapy" (see Kornerup 2009). Milieu-therapy embraces the idea that the carefully arranged setting in itself composes a vital part of the treatment, e.g. that "safety" and "predictability" on the daily organizational level is a prerequisite for working with children's inner feelings of order and meaning (Egelund and Jakobsen 2009b). In that sense, the milieu-therapeutic institution clearly meets the definitional criteria of providing "a purposefully constructed, multi-dimensional living environment" for children suffering early-age trauma.

However, I would like to argue that the discussion of TRC from a Nordic perspective should not limit itself to milieu-therapy interventions in specialized treatment homes. At least from a Danish perspective, the diversity of the institutional care sector calls for expanding the notion of TRC and to include other and less programmatic interventions. The difference between therapeutic and "non-therapeutic" interventions, I suggest, is not a matter of employing particular theories (e.g. on children's traumas) or building certain types of institutional regimes. Rather, what unites TRC across the board of interventions is the will to work purposefully and strategically with "theories of change" for the positive development of children in care with pronounced and well-described difficulties. In terms of contents, such strategic interventions may go in a number of directions, which is actually a point in itself if we want to leave behind the idea that TRC can be narrowed down to a few models or programs. It seems more fruitful to probe some of the *guiding principles* in current practices and the *active ingredients* of therapeutic services. Based on Danish findings, the final section below seeks to carve out and discuss some of these principles and ingredients.

Therapeutic residential care: towards an account of "active ingredients"

To provide a tentative template for understanding the "active ingredients" of TRC—and to demonstrate the complexity of the matter—I would like to present two brief cases from an ethnographic study of Danish residential care (Egelund and Jakobsen 2009a, 2011). The cases concern the work of two concrete institutions that are not, according to most definitions, providing "therapeutic" services for children and young people in care. Nonetheless, as cases they are helpful in terms of opening up the debate about what "therapeutic" actually entails.

The first case concerns a residential setting for 12 children and young people. At the time of the study, the residents were aged 6–17 years. The institution was run by the municipal social authorities and situated in a residential neighborhood in one of Denmark's largest cities. The children were described as suffering from "a fundamental lack of proper care," resulting in "attachment disorders" and "emotional difficulties," and they typically came from families struggling with alcohol or drug abuse, mental illness and issues of intimate partner violence. The staff employed a number of socio-pedagogical approaches, inspired by various theoretical understandings of troubled children, and they held high an open-minded professional atmosphere, discussing current challenges they were experiencing with particular children in joint meetings on a weekly basis.

In terms of the residential living environment, a number of principles were firmly applied. Most importantly, schooling had a very high priority among the professionals. "In this place, all children go to school," staff kept repeating. Most children attended ordinary public schools in the neighborhood, while a few went to special schools further away. Great efforts were put into not only making sure that every child came to school every morning, but also that school work was prioritized more generally: staff would engage actively in meetings with teachers, in helping children with their homework in the afternoon, in preparing children for particular school activities, etc.

Moreover, involving and including biological families in the everyday life of children in care was kept as a vital working principle. On the practical level, children were encouraged to visit families. For example, if a child had worries about younger siblings who lived at home with a single mother, staff would make sure that frequent visits took place. Also, staff strived to engage not just parents, but also other family members actively in children's lives—such as when a grandfather was committed to taking his grandson to football every week, or when an arrangement was made with a maternal aunt and her husband for a girl to go on visits every second weekend. In some cases, such endeavors actually resulted in children experiencing more intensive and continuous family contact than before the placement.

On a more general note, social relations were preserved and extended by staff members who perceived themselves as "mediators" between the everyday lives of cared-for children and their broader social network of kinship and friendship. This is not to ignore the fact that close personal relations would also at times arise between children and the caretakers with whom they shared large parts of their daily life, but the staff never seemed to lose sight of the fact that their own role was temporary and determined on the task of "building relations" within and across social arenas in collaboration with the individual child.

The second case concerns a very different kind of residential setting— one that, apart from providing a countryside living environment for five teenage girls in care, also comprised a special school for children with special needs as well as a riding academy. The residential setting was privately owned and thus classified as a "socio-pedagogical home," admitting young girls from various municipalities in the region. The girls were described as children with "a variety of social and emotional difficulties"—some with early traumas and damage due to parents' drug and alcohol abuse. Most of the girls had been placed in other settings—

residential homes, therapeutic units or foster families—before coming to the socio-pedagogical home.

Similar to our first case, schooling activities were a key point of attention in the residential setting, yet in a somewhat different manner. Girls who were newcomers would consistently be enrolled in the internal school, but always with a view to entering the public schools in the vicinities. While in the internal school, each child would be systematically tested, involving frequent follow-ups, to determine his/her particular learning needs. Interestingly, children who had been deemed as "incorrigible cases" by previous schools typically turned out to possess fair skills in certain areas of the curriculum, while displaying great difficulties in others. The testing allowed for much more refined and purposeful schooling measures and the prospect of attending an ordinary public school would often not appear as overwhelming as before.

The schooling program of the socio-pedagogical home is best understood as a strategy for social inclusion. However, the particular living environment of the care setting allowed for other processes of integration as well. The organizational composition of a residential home and a riding academy on the same premises provides an intriguing example. Generally, one of the major critical concerns of residential care is the potentially segregated nature of institutional practices and, accordingly, the ominous gap between residential and non-residential life. In a sense, the socio-pedagogical home had turned this conflict upside down by "inviting" the local community to take part in the everyday life of the residential setting. Most days the home would buzz with life, particularly as young girls from the local area would come to ride on the horses. Along with them came friends, parents and siblings, not to mention the children attending the special school and *their* parents, accompanied by the occasional plumber, painter or horse dealer.

On the face of it, the residential home in many ways composed a messy enterprise. Beneath the cluttered surface, however, the daily disorder would seem meaningful rather than chaotic. The everyday life of the institution provided an excellent platform for *doing* social inclusion of socially disadvantaged children rather than just talking about it or practicing skills in an isolated space.

I am aware that this last example comes a long way from a nominal definition of TRC. Indeed, the two cases could easily be dismissed as saying very little about therapeutic residential settings altogether. I want to suggest, however, that we take seriously the efforts of skilled practitioners to create "therapeutic" living environments in a variety of meaningful ways. Also, I believe there are general lessons to be taught from the concrete therapeutic strategies found in these cases. These potentials become clearer if viewed through the lens of a "social capital" approach.

Derived originally from the work of Pierre Bourdieu, social capital points to "the reciprocal set of connections, norms and obligations shared between network members, whether at the level of individuals, households or neighborhoods/communities" (Gilligan 2012, p.120). The particular relevance of the concept in connection to children in care concerns the argument that an essential part of the difficulties of these children has to do with a "social capital deficiency." Importantly, this understanding does not undermine or ignore the material reality of the troubles experienced by cared-for children and their families (poverty, unemployment, etc.). Rather, its focus on social capital brings into play the grave implications of lacking social relations as a valuable asset—while also pointing to the prospects of focusing in social work on the strengthening of the child's most vital social relations.

An important analytical distinction has been drawn in the literature between "bonding" and "bridging" aspects of social capital:

> Bonding entails strong connectedness with people similar to yourself in important ways. Bridging social capital, on the other hand, involves fewer close contacts with people who are different from yourself. Bonding capital may provide a lot of support, yet may sometimes prove restrictive. Bridging capital can help in moving on from a predicament, in finding additional resources to break out of a stalemate. (Gilligan 2012, p.120)

Put differently, bonding social capital is good for "getting by," while bridging social capital is good for "getting on" (Forbes and McCartney 2012, p.277).

This is a helpful distinction for our purposes. Thus, one might argue that the ability to provide severely troubled children with both bonding and bridging social capital is a defining characteristic of successful therapeutic residential interventions. Bonding social capital concerns the kind of support that enables children to stay anchored in strong emotional ties—as when social pedagogues take on the role of "mediators" between children in care and their family relations. Bridging social capital concerns the kind of support that gives children the opportunity to develop by becoming part of a broader and more differentiated social network—as when the local community is "brought into the institution" or when the proper requirements are met so that cared-for children can thrive in the ordinary schooling system.

Clearly, providing support for troubled children along the lines of a social capital approach is not restricted to TRC. In many ways, successful foster care families do just that, creating at once an emotionally positive home environment, a pathway for the child to keep contact with his/her biological family and windows of opportunity for the child to develop new skills and competences in a variety of settings. This is no different from what we strive to offer naturally to our own children.

What sets TRC apart, however, is the *purposeful employment* of such strategies. Children in TRC generally struggle with such grave difficulties that systematic approaches are called for. "Systematic," however, should not be confused with "programmatic." Looking at the Nordic landscape of residential care, some of the most promising examples are not manual-based interventions, I would contend, but professionalized services, building on extensive experience and displaying a range of inventive practices. Despite their differences, these residential care services find a common ground in working purposefully towards the social and societal anchoring of troubled children, and they do this work on the basis of clearly defined strategies for conjuring up bonding and bridging social capital. We need to tap into these long-stretched professional practices if we are to pave the way for a promising and enduring road for TRC.

Varieties of Nordic Residential Care: A Way Forward for Institutionalized Therapeutic Interventions?

TURF BÖCKER JAKOBSEN

Turf Jakobsen raises some important theoretical and conceptual issues, extrapolating from a few specific instances of Nordic (especially Danish) residential care. At the heart of his discussion is a concern with defining what we mean by *therapeutic* across the wide diversity of residential settings. A number of other significant issues are raised as well, including the role of "purposiveness" in the provision of care, the importance of being strategic and the balance of experience-based and evidence-based practice.

Earlier in my career, I was charged with drafting standards for residential facilities in Ontario, Canada, and one of the key issues was what constituted residential *treatment* as opposed to "regular" or "basic" care. Today, I would maintain that all residential care needs to be therapeutic, but only some care facilities should be designated as providing a residential treatment program characterized by a highly *medical* focus and under the overall direction of a physician. In a therapeutic approach, the medical aspects constitute one dimension alongside many others, and as Jakobsen notes, the overarching focus is *social pedagogic* (child and youth care), which focuses primarily on the social-emotional and developmental-learning needs of the young residents. It is to be hoped that all treatment programs would also have therapeutic characteristics.

Jakobsen purposely passes quite lightly over the significance of trauma in the therapeutic care of young people. My own research (Anglin 2002) suggests that virtually all young people in residential care experience deep and profound psycho-emotional pain as a result of various traumatic experiences, and that too often this aspect is not being consistently or effectively addressed. While social capital and competencies need to be fostered, we must not ignore the fact that many of the challenging actions of the residents can be understood as "pain-based behavior" (Anglin 2002, pp.107–114). In addition, care workers need to be aware of their own pain-based anxieties, in order to be responsive rather than reactive or coercive.

Jakobsen indicates that all residential care needs to be *purposive*, which I take to mean that all events of daily life can be understood in terms of their therapeutic potential for each child. In this sense, milieu-therapy is still a powerful notion as long as it is informed by recent research. As

Jakobsen observes, care also needs to be *strategic*. While I am a strong proponent of good strategic thinking as a vital aspect of managing complexity, we also need to heed the business mantra "culture eats strategy for breakfast". Research over the past decade (Anglin 2002, 2012; see also Holden, Anglin, Nunno and Izzo, Chapter 20, this volume) identifies the critical importance of creating congruence across the entire culture and operation of an agency. Strategies alone cannot overcome weaknesses in the organizational cultural fabric.

Lastly, I agree strongly with Jakobsen that we need to value practice wisdom as well as research evidence in the provision of residential care. Research evidence does not always capture the differences that make a difference, and we must always respect and develop the professional judgment of residential staff.

CHAPTER 7

MultifunC
Multifunctional Treatment in Residential and Community Settings

Tore Andreassen

In most countries, youths with serious behaviour problems are placed in residential treatment institutions. Generally, it has been a problem that the residential treatment has been poorly described and appears to be like a 'black box'. In addition, there has been a lack of outcome studies of treatment effectiveness.

In 2000, the Norwegian Ministry of Children, Family and Equality initiated a review of the research on residential treatment of youths with serious behaviour problems. Based on this review, conducted by the author of this chapter, the residential treatment model 'MultifunC' or 'Multifunctional Treatment in Residential and Community Settings' was developed. The model is implemented in Norway, Sweden and Denmark, and an effectiveness study of the model is underway in these countries. This chapter presents the main conclusions from the review of the research, along with a presentation of the treatment model.

Residential treatment as an intervention for youths

Youths may be placed in residential treatment for different purposes. Some placements are a result of abuse or poor care conditions. The aim of such placements is to secure good daily care for the youths. Another reason for placement may be the youths' antisocial behaviour, including criminality, violence or substance abuse, and the aim is to intervene in order to reduce these problems. The contents, standards and effectiveness of residential treatment have not been well documented in the research literature, therefore, the Norwegian Ministry of Children, Family and Equality in collaboration with the National Board of Institutional Care and the Centre for Evaluation of Social Services in Sweden initiated a comprehensive review of the topic (Andreassen 2003). Following the publication of the review, those same authorities funded the establishment of a residential treatment model called 'MultifunC'. Currently, the model has been implemented in nine residential units in Norway, Sweden and Denmark.

Research on residential treatment

The research on residential treatment has increased over the years, and a substantial number of experimental and quasi-experimental studies have been conducted. In addition, several meta-analyses and even meta-analyses of meta-analyses have been published. The research indicates that the effects of residential treatment may vary from the negative (Whitehead and Lab 1989) to the uncertain (Gottschalk *et al.* 1987) and to the more positive (Andrews *et al.* 1990). The important question seems not to be whether residential treatment may have positive effects or not, but rather what type of residential treatment does work. Some research also indicates that treatment that works for some youths may not work, or may even be harmful, for others (Lowenkamp and Latessa 2008). This implies that the main question is 'What works for whom?' Both longitudinal studies of influences on the development of behaviour problems (risk factors) and meta-analyses of treatment studies shed some light on this question. For instance, a group of researchers at Carleton University in Canada formulated several theoretical 'principles of effective treatment', based on research on treatment of serious behaviour problems (Andrews *et al.* 1990). These are the principles of Risk, Need and Responsivity (RNR). Several meta-analyses support these principles (Andrews and Bonta 2006; Andrews, Bonta and Wormith 2011; Dowden and Andrews 2000; Joy Tong and Farrington 2006; Koehler *et al.* 2013; Latessa and Lowenkamp 2006; Lipsey 2009; Lipsey and Wilson 1998; Lipsey, Landenberger and Wilson 2007; Lipsey *et al.* 2010; Lowenkamp *et al.* 2010, and others). Even if some principles have been added, these three still seem to be the most important ones when it comes to describing effective interventions. Among the principles added is the fidelity or integrity principle, which refers to the therapeutic integrity of the programme. An increasing amount of research has documented significant associations between treatment fidelity or integrity and treatment effectiveness (Lipsey 2009; Lowenkamp and Latessa 2004; Lowenkamp *et al.* 2010).

The risk principle

The risk principle predicts that residential treatment and other intensive interventions work best for high-risk youths, that is, youths with many risk factors. Important risk factors for serious behaviour problems are known from longitudinal studies (Cottle, Lee and Heilburn 2001; Loeber and Farrington 2000; Pardini and Frick 2013). Longitudinal studies have identified major risk factors under the heading of 'The Central Eight' (Andrews, Bonta and Wormith 2006). Among these are a history of antisocial behaviour, antisocial personality pattern, antisocial cognition, antisocial associates, specific family conditions, specific school conditions, leisure activities and substance abuse. High-risk youths have more needs and, in accordance with this principle, should be offered more resources and more intensive treatment than low-risk youths.

Some research indicates that residential treatment may have unintended or iatrogenic effects through reciprocal negative influence and through mutual reinforcement of negative behaviour and attitudes among youths (Dodge, Dishion and Lansford 2006). This risk factor seems to be operating specifically when low-risk youths are placed together with high-risk youths (Lowenkamp and Latessa 2008). When low-risk youths are placed in residential facilities, contact with positive factors at home (school, peers and family) is reduced and in the company of high-risk youths, they may be even more at risk. For high-risk youths, such placement seldom implies loss of positive influence or increased risk level due to their multi-problem status.

The need principle

The risk factors may be divided into static and dynamic factors. The need principle states that the dynamic or malleable risk factors are promising targets for treatment and are often referred to as 'criminogenic needs'. This implies that promising targets for treatment may be individual behaviour, skills and attitudes, but also transactions with family, peers and school. This is also in agreement with the research on predictors of criminal behaviour, which recommends that effective interventions should target factors within several domains. If the treatment reduces the number of risk factors, the probability of future antisocial behaviour decreases. In other words, effective treatment should be systemic and address factors such as family function, peer relations and school functioning.

The responsivity principle

The responsivity principle makes a distinction between general and specific responsivity. General responsivity implies that well-structured programmes based on cognitive behaviour theory and social learning theory are more effective than other approaches if the programme targets risk factors such as social skills deficits, poor anger management and antisocial attitudes. Several meta-analyses support the effectiveness of such interventions (Armelius and Andreassen 2007; Lipsey *et al.* 2007). The learning of new skills and behaviours requires that youths are motivated to apply what they have learned in the real world. Therefore, programmes based on cognitive behaviour theory should be combined with motivational techniques such as token economy, which rewards pro-social behaviour, and Motivational Interview (MI) (McMurran 2009; Miller and Rollnick 1991). The latter is a therapeutic approach that motivates youths to reflect on the disadvantages of their problem behaviour.

Youths with serious behaviour problems have some common characteristics such as lack of social skills, antisocial attitudes and weak problem-solving skills. Still, in other domains, they are unique individuals who vary as much as other adolescents. Specific responsivity indicates that youths respond individually to treatment efforts based on their personality characteristics such as anxiety, mental capacity, mental health problems and others. In accordance with the Responsivity principle, such individual differences should be taken into consideration (Andrews and Bonta 2006; Kennedy 1999). For example, reflections on moral dilemmas should be presented differently for youths with weak cognitive skills compared with other youths. In social skills training, the anxiety level of the youth should be considered in role-plays.

Treatment culture / climate

No methods or principles, regardless of their empirical support, work in a vacuum (Fretz 2007). Fretz (2007) claims that effective use of the RNR principles approach requires a treatment culture that is pro-social, highly structured and mutually respectful. The staff and administrators should continuously monitor the culture of a programme, because effective treatment cultures depend on the entire programme for their sustainability. Others have also concluded that the treatment climate needs to build on good relations, be respectful and involve the youths in their own treatment (Andrews and Dowden 2004). Scholte and Van der Ploeg (2000) found the best effects occurred if there was a balance between adult control and youth autonomy.

Family work and aftercare

Residential treatment of high-risk youths is very complicated because of the complexity of the problems and because the different topics demand different approaches and competencies. For the families or the parents, the same methods and principles that have proven effective in home-based interventions also seem to work in residential treatment approaches. Both Parent Management Training (PMT) and Multi-Systemic Therapy (MST) target family factors that influence the youth's behaviour problems (Borduin *et al.* 1995; Kazdin 2005; Ogden and Hagen 2006). PMT's focus on communication and control of behaviour and MST's focus on systemic factors that influence behaviour problems seem to be equally applicable to residential treatment approaches.

The home environment that the youth returns to after residential placement is of critical importance in order to sustain the positive changes achieved during placement. The quality of the environment, especially pro-social peers, positive family function and involvement in school, seem to be important factors in success (Liddle and Rowe 2001). Behavioural changes during the residential stay may be of short duration if the treatment does not include efforts to change the ecology of the youth outside the institution (Hollin 2000).

The family is in need of help and support both during residential placement and afterwards. A review by Frensch and Cameron (2002) highlighted the importance of aftercare and working with the family in order to improve the effectiveness of residential care. Another review by Hair (2005) concluded that children and adolescents with severe emotional and behaviour disorders can benefit from and sustain positive outcomes from residential treatment if it is multi-modal, holistic and ecological in its approach. Aftercare seems to be as important as the residential treatment itself, and should be an integrated part of residential placement (Altschuler 2008; Liddle and Rowe 2001). In accordance with the Risk principle, high-risk youths should receive more intensive aftercare than low-risk youths in programmes targeting dynamic risk factors (Lowenkamp and Latessa 2005). Consequently, programs such as MST and Family Integrated Transitions (FIT) could be used as aftercare interventions (Trupin *et al.* 2011).

MultifunC

The review of the research has identified important characteristics of effective residential treatment interventions for youths with serious behaviour problems. Based on the messages from research, it has been possible to develop standards for effective residential treatment approaches, such as MultifunC (which stands for 'Multifunctional Treatment in Residential and Community Settings') (Andreassen 2004). The name of the model signals the importance of targeting individual as well as environmental risk factors and of including integrated aftercare in community settings. The first MultifunC units were established in 2005 in Norway and Sweden, and MultifunC units have also been established in Denmark. Each residential unit may have up to eight youths at the same time, separated into two sections. Several written manuals describe the treatment model, including the theoretical basis, principles for assessment, treatment, organisation of the treatment process and quality assurance of the model (Andreassen 2004). A training programme describing the theory and practice of the MultifunC model has also been produced. In these units, the whole staff is trained in MultifunC as a model, and additionally, some employees receive special training in risk-assessment, Aggression Replacement Training (ART), MI, MST, PMT, therapeutic management of violent behaviour, etc.

MultifunC targets high-risk youths with serious behaviour problems. A standardised assessment instrument (Youth Level of Service/Case Management Inventory) is used to assess the risk level (Hoge and Andrews 2002). Based on conclusions from research on the need for intensive support following the residential placement (Lowenkamp and Latessa 2005), plans for their future care situation are required. The future care situation may be the family of origin, but may alternatively be relatives or foster parents.

The residential units are open (not secure), but the youths' opportunities to leave the units are regulated by the staff. Whenever a youth is outside the residential area, the staff will monitor where he or she is. If the youth runs away, he or she is brought back, if necessary with assistance from the police. If possible, youths attend ordinary schools in the area and they participate in pro-social leisure activities outside the unit. Such activities are training grounds, and may increase the possibilities to succeed when the youths progress into aftercare. Those who at first do not manage to adapt to an ordinary school situation are offered education within the residential unit. In all cases, there is a focus on gradually progressing into an ordinary school setting.

The treatment process is organised in two main parts. The first takes place within the institution and the other takes place in the home environment (aftercare). The duration of the residential treatment depends on the youth's individual development, but is usually about six months.

The duration of the integrated aftercare is about four to five months so that totally treatment duration amounts to 10–12 months.

Stages during the residential placement

The residential placement is divided into three main phases or stages. These are the 'intake stage', the 'treatment stage' and the 'transfer stage'. During the Intake stage, the youth's treatment needs are assessed (the risk factors relevant to each youth) in addition to responsivity factors (personality factors that may influence the responsivity to treatment efforts). This assessment provides the basis for individually tailored treatment plans. This stage includes a meeting with the youth, the family and other relevant participants to agree on treatment targets and treatment plans.

As soon as the treatment plans are developed, the treatment stage begins. In this stage, the treatment systematically targets change of behaviour, training in new skills, change of attitudes, performance in school settings, decreasing contact with antisocial peers, increasing contact with pro-social peers and leisure activities. At the same time, the parents receive guidance and training in communication and setting limits. They also receive support in the planning and management of the youth's home visits.

In the last phase – the transfer stage – the youth visits their home more often; their behaviour at home is an important factor in making decisions about progressing to aftercare. It is considered more important that the youth functions well at home than in the residential setting. This means that youths who misbehave in the residential setting but not at home should spend more time at home than other youths. It also means that youths who behave well at home and in school settings may progress to the aftercare (finishing their residential stay), even if their residential behaviour is negative.

The residential treatment is further divided into five levels, each with a different focus and structure. Level 1 focuses on daily routines and rules and matches the Intake stage with a focus on assessment, while the other levels additionally focus on treatment targets according to the treatment plan. The youths may, during their stay, earn tokens that can be exchanged for privileges or goods. Progression from one level to another is a function of the number of tokens earned and reflects the youth's level of development. It is not possible to lose tokens or to 'fall down' a level. The levels are designed so that a youth at Level 1 earns token on a card with daily rewards, while a youth at Level 2 gets weekly rewards. At Levels 3, 4 and 5 there is increased focus on individually tailored treatment targets and the use of behavioural contracts instead of cards. The behavioural contracts are written agreements between the youth and the staff and include what the youth and staff should do respectively. Level 5 is designed so that the parents may take over when the youth moves home.

Methods in the milieu-therapy

The milieu-therapy focuses on predictability and structure, systematic and targeted change efforts, and attempts at striking a good balance between the youth's autonomy and adult control, in addition to more concrete methodological approaches. The youths' daily lives are predictable and structured in the form of daily and weekly plans. Staff seek to control negative behaviour such as violence, substance abuse and other unacceptable behaviours. Staff also monitor the youths and always know where they are and with whom they spend time when they are outside the residential unit. In accordance to the youths' development, the methods of control change from close physical staff monitoring to other forms of monitoring (phone contact, etc.). The youths are involved in their own treatment process, both through opportunities to express their opinions and needs and through involvement in problem solving. The youths are allowed to discuss and make suggestions about how unacceptable behaviour may be changed and how treatment targets could be reached. The staff approach the youths with respect and are good role models – this includes representing and modelling the skills and behaviours that the youths are learning.

The youths get training in social skills, anger management and new attitudes through ART (Goldstein, Glick and Gibbs 1986). This is a structured training programme that consists of three elements. Each element is scheduled in groups once a week. Anger management training is the emotional component and involves a stepwise training where the youths learn about which situations make them angry, their own signals and how to manage their anger. They also learn alternatives to aggression through the social skills training, including role-playing, modelling and guidance. The training in new skills is connected to the reward system and they are rewarded for using these skills. In moral discussion groups, fictional and real-life dilemmas are discussed.

Every week, there are concrete treatment targets for each youth, related to behaviour, skills, performance in school and making pro-social contacts. The staff and youths evaluate the degree of weekly success together. This ensures focus and intensity in the treatment. If no success in reaching the treatment targets is observed, they analyse potential barriers, and the next week's target will be to change the barriers. In order to assess change over time there are monthly evaluations.

Family support and aftercare

The parents are involved during the whole treatment process, including both the residential placement and the aftercare. They are considered to be a resource more than a problem. At the intake stage, they are involved in discussing the treatment targets and needs. While the youth is in the institution, the parents receive training and guidance based on principles from PMT and MST. The institutions have family apartments where the parents can practise with their son or daughter before they practise at home. The youth's home visits are thoroughly planned and evaluated. When the youth is moving home, the parents get support from the family team through regular weekly contact. Family therapists are available by phone 24 hours a day, both when the youth visits the home and during the aftercare.

Organisation of MultifunC

Each MultifunC unit consists of one leader and four different teams (Assessment team, Milieu treatment team, Pedagogical or School team and Family/Aftercare team). Each team has a team leader who, together with the institutional leader, the constitutes 'leader team' of the unit. In addition to these teams, an external Quality Assurance team monitors drift from the treatment principles.

The Assessment team consists of psychologists who assess the youth's needs and responsivity factors and develop treatment plans. They assist the other teams through the treatment process regarding both weekly treatment targets and personality factors that may influence the treatment (e.g. ADHD, anxiety, cognitive level and others). They also make a new assessment of risk level before ending the treatment and are central in deciding when the residential placement, as well as the total treatment, should end.

The Milieu team consists of milieu-therapists who are responsible for the daily milieu-therapeutic work, the ART training and the communication and limit setting regarding the youths. They also perform the reward system or token economy and follow up the weekly treatment targets through the week with daily meetings and discussions together with the youths about how to reach the targets. At least 75 per cent of this team should have a minimum of three years' education in social work.

The Pedagogical or School team consists of pedagogues who are responsible for pedagogical assessment and give support and guidance to the school during the residential placement. They also support the youth regarding school. This team develops weekly treatment targets in cooperation with the youth and the teacher, and has contact with the teacher to get feedback about the youth's behaviour in the school setting. Before finishing the institutional placement, it transfers necessary information and preparations to the new school at home.

The Family/Aftercare team consists of therapists who are responsible for family work based on principles and methods from PMT and MST. They support the parents by training them in parental skills and planning the youth's visits home, and they support parents during aftercare. After the youth leaves the institution and moves home, there are weekly meetings between the family therapist and the parents. In addition, the parents may contact the therapists whenever they need (24 hours a day). The therapists are trained in MST and PMT.

In each country, there is an external Quality Assurance team, which supports the MultifunC units. The team consists of specialists who are responsible for training the staff at the MultifunC units. They also follow up each unit with weekly phone consultations, which include checking documentation (weekly targets, analyses, etc.) that is given to the team in advance and discussing different problems the staff may have. The team also do regular 'boosters' for the treatment teams.

Evaluation of MultifunC

Even if MultifunC as a model is grounded on research about which principles and methods are most effective in treatment of serious behaviour problems in youth, it was not possible to know whether this complex model could work in real life or if it would give the expected positive results. Implementation studies were completed both in Norway and in Sweden. These showed, in both countries, that it was possible to implement the model into practice, but also that practice varies through time. Both studies of the treatment effects were designed as quasi-experimental, matched control group studies and are expected to be completed during 2014 in Sweden and 2015 in Norway. The control group consists of youths with similar risk levels who get 'treatment as usual' in other Norwegian and Swedish institutions.

Finishing comments

MultifunC is a complex treatment model that focuses on many topics at the same time. The youths have problems in several different areas that all influence the behaviour problems. The model has high standards of staff competence, structure, intensity, systematic treatment and functional cooperation between different groups (teams) of staff, which consist of different professionals.

The process of implementing the model in real life according to the written manuals has been demanding and challenging. In addition to the challenges of establishing new institutions for this target group, the challenges have specifically been on two topics.

1. Transferring theory (manual-based methods and principles) into practice (to integrate theoretical understanding and new skills, follow the principles in the model, work with different external conditions and support, etc.).

2. To sustain high-quality treatment according to the manuals over time.

Implementation research points to important factors in successful implementation of new programmes (Fixsen *et al.* 2005). Among these factors are support from decision makers, training of the staff (both information and practical training), supervision of practice performance, assessment of practice, development of leaders, plans for development of staff, internal procedures that sustain the practice and establishment of a quality assurance or implementation team. In the implementation of MultifunC, these factors have been more or less present. The process has also been challenged by high costs compared with treatment as usual because of the specialist teams and an ongoing discussion about the institutions' existence because of this, especially since the model has not yet been evaluated. The experiences so far show that the total costs per youth may be less than in treatment as usual because of the shorter duration of the residential stay. Preliminary data seems to document shorter stays in residential placement than usual, lower costs per youth and fewer re-placements than usual for this target group.

So far the experiences show that the model is possible to implement in 'real life', but also that this is a challenging process. In addition, the implementing process is ongoing and never ends. Even if all the units succeed in implementing the model, there is regular turnover and a tendency to drift. To sustain the model in practice, there is a need for continuous support and training.

MultifunC: Multifunctional Treatment in Residential and Community Settings

TORE ANDREASSEN

In policy and practice, residential treatment is often referred to as a defined intervention. In fact, however, much of residential treatment is poorly described, and evaluation results are mixed. In this context, it is very encouraging to learn about a model of residential treatment that is based on a review of the research, includes practices that have demonstrated evidence and other emerging promising practices, is carefully described in manuals and is undergoing a quasi-experimental implementation and outcome trial.

First of all, the model is based on a general intervention framework called Risk, Need and Responsivity (RNR). As the author states, evidence has been accumulating that youths at the highest level of risk are those who benefit most from residential treatment. These high-risk youths often have multiple risk factors and failed placements, but they present with different characteristics and risk profiles. The MultifunC model is designed to target malleable risks and match evidence-based or promising practices to them, creating individualised treatment for each youth.

Some of the evidence-based practices that have been incorporated into the model include motivational interviewing; behavioural contingency management; social skills training; aggression replacement training; problem solving; parent management training; and ecological intervention. Promising practices that have also been incorporated into the programme include youth and family engagement and involvement; staged treatment progressing from an emphasis on daily routines and structure to logical and natural consequences applied in the youth's home environment; treatment progress monitoring; aftercare support in family, school and peer settings; and ongoing quality improvement, training and support.

This is a great example of a systematic and thoughtful approach to the design of residential care and treatment, and an important contribution to the knowledge base for residential treatment as a viable, evidence-based intervention for high-risk youths. However, a few thoughts are offered for consideration. First, the author notes that two prime reasons that youths enter residential treatment are adverse child care experiences such as abuse and neglect and the development of disruptive and antisocial behaviour. Yet the majority of the literature cited relates interventions for disruptive and antisocial behaviour. It may also be helpful to consider the demonstrated life-long risk related to adverse experiences. Intervention practices with some promise include approaches to promote emotion regulation and cognitive behavioural techniques focused on reframing traumatic experiences. Second, the evaluation results suggest that the model is expensive and challenging to implement, requiring professionally trained staff and ongoing training and support. To make the model feasible to implement on a broad scale, it may be necessary to conduct studies to determine the added value of each of these evidence-based and promising practices and the feasibility of having staff with less formal university training implement them with the support of more highly trained professional staff. Finally, it will also be important to evaluate the efficacy of this residential model with the most rigorous research designs such as randomised controlled trials that include moderation and mediation analyses and assessment of long-term effects to continue to address the question, 'What works with whom?'

CHAPTER 8

The Family Home Program
An Adaptation of the Teaching Family Model at Boys Town[1]

Ronald W. Thompson and Daniel L. Daly

The Boys Town Family Home Program has its roots in a home for orphaned and troubled youth, founded in Omaha, Nebraska in 1917 by an Irish American priest named Father Edward J. Flanagan. Father Flanagan's approach had the following characteristics: nurturance, education, vocational training, spiritual development, and self-government. He was one of the original child advocates concerned about permanency, safety, and well-being. Boys Town became a long-term home for children otherwise homeless—providing not only permanency but also safety and care to needy children. He helped to close abusive programs all over the country and developed monitoring systems to ensure safety. Youth left with high school graduation and/or trade skills and became productive citizens. Boys Town grew into an incorporated village located just outside the city of Omaha. By the 1930s, Boys Town was featured in an academy-award winning movie and also soon became known internationally as a state-of-the-art youth care program. As a result, President Truman asked Father Flanagan to provide advice to countries in Western Europe about their youth care systems and practices in the late 1940s due to the prevalence of European orphans following World War II.

By the 1960s and 1970s, however, there was a need to incorporate a model of care to guide program development and evaluate outcomes. At that time approximately 600 youth were placed at Boys Town. The

---

1   The authors would like to acknowledge Beth Chmelka and Jon Huefner at the Boys Town National Research Institute for their assistance with this manuscript.

approach had become long-term, congregate care with counseling provided by professionally trained social workers and counselors. Runaways and other youth problems had become common, and there was no systematic approach to the intervention. The Boys Town Board of Trustees, staff and consultants searched for effective programs for at-risk youth and chose an applied research project called Achievement Place at the University of Kansas. Achievement Place psychologists had developed a behaviorally based, family-style community group home model as an alternative to detention centers and state training facilities for youth involved in the juvenile justice system (Phillips *et al.*1973).

At the Achievement Place site, intervention methods were tested and refined. From the very beginning, program development focused on identifying adult behaviors functionally related to teaching social, academic, and life skills to delinquent and behaviorally disordered youth. The elements that define the Teaching Family Model and the Boys Town adaptation stem from this work. For instance, an early study by Willner *et al.* (1977) found that if adults engaged in "youth preferred" behaviors, youth could be more effectively taught important skills. A model component known as the "teaching interaction" ensued. The teaching interaction prompted adults to praise often, stay calm, give reasons for instructions, avoid power struggles, and teach skills directly. These adult skills were related to youth behavior gains. For instance, studies indicated that this teaching interaction could increase social skills (Phillips, 1968; Phillips *et al.* 1971), and the components of the teaching interaction were positively related to youth satisfaction and negatively related to youth delinquency (Bedlington 1983).

Additionally, a behavioral self-government practice was developed, and evaluation results suggested that at-risk youth could successfully establish rules and consequences for peer behavior (Fixsen, Phillips and Wolf 1973). This was a radical approach in the field of juvenile justice at the time, and it was consistent with and enhanced Father Flanagan's original practice using functional, behavioral psychology. Another practice example, known as the "school note," was developed. It was designed to integrate school-based and home-based behavioral teaching. Consistent with applied behavioral analysis, which at the time was enjoying wide-scale success in working with at-risk youth, these practices were carefully described so they could be trained and evaluated to ensure fidelity of implementation by staff.

Implementation of the Achievement Place model at Boys Town took place over several years. It included retraining and sometimes replacing staff, construction of single-family homes, recruiting married couples to serve as in-home primary intervention agents, and the development of methods to train and evaluate staff and measure youth outcomes on a much larger scale than was used at the original site in Kansas (e.g. Fixsen *et al.* 1978). Other Teaching Family Model agencies also continued to develop program implementation methods and strategies (Fixsen *et al* 2001). A national association, called the Teaching Family Association, was formed to facilitate and support this national replication of the Teaching Family Model. During this time the model continued to evolve and be replicated at Boys Town sites, and because of some unique methods developed and implemented, we felt it was necessary to rename the Boys Town adaptation the "Family Home Program."

Family Home Program model

Currently the Boys Town Family Home Program serves approximately 1200 youth annually at ten sites around the country spanning from New York City to Orange County, California. There are five core program elements: teaching skills, building healthy relationships, supporting religion and faith, creating a positive family environment, and promoting self-determination (see Table 8.1). Family-style living is one element of the model that clearly distinguishes it from other types of residential care, sometimes called congregate care (Child Welfare Strategy Group 2013). Family-style living and other program elements, while clearly specified, are experienced by youth and families as a natural, family-focused living arrangement rather than a prescriptive curriculum. Trained married couples, called Family Teachers, live with children 24 hours per day. They implement the intervention strategies with youth and are the primary contact for the child's family. This model is more similar to treatment foster care than to traditional residential care. The context is a family-style setting, but it also includes well-specified, evidence-supported practices that are implemented with intensive supervision, monitoring, and support. Family Teachers are professionally trained to teach living skills to youth and parenting skills to their family. Youth attend public or private schools, play sports, act in plays, shop in malls, and interact with their own family. Because youth develop close relationships with caring adults in a family setting, life-long aftercare relationships develop. This was part of the original design of the Teaching Family Model (Wolfe, Braukmann and Ramp 1987).

TABLE 8.1: Family Home Program model elements

MODEL ELEMENT	BRIEF DESCRIPTION
Teaching skills	Teaching skills is a core element of the model and has been demonstrated to produce positive results. It allows both youth and adults to learn and practice new ways of thinking, feeling, behaving, and interacting with people. Skills taught range from basic (e.g. greeting others, following instructions) to complex (e.g. positive peer reporting, social problem solving).
Building healthy relationships	Building healthy relationships is another core component of the model. Therapeutic alliance has been repeatedly linked to positive mental health outcomes for both adults and children. In the Family Home Program, specific strategies and methods to enhance adult–child and peer-to-peer relationships are trained, supervised and evaluated for adults working most closely to the children and their immediate supervisors.
Supporting religion and faith	This is a value that dates back to Father Flanagan and continues to be emphasized today. Spiritual and moral development for youth and family members is encouraged without proselytizing specific religious doctrines. All youth are encouraged to attend religious services of their choice regularly.
Creating a positive family environment	Families are where youth first learn how to interact with others. The goal is to provide a model of healthy, family-style living for youth without trying to replace their birth family or adoptive family. This includes cooking meals in the home, grocery shopping as a family, taking care of home cleaning and minor repairs, conducting family meetings, going on outings and vacations, etc.
Promoting self-determination	Youth involvement is supported by specific practices such as self-government, participation in goal-setting, and cognitive problem solving. These practices promote internalization of learned skills, behavior, and values. Youth are also directly involved in discussions about their permanency, safety, and well-being. For example, youth are encouraged to learn about their primary health-care needs, and youth who are preparing to age out of the program are involved in a year-long process of self-directed planning for transitioning to adulthood.

Note: Each of these model elements entails specific adult behaviors that are monitored to ensure adherence to methods that promote youth progress.

The theoretical foundation for the program continues to have its roots in Social Learning Theory (Bandura 1977), Social Interaction Theory (Patterson, Reid, and Dishion 1992), and Coercion Theory (Patterson 1982), but an ongoing process of evaluation, research, and continuous quality improvement have resulted in a number of refinements to the program. The most recent model enhancements were made in 2011–12 in a comprehensive, national program development effort involving hundreds of Boys Town staff from program sites and national support systems. The most aggressive program refinements were made in areas reflecting current research and policy developments related to residential care and treatment. One example is the work that has been done on community-based systems of care for children's mental health (Friedman 2003). A Family Home Program model enhancement directly related to this community-based movement is an increased emphasis on family engagement and involvement. Recent research suggests the benefits of family involvement, and promising practices have been developed and advocated nationally (Walter and Petr 2008; Williamson and Gray 2011). In the Family Home Program, family involvement currently takes two forms. First, families frequently communicate with their child and program staff. Communication occurs proactively and is assessed regularly. Second, for families and children for whom reunification, relative placement, or foster placement is planned, transition planning and intervention begins at intake and is ongoing. A key element is a gradual transition from brief family visits to overnight stays at the parent or relative's home. When indicated, Boys Town In-Home Family Services[SM] staff also assist the permanent family and youth with preparation for successful transition.

A second priority was to enhance youth assessment and service planning in order to individualize each youth's goals, with an emphasis on helping youth and family members prepare for permanency as quickly as possible. In order to identify the need for specialized treatment, youth are screened at admission for behavior, mental health, and substance use problems. Youth are also screened for symptoms of trauma history such as anxiety, sleep problems, and physical health symptoms that may be psychosomatic. The result is an assessment-driven individualized service plan focused on the needs identified at intake, measurement of progress during care, discharge planning, and support for family reunification, adoption, or successful transition to adulthood. These program enhancements are clearly specified in training manuals, supervision strategies, and evaluation methods to create an infrastructure to support program implementation and ongoing continuous improvement.

National program replication and implementation

What has evolved along the way is a set of quality standards for residential care (Daly and Nordingler 1997) and program implementation strategies that have guided and enhanced Boys Town's own national replication of this model of family-style residential care across the country. This required the development of an even more elaborate process to make sure that staff were trained, supervised, and certified to implement the model, not to mention the creation of a national database to monitor data about the safety of the youth and progress during their residential stay. One of the most crucial components of the program implementation strategy is intensive supervision of direct care staff. This is widely recognized in current implementation and dissemination science and practice as one of the most critical components of program effectiveness (Schoenwald *et al.* 2013). Another important component is facilitative leadership to ensure ongoing administrative support for model implementation. The development of this infrastructure began at Kansas University in the early 1970s and continues to evolve. The core components of this support system are consistent with current accepted best practices in dissemination and implementation science (Fixsen *et al.* 2009; Proctor *et al.* 2007) and the unique features of these components are described in Table 8.2.

TABLE 8.2: Family Home Program implementation components

IMPLEMENTATION COMPONENTS	UNIQUE FEATURES
Staff recruitment and selection	Human resources staff, who often have direct care experience themselves, recruit, screen, and collaborate with hiring managers to select the best candidates for direct care positions. Applicants are screened with structured progressive interviews. Supervisors are frequently selected from candidate pools made up primarily of successful direct care staff who have demonstrated leadership potential.
Pre-service and in-service training	All staff have two weeks of pre-service training about model elements and specific skills related to their positions. All training is competency based. Staff are required to pass paper and pencil tests covering essential knowledge and successfully demonstrate skills during role play sessions with experienced staff. Direct care staff serve as the primary intervention agents, and it is expected that their first year of employment is primarily developmental. Specific follow-up training is provided throughout employment either through competency-based online courses or site-based workshops.
Supervision and consultation	Supervisors are also required to complete competency-based training in the supervision model. Since direct care staff are the primary intervention agents, the focus of supervision is the development of direct care staff, continuous quality improvement, and model fidelity. Staff observation for model fidelity is a critical supervisory skill. A second important responsibility for supervisors is to ensure safety of youth and staff.

Evaluation and data support	Direct care staff and immediate supervisors receive an annual, performance-based credentialing evaluation known as certification. Supervisors and other leaders have a number of data reports at their disposal to provide information about the youth and family needs and strengths, progress on goals and objectives, critical incidents, program management indicators, and outcomes. These data are available in real time via an internal national network. Finally, data from structured follow-up interviews conducted at 6, 12, and 24 months post-discharge are used to inform quality improvement initiatives as well as program evaluation and advocacy with donors and payers.
Facilitative leadership	It became more and more apparent as the Family Home Program was being developed, evaluated, and implemented on a wide scale that another critical feature was a leadership model to support it. All levels of leadership need to be experts in the model itself through training, experience, and leadership development opportunities. Also, management decision making is structured to support quality model implementation.

Research evidence

Evidence-based programs and practices have been increasingly emphasized in the United States for both intervention and prevention services over the past two decades not only by scientists but also policymakers, public funding agencies, and providers. As a result, a number of national registries of evidence-based programs have been developed, and they include scientific reviews of evidence for programs and practices and dissemination of information about evidence-supported interventions. There is very limited scientific evidence for models of residential care and treatment, however, with a small number of programs rated as having promising evidence or being supported by evidence. In a recent review of this evidence, James (2011a) concluded that the following programs fell in to these categories: Positive Peer Culture, Sanctuary Model, the Stop-Gap Model, the Teaching Family Model, and the adaptation of this model at Boys Town (Family Home Program). The article was based on scientific reviews conducted by the California Evidence-Based Clearinghouse for Child Welfare (CEBC). The Teaching Family Model and the Boys Town adaptation were described in this review as, "the most described and researched model in the literature" (p.311). The Teaching Family Model is listed on the CEBC as having promising research evidence (www.cebc4cw.org), and the Family Home Program is also listed as having promising research evidence by the Office of Juvenile Justice and Delinquency Prevention Model Programs Guide (www.ojjdp.gov/

mpg) and Find Youth Info (www.findyouthinfo.gov) national registries of evidence-based programs.

A number of outcome studies about the Teaching Family Model have been conducted by Achievement Place psychologists and other scientists, suggesting that the model has promising research evidence (Kingsley 2006). The most recent study was completed by Elizabeth Farmer and colleagues comparing data from Teaching Family and non-Teaching Family group homes in North Carolina using a quasi-experimental design. Results indicated significant differences in both process and outcome data, including the finding that youth from Teaching Family homes not only made significant progress during placement, but also continued to make progress post-discharge, unlike comparison group youth (Farmer, Murphy and Wonnum 2013).

In addition, approximately 80 papers, including peer-reviewed articles, practice descriptions, and book chapters, have been published in the past 20 years about Boys Town's adaptation of the Teaching Family Model. A number of these relate to outcome and program implementation issues. This literature will be briefly summarized in the following paragraphs.

Outcome studies

A number of outcome evaluations have been conducted. The first of these was conducted between 1980 and 1989. It was a quasi-experimental outcome study using state-of-the-art analytic methods (Osgood and Smith 1995). Results indicated significant positive long-term treatment effects related to educational success for youth served at Boys Town (i.e. post-care high school graduation rates in excess of 80%; Thompson *et al.* 1996), and placement in this type of family-style residential program did not result in long-term negative effects for social isolation and related difficulties as argued by critics of residential treatment at the time (Friman *et al.* 1996). A second follow-up study using the same participant sample conducted approximately 16 years post-discharge supported these findings and also suggested positive treatment effects for lower rates of intimate partner violence in adulthood (Huefner *et al.* 2007). A more recent analysis of follow-up data suggested that longer lengths of stay in this type of residential program were associated with more long-term positive effects for youth, contrary to popular opinion and much of current child and family policy emphasizing shorter lengths of stay in residential care (Ringle, Ingram and Thompson 2010).

In terms of moderators of outcomes, results of a series of studies have indicated that both girls and boys make significant progress during care on behavioral ratings and mental health symptoms (Larzelere *et al.* 2004). Also, girls enter the program with significantly higher levels of behavior problems than boys but make greater gains during placement (Handwerk *et al.* 2006). Finally, youth improve clinically across all measures, regardless of maltreatment histories (Brack, Huefner and Handwerk 2012).

A series of more recent studies also provides some insight about potential mediators of positive outcomes for youth in residential care. First of all, one study suggested the gains that youth make during care are actually predictive of functioning at follow-up (Lee, Chmelka and Thompson 2010). The results of a second series of studies suggest that common therapeutic process factors (therapeutic alliance and readiness to change), as well as a high level of model fidelity from the youth's perspective, mediate positive outcomes (Duppong Hurley *et al.* 2013). Finally, Boys Town scientists have also begun to study the relationships between family involvement and youth outcomes. In an initial study, results suggested that overnight at home stays were associated with immediate and long-term positive youth outcomes, whereas other types of family contact (e.g. family visits to the program, telephone calls) had neutral to negative relationships with youth outcomes (Huefner and Pick 2013).

Studies about recent criticisms of residential care and treatment

Criticisms related to placement in residential care settings have also been studied as they apply to this highly structured, family-style approach to residential care. Two examples follow. The first is a construct called peer contagion or deviancy training, which refers to youth actually learning anti-social behavior in settings with other youth who display anti-social behavior. When we have studied this construct in the Family Home Program, results suggested that it did not occur for most of the youth and, in fact, positive peer influences may be protective and inhibit problem behaviors (Huefner and Ringle 2012; Lee and Thompson 2009). A second criticism is that youth who are placed in residential care and treatment do not maintain gains made during care or after discharge. Although our outcome studies have suggested overall promising results at and after discharge, there are subsets of youth who do not progress during treatment (Lee and Thompson 2009) and some engage in risky behavior after discharge (Kingsley *et al.* 2008). Therefore we began a program of research to develop and evaluate additional, specific, family- and school-based aftercare support beginning prior to discharge and extending for several months post-discharge (Thompson *et al.* 2010; Trout *et al.* 2012). Results of a small, randomized trial evaluation suggest significant benefits for youth (Trout *et al.* 2013), and a larger randomized trial is currently underway.

Current organizational transformation and goals for the future

Along with the ongoing development and implementation of the Family Home Program, we have built on the same theoretical foundation and promising practices to create an integrated continuum of care that also includes psychiatric residential treatment, short-term residential intervention and assessment, foster family services, in-home family services, parent training, school and classroom behavior management, parent-to-parent support and empowerment, and a national crisis intervention and information and referral hotline.

In recent years we have emphasized a more pronounced effort to grow our family- and community-based intervention programs, including in-home family services, parent training, school and classroom behavior management, and parent-to-parent support and empowerment. With an emphasis on program development and research in family- and community-based intervention, Boys Town has been able to expand services from approximately 12,000 youth served in 2007 to more than 30,000 youth served in 2012. This has required us to integrate other theoretical approaches such as ecological theory (Bronfenbrenner 1979) and theory of planned behavior (Ajzen 1985), as well as adapt our practices to these different intervention settings and populations served. The common theoretical foundation and practice language across interventions, however, facilitates program integration from the perspective of youth and families. Since the Family Home Program is essentially a parenting intervention, we have found it a natural transition to family and community intervention practice and research.

Along with this emphasis, we had to build our capacity to provide these services and conduct studies in community settings. These programs have also gone through program development and implementation revisions, with an emphasis on use of evidence-based practices and refining the infrastructure to evaluate them with the most rigorous scientific methods and implement them on a wide scale (e.g., Ingram *et al.* 2013). To support this initiative we reached out to scientists who have specialized in school and family intervention and prevention and established partnerships with university-based research centers (Duppong Hurley *et al.* 2010). The new focus for our research also required substantial funding, so in partnership with these university-based research centers we began a focused effort to obtain research funding. As a result, along with our partners, we have been awarded over $13 million in research funding over the past six years, and we are currently engaged in four large, randomized intervention studies related to family- and community-based intervention. The goal is to continue to build the evidence base for these promising interventions to support the continued growth of our service network (Mason *et al.* 2013).

Our next strategic goal is to use this knowledge to partner with others who are providing compatible services and deliver enough integrated intervention in communities to achieve community-level impact for at-risk children and their families. At the same time we want to continue to focus on quality of services across our integrated continuum. As a result, our current strategic plan has five major initiatives:

1. Continue to grow services with a focus on family- and community-based interventions in communities with a high density of at-risk youth and families.

2. Continue research on evidence-based preventive programs and practices and translate findings into practice.

3. Pilot, and replicate approaches to strengthen communities by providing needs-based services to children and families.

4. Develop or adopt measures and research strategies to assess community impact.

5. Grow neurobehavioral research to help develop effective interventions for some of the most challenging youth and family problems and translate findings into practice.

The Family Home Program, however, continues to remain a vital service, especially for youth and families with some of the most challenging problems. One only needs to look at the abysmal high school graduation rates for youth placed in foster care (Blome 1997; Unrau, Font and Rawls 2012; Zetlin, Weinberg and Kimm 2004) to conclude that alternatives are needed for many at-risk youth and families. Quality, safe, family-style, evidence-supported residential care, such as the Teaching Family Model or the Family Home Program, is a vital component in a comprehensive system of care based on the values of safety, permanency, and well-being for at-risk children and their families.

The Family Home Program: An Adaptation of the Teaching Family Model at Boys Town

RONALD W. THOMPSON AND DANIEL L. DALY

This is an excellent summary of the development of a treatment model, which has been able to change during time in agreement with new knowledge. The model has incorporated new knowledge about involving the family, integrating aftercare, and implementation issues. The chapter includes a description of the history of the model, a short description of the model, the implementation process, the research evidence, and goals for the future. In my view, all parts are interesting.

It is a very unique model that is different from most group care models in that the staff consist of trained married couples as primary staff. It is also one of few such models that have undergone a lot of outcome evaluation and through this have support for positive effects. It is also interesting that studies have not found iatrogenic effects of group treatment in this model.

What I miss is a more detailed description of the treatment model. The chapter gives a good description of adult behavior and mentions the five core elements where some are in agreement with research on this topic (Andrews and Dowden 2004). Generally in the literature there is a lack of description of what "good" staff behavior consists of. Staff behavior in residential settings is the core of the treatment milieu and, as such, is very important. It makes the basis for change and seems to be important, regardless what methods that are used (Fretz 2007). But it would have been nice to get a more detailed description of the methods that are used to change youth behavior, to teach them social skills, and to train the families in addition to the staff. Some research, for example, indicates that not all family interventions work for troubled youth (Dowden and Andrews 2000). What are the methods for training the youths in social skills, what are the methods for family work within this model, how is it organized, and so on?

I also miss a more clear description of the target group for the model. How serious are the problems the youth present? Does the model work for all youth, or does it work better for specific groups of youth? Some research indicates that different target groups are in need of different forms of treatment among troubled youth. Such differences apply both to the intensity of treatment, content of treatment, targets of treatment, and risk of iatrogenic effects. This could also have been specified in more detail in the evaluation studies. Were there better results for some groups than for others?

The chapter is useful in that it describes what it takes to develop effective models, both in time and effort. The limitation is that it is unclear for whom the model works best or does not work. It clearly faces different challenges based on the youth or target group.

CHAPTER 9

A New Era in the Development of Therapeutic Residential Care in the State of Victoria

Patricia M. McNamara[1]

Introduction

Residential care for children and young people in the Australian welfare sector has often been viewed as the 'intervention of last resort' or simply as 'containment of hard cases' (McLean *et al.* 2011). Kinship care and family foster care are the preferred alternatives when caregiving by the biological family is not possible. This is evident in Victoria's out-of-home care statistics, illustrated in Figure 9.1.

Young people in the child welfare system have, until very recently, only been referred to residential programmes when all other, purportedly 'less intrusive' and 'more therapeutic' interventions have been tried (often repeatedly) and failed. Enduring negativity in relation to residential care emerges from a range of complex contextual parameters – both historical and contemporary. Clinical, political and economic factors contribute to a pervasive pessimism about the worth and impact of residential programmes for traumatised young people. Notwithstanding such a climate across Australia, and in the State of Victoria, a number of therapeutic options have emerged that challenge the 'culture of reluctance' around residential care referrals.

1   The author wishes to acknowledge support and advice from a number of professionals in Victorian therapeutic residential care during preparation of this chapter. Special thanks are due to Pauline McLoughlin PhD (Lighthouse Foundation), Jacqui Watts, (Anglicare Victoria) and Gerard Jones and Nick Halfpenny PhD, Mackillop Family Services. The views expressed herein are, of course, entirely those of the author.

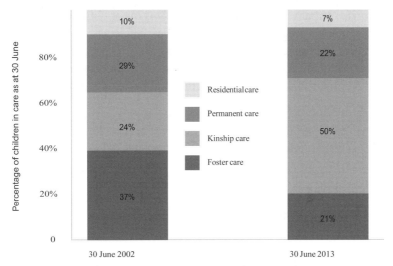

FIGURE 9.1: Out-of-home care in Victoria – A five year plan

Source: Department of Human Services, Government of Victoria (March, 2014), from www.dhs.vic. gov.au/__data/assets/pdf_file/0010/864793/Out-of-home-care_a_five_year_plan.pdf

This chapter explores the contemporary landscape of residential care, especially the 'shift' to therapeutic approaches. Three prominent models of Therapeutic Residential Care (TRC) are presented, along with their similarities and differences. The chapter then considers opportunities and challenges for future policy and programme development. It concludes with implications for research – locally and internationally.

For the purposes of this chapter the definition of TRC is that articulated at the outset of this volume. It is also informed by Australia's National Therapeutic Residential Care Working Group's definition:

> Therapeutic Residential Care is intensive and time-limited care for a child or young person in statutory care that responds to the complex impacts of abuse, neglect and separation from family. This is achieved through the creation of positive, safe, healing relationships and experiences informed by a sound understanding of trauma, damaged attachment, and developmental needs. (McLean *et al.* 2011, p.2)

A therapeutic shift

Therapeutic residential programmes have emerged relatively recently in Victoria. Their appearance is somewhat surprising perhaps, in light of contemporary exposure of past abuse in residential care (Parliament of

Victoria, Australia 2013), well-placed concerns about current standards and compelling scepticism regarding cost effectiveness (Bath 2009). However, Victorian child welfare has, over the past decade, become more developmentally and ecologically responsive (Bronfenbrenner 1979). This orientation is manifest in the legislation and policy that currently informs practice:

- *Victoria's Vulnerable Children: Our Shared Responsibility Strategy 2013–2022* (Victorian State Government 2013)

- Victorian State Government *Children Youth and Families Act* (VIC) 2005

- Victorian State Government *Child Wellbeing and Safety Act* (VIC) 2005

- Best Interests Framework for Vulnerable Children and Youth, Department of Human Services 2007 – updated 2013 (Victorian State Government 2007/2013).

That context appears to have given rise to optimism about the therapeutic potential of residential care. The 'new neuroscience' for healing attachment disruption has clearly had a key role to play in this evolving chapter (Perry 2006, 2008; Van der Kolk *et al.* 2005), along with a growing awareness that the reciprocity demanded in a family situation cannot be accommodated by all traumatised young people, at least not immediately. Building strong and enduring community support networks around young people whilst they are within residential programmes, and after they leave, has also become a priority. Combining periods in residence with respite foster care and mentoring programmes is being actively promoted in the belief that 'it takes a village to raise a child' (Brunner and O'Neill 2009). Young people are now able to stay longer in Victorian residential programmes to heal and mature; they are also offered better preparation for leaving residential programmes and more supports as they move into the community. There appears to be new energy and hope that privileges TRC as an option of first choice for some traumatised young people (Clarke 2011; McLean *et al.* 2011).

Three contemporary models

The three programmes described here dominate the contemporary Victorian TRC landscape. First, we consider the Sanctuary model of TRC, developed by Dr Sandra Bloom and her colleagues at the Andrus

Centre in New York State. This model has recently been universally applied by Mackillop Family Services, the largest provider of residential care in Victoria (Abramovitz and Bloom 2003; Bloom 2005; Bloom and Farragher 2013; Rivard *et al.* 2005). The next model is represented by 12 government-funded pilot TRC programmes recently developed by the Victorian Government's Department of Human Services and implemented by a range of non-government service providers. Rigorous longitudinal evaluation of these pilots has produced overwhelmingly positive findings, resulting in substantial state-wide programmatic extension (DHS-Verso 2011). A third feature on the TRC landscape is the Lighthouse Foundation, which arguably operates the longest running therapeutic residential programme in the state. Lighthouse services homeless young people aged 15–22 years (Barton *et al.* 2012), whilst the two more recent models of care are geared to a slightly younger, mainly child protection cohort (12–18 years). Inevitably there is overlap between the cohorts despite the organisations' slightly different service orientations.

The Sanctuary model

The Sanctuary model of TRC is a trauma-informed systems approach. It aims to heal extensive trauma – especially that resultant from abuse and family violence (Clarke 2011). The Sanctuary model has been implemented in over 100 programmes across the world. It is designed to promote and maintain conceptual and operational congruence across organisations providing a range of services, including residential programmes. Sanctuary was adopted by Mackillop Family Services in 2012 for 'whole of organisation' application to all of its programmes. Mackillop is a large, faith-based, non-government organisation that provides a broad range of child and family welfare services. It is under the auspices of the Roman Catholic Church and was incorporated 20 years ago by several religious orders that had historically provided residential services for over a century. Mackillop is the largest provider of residential services in the State of Victoria. Its units each accommodate around four to six young people; it aims to preserve placements in these units for as long as is deemed therapeutically necessary. Mackillop's residential clients fit the profile targeted by the Sanctuary's developers – that is, young people facing major problems in the biological, affective, cognitive, social and existential domains (Bloom 2005; Rivard *et al.* 2004). These young people are prone to self-harm and can be abusive of others (Clarke 2011). Sandra Bloom has described Sanctuary residents thus:

chronically tense and hyperaroused with hair-trigger tempers and a compromised ability to manage distressing emotions. This emotional arousal interferes with the development of good decision-making, problem solving skills and conflict resolution skills, and as a result, the ability to communicate constructively with others does not develop properly. This results in grave cognitive, emotional and interpersonal difficulties. (Bloom 2005, p.10)

A collective understanding of attachment disruption, loss and trauma across the whole organisation and the means to respond to this is central to successful implementation of the Sanctuary model. Helping clients to develop more resilient responses to change and unpredictability is a cornerstone of the Sanctuary approach to healing. The theoretical underpinning of the Sanctuary model combines trauma theory, social learning theory, nonviolent practice and complexity theory. Clients are taught awareness of hyperarousal and how to present a nonviolent response. Utilising all four frames of reference, residential staff learn how to create a socially responsible residential environment as a therapeutic agent of change. This incorporates a high level of staff self-monitoring, reflection and reflexivity (Clarke 2011, 2012). *Seven Core Commitments* expected of staff are nonviolence, emotional intelligence, inquiry and social learning democracy, social responsibility, growth and change. Children, young people and staff commit to applying the SELF tool for healing and recovery.

- *Safety*: attaining safety in self, relationships and environment.

- *Emotional management*: identifying levels of affect and modulating in response to memories, people and events.

- *Loss*: feeling grief and dealing with personal loss.

- *Future*: trying out new roles, ways of relating and behaving as a 'survivor' to ensure personal safety and help others.

(Bloom 2005 p.13).

The model is well articulated (see Figure 9.2) and offers specific operational guidelines. Daily forums in the residential units maintain clear intra-organisational communication at all levels. Community meetings, safety plans, psycho-educational group work, self-care plans, red flag meetings and team meetings are all features of the Sanctuary Model (Clarke 2012, 2013). Red flag meetings can be called to respond to critical incidents or raise issues of concern at any level of the organisation. Everyone in the organisation, from board of directors to casual staff, receives extensive training in the model.

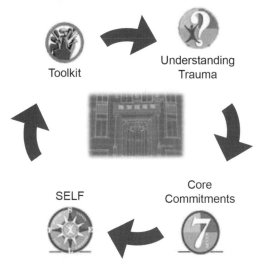

FIGURE 9.2: The Sanctuary model
Source: Mackillop Family Services Sanctuary Training Team, Melbourne, Victoria, Australia

A five-year longitudinal evaluation of 18 Sanctuary programmes in the United States has identified decreases in restraints, critical incidents and staff turnover, as well as increased positive staff perception of the organisation (Banks and Vargas 2009). Whilst it is too soon to comment on any sustained impact of the introduction of the Sanctuary model for TRC at Mackillop Family Services in Victoria, early signs are positive, especially in relation to staff retention patterns, organisational culture improvement and reduction in critical incidents. A comprehensive outcomes study is underway.

Therapeutic Residential Care pilot model

Concern about the lack of quality of out-of-home care options for children and young people with high-level complex needs led to the Victorian government's experimentation with TRC. In 2007, the Department of Human Services (DHS) in Victoria launched its first TRC pilot programme on a property located in the semi-rural outskirts of metropolitan Melbourne, Hurstbridge Farm. DHS then adopted a staged funding of TRC pilot programmes across the state between 2007 and 2009; these programmes have been delivered by a range of non-government organisations. A further

11 pilot programmes were funded by the Victorian State Government, with services being delivered by a range of experienced, non-government service providers. A training package, With Care, provides therapeutic training for workers on the programmes; the package is a non-negotiable pre-requisite to programme implementation. Each of these programmes has a specific client focus (such as gender, age and statutory orders) and housing capacity. Most TRC residences can accommodate four children/young people aged 12–18 years (DHS-Verso 2011).

The conceptual underpinning of the Victorian TRC model is influenced by the Sanctuary model. Theories of attachment and trauma, neurobiology of brain development and resilience underpin the development and practice evident in the TRCs. Figure 9.3 describes the logic of the TRC programme.

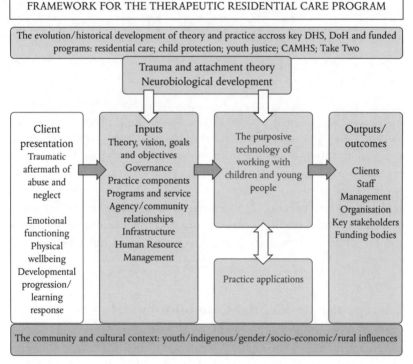

FIGURE 9.3: Framework for the Therapeutic Residential Care program (DHS-Verso, 2011)

The approach was tested programmatically and operationally at Hurstbridge Farm. Positive results for young residents there encouraged DHS and the sector to develop, pilot and evaluate TRC programmes state-wide. The evaluation was undertaken by Verso Consulting, a research consultancy with broad experience in the sector (DHS-Verso 2011).

A longitudinal evaluation took place over two years and collected data in relation to the conceptual frame of reference, programme fidelity and the effectiveness and efficiency of the programme itself (DHS-Verso 2011). Thirty-eight children and young people were assessed in relation to their progress toward desired goals at three points in time and were compared with 16 young people in general residential care. Their progress at three points prior to entering TRC (whilst they were still placed in general residential care) was also tracked. The Child Protection and Family Services Outcomes Framework (National Framework for Protecting Australia's Children 2009) provided the benchmarks with which to measure outcomes. Instruments utilised in the evaluation included the Strengths and Difficulties Questionnaire (SDQ; Goodman 1997), Health of the Nation Scales for children and Adolescents (Garralda, Yates and Higginson 2000) and Brann Likert Scales (developed specially for the Project, DHS-Verso 2011).

It appears that the children and young people in TRC made more progress in relation to quality of relationships and contact with family, and sustained significant improvements to the quality of contact with their residential carers over time in the TRC units. They also had increased community connection through recreational activities, significant improvements in sense of self, increased healthy lifestyles and reduced risk taking, enhanced mental and emotional health and improved relationships with school. These improvements contrasted with that of their peers in general care and with their own earlier progress in general residential units. In relation to the programme itself, trained and additional staff, consistent rostering, engagement and participation of the young people, client mix, care team meetings, the therapeutic specialist, reflective practice, organisational congruence and commitment, physical environment, exit planning and post exit support were considered critical to the programme's success (DHS-Verso 2011). Per person cost avoided by placement in the TRCs was assessed as AUD 44,243. On the basis of these positive findings, the TRCs have now been substantially expanded by 100 beds across the State of Victoria.

The Lighthouse model

The Lighthouse Foundation would seem to be the longest running therapeutic residential programme for young people in Victoria. It was founded 22 years ago by long-term foster parent, Susan Barton. Lighthouse Foundation is a not-for-profit organisation, based in Melbourne. It services young people aged 15–22 years. It aims to help young people who have experienced abuse and neglect – to heal and rebuild their lives.

Until very recently Lighthouse has depended entirely on charitable donations. By choice, it did not seek or receive government funding of any kind. It appears this choice aligned with Lighthouse's apparent raison d'être as a response to perceived 'system failure'. Of late, Lighthouse is in receipt of some government funding. This, along with strong sector interest in therapeutic residential programmes, has meant its work is becoming better known and more integrated with mainstream child and family welfare. There are nine Lighthouse homes in Melbourne, and one in regional Victoria; each is home to about four young people.

Lighthouse Foundation has developed its own Therapeutic Family Model of Care (see Figure 9.4). It provides long-term TRC and specialist mental health support for children and young people who have experienced complex trauma as a result of childhood abuse and neglect.

The Lighthouse Therapeutic Family Model of Care is based on attachment theory and addresses the biological and psychological need of individuals to bond with and relate to primary caregivers as fundamental to the survival and future development of human beings. Each young person is encouraged to be active in school, work and personal development, while undertaking programmes to address individual barriers. The continuing support and access to these programmes from within the home and on an outreach basis ensures that a sense of belonging within a community is maintained and strengthened.

Young people are usually cared for in a Lighthouse home for at least two years and are highly supported when they transition from the programme; they are strongly encouraged to remain connected with the organisation for life. They are offered life membership to Lighthouse as they transition to independent living via the Outreach and Aftercare Programme. Many young people regularly check in to Lighthouse, especially at important family gathering times, such as Christmas. Lighthouse Home Committees of trained local volunteers support professional staff by assisting with home maintenance and by socialising and building mentoring relationships with the young residents.

The organisation has developed a psychodynamic, attachment and trauma informed approach to its work (Barton *et al.* 2012). The Lighthouse Therapeutic Family Model aims to offer traumatised children and young people a safe and consistent physical living environment, with positive and consistent parental role models, as well as clinical and support services so they can (re)build their sense of self, learn new ways of trusting and relating to others and develop pro-social connections within their broader communities (Bowlby 1980; Becker-Weidman and Shell 2010; Dockar-Drysdale 1990; Scharff and Scharff 1991). The Therapeutic Family Model of Care is grounded in the belief that new and constructive behaviours can be learned by children and young people from carers, who act as 'therapeutic parents' (Pughe and Philpot 2007).

Family-like settings, strong relationships with carers and the support of other specialists, including psychotherapists, encourages children and young people to confront and work through the complex impacts of childhood trauma. A key element of the Lighthouse model is that children and young people are assisted to form and sustain positive and reciprocal relationships with others in and beyond the programme that will extend throughout their lives. This is facilitated by developing the young residents' coping and life skills, support networks, helpful attachments and broader community networks. The Lighthouse model targets multiple domains that aim to shape young people's positive overall development. The Therapeutic Outcomes Assessment tool measures the recovery of children and young people across eight developmental areas:

- learning

- physical development

- emotional development

- attachment

- identity

- social development

- autonomy/life skills

- relational and community connectedness.

The success of the Therapeutic Family Model of Care is measured by monitoring the number of young people in care, the number of active homes and active individual development plans, the number of young people in education and employment and reduction in young people re-entering youth homelessness services; staff retention is also considered an important measure of success. A formal outcomes study is currently being developed at Lighthouse.

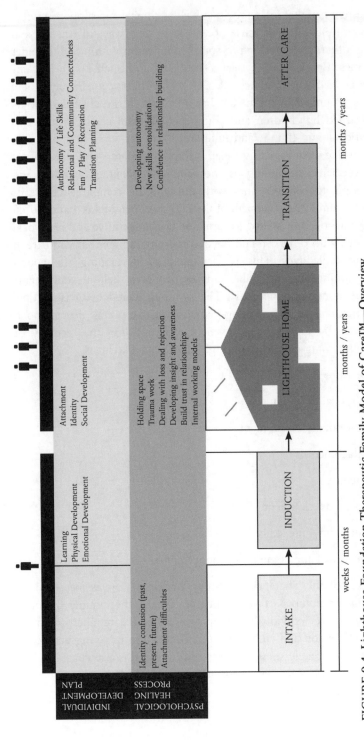

FIGURE 9.4: Lighthouse Foundation Therapeutic Family Model of Care™—Overview
Source: Gonzalez and Tomlinson (2011, p.x). Copyright 2011 Lighthouse Foundation.

The following text appears within the figure:

INDIVIDUAL DEVELOPMENT PLAN

PSYCHOLOGICAL HEALING PROCESS

Learning
Physical Development
Emotional Development

Attachment
Identity
Social Development

Autonomy / Life Skills
Relational and Community Connectedness
Fun / Play / Recreation
Transition Planning

Identity confusion (past, present, future)
Attachment difficulties

Holding space
Trauma work
Dealing with loss and rejection
Developing insight and awareness
Build trust in relationships
Internal working models

Developing autonomy
New skills consolidation
Confidence in relationship building

INTAKE

INDUCTION

LIGHTHOUSE HOME

TRANSITION

AFTER CARE

weeks / months

months / years

months / years

Overview

This brief overview of three key models of TRC for children and young people operating in Victoria is indeed hopeful. The models all appear well informed by current neuroscience around the impact of trauma and abuse on brain development. All three are purposefully focused on this impact, and on attachment disruption, in order to respond therapeutically. There is clearly generalised understanding that such complex issues cannot be addressed with short-term interventions. It is recognised that years, rather than weeks or months, are needed for children and young people to heal and be supported to move forward developmentally and systemically. There is also recognition that if residential care ends at the point of leaving formal care, detailed planning and long-term support will be required.

Along with the similarities between the programmes, differences clearly exist. The first two models described here developed in Victoria quite recently and are still in evolution. The third has been functioning for almost a quarter of a century. Conceptually, it would appear that the newer models are much influenced by the Sanctuary. Mackillop Family Services identifies fully with this approach and has applied it to all of its many programmes – residential and non-residential. The Lighthouse model appears to be underpinned by psychodynamic theory, especially object relations, which is manifest in 'family-like' group dynamics, 'in-house' individual psychotherapy, clinical supervision and community wellness. The Lighthouse Community Home Committees reflect an emphasis on community connectedness that is seemingly unique to that model. A holistic, trauma-informed, therapeutic approach clearly characterises each of the three models with important roles for therapeutic specialists as consultants. However, there appears to be more emphasis on formal 'in-house' psychotherapy in the Lighthouse approach. 'Connections for life' are also a Lighthouse feature not 'built in' to the other models, though clearly lifelong relationships do sometimes develop spontaneously.

Organisational and programmatic congruence are clearly core features of effective therapeutic care and all models privilege this (Anglin 2002, 2003). Mackillop's recent 'whole of organisation' adoption of the Sanctuary model incorporating residential care and the Therapeutic Family Model of Care developed over many years by the Lighthouse Foundation, are both strongly suggestive of organisational congruence (Anglin 2003). With TRC, a range of non-governmental organisations (NGOs) and government services are involved in service delivery (DHS-Verso 2011). Sometimes one organisation is responsible for day-to-day operations in partnership with another that delivers therapeutic services. The quest for congruence is perhaps likely to be more challenging where a range of organisations are simultaneously involved.

The future

Optimism and energy characterises contemporary residential care in Victoria. Great progress is being made in developing high-quality therapeutic responses that can become options of first choice, rather than avenues of last resort, for traumatised young people requiring out-of-home care. Much developmental work is still required, however, in policy, practice and research.

The public policy shift toward TRC has been strongly supported by convincing research evidence about the effectiveness of TRC (DHS-Verso 2011). This has resulted in the recent funding of a further 100 therapeutic residential beds across the state. Many more beds are still needed, including those specifically geared to the culturally competent care of Aboriginal children and young people (Atkinson 2013). Culturally and linguistically diverse (CALD) young people, especially refugees (including unaccompanied minors), require specialised therapeutic residential programmes. Policy development is also needed to break down service silos and advance congruence at the macro level, especially between residential services and mental health, immigration and education (Atkinson 2013).

More comprehensive training programmes are required to prepare residential workers for the complex practice of healing trauma in children and young people who have experienced serious abuse and attachment disruption (Centre for Excellence in Child and Family Welfare 2013). Many of Victoria's residential workers still have minimal theoretical and/or clinical training. Expert supervision and support to staff, both in crisis and on an ongoing basis are also essential if retention of staff and continuity of care for young people is to reach appropriate levels. No residential programme can be deemed therapeutic if staff turnover is high. Ensuring goodness of fit between different theories, models of care and the complex needs of individual young people is rarely well orchestrated; this must almost certainly impact negatively on outcomes and effectiveness.

There are also a number of important priorities for research. First, ongoing longitudinal monitoring of outcomes is essential so that programmes can be refined to address the complex and changing needs of young people in care. Cost effectiveness of residential programmes (compared with therapeutic foster care, secure welfare units and other similar options) must be demonstrated to convince policymakers and funders of the credibility of TRC programmes.

Embedding TRC in local communities is consistent with the long-established, ecological-developmental approach to healing trauma (Bronfenbrenner 1979). The creation of 'heart connections for life' in communities is vital for young people whose birth family supports have been seriously disrupted, in some cases irreparably (Brunner and O'Neill 2009). The development of 'therapeutic mentoring' within a framework of education (especially literacy and numeracy) and recreation (including the arts) is a possible means of drawing residential care programmes and local communities much closer together. Establishing a best practice model for therapeutic mentoring, and then testing that model, is currently on the research agenda for La Trobe University and the Lighthouse Foundation. Should this model be successful, programmatic extension and larger scale testing may be possible – locally and internationally. Cross-national testing of the model might potentially develop under the auspices of IAOBER, the International Association for Outcome-Based Research and Evaluation in Family and Children's Services.

Educational outcomes for young people in residential care are notoriously poor in Australia. Very few young people leaving residential care have completed formal secondary education. Redressing this has been a key focus for several Victorian service providers (Good Shepherd Youth and Family Service, Jesuit Social Services and MacKillop Family Services 2012). A more aspirational approach to learning is needed with greater investment in the specialist teacher training required to operationalise this. Improvement of formal and informal learning outcomes needs extensive research and development.

Family reunification from residential care must also remain on the practice and research agenda. As children and young people experience better opportunities for healing, their families, too, must be offered therapeutic interventions where possible. Most often, children's trauma is part of a trans-generational pattern. An evidence base, acquired through rigorous research, will be required to develop and refine reunification best practice.

A New Era in the Development of Therapeutic Residential Care in the State of Victoria

PATRICIA M. MCNAMARA

Viewed from the Australian context, this chapter provides an important perspective on the current state and potential future of TRC. Patricia McNamara locates an interesting and somewhat surprising turn in the general understanding of residential care as an 'intervention of last resort' to a 'first choice for some traumatised young people'. She goes on to demonstrate the ways in which this new path of 'energy and hope' for residential services is unfolded in three models of care, all with considerable impact in contemporary Victoria. While some differences prevail, the models clearly share some significant characteristics by being well described (e.g. in terms of target groups and the nature of interventions), theory driven (incorporating novel insights from fields such as neuroscience) and grounded in a holistic and ecologically responsive understanding of child development.

Even if this recent restoration of TRC is highly promising, history teaches us to be humble about our expectations for massive leaps forward in this area. In retrospect, child care practices of the past can easily be dismissed as inadequate and of poor quality. Conversely, we tend to look with much more favourable eyes on current attempts to deal with the same fundamental issues. In that light, a critical approach to new models and their general applicability is crucial, something that McNamara seems to acknowledge in her call for better training of professionals and more longitudinal research on outcomes for children and young people in (therapeutic) care.

The models presented are not only theory and research based, but evaluations have also been undertaken with promising results and outcomes studies are currently being developed in both the Sanctuary and the Lighthouse models. One could hope that such outcome studies in their design would demonstrate the kind of holistic approach to the developmental challenges of children and young people in care that the models presented reflect. So far, evidence on the results of child care models and programmes have tended to focus rather narrowly on outcomes, often providing little explanatory power in terms of the 'differences that make a difference' for troubled children and their families.

The description by McNamara of the three promising models resonates with intriguing examples of the basic *elements* of care that could be expected to make exactly such differences. For example, in the Lighthouse model a key component appears to be a targeted professional effort on safeguarding that young people leaving care 'are assisted to form and sustain positive and reciprocal relationships with others in and beyond the programme that will extend throughout their lives'. Arguably, this kind of long-term, social/societal support is exactly what 'effective' interventions are all about. Clever research on outcomes (and their reasons) may come to prove that such active elements in TRC have little bearing on specific models and all to do with more general strategies for supporting troubled children, young people and their families.

CHAPTER 10

Evidence-Based Practices in Therapeutic Residential Care

Sigrid James[1]

Introduction

It could be argued that evidence-based practice in residential care is an oxymoron. Evidence-based practice encapsulates a paradigm in which research evidence is used as a key determinant in clinical practice decisions to be integrated with practitioners' experiences and the specific needs, values and preferences of consumers (Sackett *et al.* 1997). Research evidence is defined by clearly delineated standards that are steeped in the scientific method, such as treatment specification and the testing of an intervention's effectiveness in controlled trials (Chambless and Hollon 1998). More recently, the term evidence-based practice[2] has been used to capture specific treatments or interventions, which have been deemed to have a sufficiently developed empirical evidence base (Rosen and Proctor 2002).

Residential care, on the other hand, has a comparably slim evidence base, judged by scientific standards. It is a field that has been shaped

1   The preparation of this chapter was supported in part by grant NIMH K01 MH077732-01A1 (PI: Sigrid James) and further grows out of a Fellowship completed at the Implementation Research Institute (IRI)/George Warren Brown School of Social Work, Washington University in St. Louis (R25 MH080916-01A2) and the Department of Veterans Affairs, Health Services Research and Development Service, Quality Enhancement Research Initiative (QUERI).
2   The literature sometimes distinguishes between evidence-based practice—a practice paradigm—and evidence-based practices, which connote specific treatments, interventions, or even policies, which have been found to be effective according to scientific standards (e.g., Rosen and Proctor 2002).

over time by policy and practice developments in child welfare, mental health, juvenile justice and education, and has been subject to ideological debates reflecting the socio-political stirrings of various time periods. In the current service delivery climate, which emphasizes cost, effectiveness, and data-driven decision-making, residential care seems like an outdated, expensive, and ineffectual approach to treating some of the most disordered youths in our child-serving systems (Sowers 2009).

The concerns about residential care are numerous and serious. They include: a limited capacity to provide developmentally appropriate and culturally relevant community-based care (Steiker 2005); failure to adequately engage the family of origin (Geurts *et al.* 2012); insufficient post-discharge planning (Barth 2005); an inadequately trained workforce with high rates of turnover (Colton and Roberts 2007); a high risk for abuse and revictimization (Colton, Vanstone and Walby 2002; M. Smith 2011); and concerns about iatrogenic effects when children with behavior problems are pooled (Dishion *et al.* 1999). A primary and more recent criticism of residential care has been the lack of established effectiveness, especially in light of its high cost (Frensch and Cameron 2002; New Freedom Commission 2003). Research and funding priorities in the United States have, for the most part, settled on the development and testing of interventions that keep youth in their families and communities. Given the growing number of community-based treatments that are considered to be viable and evidence-based alternatives for children with emotional and behavioral disorders, such as wraparound services (Bruns 2008), Multi-Dimensional Treatment Foster Care (MTFC) (Chamberlain 2003), and Multi-Systemic Therapy (MST) (Henggeler *et al.* 2009), efforts have been made in many youth-serving systems to drastically reduce the number of residential care facilities (Courtney and Iwaniec 2009). As a result, many agencies have closed their doors or have reduced their residential beds while focusing on diversifying their program offerings in order to ensure financial viability (Lee and McMillen 2007). As some have stated, residential care is in urgent need of reconceptualization in order to stay relevant (Leichtman 2006; McCurdy and McIntyre 2004; Whittaker 2004).

In 2009, the American Association of Children's Residential Centers (AACRC) wrote that "residential agencies across the country are making efforts to implement EBP…into their programming; introducing milieu-wide interactive approaches…and working with community partners to send youth to evidence based treatments offered in community settings" (AACRC 2009a, p.249). While this statement signaled the arrival of the evidence-based practice movement in the residential care arena, the question is to what degree such efforts are indeed occurring and whether anything is known about the successes and challenges of these efforts. In 2010, our research team conducted a survey of residential care facilities in California and asked participants about their use of evidence-based practices (James 2011b). Results suggested that almost every program used multiple, and in some cases many, evidence-based treatments. A follow-up phone survey to ascertain whether evidence-based practices were indeed being used shed doubts on the validity of the initial findings. Responses by participants highlighted how questions about the use of evidence-based treatments may be confounded by definitional disagreements and confusion about what standards to apply when designating an intervention to be evidence-based. Clearly, all newly developed or implemented treatments and interventions start with a claim of effectiveness, and it is apparent that a discrepancy exists in practice, policy, and research communities about the appropriate use of the evidence-base label (e.g., DiGennaro Reed and Reed 2008; Rycroft-Malone *et al.* 2004). To further complicate the debate, clearinghouses and organizations that appraise interventions for the practice and policy community apply different standards and rating systems, resulting in some interventions being included on one list yet omitted from another. Publications regularly appear that promote best practices, promising approaches, and evidence-based treatments, creating a conceptual maze for those entrusted with choosing treatments for some of the most troubled children and youths (Ellis 2009).

Yet in the research arena, treatments that are deemed to be evidence-based have relatively clearly defined parameters: they are based on a carefully developed research protocol, which is steeped in sound theory; their results are supported by controlled treatment studies, which implies a comparison group and/or random assignment to different treatment conditions; and, they have guidelines and procedures for their implementation, which means they are manualized and clearly specified in their treatment procedures and elements.

This chapter is structured around the three-part statement made by the AACRC in 2009, and as such addresses the following questions.

1. What is known about the effectiveness and implementation of (evidence-based) client-specific models into residential care settings?

2. What is known about the evidence for milieu-wide treatments?

3. What, if anything is known about sending youth to evidence-based treatments in the community?

We had started pursuing these questions about three years ago, not knowing whether any information could be found. There was also uncertainty about how to begin the search, given the lack of a list on evidence-based treatments in residential care, and the variability with which specific treatments are included on various lists of evidence-based practices.

This chapter is based in part on two previously published articles, which used scientific methods to review the peer-reviewed literature for client-specific and milieu-wide treatments in residential care (James 2011b; James, Alemi and Zepeda 2013). For the purposes of this chapter, we expanded our search to address the third question. The search was restricted to the peer-reviewed literature for two reasons: it is the most authoritative literature shaping a knowledge area and, given the exploratory nature of the questions, it would have been neither feasible nor substantively advisable to also include grey or white literature. However, this means that there may be ongoing efforts described outside the peer-reviewed literature that are not presented here.[3]

Adding client-specific models into residential care

What do we know about the effectiveness and implementation of evidence-based client-specific treatments into residential care settings? Client-specific treatments are different from milieu-based models in that they are contained and more narrowly focused on specific diagnoses or presenting problems, e.g. depression, trauma. Trauma-Focused Cognitive Behavioral Therapy or Dialectical Behavior Therapy would fall into this category. Treatments may not have been developed specifically for residential care, but could theoretically be transported into such a setting. Implementation may not require significant organizational restructuring and may have a limited effect on the overall treatment orientation of a setting. The idea is compelling. Being able to improve outcomes of youth by transporting efficacious diagnostic-specific interventions into a residential care setting may be more cost-effective and feasible than changing the structure or orientation of an entire treatment milieu.

In a structured review conducted between February and April 2012 (James *et al.* 2013) we aimed to identify psychosocial interventions with some level of established effectiveness for children and youth with

---

3 Due to space limitations this chapter will omit details of the methodological procedures used in the reviews, and readers are advised to consult the referenced articles.

emotional and behavioral disorders. The review further tried to determine whether such interventions, which may not necessarily have been developed for residential care, had subsequently been tested in short- or long-term residential care settings.[4] To identify studies, this exploratory review followed a multi-phase search strategy that began with a screening of popular clearinghouse sites (SAMHSA's National Registry for Evidence-Based Programs and Practices, California Evidence-Based Clearinghouse for Child Welfare, etc.), which publish descriptions and ratings of psychosocial interventions for children and youth. The search spanned the peer-reviewed literature from 1990 to 2012. Given the preponderance of non-randomized evaluation designs in the field of residential care, we included pre-experimental studies in the review. Thirteen studies were identified, which reported on ten interventions examined in the context of different residential care settings. They included: Adolescent Community Reinforcement Approach (A-CRA) (Godley *et al.* 2002, 2006), Aggression Replacement Training (ART) (Coleman, Pfeiffer and Oakland 1992; Nugent, Bruley and Allen 1998), Dialectical Behavior Therapy (DBT) (Sunseri 2004; The Grove Street Adolescent Residence 2004; Wasser *et al.* 2008), Ecologically-Based Family Therapy (EBFT) (Slesnick and Prestopnik 2009), Eye Movement and Desensitization Therapy (EMDR) (Soberman, Greenwald and Rule 2002), Functional Family Therapy (FFT) (Slesnick and Prestopnik 2009), Multimodal Substance Abuse Prevention (MSAP) (Friedman, Terras and Glassman 2002), Residential Student Assistance Program (RSAP) (Morehouse and Tobler 2000), Solution-Focused Brief Therapy (SFBT) (Koob and Love 2010), and Trauma Intervention Program for Adjudicated and At-Risk Youth (SITCAP-ART) (Raider *et al.* 2008). Half of the interventions were not specifically designed for residential care (DBT, EBFT, EMDR, FFT, SFBT), two interventions included residential care as one of the target delivery settings (ART, SITCAP-ART), and the remaining interventions were specifically developed for youth in residential care (A-CRA, MSAP, RSAP). The interventions covered a range of treatment approaches and studied both case status (e.g. premature discharges, placement stability, program completion) and youth functioning outcomes (e.g. trauma, depression, aggression, substance abuse, family functioning). The majority of studies focused on substance use/abuse reduction.

A standardized quality appraisal of the studies indicated significant variation in methodological rigor across multiple domains (e.g. study

---

4   Studies focused solely on inpatient psychiatric care settings, and secure juvenile detention or correctional facilities, were not included in the review.

design, representativeness of the study sample, quality of measurements, and outcomes). While this chapter cannot go into detail on these issues, a few points deserve noting. Ten of the 13 studies involved comparison group designs, seven of which included randomization. Four studies relied on archival data and were therefore able to include all youth within a given time period. The remaining studies used convenience samples, and in most cases participants were recruited or selected from one residential care setting, limiting generalizability. Of note are also important exclusion criteria. The otherwise most rigorously conducted studies involving A-CRA (Godley *et al.* 2002, 2006) and a comparison of EBFT and FFT (Slesnick and Prestopnik 2009) excluded youth who were wards of the state, and in the case of Slesnick and Prestopnik's study also excluded youth who had no family to return to. Thus, the two studies excluded youth with characteristics that are very common to a significant portion of the residential care population.

Overall, the studies reported significant improvement in most target areas. However, due to considerable bias introduced through methodological weaknesses, along with a lack of methodological clarity in some studies, findings about some of the interventions are at best preliminary.

The review also examined the challenges and barriers of implementing evidence-based treatments in residential care settings. The lack of information about feasible and applicable implementation models for residential care has been previously noted (Bright *et al.* 2010). The review pointed to many complexities in the implementation process, ranging from general receptivity among staff and clients to treatment factors (e.g. effect of placement instability on treatment, parent involvement) and structural/organizational barriers. Several barriers were noted, some of which appear to be particular to implementation efforts in residential care settings. They included: lack of continuity in group leadership due to shift work and overtime regulations; logistic problems, such as transporting youth to off-site meetings and finding suitable meeting rooms; budgetary constraints; high staff turnover; and lack of leadership support.

We also examined how residential care settings addressed treatment adaptations, training and supervision, and treatment fidelity. Several studies reported making adaptations to the treatment protocol to improve fit with the setting or accommodate the perceived characteristics of the target population. With regard to training and supervision, several models were utilized:

1. The use of expert trainers to provide initial training to either all or some staff with subsequent delivery of the intervention by all or partial residential care staff.

2. Attendance of external workshops and trainings by select staff.

3. Delivery of the intervention by trained and certified experts or therapists.

4. Training, administration, and supervision of an intervention through an external liaison organization.

Several studies addressed treatment fidelity, albeit with great variability. Methods included youth feedback about services received, expert observation and feedback, daily group leader logs, videotaping and periodic review of sessions, weekly meetings between experts and counselors, follow-up visits by developers of an intervention, and use of a fidelity checklist.

The review demonstrated that evidence-based interventions can be implemented and tested within the context of residential care, even using comparison group designs. While a behavioral and trauma-focused orientation was common, treatments utilized a range of methods and were steeped in different theoretical approaches. They addressed severe emotional and behavioral disorders as well as substance abuse problems and facilitated service continuity beyond residential care. Three interventions had an explicit parent component.

Much was learned about potential barriers to the implementation of evidence-based practices in residential care. Several conceptual articles point to the need for organizational buy-in and collaborative implementation teams, as well as the crucial role of opinion leaders to introduce an evidence-based intervention into the treatment milieu (Bright *et al.* 2010; Little, Butler and Fowler 2010: Lovelle 2005; Stewart and Bramson 2000). Interventions that are carefully planned and are gradually phased in may have more success in gaining acceptance among staff (Sunseri 2004). Reimbursement policies, budgetary constraints, and funding streams may also undermine the implementation of evidence-based treatments. Despite formidable barriers, residential care settings with their treatment milieu and embedded child care staff are seen by some as an ideal resource and opportunity to teach and reinforce new interventions (Lovelle 2005; Wasser *et al.* 2008). However, if an evidence-based treatment is implemented and brought in by external staff, orientation of child care staff and internal opinion leaders to the treatment model becomes essential to ensure successful implementation (Little *et al.* 2010; Lovelle 2005).

Milieu-wide treatments

Residential care settings also implement evidence-based milieu-wide interactive models, according to the AACRC. In contrast to client-centered treatments, adopting such models would most likely require significant organizational restructuring, since adoption of a milieu-wide model may constitute an ideological and service delivery shift. In collaboration with the California Evidence-based Clearinghouse for Child Welfare (CEBC) (www.cebc4cw.org) we identified residential care models, and assessed and rated their effectiveness using CEBC's scientific rating criteria (James 2011b). Five models were identified: Positive Peer Culture, Teaching Family Model, Sanctuary Model, Stop-Gap Model, and Re-ED. Each model was specifically designed for residential care and was generally developed in response to perceived failures or gaps in traditional residential care treatment.

Positive Peer Culture (PPC) was developed by Vorrath and Brendtro (1985) to create a culture of positive peer influences aimed at increasing mutual caring, prosocial behaviors, and self-worth among youth. This is accomplished through treatment elements (e.g., building of group responsibility, service learning) that are built around a program management paradigm of teamwork between and among staff and youth. PPC is delivered in a group format multiple times a week, and has been implemented in residential care, outpatient facilities, and schools. PPC was considered to be supported by research evidence, having been evaluated in one randomized trial.

The Teaching Family Model (TFM) (Phillips *et al.* 1974) uses a married couple or other "teaching parents" to offer a family-like environment in the residence. The teaching parents help with learning living skills and positive interpersonal interactions. TFM is characterized by clearly defined goals, integrated support systems, and a set of core elements, which beyond the teaching parent include peer leadership, skill-based training, and evaluation. While the TFM is probably the most described and researched residential care model in the literature, at the time of our review it was only given a rating of "promising" as it lacked evaluation in randomized trials. Since then, Elizabeth Farmer has completed her study comparing the effectiveness of the TFM with regular residential group care. Findings from her work will significantly advance the knowledge base on TFM's effectiveness.

The Sanctuary model developed by Bloom (1997) represents a trauma-informed method for creating an organizational culture and developing structures, processes, and behaviors among staff and community aimed at counteracting the effects of trauma among children and youth. While initially developed within the context of an acute inpatient psychiatric setting, the model has been implemented and adapted in other settings, including residential care. The model has several key features and is conceptualized as occurring in four stages, but essentially combines cognitive-behavioral strategies within a trauma-recovery framework. Evaluative research of this model is very limited, but a quasi-experimental study comparing the Sanctuary model to other residential care programs reported significant differences in targeted outcomes (Rivard *et al.* 2005), such as trauma symptoms, self-esteem, behavior problems, and parent and peer attachment, as well as coping and problem-solving skills.

The Stop-Gap Model described by McCurdy and McIntyre (2004) reconceptualizes residential care as a short-term arrangement aimed at stabilizing youth sufficiently for discharge to lower-level, community-based care. The model emphasizes the integration of evidence-based treatments (e.g., Intensive Case Management, Parent Management Training) within a three-tiered approach of service delivery. While considered promising, evaluative work on this model has not progressed, to the best of our knowledge. However, Stop-Gap's key premise is important for residential care settings aiming to stay relevant in the current evidence-based and short-term treatment climate.

The final model included in the 2011 review was Re-ED (originally called Re-Education of Children with Emotional Disturbance) (Hobbs 1966). Re-ED has gone through multiple modifications since the early 1960s, but its importance lay in a paradigmatic shift in service delivery to youth with emotional and behavioral problems, emphasizing a strength-based approach, an ecological orientation, a focus on competence and learning, an emphasis on relationship-building, and the development of a culture of informed or data-driven decision-making. Re-ED was initially implemented and tested in short-term residential treatment programs as well as public school support services programs, and has been adapted to a variety of community needs since then. Re-ED is implemented as a group approach and is intended as a short-term intervention (about four to six months) with rapid return to the community. Given the lack of comparison group studies, the effectiveness of Re-ED could not definitively be determined although pre-post designs have reported improvements in various domains of functioning.[5]

The review of residential care models indicated a painfully small knowledge base considering the decades that some models have been in existence and an overall lack of knowledge advancement. At this stage, far too few rigorous studies have been conducted to make a strong recommendation for one or the other treatment model.

Evidence-based treatments for residential care youth in the community

Several searches were conducted to identify any systematic knowledge about the use of evidence-based treatments in the community by residential care youth. It was evident from the start that such a search would be difficult, as no studies to date have specifically addressed this question. As such, any knowledge would have to be derived from studies that included residential care youth in their community-based samples and conducted separate analyses for residential care youth. Given that only a fraction of mental health care consumers in the general population have access to evidence-based treatments (e.g. Shafran *et al.* 2009), and that little is known about their experiences and outcomes, even less would be known about sub-populations, such as residential care youth. Usual community-based care tends to be eclectic (Weersing, Weisz and Donenberg 2002) and discrepant from the structured treatment procedures and guidelines required in evidence-based care (e.g. Garland *et al.* 2010; Kramer and Burns 2008). To answer the target question, studies would have to be carefully designed not only to track residential care youths' access and use of community-based treatments, but also to determine the quality and nature of these treatments.

---

5   A residential treatment model that was not included in the 2011 review due to its primary focus on substance abuse, is the Phoenix House Academy (PHA) model developed for youth, aged 13–17, with substance abuse and co-occurring mental health disorders (Morral, McCaffrey and Ridgeway 2004). It employs the concept of the therapeutic community and applies it to youth, integrating residential treatment with on-site school or vocational training. The PHA model is based on social learning principles and intervenes in every aspect of a youth's ecology, involving multiple treatment components, such as case management, individual, group and family counseling, milieu-therapy, and trauma-specific treatment. PHA is considered a promising residential treatment model, having been tested in a quasi-experimental outcome study with superior substance abuse and psychologically functioning outcomes compared with youth in other residential settings.

As expected, we were unable to identify any studies even after employing several different search strategies. The lack of systematic knowledge in this area opens up a new line of inquiry, which can only be pursued through collaborative relationships between residential care settings and researchers interested in addressing this knowledge gap.

Conclusion

The idea that evidence-based treatments could be implemented in residential care settings is intriguing, but may never be convincing to those who view evidence-based treatments as a much needed alternative to residential care. To those who believe that residential care continues to play a role in the continuum of services for children and youth with severe emotional problems, this is a new area of inquiry with a very small knowledge base to date.

Our two previous reviews yielded a very modest body of knowledge that indicates the existence of a few promising residential care treatment models and supports the feasibility of implementing and testing evidence-based treatments in residential care. However, it is evident that the research lags far behind the needs of the residential care practice and policy community. Discussions with residential care providers indicate growing interest and efforts in the implementation of evidence-based treatments. However, there also seems to be uncertainty and many questions about the process of identifying and implementing an evidence-based treatment. Some providers are looking to the literature to guide these efforts, yet unfortunately they will be mostly disappointed. While the emergent field of Implementation Science has been flourishing, there are no implementation models that have been tested for residential care, and our review was the first to identify barriers to successful implementation in residential care across studies. Some of these barriers may be unique to residential care, but others may be shared by other organizational settings, and as such lessons learned may be applicable across contexts. However, such information needs to be distilled from the larger body of knowledge on implementation, and subsequently applied and disseminated to the residential care community. To advance knowledge in this area, partnerships between researchers and residential care providers who are already in the process of implementing evidence-based treatments will be essential. At the moment, many residential care settings are learning invaluable lessons about the use and implementation of evidence-based treatments in their specific practice contexts. It is this knowledge that needs to be captured and systematized in order to advance this field and provide guidance to other programs interested in the integration of evidence-based treatments in residential care.

While there is need to advance knowledge in all identified areas, we see urgency in answering the following questions.

- What percentage of residential care settings is implementing evidence-based treatments?

- What evidence-based treatments are most appropriate and/or effective to meet the needs of youth in residential care, and which ones lend themselves to implementation in residential care settings?

- What factors facilitate or hinder the implementation of evidence-based treatments, and what implementation models may be most relevant for residential care?

Finally, more rigorously conducted outcome research is needed to definitively determine the relative effectiveness of milieu-wide and client-specific evidence-based treatments in residential care. This needs to be accompanied by studies that empirically (not just conceptually) address issues of implementation.

COMMENTARY BY JAMES K. WHITTAKER ON:

Evidence-Based Practices in Therapeutic Residential Care

SIGRID JAMES

Sigrid James provides an extraordinarily valuable assessment of the current state and source of knowledge undergirding contemporary Therapeutic Residential Care (TRC) in a United States context. She draws heavily on her two previous systematic reviews of peer-reviewed literature on client-specific and milieu-wide treatments in residential care (James 2011b; James *et al.* 2013) to paint a picture that at one and the same time elicits optimism and pessimism in the reader. On the client-specific side of evidence-based interventions, her team identified a range of studies documenting the uptake of ten discrete evidence-based interventions in residential care settings. These included such familiar interventions as: Aggression Replacement Training (ART), Dialectical Behavior Therapy (DBT), Functional Family Therapy (FFT), Solution-Focused Brief Therapy (SFBT), Trauma Intervention Program for Adjudicated and At-Risk Youth (SITCAP-ART), and Ecologically-Based Family Therapy (EBFT) among others. This activity reflects a growing interest among residential providers—also documented by the author—in the identification and integration of evidence-based practices into existing treatment programs: discussions with residential care providers indicate growing interest and efforts in the implementation of evidence-based treatments. However, there also seems to be uncertainty and many questions about the process of identifying and implementing an evidence-based treatment. Some providers are looking to the literature to guide these efforts, yet unfortunately they will be mostly disappointed.

James makes a strong plea for rigorous empirical studies of the implementation process, including identification of barriers/incentives in residential settings, and outlines a series of potentially fruitful questions to explore. This is the part of the review that elicits optimism.

It remains for her review of milieu-wide treatments (program models) to pinpoint the inadequacies of the current state of knowledge in therapeutic residential care in providing bright and clear guidelines for either policy makers or practitioners: the review of residential care models indicated a painfully small knowledge base considering the decades that some models have been in existence and an overall lack of knowledge advancement. At this stage, far too few rigorous studies have been conducted to make a strong recommendation for one or the other treatment model.

This conclusion echoes similar observations made in the introduction to this volume about the corrosive effects of atrophied model development in TRC and the absence of both government and private philanthropic resources for new initiatives in research and development of novel approaches within residential services. In my view, milieu-wide (or whole cloth) models of TRC will not emerge solely from an inductive approach: in this instance, the ever-more refined knowledge gained through research on the serial integration of client-specific evidence-based practices. As James notes, evidence-based treatments have clearly defined parameters including that they are *steeped in strong theory*. To paraphrase philosopher of science, Steven Jay Gould, doing science without theory is like building a building brick-by-brick without a blueprint. The field of TRC is sorely in need of both client-specific and milieu-wide pathways of research identified so clearly by James who, in addition, makes a strong plea for a closer cooperation between researchers and practitioners to achieve both ends. The fruits of her own carefully constructed and rigorously implemented research in TRC—as well as that of a small but growing band of researchers committed to this critical area of service—make the case for doing more.

CHAPTER 11

Creating and Maintaining Family Partnerships in Residential Treatment Programs

Shared Decisions, Full Participation, Mutual Responsibility

Richard W. Small, Christopher Bellonci and Susan Ramsey

Introduction

There is an accumulation of evidence that family involvement and family-centered practice make a difference in outcomes of residential treatment. Whittaker (2012) reviews a number of North American sources dating back to the 1960s, all supporting the critical role of active family and community involvement in enhancing positive outcomes. Geurts *et al.* (2012), with more emphasis on the European literature on residential treatment, similarly identify a range of papers connecting family involvement to better conditions in care and better overall outcomes. This emerging consensus in the scholarly literature is also supported by the values of current national policy formulations, including Systems of Care principles (Stroul and Friedman 1986), the Building Bridges Initiative (www.buildingbridges4youth.org) and the Federation of Families for Children's Mental Health (www.ffcmh.org), among others. (See also Walter and Petr, 2008 and AACRC 2006; 2009b). Whittaker sums up this present context for practice in residential treatment succinctly:

The weight of the empirical historical evidence as well as the experience of countless residential treatment programs is that a robust and encompassing set of avenues for family engagement constitutes, if not a *sufficient* element in achieving positive outcomes, clearly a *necessary* one: both to meet the goals of permanency and treatment efficacy previously cited and to fulfill the widely shared value commitments to include parents as full partners in the treatment process. (Whittaker 2012, p.260)

Yet what does all this mean in terms of real-life practice? This chapter draws on our own collective range of experience with Therapeutic Residential Care (TRC) (including the perspectives of chief executive management, senior clinical leadership, and experienced parent leadership), as well as on concepts from the Building Bridges Initiative to describe how the implementation of full value family partnerships requires changes in structure and culture within the residential program from pre-admission to discharge planning and aftercare, and also requires new skills for professional helpers and family members alike. Again based on our experience, we will highlight the critical role of the Professional Parent Liaison (PPL) in maintaining effective teamwork between staff and empowered family members in the high tension environment of the residential treatment center. First, we submit a working definition of family-centered practice specific to therapeutic residential settings for children and youth.

Working definition

Family-centered practice in therapeutic residential care is characterized by a set of pervasive institutional structures and a range of services, supports, and professional practices designed to:

- preserve and, whenever possible, strengthen connections between the young person in care and his/her extended family, most broadly defined

- facilitate and actively support full participation of family members in the daily life of the program

- promote shared responsibility for outcomes, shared decision making, and active partnership between family members and all helpers.

We believe that TRC programs effectively re-engineered with this practice blueprint can be powerful environments for families to begin the work of connecting and reconnecting, especially where other factors related to safety and stability have made residential treatment the best option. Of course, implementation of the above blueprint requires significant, even transformational, changes in practice.

Self-assessment as a platform for agencies developing family-centered approaches

Implementation of a family-centered approach means first assessing the organization's readiness for and commitment to family-centered practice. The Residential Child Care Project (CARE) at Cornell University (Holden *et al.* 2010) developed a Family Involvement Survey in 2011 that was based on earlier work by Walker's Trieschman Center Carolinas Project (Alwon *et al.* 2000), supported by the philanthropy of the Duke Endowment. The survey was designed for organizations looking at how to engage families in key aspects of the organization's functions and to support meaningful family involvement in their child's treatment during their residential stay. The CARE survey is completed by agency staff and asks questions about how the organizational culture and policies address family engagement practices (e.g. written policies and procedures, mission statement, staff orientation, professional development, roles for family members in corporate governance); the admissions process starting from referral to entry into the residential program; the care of the child and communications with the family once the child is admitted to the program; and how the transition planning and discharge is managed (http://rccp.cornell.edu/caremainpage.html). Although not designed to be used with families or funders, it could be adapted for that purpose in order to provide a critical outsider's perspective on how well the agency is meeting their family-centered goals.

A second approach to getting ready for family-centered practice was developed through the Building Bridges Initiative (BBI). BBI is a national initiative in the US—federally sponsored by the Substance Abuse and Mental Health Services Administration (SAMSHA)—working to identify and promote practice and policy that will create strong and closely coordinated partnerships and collaborations between families, youth, community and residentially based treatment and service providers, advocates, and policymakers to ensure that comprehensive mental health services and supports are available to improve the lives of young people and their families. The BBI outcomes work group developed a number of products to support the development and enhancement of family-centered approaches to residential interventions. Similar to the CARE approach, BBI focused on assessment first, developing a self-assessment tool that has versions for youth and families as well as staff and advocates (Spanish language versions are also available) (BBI 2010). The BBI tools look at the issue of family-centered practice at a much more granular level than the CARE survey. Both approaches bring a "family-centered lens" to examine policies, programs, and practices from pre-admission through the residential stay and including the discharge and aftercare experience. In addition to the self-assessment tool, BBI developed a performance guidelines and indicators matrix for agencies to use as a quality improvement tool, measuring adherence to family-centered practice (BBI 2009).

Family-centered practices in residential treatment centers

We have found the BBI matrix of performance guidelines most useful in mapping out practices in support of real, measurable family partnerships. Examples of pre-admission practice guidelines include asking families, residential staff, and referral sources whether marketing materials accurately reflect the program's outcomes data; policies and utilization rates of emergency safety procedures like restraint or seclusion are available to families; admission and intake procedures are developed for the family and child's convenience and comfort; there is outreach to community providers who have worked with the family in order to capitalize on their insights and treatment relationships with the family; the agency uses current and alumni parents and children as "ambassadors," welcoming new families and children to the Residential Treatment Center (RTC); transportation and other barriers are addressed and plans developed to ensure frequent opportunities by parents and siblings to spend time with the child at the program, home, and community.

Pre-admission family-centered practices in particular look at possible barriers to full partnership between families and residential providers at the outset of the treatment. Written and oral communication emphasizes that the work will not be successful without the family being fully engaged in the treatment. The family gets to identify who its members are and what roles they will play in the treatment. If a child is referred to a residential provider with no identified family members, the residential provider immediately works with the referring agency and guardian (typically the state child welfare department) to identify someone who can serve in this role. This may involve intensive efforts to identify biological family members not previously involved; identifying a foster family where the child can go after discharge; or minimally, identifying a visiting resource for the child even if this person will not ultimately be a full-time caregiver (see Louisell 2007 for a well-articulated description of family finding in the US). The treatment plan should always be focused on what it is going to take to return this child to their home and community safely, and with enduring family ties even if the child and family cannot live together full time.

Family-centered practices emphasize the full participation of the family throughout the child's residential stay. Guidelines looking at the experience of the child and family during the residential stay include parents not being treated as guests but being granted 24/7 access to their child with visits not being conditionally based on the child's progress within the program; parents get to decide the members of their child and family team; there are clear protocols developed with the family about how often and what information will be communicated about their child; community partners who have worked with the family are encouraged to remain involved during the residential stay and are seen as partners in the family's care; decisions are reached by consensus, with the family seen as the expert regarding their child, and professionals are used as consultants to the family and child; shared formulation of the problem and shared vision of the solution; only interventions that can be meaningfully replicated in the home and community are utilized; goals are youth/ family driven, strength-based, oriented to the least restrictive options, and used to regularly measure progress; assessment and utilization of natural supports is emphasized; cultural and linguistic preferences of the family are respected and attended to; youth are encouraged to be home and in the community as much as they are able to do so safely.

Discharge planning from a family-centered perspective starts at admission by asking "What will it take for the child to be safe and behaviorally stable in the home and community?" All interventions are then oriented around this goal. Discharges should not be made arbitrarily based on a certain date or duration of treatment but based on achieving the treatment goals. Frequent progress meetings should occur to ensure the child is reunited with their family and returned to the community as quickly as is safely possible. Delays in progress should be a cause for alarm by the treatment team and reconsideration of the formulation of the problem and reconsideration of the treatment plan may be needed if a child's stay becomes prolonged or progress towards goals is not achieved. Management of risks associated with treatment decisions becomes shared between the family and residential provider, community resources, funding agency and any other systems involved in the child and family's care. This allows for the development of mutual responsibility in the context of shared decision making. Aftercare guidelines include detailing what services and supports will be provided to the family post-discharge; developing an aftercare crisis plan with specificity and practicality; lining up post-discharge respite care options; and determining what services the residential care agency can provide the family in the community either directly or in collaboration with community-based agencies.

BBI encourages the use of data to track outcomes important to families in order to understand whether the residential agency has made a lasting impact that is sustainable including educational outcomes; medication rates; response to behavioral and clinical interventions as established by the child's individual treatment plan; use of emergency behavioral interventions including restraint and seclusion; length of stay; and discharge outcomes. Systemic measures would also look at the role of parents in hiring, training, and evaluating residential staff and whether family members have a meaningful role on agency governance structures.

Implementation of family-centered practice means constructing a system that prioritizes the needs of the family over those of the residential provider. It means the system is designed and built from the ground up with a singular focus on what families want and need to treat their child. This is not to say that there won't be times when there are competing needs or values creating conflict between families and providers. How these conflicts are addressed and resolved is the true measure of family-centered practice.

Beyond advocacy: the essential role of the Professional Parent Liaison

With the increased policy emphasis on family-centered care, a new role, sometimes called Parent Partner or Family Advocate, has emerged in the behavioral health workforce in the US (Obrochta *et al.* 2011; Purdy 2010). For the purposes of this chapter we refer to this position as Professional Parent Liaison (PPL), in part to emphasize the role as a resource to families and to staff members working to fully include families in the helping process. Optimally, the PPL draws from his/her lived experience, in combination with formal training and/or professional education, to guide, empower, and plan with families who are navigating service systems. Family partnership staff, whatever their formal title, have been part of the outpatient and community mental health landscape for many years and continue to gain recognition as influential members of care teams. In the residential treatment program, we think the role of the PPL is particularly critical.

Ideally, the residential program's PPL is a member of the agency's senior management team. This gives families a prominent, visible presence from top to bottom in the program, sending the clear message that commitment to family partnership is one of the highest priorities of the organization. In turn, the therapeutic residential setting gains a resident expert whose "insider" views and background are represented in decision making at every level. By strategically sharing their own experiences, the PPL at a senior level is positioned to challenge myths and assumptions about families who are parenting children with severe emotional disturbance, to help both staff and family members be heard rather than misunderstood, and to push care teams to plan helping strategies from a real-life, strengths-based approach.

The PPL also plays a key role in maintaining the culture of full family partnership over time. Once a new practice paradigm is in place it has to be sustainable, and the truth is that managing a changing culture of professional practice, with family members as true, active partners, is not so easy. Real partnerships with families of young people placed in residential treatment require that everyone involved be respectful, honest, and trusting in the highest of high-stress contexts. Thorny issues can arise as partnerships evolve and cultures change.

- Communication between direct care workers, clinical staff, family members, and youth in care can get complicated at the least. Roles and responsibility lines are sometimes blurred or miscommunicated.

- Families and direct care staff may be hesitant to be open and honest with each other, or may lack the skills to manage conflict if it arises. Staff turnover may affect relationships and progress.

- Stress and trauma may adversely affect teamwork, especially when there are perceived power differentials. Families are worn out from looking for help and may appear resistant.

- Families may be invited, but they may not feel welcome or supported to fully participate in the program.

In all of these situations, the PPL can play an essential role in helping all sides of the partnership work together. Functionally, the PPL goes far beyond advocate to serve as resource, mediator, consensus builder, coach, and innovator for families but equally so for residential treatment staff. The PPL represents the family perspective—most especially the diversity of families and family perspectives—throughout the organization, from employee hiring, orientation, and training to case consultation, and participation in treatment and risk management meetings, program and policy conversations, proposing new programs, and transition planning services. The PPL must be ready to balance multiple roles at all phases of treatment—admission, during stay, transition, and aftercare.

The role of the Professional Parent Liaison in the admission phase

Completing the admissions process is an especially vulnerable time for family members in crisis who are coping with uncertainty about the present and future. It is an equally vulnerable time for the admissions staff pressured to complete contracts necessary to initiate service and reimbursement and keep beds filled. These competing stressors can inadvertently derail the optimum time to begin shaping a partnership with the family. Including the PPL in this process can help to ensure the relationship has a positive start or at best a "jump start" in collaboration. The PPL can instill credibility and confidence that the residential treatment program values the family member's expertise about the child. The PPL is a symbol of hope and relief. By having a true appreciation for and listening to the family's journey at the outset, they can begin to identify ways to help the whole care team understand each family's unique history and move forward together.

The role of the Professional Parent Liaison during the residential treatment stay

As noted above, on-going shared decisions and mutual responsibility for the care plan are attainable throughout placement when organizational culture supports engaging families as full partners. Keys to success include being able to develop a partnership with a family free of power differentials and respectful of cultural diversity; an ability to reach consensus on goals, roles, and responsibilities; and sharing knowledge of practices and resources that work in the real world. The PPL can be an important facilitator of all of these activities.

A stay in residential treatment is just that: a defined period of time during which a child and family will stabilize and learn new skills, and the child will return home as soon as possible. RTCs should seize natural opportunities to shift from doing things for parents (enabling) to having parents continue expected child rearing responsibilities (empowering). For example, parents could be asked to schedule haircuts, choose afterschool activities, and/or manage their child's medical care. These situations allow for maintaining community connections, continuity of care, and easier transitions at discharge. As a matter of course, family members have not been included in daily routines in residential treatment programs, but family-driven care practices prescribe welcoming family members into this culture. Allowing family members unfettered access to the milieu, however, can be particularly stressful for both staff and family members. Embracing this opportunity, however, is one of the most ideal ways for both parents and temporary caretakers to learn from each other. The PPL can facilitate by guiding and modeling for both partners.

For staff members, most of whom are recent college graduates with little to no parenting experience, having family members around can be intimidating. Workers may be fearful they may be judged or criticized for doing something wrong. Inevitably, the answer to the question "Who is in charge?" (staff or parent) may become unclear. Interestingly, family members also experience a similar range of concerns. The PPL can be a tremendous resource here. Having both an established relationship with family members and familiarity with the residential treatment program staff and routines allows the PPL to pose recommendations and coach staff and family members through stressful situations in the moment.

The role of the Professional Parent Liaison in transition planning and aftercare

At transition we know a lot about the child's behavior. Harder to judge is the parent's readiness to have their child at home. The PPL, having travelled this anxious road, is in a position to understand and allay a parent's fears while assisting staff in developing a plan that continues to move forward while acknowledging the legitimacy of family member worries. This may include, but not be limited to, visiting school programs with family; mediating staff and family priorities; suggesting staggered transitions to home (weekends first, once mastered adding a day at a time until home full time); negotiating staff support for visits to home and community; and helping to craft crisis safety plans. Encouraging parents to practice self-care and make room for their own social interests as crucial parts of the discharge plan is also a helping function uniquely suited to the PPL.

The PPL can be helpful in designing and overseeing discharge surveys and tracking a family's progress at home. By remaining in touch with families, the PPL is able to develop an informal network of parents and offer updates to staff. Parents can become referrals for current families looking for information on services or schools. For staff, hearing that a child and family they worked with is doing well offers a tremendous sense of pride. Also, potential exists for the PPL to recruit and train family members to stay connected to former helpers as volunteer mentors and trainers to new families.

Questions for future research

As noted above, it seems clear that extant research over many years supports the finding that active family participation in therapeutic residential settings is connected to better outcomes. We also have lots of ideas—with lots of variance—about how this full participation should look in practice settings. Our colleague John Lyons at the University of Ottawa describes successful family partnership as remaking the residential treatment program to be "fully permeable" to families—empowering them as team members, but going beyond shared decision making to actively support family participation in the day-to-day life of the program (John Lyons, personal communication to R. Small 2012). This seems to us exactly right from the point of view of the residential center as a potentially powerful environment for connecting and reconnecting families, but it also raises many interesting questions for further exploration.

- Just how powerful are the ecological effects of frequent family participation in the life space?

- Should we think in terms of a bottom-line minimum of family contact with youngsters in care (including by phone, internet, and face to face), or is this best left to individual care planning?

- What are the implications for communication and information technology here, including privacy issues?

- Is frequency of family participation in the residential milieu an "active ingredient" of effective practice in and of itself?

- If family members are in more frequent direct contact with care staff, does this change communication patterns for the care team as a whole?

- Does more frequent family participation in the residential milieu change the behavior of the young people in care?

- Finally, do presumed positive effects related to frequent, direct family participation in the residential milieu enhance the impact of evidence-based family therapy interventions on offer to families in the program?

Exploring these questions and learning what we can from whatever answers we generate seems to us to be very promising for transformative future research and model building.

There are, of course, other potentially researchable questions raised by the practice realities of implementing full partnerships with families in therapeutic residential settings. In brief, some of the questions we think most suggestive for more practice research are as follows.

- How do family-centered teams, with parents as full partners, make decisions in real life? Our values tell us that fully shared decision making is best, but what does "shared" look like in practice? Do staff and family members always have the tools they need to work together in the high-stress context of residential treatment? What is the best way to empower staff and family members to be good, team decision makers, especially when there is disagreement or conflict? As noted above, the PPL may have a significant role to play here, helping struggling care teams as a mediator and coach. In our experience, most family-centered care teams work pretty well, but some don't. We need to learn more here.

- How do family-centered care teams make decisions about risk, especially perceived risks associated with the young person in care spending increasing amounts of time at home? Differing risk assessments between family and staff team members can create some difficult situations, with anxious family members feeling that their voices are not being heard, and program staff mistaking anxiety and trauma for lack of commitment to the young person in care. This can bring the whole care plan to a halt. We need to find more and better ways for family-centered teams to reach consensus about risks, as well as about what real supports will need to be in place for families to feel safe as the care plan moves toward discharge.

- Also noted above, there are many versions of what we have defined as PPL in use throughout the system of care as a whole.

Now would be a good time for a comprehensive review of the varied roles and essential functions of parent liaisons as they are utilized specifically in therapeutic residential settings.

- Finally, what is best practice in therapeutic residential settings when families opt not to participate as active partners, even when programs make concrete, honest attempts to identify and eliminate barriers to participation? This seems to us to be a compelling question for practice and practice research. Do we know everything we need to know about who the families we struggle to connect with are? Does every family need to be an active partner at the same level? What are the rock-bottom, minimum ways we need to support families to work with the care team?

Answers to these questions and others like them will be very important as those of us in the field continue efforts to transform uninformed, ineffective program models of TRC into powerful environments for family connection and support. As the present volume attests, we have come a long way here, but we still have lots to learn.

Creating and Maintaining Family Partnerships in Residential Treatment Programs: Shared Decisions, Full Participation, Mutual Responsibility

RICHARD W. SMALL, CHRISTOPHER BELLONCI, AND SUSAN RAMSEY

It has been this writer's long experience that family engagement can be something of an "Achilles heel" for residential programs. As a practicing social worker and family therapist in residential psychiatric milieu I often felt compromised by protocols that enforced family attendance at weekly family sessions as part of the standard contract for admission of the young person. No family therapy, no admission! This hardly seemed the optimum starting point for meaningful collaboration with families. Indeed, that authoritarian approach at times quietly echoed for me Bettelheim's infamously pathologized view of residents' families that dominated the Orthogenic School at its outset (Bettelheim 1974).

In sharp contrast, Small, Bellonci, and Ramsey embrace here a strengths approach to engagement of family and community in residential therapeutic work. That approach is located convincingly within an ecological systems practice orientation. The authors stoically engage with the very complex challenge of identifying effective organizational processes that can facilitate true partnerships with families to promote "both the goals of permanency and treatment efficacy" (Whittaker 2012). They draw on their own broad collective experience along with the Residential Child Care (CARE) Project and the Building Bridges Initiative (BBI) to describe how achievement of optimum family partnerships requires changes in structure and culture within the residential program from pre-admission to discharge planning and aftercare. They argue that it also requires new skills for professional helpers and family members alike. The authors wisely advocate for the broadest possible set of meanings of "family." This perspective is clearly going to be most productive in the residential care context where attachment disruption, abuse, neglect, and other trauma have often undermined family functioning over generations. Identifying and actualizing extended family and family-like connections (sometimes described as kith) can be most important.

Many, including these authors, argue that discharge planning should begin from the outset of a residential admission. There is little contest with the assertion made here that positive discharge outcomes are more likely with a family-centered approach to goal attainment. All interventions can then be firmly aligned with the targeted goals and reviewed collaboratively by staff and family members. The authors also champion the role of Professional Parent Liaison (PPL); this seems well justified. The PPL role is clearly vital in supporting all team and family members throughout the treatment process—from intake to aftercare. There would appear to be considerable potential for this role to be adopted internationally.

The chapter concludes by raising areas for further research. These largely emerge from speculation about the ecological impacts of developing greater "permeability" to families in therapeutic residential care programs. How collaborative decision making between staff and family members in situations of risk can be best managed is clearly a key knowledge gap. "Bottom-line" expectations of the resident's family, especially when a family is reluctant to engage with the therapeutic residential program, is another area requiring rigorous investigation.

Residential therapeutic programs can offer an important (and in some cases, possibly a last) opportunity for young people to build strong, protective relationships with family members. This chapter reminds us that this is an opportunity too important to miss; it also offers practical suggestions about how best to seize the moment.

Preparing Youth for Successful Transitions from Therapeutic Residential Care

Relationship between Adult Outcomes of Young People Making the Transition to Adulthood from Out-of-Home Care and Prior Residential Care

Nathanael J. Okpych and Mark E. Courtney

Introduction: general survey of residential care in the US

The convention of raising or treating children in congregate settings apart from their families is a practice that stretches back over two-and-a-half centuries in the US (Courtney and Hughes-Heuring 2009). Orphanages and reformatories emerged in the 18th century and expanded throughout the 19th century, coinciding with a cultural shift in the perception of children as vulnerable and in need of social protection (Wolins and Piliavin 1964). Although residential care was met with admonition as foster care became increasingly formalized and common, these institutions continued to serve children well into the 20th century. By 1910, more than 1150 institutions were in operation that housed over 111,000 children (Ashby 1997). It was not until 1958 that the number of dependent children who were served by residential care institutions was surpassed by the number of children placed in foster care arrangements (Ashby 1997), and the reliance on group care continued to decrease (Whittaker 2006). Within the contemporary US foster care system, for example, the 58,000 children placed in a group home or institutional setting comprised just 15 percent of all placements in 2012 (US Department of Health and Human Services 2013).

Preserving a family caretaking environment versus placing children in a congregate care setting is a tension that has run through the evolution of out-of-home care in the US and continues to be hotly debated. In addition to moral and ideological viewpoints that have animated the debate in the past, current discourse takes place in a context of increased accountability. Attention to whether group care "works" and how much it costs in relation to other services have become key points of consideration. The remarkable diversity of programs and services that fall under the umbrella of residential or group care and the populations they serve complicates assessment of effectiveness. Placement in residential settings is a staple treatment modality in three major US service systems: child welfare; juvenile justice; and mental and behavioral health, which includes alcohol and substance abuse treatment (James 2011a). Residential care is also utilized with other populations, including children with disabilities and runaway and homeless youth. Programs range in size from large institutions to small group homes that serve only a small handful of children (Courtney and Hughes-Heuring 2009). Placements also vary in terms of the range and intensity of services, the use of formal programmatic or treatment models or approaches, level of restrictiveness, the duration that children remain in the placement, staff credentials, supervisory structure (e.g. live-in versus shift work), contact with and connection to the community, use of public versus specialized schooling, and other characteristics (Barth *et al.* 2009; James 2011a; Lee and Barth 2011; Lee *et al.* 2010).

Despite this diversity, there are some trends that can be discerned in residential care as a whole. Over the years, facilities have become more numerous and smaller, lengths of stay have decreased, children entering care are more likely to be males and tend to be older, and since group care is often viewed as a last resort to be used when less restrictive treatments have not worked, children admitted are increasingly troubled and have multiple problems (Baker, Archer and Curtis 2005; Barth 2002, 2005; Lee *et al.* 2010; Whittaker 2006). Concerns have been raised about the potential for deviance contagion and deviance training in residential settings, but clear and compelling evidence for this has not been consistently produced (Whittaker 2008).

Although residential care is a mainstay of services for children and adolescents, there has been a dearth of nuanced and rigorous research that gauges its effectiveness. Most studies on residential care inadequately specify program characteristics, measure disparate outcomes, lack control or comparison groups, do not randomly assign participants or correct for selection biases, and rarely assess long-term outcomes (James 2011a; Lee *et al.* 2010; Whittaker 2006).

In reviews that have considered the effectiveness of residential care in improving various developmental outcomes, the findings are mixed (e.g. Lee *et al.* 2010). Some research indicates that youths' behavior and mental health do improve, as do their optimism and life satisfaction, while in care (e.g. Gilman and Handwerk 2001; Lee and Thompson 2008; Lyons, *et al.* 2001). Conversely, other studies have found that residential care services have little or no impact on outcomes (e.g. Barth *et al.* 2007; Chamberlain and Reid 1998; Lee *et al.* 2011; Ryan *et al.* 2008). Lee and Barth (2011) astutely caution against making sweeping conclusions about the effectiveness of residential care based on aggregations of disparate programs. Not only does this fail to identify specific types of residential care that verily improve outcomes, but it also will not separate out other programs that may be ineffective or even have iatrogenic effects. Thus, while studies that cast doubt on the effectiveness and efficiency of residential care have brought its widespread utilization in the US into question, it has also been recognized that more fine grained and rigorous evaluation research is needed to draw specific conclusions about the effectiveness of group care.

Three recent responses to the questionable effectiveness of residential care and the need for nuanced evaluation research include: seeking to identify programs and models with strong empirical support, teasing out common elements, and considering community-based alternatives to residential care. In response to increased calls for identifying evidence-based practices, a growing number of treatment models utilized in group care and residential settings are being rigorously evaluated. For example, James (2011a) reviewed four models that received either a "supported by research evidence" or a "promising" designation by the California Evidence-Based Clearinghouse for Child Welfare: Positive Peer Culture, Teaching Family model, Sanctuary model, and the Stop-Gap model. Additionally, researchers have begun to create indices of reporting standards that will help standardize the evaluation of group care treatment models (e.g. Butler and McPherson 2007; Lee and Barth 2011).

A second response entails identifying common elements—the critical ingredients that are present across treatment models which appear to drive favorable outcomes. Using family-style or family-oriented program structures, engaging the youth's caretakers in treatment, and coordinating post-discharge services to support the youth as they transition out of congregate care are examples of promising common elements that have garnered some support from the evaluation literature (James 2011a; Lee and Barth, 2011; Whittaker 2006).

Community-based alternatives that are less intrusive and less expensive than residential care is a third response that has emerged. Multi-Dimensional Treatment Foster Care (MTFC), the wraparound model, and Multi-Systemic Therapy (MST) are examples of community-based treatment approaches used with youth who would traditionally be placed in group care settings (Barth *et al.* 2009). The high degree of monitoring and service intensity afforded in residential programs is substituted with intensive and coordinated services that are intended to support youth with complex needs in a less-restrictive setting. The California Evidence Based Clearinghouse has classified MTFC and MST as being "well-supported" interventions, while the wraparound model received a rating of "promising" and requires further evaluation.

Recent programmatic developments that seek to make residential care models more family-like and family-oriented, and community-based interventions that expand the arc of support are blurring hard-and-fast divisions between residential care services and family-centered services. Indeed, some scholars have challenged the field of health and human services to envision "a new service continuum that softens the differences and blurs the boundaries between in-home and out-of-home options such as shared care, respite care, and partial placements" (Whittaker 2008 p.259; Whittaker and Maluccio 2002).

Analysis of outcomes of older youth in foster care who lived in residential care

We now turn from a general survey of residential care in the US to an analysis of the long-term outcomes of older youth involved in the US foster care system. As discussed above, child welfare is one of the major social service systems that utilize congregate care placements as a common type of service. We draw on data from the Midwest Evaluation of the Adult Functioning of Former Foster Care Youth (Midwest Study) to assess the impact being placed in residential care has on a wide variety of outcomes in young adulthood. At the time this chapter was written, the Midwest Study was the largest study of its kind in the US, following over 700 young people, for nearly a decade, who resided in three Midwestern states. As such, the Midwest Study provides a unique opportunity to examine long-term outcomes of youth who had lived in a residential care setting at some point during their time in foster care.

The baseline sample (n=732) was first interviewed in 2002 when participants were 17 or 18 years old, and they were followed up in four subsequent waves spaced approximately two years apart. To be eligible for the study, adolescents had to be in foster care in Illinois, Iowa, or Wisconsin for at least one year prior to their 17th birthday. The last wave of interviews took place in 2010 and 2011 when respondents were in their mid-20s (n=596, response rate=83 percent excluding 12 respondents who had died by wave 5). For more information about the Midwest Study, the reader can refer to the five reports that correspond to each wave of data collection (Courtney, Terao and Boast 2004; Courtney *et al.* 2005, 2007, 2010, 2012).

The central question guiding our present analysis is whether living in a residential care setting impacts educational, employment, economic, social support, delinquency, life satisfaction, and health and mental health outcomes later in early adulthood. At age 17, about 6 in 10 Midwest Study participants (n=353) reported that they had lived in residential care (group care or a residential treatment center) at some point prior to the interview. Data on outcomes are drawn from wave 5 of the study, when participants were 25 or 26 years old. Since it is likely that living in a residential care placement and the various outcomes of interest are influenced by a number of characteristics and conditions, we control for a broad range of factors in our analyses. Only respondents who were interviewed at both wave 1 and wave 5 are included in the analysis (n=595). Before presenting these results, we briefly summarize the variables.

TABLE 12.1: Descriptive statistics of control variables

	TOTAL SAMPLE		RESIDENTIAL CARE		NO RESIDENTIAL CARE	
CONTROL VARIABLES (WAVE 1)	N N=595	% OF SAMPLE	N N=352	% OF RES. CARE	N N=243	% OF NO RES. CARE
Race						
White	190	32.0%	127	36.1%	63	25.9%
Black	337	56.6%	184	52.3%	153	63.0%
Other	68	11.4%	41	11.7%	27	11.1%
Female	327	55.0%	168	47.7%	159	65.4%
Age						
17	360	60.5%	215	61.1%	145	59.7%
18	235	39.5%	137	38.9%	98	40.3%
State						
Illinois	375	63.0%	221	62.8%	154	63.4%
Iowa	53	8.9%	41	11.6%	12	4.9%
Wisconsin	167	28.1%	90	25.6%	77	31.7%

cont.

	TOTAL SAMPLE		RESIDENTIAL CARE		NO RESIDENTIAL CARE	
CONTROL VARIABLES (WAVE 1)	N N=595	% OF SAMPLE	N N=352	% OF RES. CARE	N N=243	% OF NO RES. CARE
Ever spent one night incarcerated†	193	32.4%	160	45.5%	33	13.6%
WRAT reading ability score						
<6th grade	209	35.1%	125	35.5%	84	34.6%
6th–8th grade	148	24.9%	95	27.0%	53	21.8%
High school	142	23.9%	83	23.6%	59	24.3%
Above high school	96	16.1%	49	13.9%	47	19.3%
Ever repeat a grade	223	37.5%	138	39.2%	85	35.0%
Ever placed in special education	291	48.9%	208	59.1%	83	34.2%
Had a child†	89	15.1%	46	13.1%	43	17.8%
Ever had a job	488	82.0%	289	82.1%	199	81.9%
Perceived health rating						
Poor or fair	82	13.8%	49	13.9%	33	13.6%
Good, versus good, or excellent	513	86.2%	303	86.1%	210	86.4%
Internalizing (depression and/or PTSD)†	130	23.5%	84	25.9%	46	20.1%
Substance and/or alcohol problems†	113	21.0%	89	28.3%	24	10.8%
Ever neglected†	350	61.8%	210	63.1%	140	60.1%
Ever abused†	200	35.9%	135	41.2%	65	28.4%
Ever raped or sexually molested†	182	30.7%	118	33.7%	64	26.4%
	RANGE	MEAN	S.D.	MEAN	S.D.	MEAN	S.D.
Number of placements†	1–25	5.68	5.33	7.53	5.81	2.99	2.91
Number of runaways	0–21	2.79	5.68	4.28	6.82	.62	1.95
Total number of delinquency behaviors†	0–43	7.63	6.63	9.13	7.06	5.47	5.23
Receipt of ILS services	0–8	3.06	2.35	3.39	2.37	2.59	2.24
Social support average†	0–4	2.91	0.92	2.80	.97	3.06	.83

† Variables had some missing data. Percentages were calculated excluding missing cases.

Table 12.1 displays data on the control variables included in our regression models. Most of the participants were black, followed by white and other races. There were more females than males, and most respondents were 17 years old. The majority of youth lived in Illinois. On average, respondents had lived in nearly six placements while in foster care and had run away nearly three times. About one-third of respondents had ever spent one night in jail or prison by the time of the baseline interview. On a scale of engagement in delinquent behaviors that ranged from 0 to 43, the average score was 7.63. The Midwest Study included 47 questions about receipt of independent living services (e.g. SAT instruction, financial literacy, job interview preparation, daily living skills, etc.), which were converted to an eight-point scale (0=no services, 1=1–5 services, 2=6–10 services, 8=36 or more services). The average score on the eight-point scale was 3.06, or receipt of roughly 11–15 services. More than half of respondents scored below a high school reading level on the Wide Range Achievement Test (WRAT), more than one-third had ever repeated a grade, and just under half had been placed in special education.

Fifteen percent of respondents had a child at the time of the baseline interview. About four-fifths of respondents had held a job. Social support was measured with the Medical Outcomes Study (MOS) questionnaire, which consists of 19 items that measure amounts of perceived emotional/informational, affectionate, tangible, and positive social interaction support. A scale was created that ranged from 0 (no social support) to 4 (a high degree of social support), and the average score for Midwest Study participants was 2.91. The majority of adolescents reported being in good, very good, or excellent health. The World Health Organization's Composite International Diagnostic Interview (CIDI) was used to assess mental health conditions. Roughly one-quarter of respondents had a positive screen for depression and/or post-traumatic stress disorder (PTSD) and about one-fifth screened positive for alcohol or substance abuse or dependence. An "internalizing" dummy variable was created, and respondents were assigned a 1 if they scored positive on depression and/or PTSD. Similarly, a dummy variable was created for substance/alcohol problems, and respondents were assigned a 1 if they screened positive for alcohol abuse, alcohol dependence, substance abuse, and/or substance dependence. Most respondents reported ever being neglected while substantially fewer reported ever being abused or raped or sexually molested. Please refer to Courtney, Terao and Boast (2004) for more detailed information about measures taken at baseline.

Some marked baseline differences emerge between respondents who had been in residential care and respondents who had not been in residential care on a number of variables. The former group has larger proportions of individuals who were males, had been incarcerated, were ever placed in special education, had a substance and/or alcohol problem, and were ever abused. Chi-squared analyses yielded a statistically significant difference in the distribution of races between youth who had and had not resided in a group care setting.

TABLE 12.2: Descriptive statistics of outcome variables

OUTCOME VARIABLES (WAVE 5)	TOTAL SAMPLE		RESIDENTIAL CARE		NO RESIDENTIAL CARE	
	N N=595	% OF SAMPLE	N N=352	% OF RES. CARE	N N=243	% OF NO RES. CARE
Housing situation†						
Group home/jail/hospital	33	5.6%	25	7.2%	8	3.3%
Homeless/couch surfed	165	28.2%	109	31.5%	56	23.3%
Normative living situation	388	66.2%	212	61.3%	176	73.4%
Educational attainment†						
Some high school	107	18.1%	69	19.8%	38	15.7%
High school credential	248	41.9%	159	45.6%	89	36.6%
Some college	188	31.7%	99	28.3%	89	36.6%
2-year degree	26	4.4%	15	4.3%	11	4.5%
4-year degree or higher	23	3.9%	7	2.0%	16	6.6%
Disconnected from the labor force over past 12 months†‡	130	23.64%	108	31.7%	51	21.3%
Employed 10+ hours per week†‡‡	273	51.22%	142	46.7%	131	57.2%
Owns a car	288	48.3%	152	43.2%	136	56.0%
Food stamp receipt in past 12 months†	329	55.67%	196	56.2%	133	55.0%
Description of health						
Fair or poor	105	17.6%	75	21.3%	30	12.3%
Good, very good, or excellent	490	82.4%	277	78.7%	213	87.7%
Internalizing symptoms (depression and/or PTSD) †	243	41.26%	145	41.5%	98	40.8%
Substance and/or alcohol problems	216	36.3%	128	36.4%	88	36.2%

Spent a night in jail/prison since baseline	276	46.4%	189	53.7%	87	35.8%
Victimized since last interview†	84	14.97%	64	19.3%	20	8.7%
Life satisfaction†						
Very dissatisfied	37	6.23%	29	8.3%	8	3.3%
Dissatisfied	73	12.29%	48	13.7%	25	10.3%
Neither satisfied nor dissatisfied	111	18.69%	68	19.4%	43	17.7%
Satisfied	239	40.23%	124	35.3%	115	47.3%
Very satisfied	134	22.56%	82	23.3%	52	21.4%
	RANGE	**MEAN**	**S.D.**	**MEAN**	**S.D.**	**MEAN**	**S.D.**
Economic hardship†	0–9	2.03	2.28	2.13	2.34	1.88	2.18
Total social support	0–8	5.82	2.25	5.56	2.39	6.19	1.97

† Variables had some missing data. Percentages were calculated excluding missing cases.
‡ Excludes prisoners incarcerated for 12 or more months and those unable to work (e.g. disabled, in the military).
‡‡ Excludes prisoners and those unable to work (disabled and in the military).

Table 12.2 presents data on the 14 outcome variables included in our analyses. With regard to place of residence, we created two measures that can be considered deviations from normative living situations. Most respondents (66.21%) lived on their own or with a spouse, family member, foster family member, friends, or other acquaintances (referred to as "normative living situation"). In contrast, a small proportion of participants were currently living in a group home, correctional, or hospital setting (5.6%). A third residential category was created consisting of respondents who were currently experiencing or who had recently experienced housing disruption. About 28 percent of respondents were either currently homeless or had been homeless or had couch surfed at least once since the last time they were interviewed. Roughly one-fifth of respondents never completed high school (18%), two-fifths earned a high school credential (41.9%), and the remaining two-fifths completed some college or earned a postsecondary degree (40.0%). Slightly more than half of the young adults were currently employed for at least ten hours per week or more (51.2%). Almost one-quarter of respondents had not been employed at any time over the past 12 months (23.6%). Just under half of participants reported owning a car. Over half of participants indicated that they had received food stamps at some point over the past year (55.7%). A composite measure of economic hardship was created from the count of affirmative responses to nine items (e.g. not enough money to buy clothing or shoes, utilities shut off because they could not pay the bill, had to eat less because they did not have enough for food). Chronbach's alpha was 0.825, indicating that there is was good degree of internal consistency between the items. The average score of economic hardship for Midwest participants was 2.03 on a scale from 0 to 9.

Most respondents rated their health as being good, very good, or excellent (82.4%). The full CIDI instrument was not administered for all diagnoses during the wave 5 interviews. Three symptoms of major depression taken from the CIDI (dysphoria, loss of interest, suicidality) were converted into a dummy variable. Respondents were given a 1 if they endorsed one or more of the symptoms. A dichotomous measure was also created for PTSD, and respondents were marked with a 1 if they reported at least one symptom on each of the five symptom clusters for the disorder (experienced a traumatic event; felt shocked, terrified, or helpless at the time of the event; re-experienced the event; persistent avoidance; and persistent symptoms of increased arousal). The two dummy variables were then combined into an internalizing symptoms dummy variable that was used in the regression model. Respondents were given a 1 if they screened positive for PSTD and/or depression symptoms, and they were given a 0 if they screened negative on both PTSD and depression symptoms. Overall, 41.3 percent of respondents endorsed positive symptoms of depression and/or PTSD. The CIDI screen for substance and alcohol abuse and dependence were administered in full at wave 5, and 36.3 percent of respondents screened positive for abuse and/or dependence.

To measure involvement with the criminal justice system, we used data from waves 2 through 5 to determine whether respondents had spent a night in jail or prison since the baseline interview. Nearly half of the respondents indicated that they had been incarcerated at some point since they were 17 or 18 (46.4%). Approximately 15 percent of respondents stated that they had been victimized since the last time they had been interviewed (e.g. saw someone being shot or stabbed, were beaten up). During wave 5, respondents were asked about the adequacy of available social support (people to listen, people to help with favors, people to loan money, people to help meet goals). Respondents could select "no one," "too few," or "enough" for each item. The combined score of all four questions created a range of 0 to 8, with the average score being 5.82 (Chronbach's alpha=0.869). In terms of life satisfaction, most respondents were either very satisfied or satisfied (62.8%), about one-fifth were dissatisfied or very dissatisfied (18.5%), and about one-fifth were neither satisfied nor dissatisfied (18.7%).

A two-step analytic procedure was used to gauge the influence of ever residing in group care on the 14 outcome variables. First, we regressed each outcome variable onto the wave 1 residential care variable without adjusting for any of the control variables (Reduced Model in Table 12.3). In the second step, all of the wave 1 control variables were added to each of the regression models (Full Model in Table 12.3). Only the regression coefficients for wave 1 residential care status are presented here. As listed in Table 12.3, different regression models were used based on the measurement scale of each outcome variable. Ordinary Least Squares (OLS) regression was used for two continuous variables (adequacy of social support and life satisfaction). Poisson regression was used for the count variable economic hardship. Ordinal logistic regression was used for the five ordered levels of educational attainment (no high school credential, high school credential, some college, two-year degree, and four-year degree). Multinomial logistic regression was used for the outcome variable that measured respondents' wave 5 housing situation. The reference group is normative living situation, and this condition is compared with the two alternative living situations (group care/institution/incarceration and homeless/couch surfing). Logistic regression was used for the remaining nine outcome variables, which were all binary. For the Poisson, ordinal logistic, multinomial, and logistic regression models, the beta coefficients were exponentiated to yield more interpretable results (i.e. they are presented as incidence rates [Poisson], the odds ratio of moving to the next ordered level [ordinal logistic], and odds ratios [logistic and multinomial logistic]).

Some wave 1 variables (e.g. mental health, substance/alcohol use, and maltreatment) had missing data. We ran regression models with all of the control variables and then regression models in which these four variables (internalizing, substance/alcohol problems, abuse, neglect) were excluded. In all but one regression model (current employment), removing the coefficients did not significantly affect the overall fit of the model. The coefficients and significance levels reported here include the mental health, substance/alcohol use, and the maltreatment variables.

TABLE 12.3: Results from regression analyses

OUTCOME VARIABLE		TYPE OF REGRESSION MODEL	REDUCED MODEL		FULL MODEL	
			β	p-value	β	p-value
Housing situation	Residential care	Multinomial logistic	2.594	.023	1.627	.517
	Homeless		1.616	.013	1.116	.701
Educational attainment		Ordinal logistic	.6014	.002	.9723	.899
Labor force disconnection†		Logistic	1.655	.017	1.856	.039
Current employment‡		Logistic	.6557	.017	.8114	.420
Owns a vehicle		Logistic	.5979	.002	.5819	.039
Economic hardship		Poisson	.1268	.035	-.0498	.567
Receipt of food stamps		Logistic	1.050	.772	.9443	.825
General health		Logistic	.5202	.005	.6810	.288
Internalizing problems		Logistic	1.030	.863	1.278	.350
Alcohol/substance problems		Logistic	1.006	.970	.7979	.377
Ever incarcerated since 18		Logistic	2.079	<.001	.8881	.657
Recent victimization		Logistic	2.496	.001	1.694	.202
Adequacy of social support		OLS	-.6317	.001	-.2733	.233
Life satisfaction		OLS	-.2140	.025	-.0267	.832

† Analysis excludes respondents who are currently unable to work (e.g. disability, serving in the military) and respondents who have been incarcerated for more than 12 months.
‡ Analysis excludes respondents who are currently unable to work (e.g. disability, serving in the military) and respondents who are currently incarcerated.

In the reduced model that did not include control variables, we see that youth who had been in group care by their baseline interview of the Midwest Study fared worse on nearly all of the 14 outcomes that were measured in their mid-20s, though no group differences were found between youth who had been in residential care and never been in residential care in the areas of receipt of food stamps, internalizing mental health problems, and substance and alcohol use problems.

As displayed in the Table 12.3 under the Full Model, most of the significant group differences in outcomes disappear once the control variables are added to the model. After controlling for the covariates, youth who lived in residential care are significantly more likely to have been disconnected from the labor force over the past 12 months and are less likely to own a vehicle than youth who had not been in residential care.

Limitations

While the Midwest Study covers a wide range of functional domains that are relevant to assessing the relationship between residential care placement and later adult outcomes, interpretation of the study findings should include the usual caution regarding the consequences of omitted variables. In addition, while the temporal ordering of residential care placement and later outcomes is clear, that is not the case for the relationship between residential care and all of the control variables. In other words, it is possible that the functioning of youth at baseline was to some extent a result of their prior experiences in group care.

Conclusion

Comparisons of young people who had ever resided in residential care with individuals who have not indicate that these two groups differed in important ways at the time of the first interview wave. The residential care group was disproportionately comprised of white adolescents and males, and these individuals were more likely to have spent a night in jail or prison, to have been placed in special education, and to have problems with substances or alcohol. When looking at their prior experiences, these youth reported higher instances of physical abuse and being sexually violated. On average, they had been placed in over seven different placements and had run away over four times while in foster care. It is little surprise that results from the simple regression models predicted that youth who resided in residential care settings fared significantly worse on measures of housing stability, educational attainment, employment, economic hardship, health, involvement with the law, victimization, social support, and life satisfaction. However, once a wide array of personal and situational characteristics was accounted for, the independent effect of residential care disappeared from all but two outcomes: the likelihood of owning a car and the likelihood of being disconnected from the labor force.

A few important implications can be drawn from the analyses above, which resonate with findings and observations made by other scholars. Youth who enter residential care are likely to be more troubled and have more problematic histories and experiences than youth placed in other out-of-home settings. The drastic reduction in statistical significance that was observed in the second set of regression models once these characteristics were accounted for suggests that it is these characteristics, and not just the residential care setting per se, that contribute to the bleak outcomes observed later in life. This represents both an opportunity for and places an onus on the future of residential care. Knowing that more troubled children will enter these settings, and that their time in placement could potentially solidify or disrupt the trajectories toward unfavorable outcomes, more intentional and data-driven approaches to residential care are called for.

Although the breadth of domains covered in the Midwest Study precluded the collection of more specific information on group care placements (e.g. exact age of admission, duration of stays, characteristics of the facilities, etc.), the youth participating in the study likely encountered some of the primary types of placements that fall under the umbrella of residential care. For some higher functioning youth, placement in a residential setting may have been a temporary arrangement utilized until a more appropriate and long lasting placement became available. For others, placements were likely shelters for periods of homelessness, juvenile justice placements meant to target delinquency, treatment programs that addressed mental health or substance use problems, or congregate care facilities used as a last resort after several other failed placements. Future directions for residential care in the US will likely be a combination of identifying and refining existent models that are promising to be effective and developing new models that may defy strict boundaries between congregate and community-based approaches.

Relationship between Adult Outcomes of Young People Making the Transition to Adulthood from Out-of-Home Care and Prior Residential Care

NATHANAEL J. OKPYCH AND MARK E. COURTNEY

Okpych and Courtney make two important contributions to our understanding of therapeutic residential care (TRC) viewed from a US perspective. First, in a carefully written introductory section, they delineate both the historical shifts that have taken place within the residential sector and underscore how preserving a family caretaking environment versus placing children in a congregate care setting is a tension that has run through the evolution of residential care in America. They identify many of the factors that continue to make residential services a contested arena and highlight both the varied range of programs and services that fall under the umbrella of residential care and the variability of individual programs within any specific type of residential service. They point out the general trajectory of decreasing lengths of stay and smaller sized living units, as well as the multiple challenges that youth entering residential services typically present. Like other contributors to this volume, they identify the dearth of effectiveness research and empirical studies that specify key details about program characteristics. Like others they call for more fine grained analyses and rigorous evaluation research to draw specific conclusions about the effectiveness of residential services. Finally, they identify three promising pathways for improving the knowledge base for TRC including:

1. a rigorous, critical examination of existing program models

2. a search for common elements—critical ingredients—that appear to be linked with successful outcomes

3. a closer examination of such community-centered alternatives as MST, MTFC and wraparound—their similarities, differences and potential connection to therapeutic residential care.

Their second contribution flows from a subsequent empirical analysis of Mark Courtney's widely acclaimed and ambitious study of the adult functioning of former foster youth in several Midwest states. As the authors note, this study was the largest evaluation of its kind in the US, following over 700 young people for nearly a decade who resided in three

Midwestern states. Here, Okpych and Courtney analyze the outcomes of nearly 600 youth (n=595) who resided in residential care at some point in their out-of-home experience and were included in the study sample at wave 1 and wave 5 of the overall study process. While an independent effect of residential care was identified in a first stage analysis, this effect seemed to disappear once a "wide array of personal and situational characteristics" was accounted for. Okpych and Courtney account for this thus:

> The drastic reduction in statistical significance that was observed in the second set of regression models once these characteristics were accounted for suggests that it is these characteristics, and not just the residential care setting per se, that contribute to the bleak outcomes observed later in life.

The authors go on to say that in anticipation that youth with these challenging characteristics and experiences will be presenting for therapeutic residential care, we must intensify our search for "more intentional and data-driven approaches to residential care." I heartily concur.

CHAPTER 13

Supportive Pathways for Young People Leaving Care
Lessons Learned from Four Decades of Research

Mike Stein

Introduction

For most young people today, their journey to adulthood takes place over time and includes a number of different but connected and reinforcing pathways: moving into accommodation of their choice; entering further or higher education, or training; finding satisfying employment; achieving good health and a positive sense of well-being; and, for some young people, becoming a parent. It is usually a time of expectation and excitement as well as apprehension and uncertainty.

As a group, young people leaving care may face more difficulties than other young people on these pathways to adulthood. Their journey may be shorter, more severe and often more hazardous than for those young people leaving their family home, and they may have been burdened by earlier negative experiences of poor parenting, including maltreatment, and social disadvantage (Davies and Ward 2011). For some young people, the quality of care they have experienced may have failed to compensate them for past difficulties and they may lack the ongoing support that many young people can expect from their families (Hannon, Wood and Bazalgette 2010; Sinclair *et al.* 2007).

This chapter explores how young people may be supported on their main pathways to adulthood. It begins by discussing the foundation stones upon which effective support needs to be built whilst young people are in care. It then focuses upon young people's transitions from care, setting these in the context of normative processes and experiences. Finally, it considers their main pathways from care to adulthood: accommodation; careers, education, employment and training; and health and well-being, including the needs of specific groups of care leavers.

In reflecting on the 'lessons learned from four decades of research', the chapter will draw upon studies completed since the mid-1980s. These studies, in the main, include young people leaving care – or ageing out of care – many having lived in different placements including family foster care and children's homes, and although the evidence is not derived from young people leaving therapeutic residential care (TRC), the main messages may well have relevance for this group of young people.

Conceptually, the chapter will be informed by a resilience perspective – how the resilience of young people can be promoted through the quality of care they receive and how they can be supported on their pathways to adulthood through the services they receive. But it will also draw upon other concepts and theories, including attachment, focal theory and social transition. The empirical and theoretical work discussed in the chapter is explored more fully in Stein (2012).

The foundation stones for effective support

The critical importance of providing young people from care with stability has been a consistent finding in research studies for nearly 30 years (Biehal *et al.* 1995; Dixon and Stein 2005; Stein and Carey 1986). A correlated review of 92 international studies of children in care identifies placement stability as a key mediator for a wide range of adult outcomes including physical and mental health and employment (Jones *et al.* 2011). Young people who experience stable placements providing good-quality care are more likely to succeed on their pathways to adulthood than those who have experienced further movement and disruption during their time in care. Stability has the potential to promote resilience in two respects. First, by providing the young person with a warm and redeeming relationship with a carer – or a compensatory secure attachment, which may in itself reduce the likelihood of placement breakdown (Sinclair *et al.* 2005). Second, and not necessarily dependent on the first, stability may provide continuity of care in young people's lives – especially in respect of older entrants to care – which may give them emotional security and contribute to positive educational and career outcomes (Jackson 2002).

The provision of stable, high-quality placements may assist young people with mental health problems who are overrepresented within the care population: entering the care system later; more reported changes of placement within the past year and having lived for less time in their current placement are established risk factors (Ford *et al.* 2007; Stein and Dumaret 2011). Disrupted care experience may also contribute to a sense of connectedness and poor psychosocial outcomes (Ward 2011). Research shows that Multi-Dimensional Treatment Foster Care (MTFC) can reduce the behaviour problems of those young people with the most serious anti-social behaviour (Biehal *et al.* 2012). There is evidence from Germany of the positive contribution made by a socio-pedagogical approach within residential care, although a pilot study in England comparing behavioural, emotional and educational outcomes in homes that used social pedagogues and ordinary children's homes showed little difference. Both good-quality care and poor practices were found in both pilot and comparative homes (Berridge *et al.* 2011; Kongeter, Schroer and Zeller 2008; Petrie *et al.* 2006).

Helping young people develop a positive sense of identity, including their self-knowledge, their self-esteem and self-efficacy, may also promote their resilience (Stein 2012). This will be furthered first, by the quality of care and attachments experienced by young people – a significant resilience-promoting factor discussed above; second, by their knowledge and understanding of their background and personal history; third, by their experience of how other people perceive and respond to them; and finally, how they see themselves and the opportunities they have to influence and shape their own biography (Biehal *et al.* 1995; Stein 2011).

Research evidence dating back to the 1980s has shown that many children and young people who are in care have lower levels of educational achievement than children in the general population (Jackson 1987). They are also more likely to have a statement of special educational needs, be excluded from or miss school, and be far less likely to go on to higher education – as discussed below (SEU 2003). Poor school performance has been identified as the major risk factor of future psychosocial problems and thus a barrier to resilience (Berlin, Vinnerljung and Hjern 2011; Rutter 1999; Rutter, Giller and Hagell 1998). The reasons for underachievement are multifaceted and include social disadvantage, maltreatment and poor birth parenting, often contributing to social, emotional and behavioural problems, as well as the failure of care and education to compensate young people (Berridge *et al.* 2008; Jackson *et al.* 2011). 'Lessons learned' and initiatives to address the latter include: reducing placement movement; improving school attendance; providing additional help with education, both at school and from care; increasing the awareness and monitoring of the educational needs of children in care; and responding to young people's emotional and mental health needs (Brodie and Morris 2011).

School or being in care itself may also provide turning points for young people. They may open the door for participation in a range of leisure or extra curricula activities that may lead to new friends and opportunities, including the learning of competencies and the development of emotional maturity – and thus promote their resilience (Gilligan 2009; Rutter *et al.* 1998). Indeed, resilient young people had often been able to turn their negative experiences into opportunities, with the help of others. Recent developments include young people from care acting as peer mentors to young people in and leaving care and participating as peer researchers (Clayden and Stein, 2005; Munro *et al.* 2012; Stein and Verweijen-Slamnescu 2012).

Preparation for leaving care may also provide young people with opportunities for planning, problem solving and the learning of new competencies – all resilience-promoting factors. This may include the development of: self-care skills – personal hygiene, diet and health, including sexual health; practical skills – budgeting, shopping, cooking and cleaning; and inter-personal skills – managing a range of formal and informal relationships. Evaluations of good practice over several decades highlight the importance of: a holistic approach, attaching equal importance to practical, emotional and interpersonal skills; assessment; involving young people fully; providing opportunities for risk taking; the gradual learning of skills; continuity of carers; and carers being trained to assist young people (Biehal *et al.* 1995; Dixon and Stein 2005; Morgan and Lindsay 2012; Stein and Carey 1986).

Young people's transitions from care

Research evidence dating back to the 1980s shows that many young people are expected to undertake their journey to adulthood far younger and in far less time than their peers: leaving foster care or their children's home and setting up a new home, often in a different area, and, for some young people, starting a family as well; leaving school and finding their way into further education, training or employment, or coping with unemployment (Biehal *et al.* 1995; Dixon and Stein 2005; Stein and Carey 1986). In short, their journey to adulthood is both accelerated and compressed. Also, for many of these young people, leaving care is often a final event – there is no option to return in times of difficulty.

The empirical testing of 'focal model of adolescence' shows that having the opportunity to deal with interpersonal issues, spread over time, is how most young people cope successfully with the challenges of transition to adulthood (Coleman and Hendry 1999). Conversely, those young people who have to face a number of interpersonal issues at the same time are likely to experience significant problems of adjustment. Research on transitions from care, drawing on an anthropological perspective, complements focal theory and the arguments for giving young people from care normative experiences (Hart 1984).

The process of social transition has traditionally included three distinct but related stages: leaving or disengagement; transition itself; and integration into a new or different social state. In post- or late-modern societies, providing more opportunities but also more risks, this process has become more extended and less structured for most young people, although the psychological 'activities' associated with the three stages still remain (Giddens 1991). However, as detailed above, for many young people leaving care there is the expectation of instant adulthood. They often miss out on the critical preparation stage, transition itself, that gives young people an opportunity to 'space out' and provides a time for freedom, exploration, reflection, risk taking and identity search.

For a majority of young people today this is gained through the experience of further education (post-16) and, especially, higher education (post-18) but as discussed below, many care leavers, as a consequence of their pre-care and care experiences, are unable to take advantage of these educational opportunities. Also, in the context of extended transitions, the family plays an increasing role in providing financial, practical and emotional support but for many care leavers their family relationships at this important time may be missing or problematic rather than supportive (Biehal and Wade 1996; Sinclair *et al.* 2005). In this context, the support provided by leaving care services and informal social networks is very important to young people.

The main 'lessons learned' from these different perspectives on transition are: first, services should be organised to reflect the nature and timing of young people's transitions from care, more akin to normative transitions; this should include opportunities for young people to remain in placements where they are settled. Second, the organisation and culture of services and placements should recognise the need young people have for psychological space, in order to cope with changes over time; this should include recognition of the different stages of transitions, especially the significance of the middle stage – transition itself.

Supportive pathways to adulthood

As suggested at the beginning of this chapter, young people's main pathways to adulthood are often connected and reinforcing: for example, it is very difficult for young people to cope with their studies or settle into a new job if they are living in poor housing or are having difficulties in finding somewhere to live, and these circumstances will affect how they feel about themselves. As detailed above, most families support young people on their pathways to adulthood but such support may not be available for young people from care.

In this context, in the UK, specialist leaving care schemes have developed from the mid-1980s onwards to respond to the core needs of care leavers for assistance with accommodation, finance, education and careers, personal support networks and health and well-being (Stein 2012). In England, for example, young people can be supported up to 25 years of age by a personal adviser who is responsible for carrying out a needs assessment and a pathway plan (Stein 2012). An important part of the work of specialist teams is the development of formal interagency links, to ensure an integrated approach to assisting young people with a range of different needs. Their work may also include the development of support by former carers, as well as positive informal family and friendship support networks (Stein 2012). The specific support issues arising from young people's pathways are explored below.

Accommodation pathway

Research studies that include the views of young people about being in 'settled, safe accommodation' suggests that it can be viewed as part of a process involving a number of different stages: first, having a choice of when to leave care placements – not just being expected to leave at 16, 17 or 18 years of age; second, as discussed above, being well prepared in practical, self-care and emotional and interpersonal skills and feeling ready to move on; and third, having a good choice of accommodation matched to their assessed needs and taking into account any additional needs they may have (Stein and Morris 2010).

Research based on the views of young people suggests they benefit from: being in a safe neighbourhood in accommodation in good physical condition and close to amenities, including shops, educational and leisure facilities; being well supported – by leaving care workers, by mentors and by building on positive social networks, including support by family and friend; and being in education, employment or training, having an income or receiving adequate financial assistance (Stein and Morris 2010).

Young people who remain in foster care by 'staying put' until they are prepared and ready to leave (up to the age of 21) can be assisted to make a better transition to adulthood than those who leave care early

(Courtney, Lee and Perez 2011; Munro *et al.* 2012). Young people may also be assisted by supported lodging schemes. These may include extended placements (e.g. by a seamless transfer from foster placements) and both short- and longer-term options for young people. However, research shows that 'staying put' options are less likely to be available to young people with more complex needs and those young who are unemployed (Munro *et al.* 2012).

There is evidence that both foster and residential carers do often provide ongoing support to young people who have left their care, although this often receives little formal recognition in terms of pathway planning (Sinclair *et al.* 2005; Wade 2008). There is very little UK research on young people leaving care either by moving into, or moving on from, kinship (family and friends) care. However, the limited evidence does suggest that it is seen very positive by young people. Its potential should, therefore, be further explored (Broad, Hayes and Rushforth 2001).

Positive birth family relationships often provide young people with both practical and emotional support, but negative family relationships can be very damaging for young people (Dixon and Stein 2005; Simon 2008; Sinclair *et al.* 2005). Young people also identify a wide range of family members beyond their birth families who they see as their 'closest family' and who could also be seen as a potential source of support, including aunties, uncles and grandparents (Wade 2008). But again, there is little evidence of their involvement in the pathway planning process. There is evidence that good-quality assessments and using family group conferences as part of pathway planning is the key to identifying supportive family and social networks (Marsh and Peel 1999).

Research shows that care leavers are overrepresented among young homeless people – about one-third of care leavers move in and out of homelessness over a two-year period (Dixon and Stein 2005; Wade and Dixon 2006). The provision of more emergency accommodation (e.g. short-term lodgings, supported care placements) and better planning may prevent this happening. However, a smaller group of young people are vulnerable to more entrenched housing problems. This includes young people who leave care very early (at just 16 or 17), those who move frequently for negative reasons (breakdown of relationships), those who have mental health problems and social, emotional and behavioural difficulties, and those who leave secure accommodation (Stein and Morris 2010).

Leaving care services are effective in assisting most young people in accessing housing and in providing ongoing support, although research shows variations between local authorities in the provision of 'suitable accommodation' (Stein and Morris 2010). The main implication arising from research studies are a need for early identification and prevention of problems and agreed multiagency interventions, including joint working between leaving care services, housing providers and adult services. Where problems persist during and after care, the evidence shows that there is a shortage of more specialist accommodation for young people with higher support needs (Stein and Morris 2010).

Careers pathway

As discussed above, research dating back four decades shows that many young people from care do poorly at school in comparison to their peers (Jackson 1987). Making progress and achieving success at school lays the foundations for post-16 further and higher education, training and finding satisfying employment. European research has identified the main facilitating factors and obstacles to improving post-16 educational outcomes as identified in Table 13.1 (Jackson *et al.* 2011).

Research has also identified what can contribute to good employment outcomes: building on educational success; encouragement by carers; stability; fewer moves after leaving care; being settled in accommodation and targeted career support (Bilson, Price and Stanley. 2011; Wade and Dixon 2006). In England, in response to the high rates of unemployment of young people from care – care leavers are about three times more likely not to be engaged in education, training or employment than their peers – the Government has funded the National Care Advisory Service (NCAS) to run the From Care2Work Project. This programme began in 2009 with the aims of improving the employment opportunities for care leavers, raising their aspirations and closing the gap between young people leaving care and their peers in the general population. Through working in partnership with local authorities and national and local employers, it is succeeding in increasing employment opportunities (NCAS 2011).

TABLE 13.1: Managers' view on facilitating factor and obstacles for young people from care continuing in post-compulsory education in England

FACILITATORS	OBSTACLES
Placement stability	Multiple placements
Early support for catch-up learning	Disrupted schooling and failure to compensate for gaps
Action-orientated Personal Education Plans (PEPs)	Problems in birth families
Priority given to education by social workers and carers	No emphasis on education or interest in school experience
Personal motivation and persistence	Low self-esteem and lack of aspiration
Individual tutoring to compensate for gaps in schooling	Lack of basic skills especially literacy
Support from family, carers and professionals	Poor conditions for study
Financial resources and practical help	Leaving care/independent living
Sympathetic schools	No understanding of care problems
Positive community and cultural influences	Knowing no-one with Higher Education experience
Clear protocols agreed with colleges and HEIs	Lack of information and guidance
Staying in placement after 18	Rejection by foster carers, having no one who cares
Leaving care team promotes education over employment and includes an education specialist	Anxiety about lack of money – few part-time jobs

Source: *Jackson et al. (2011, pp.28–39)*

Health and well-being pathway

As discussed above, the foundations of good mental health and well-being should be built when young people come into care. However, there is evidence that for many young people, coping with the demands of transition itself – settling in new accommodation, often in a strange area, moving on to college or beginning a new career, often at a very young age – can combine with earlier pre-care and in-care difficulties or new challenges during transition that affects young people's overall health and well-being (Dixon 2008).

The psychological demands of accelerated and compressed transitions, including the demands of living independently, may increase young people's mental health problems (Dixon 2008; Ford *et al.* 2007). Young people may be assisted by: more gradual transitions from care, ongoing support into adulthood by leaving care services; and maintaining positive family and kinship networks. Some young people may require specialist mental health services. There is also evidence that specific groups of care leavers may benefit from additional support services to promote their resilience on their pathways to adulthood.

In the UK, there has been very little research into the experiences of young disabled people leaving care, even though they are overrepresented in the care system (Baker 2007, 2011). The limited evidence shows poor planning, coordination and consultation and that their transition from care may be very abrupt or delayed by restricted housing and employment options (Harris, Rabiee and Priestley 2002; Priestley, Rabiee and Harris 2003). Many disabled young people would benefit from additional support and those with complex needs will require the early involvement of adult services and a coordinated multiagency response (Baker 2011; Sloper *et al.* 2011).

There is evidence of high rates of teenage parenthood among young people from care associated with negative birth family experiences and poor-quality care (Barn and Mantovani 2007; Dixon *et al.* 2006). Research has shown the importance of stability and continuity of care and young parents receiving both practical and personal support – for example, mutual support groups, mentoring and advocacy schemes by mothers who were formerly in care (Mendes 2009).

Young people from black and minority ethnic groups, including those of mixed heritage, face many similar challenges to other young people on their pathways to adulthood, although research suggests it is important to recognise differences between ethnic groups (Dixon *et al.* 2006). Additional needs include recognition of and policy and practice responses to: identity issues, especially for young people of mixed heritage; the impact of racism; building on positive family and community links; and having an ethnically diverse workforce (Barn, Andrew and Mantovani 2005; Biehal *et al.* 1995; Dixon *et al.* 2006).

One indication of the global context of pathways to adulthood is work with unaccompanied asylum-seeking children. Research shows that this often means working with uncertainty while their asylum claim is being processed – personal advisers have to identify and respond to the needs of young people making the transition from care to adulthood, having both a 'leaving care' and an 'immigration' status (Wade 2011).

The former will involve the personal adviser in needs assessment and pathway planning, taking into account the background of each young person and any specialist needs arising from their circumstances. The latter will involve supporting young people during their asylum claim and its resolution (Wade 2011).

There has been very little research on the support needs of lesbian, gay, bisexual and transgendered young people leaving care in Europe. Drawing on research from the United States, Smith highlights the neglect of this group of young people and suggests this group of care leavers will be assisted by more recognition of their needs within the care system, including having more staff and carers diverse in gender identity and sexual orientation, more training of the workforce, and greater recognition of their needs in assessment processes and in providing ongoing support after leaving care (B.W. Smith 2011).

Research from England shows young people living in care are overrepresented in the youth justice system. There is evidence that early entry to care and high-quality placements with good professional support, including education and health, can minimise the risk of offending behaviour (Schofield *et al.* 2012). Care leavers in the youth justice system will require a coordinated interagency response between leaving care services, youth offending teams and probation, in assisting them at arrest, on bail, on remand and on release from custody, including after they leave care (Dixon *et al.* 2006). For young people who misuse substances, it is important that there is early identification of their behaviour whilst in care and that they receive specialist help as well as support from the leaving care service and after they leave (Dixon *et al.* 2006)

Conclusions and recommendations

Reflecting upon the main 'lessons learned', from research studies carried out over four decades suggests that the foundation stones of supportive pathways to adulthood are providing young people with: stability, continuity and attachment; emotional security; a positive sense of identity; compensation for educational deficits and opportunities to maximise progress; leisure activities, new opportunities and turning points; and holistic preparation – or put simply, good-quality care.

Building on these foundations, young people should have the opportunity for more gradual transitions from care, recognising the extended and fluid stages of transition in modern societies. They should be well supported on their pathways to adulthood, beyond the time of leaving care – by leaving care services and by positive social networks – in being in safe settled accommodation of their choice, in finding fulfilment in their careers and in achieving good health and a positive sense of well-being, as well as being assisted when things don't work out.

Finally, future empirical research on leaving care should include the following:

- Evaluative and follow-up research on the effect of specific interventions using experimental designs, for example, the impact of specialised placements, such as therapeutic care settings and kinship care.

- Follow-up research on specific groups of care leavers with additional support needs, as identified above.

- Comparative research, building on the initial work carried out by members of the Transitions from Care to Adulthood International Research group (INTRAC) (Stein and Munro 2008; Stein, Ward and Courtney 2011).

COMMENTARY BY JORGE F. DEL VALLE ON:

Supportive Pathways for Young People Leaving Care: Lessons Learned from Four Decades of Research

MIKE STEIN

Mike Stein has introduced an extremely important topic, not only in residential care but also in child care. Child welfare programs were traditionally intended to protect children (minors) until they became adults (usually at 18 years) and only in the last decades has an international movement started to recognise the needs of those same young people when leaving care. The excellent research review presented in this chapter shows clearly that young people leaving care suffer a transition to adulthood that is compressed and accelerated, without time to get well equipped to face new challenges and be integrated into society.

The chapter informs the process of transition in the perspective of resilience. I agree that this should be a core concept, as children in care have to overcome a series of traumatic experiences, from family abuse or neglect to living in substitute care that often involves adaptation to strange situations, instability, changes and difficulties to enjoy proper attachments. Promoting resilience during staying in care is extremely important, particularly the level of qualification achieved. As Stein concludes, 'poor school performance has been identified as the major risk factor of future psychosocial problems and thus a barrier to resilience'.

However, the chapter is focused on a later process of leaving care and achieving social integration by means of getting a job, having a home and a good social support network. Although previous supports are important, this transition to adulthood has its own challenges and three stages can be distinguished: leaving or disengagement; transition itself; and integration into a new or different social state. These stages in post-modern societies have become more extended for youth in general but for young people leaving care there is an expectation of instant adulthood that represents a really unfair situation. As the international review edited by Stein and Munro (2008) shows, there are significant differences in the way that different countries support this process of transition from leaving care, ranging from including specific regulations for care leavers to just transferring them to social services for adults.

Finally, related to the main aim of this book, this chapter shows that there is scarce research on leaving care from TRC. In fact, young people with disabilities or mental health disorders become a particularly vulnerable group that would need special support and a more gradual transition. In these cases, the role of adult services (mental health or disabilities) is essential, as they have to continue the treatment and support of care leavers. International research shows that a vey high percentage of young people in residential care are receiving mental health services, and further research is needed to know if these supports have the required continuity when leaving care.

CHAPTER 14

Listening to Young Alumni of Care in Israel

A Brief Note from Research about Successful Transitions to Adulthood

Anat Zeira

Out-of-home care includes a variety of forms, including foster families and campus-based residential centers. Generally, residential care is considered inferior to the community-based alternatives because it suffers from an institutionalization image. Consequently, in many countries, placing children in residential facilities is less favored and family (or kinship) foster care is the preferred alternative (Courtney and Iwaniec 2009). Contrary to many Western countries, Israel has a strong tradition of placements to residential/institutional settings of two types (Benbenishty 2008; Zeira 2004, 2009). One type, supervised by the Ministry of Welfare and Social Services, is based on professional and/or court decision and is more "treatment" oriented. Of the 8000 children annually removed from home by the welfare system, about 75 percent are placed in residential settings and the rest are placed with foster families (National Council for the Child 2012). According to the intensity of care needed, children are placed in remedial, rehabilitation or post-hospitalization institutional settings (Attar-Schwartz 2008). It should be noted that most adolescents who are placed in remedial institutions usually do not suffer significant mental health and behavioral problems and typically were removed from home because of victimization to abuse and/or neglect or severe difficulties of their parents. Thus, their social and behavior functioning is not as low compared with reports on youth in residential care in other countries (Knorth *et al.* 2008b). Furthermore, in contrast to some Scandinavian countries, in which there is a large proportion of adolescents who enter care due to their antisocial behavior and conflicts with their parents (Hestbaek 2011), in Israel there are only a few hundred such adolescents annually that are placed in hostels (i.e. residential facilities) supervised by the Correction Services within the Ministry of Welfare and Social Services.

The other type of placement is voluntary and is supervised by the Ministry of Education. Educational residential settings, also known as youth villages (Grupper 2013; Rapoport *et al.* 1980), host about 17,000 children annually (National Council for the Child 2012). Educating children in youth villages was one of the ideals of the Zionism of the Jewish settlement movement before and shortly after the establishment of the state of Israel in 1948 (Kashti 1986). Since then, the youth villages have undergone many changes, reflecting developments in Israeli society (Mash 2001). Most children enter these settings in 7th grade and stay until graduating at 12th grade. Some are given the opportunity to stay in the residential facility one or even two years longer in order to finish their schooling. Placement to this system is voluntary and is often seen as an effective and non-stigmatizing response to the unmet educational and personal needs of many children and adolescents from the social and geographical periphery of Israel (Kashti, Shlasky, and Arieli 2000). New immigrants, especially from Ethiopia, are often referred to these youth villages, and there are educational programs specifically designed to address their needs.

Over the years, the residential educational system has had an overall positive impact on the life of its alumni (Golan-Cook and Sabag 1992; Grupper 2013; Rapoport *et al.* 1980). Recently, Zeira (2009) reported outcomes of about 500 young people interviewed three to five years after completing their stay in youth villages. Overall most of these young adults showed relatively positive outcomes compared with alumni of remedial out-of-home placements both in Israel and elsewhere (Stein and Munro 2008). However, another study that examined one cohort of Israeli young people showed that the alumni of youth villages have poorer educational outcomes compared with their peers in the general population, with significant differences between young people from different cultural groups (Zeira *et al.*, in press).

Transition to adulthood

Young adults in today's industrialized countries take more time to explore and consider their future. Critical decisions about life are taken in their late 20s, in contrast to the much earlier age a few decades ago (Arnett 2000).

Instead of committing themselves to a steady job, many young people are now engaged in higher education, tend to live longer with their parents and marry much later. This period is characterized by a quest for autonomy and an exploration of identity, and is considered a new important life stage for young people (Gaudet 2007). During this developmental phase, many rely on their birth families for emotional and financial support. In contrast, youth who were placed out of home lack such support in many cases and are required to make the transition to adulthood on their own (Arnett 2007; Stein and Munro 2008).

The transition to adulthood of young people in Israel differs somewhat from their peers in other Western countries. First, their life course includes the unique social responsibility of a compulsory military service at the age of 18 (three years for men and two for women).[1] This service is considered a measure of normative functioning and successful military service opens the door to many opportunities later in life (Flum 1995). Positioned at a critical developmental stage of emerging adulthood, serving in the military also allows young people to gradually become responsible adults (Seginer 1988). Serving in the military grants young people a lot of responsibility and independence, but at the same time it is an organized system with a firm schedule and very little freedom. Paradoxically, military service delays the separation from parents (Mayseless 2004). This is due to the fact that in Israel almost all recruits continue to live with their parents and return home on leave from their military duties (some soldiers return home every day, but most have leave every two or three weeks). Therefore, contrary to adolescents in most Western countries, young Israelis have an additional transition point. The first transition is from high school to the military service and the second is from the military to being civilians again. It is only after the military service that most young Israelis make critical life decisions such as entering the job market or the higher education system and moving out of their parents' home.

For care leavers, military service is both more challenging and more potentially helpful compared with other young people. On the one hand, it is more difficult for them to adjust to the military demands without ongoing familial support. On the other hand, a meaningful military service could compensate for possible social exclusion due to their placement and provide an opportunity for a positive "turning point" that will help them enter civic life less disadvantaged.

---

1   Due to certain health conditions or for religious reasons (mostly for women) young people may substitute the military duty for National Service in one of a wide variety of social organizations.

In the Israeli context, the life trajectories and the interactions with social services are much more varied and less constrained compared with other countries with more formal policies and legislation for care leavers. Therefore, out-of-home placement in Israel has some unique characteristics that offer a different perspective on the transition to adulthood and to independent living of care leavers.

Outcomes of care leavers

Adolescents who "age out" of the care system make an accelerated transition from a protected and supportive environment to independent living (Cashmore and Paxman 2006; Keller, Cusick, and Courtney 2007). Many of them must face this complex life task alone because they lack emotional and financial support from parents (Cashmore and Paxman 1996; Wade 2008). Research on the immediate-, intermediate- and long-term outcomes for care leavers consistently portrays a gloomy picture of their situation (Biehal *et al.* 1994; Cook 1994; Courtney and Dworsky 2006; Festinger 1983). For example, they have low educational achievements (Casas *et al.* 2010), are prone to becoming homeless (Biehal and Wade 1996; Fowler, Toro and Miles 2009; Pecora *et al*, 2003; Reilly 2003), become unemployed (Cashmore and Paxman 2007; Daining and DePanfilis 2007), show antisocial behaviors (Reilly 2003; Vaughn, Shook and McMillen 2008; White *et al.* 2007) and experience financial difficulties (Barth 1990; Buehler *et al.* 2000; Pecora *et al.* 2006a, 2006b). These findings emphasize the importance of improving understanding of their life course trajectories in order to inform practice and policy.

Transition from care: the experience of young Israeli care leavers

The remainder of this chapter will illustrate the transition process of care leavers in Israel by bringing the voices of young Israelis, who spent time in different types of residential care facilities. Descriptions were obtained from the qualitative segment of a larger study on needs and outcomes of a sample of vulnerable young people in Israel (Zeira, Benbenishty and Refaeli 2012). The study used semi-structured interviews with 20 young adults (aged 19–25), of which ten spent their adolescence in residential care (coercive and voluntary removal). Interviews were conducted by an experienced social worker, following the informed consent of participants who received a $40 gift certificate at the end of the interview. Eleven of the participants were Israeli born, and all but two were single. One was married and another was a single-parent mother. Most of them completed the military (or national) service, and many were still living with their biological families at the time of the interview.

The stories of three young adults were selected to represent different types of background (i.e. gender, cultural origin), residential facility (i.e. welfare and educational settings), and overall transition experience. First, the stories of Anna, Tamara and David,[2] are presented to show the different paths of transition. Second, the lessons from these trajectories are illustrated.

The stories

Anna (#1)

As a young child, Anna immigrated to Israel from Russia. She was placed in a welfare residential facility when she was six years old. She did not complete high school and is now working as a sales person in a shop. She hopes to go to college sometime in the future. This is her story:

> I did not want to go to the residential facility at such an early age. Because I never met my father, I used to stick to my mother. For example, when she was going to the bathroom, I would ask her to open the door. I had to see her all the time. I was literally glued to her. Not leaving her for a minute. I had a fear of abandonment and suddenly she sends me to the residential facility, where I could see her only once a month. I remember that day—wondering if she loves me or not. I used to beat other kids at school so they would send me home.
>
> At the age of 15 I had a crisis. I left the residential facility and went back home. There lived also my grandmother, who didn't like me. My mother did not agree to put her in a nursing home. My grandmother, every time I wanted to be at home, every time she would say I should not stay there. I had to be on the streets. When I was 16 I was madly in love with somebody, and I took the blame for a crime he committed. Eventually I ended up in correction facilities—hostels—under house arrest from the age of 16.5 to 19. It sucked. I moved from one hostel to another. I got fed up and I finally realized that I need to go back home. And the situation at home is not that good. I have a complicated family. When I was 19 I could finally return home.
>
> I was exempted from military service because of my stay at the hostels and my criminal background. Still, I wanted to help my country

---

2   All names were altered to preserve anonymity of participants.

so I decided to volunteer for National Service. I currently do my service at a youth center in the morning and I work for my living in the afternoon. It is very difficult. I am now 21 years old and will soon finish my National Service.

Tamara (#5)

Tamara immigrated to Israel with her parents from Ethiopia. She went to a youth village (an educational residential facility) from age 16 to age 19, where she acquired a full matriculation diploma.[3] She completed National Service and will soon start post-secondary professional studies to become an accountant. This is her story:

> The youth village took care of everything, food, school, we just had to come in to learn and take advantage of all the possibilities they gave us, use all the things they have invested in us. At the youth village I had a lot of fun, a good team, I wanted to go to school, no one forced me, I went to learn. All in all it was good, the best. They took care of everything. We only had to make a wish and we had it all—tutoring, anything we wanted, just to give us the best conditions to learn.
>
> When I finished high school at the youth village, all of us, we had to take care of ourselves, feed ourselves, and be responsible for ourselves. It's not easy to go without "a back" (support) and to do everything yourself. To "think big" without any support.
>
> Transition out of the youth village was not easy. It's two different worlds, one day it is your home and suddenly you go out into the world. Not all the people out there are what you're used to, not all of them are nice people. In the National Service, right after high school, you can still have a listening ear. But after that, all the support is gone. I didn't have anyone to turn to.
>
> Then I had to work to support myself. I have not left the youth village exactly at 18. I graduated at the age of 19. I did National Service for one year and then I went to visit my family in Ethiopia for almost two months. After that—work. I work in stores. It is not easy to get a job, a normal job, work that is not physical. I did the "psychometric"[4] and continued with the work and now, God willing, I will start college. I tried to enter a university, but could not. I feel that everything is on my shoulders.

---

3   The national standardized tests that are required for application to higher education and also to many jobs.

4   A minimum score on the national psychometric test is needed to enter universities and other higher education institutes in Israel.

David (#15)

David came to Israel with Na'ale.[5] He came alone when he was 15 years old and was placed in a youth village. After completing high school he served in the military for three years and immediately thereafter he started to study economics and business administration in a college. This is his story:

> At the beginning it was a little hard, a little shock, unknown language. Then slowly it got better. You come to Israel you are alone, you are independent and then you need to share a room with three other people that have the same problems. That's how we became friends. Most interesting is that five years after graduation, I am still in contact with the same friends that are the closest to me. Even in the army and till now that I am in college they are my best friends.
>
> At 18 I joined the army straight from school. The biggest problem for me was where to stay during the vacations. I considered all options, and was lucky to get a room[6] at the youth village. It's not that easy to get. In the army, at first I wanted to be a combat soldier, but maybe because I was a little younger, I decided it was not for me to be a fighter. I wanted an easier way. Eventually I joined another unit. The service moved pretty fast. I was a problematic soldier. I got "sick days" so that I can work as a waiter.
>
> Financially it wasn't bad. Because I am a lone soldier, the army sponsored two air tickets to visit to my family in Russia. There were people with more problems than I had and they received nothing. I had less problems but I knew how to get my rights. I spoke with the welfare officer and my commanders and I knew how to convince them. All I got was thanks to me. Everyone sees their parents every two weeks and I only once a year. I knew my rights and how to claim them.
>
> The army was a good experience for me, but the service was not so easy. I do not like being told what to do. I joined pretty much as a newcomer—only three years in the country, I was the only Russian in my unit. In the youth village where I studied all the students were Russian. But all in all I managed and because during this period I continued to live in the youth village, friends came to visit on weekends and it was fine.
>
> After I finished the army I decided to continue straight with higher education. I need to finish this year all. I'm now happy at school, but let's

5   The Na'ale (which in Hebrew stands for "youth immigrate before parents") program encourages disadvantaged Jewish youth around the world to come to Israel without their parents, to complete high school (www.naale.org.il/en/the-program).

6   Some youth villages provide post-care dormitories for their alumni.

see what happens when I get my degree. See what new problems I will have: Where to work? How to earn money? It's not easy, but I think I'll manage.

What do these stories tell us about transition from residential care?

The stories of Anna, Tamara and David present three different paths from residential care to independent living. They came into the residential care system from different backgrounds and for different reasons. The story of Anna illustrates two turning points in her transition process—the first when she was 19 years old and the second at 21. After spending time in residential care of the welfare system (from 6–16 in a welfare setting and from 16.5–19 in correction services hostels) she struggled to move out. She was able to use her strengths to build herself and perhaps open a new path for her future, once she completes the National Service. Anna concludes her story:

> This is a strange age period; I had conflicts, especially about what I want to do with my life. Because of the things I did before and I paid a heavy price, it was hard to get out. I learned a lot about life, about myself, and that people are not what you think they are. One learns a lot about life. This time is what shapes it.

The stories of Tamara and David highlight the benefits of the youth village as a vehicle for acquiring secondary education and emphasize the challenges experienced thereafter. Tamara is slowly struggling to achieve her goals:

> I had to work to support myself and somehow to bring myself into the "system," to do something, to move on, to have something in my hands— something professional. High school is not enough to reach anything.

David moves on along a direct path from youth village to the army and then straight to post-secondary education. In a way Tamara and David represent patterns that are typical for their group of cultural origin. In Israel immigrants from the former Soviet Union are characterized with higher motivation for education and with an ability to effectively utilize their social rights (Rapoport and Lomsky-Feder 2002). At the same time, immigrants from Ethiopia are less educated and have more difficulties to exhaust their benefits (Ringel, Ronell and Getahune 2005).

The three stories do not pretend to represent alumni of residential care in Israel. Rather, using the young people's language they portray some of the issues associated with the debate over relevance of residential care as a useful alternative for children who, for a variety of circumstances, cannot grow up with their biological families.

First, compared with "coercive removal" youth with voluntary removal report that they could better benefit from the opportunities offered by the residential services. Here, we need to keep in mind that coercive removal usually involves other issues (e.g. victimization to maltreatment or behavioral problems) that have an effect on outcomes in early adulthood. Second, participants indicate that the mandatory military (or national) service was a turning point in their life. For example, Anna describes the service as a period that allows a change in her life:

> The service taught me lots of things about myself. It changed me as a person. It strengthened me, made me change myself. The very fact that people trust you—it never happened before. Even my mother believes everything I say—it's nice that people believe in you, and then you believe in yourself. You prove you can do things. I changed only because I wanted to change, my personal choice. National Service came from a place of a change in "who I am." This is why I chose to do National Service, because I know that in the military and in the National Service you are changing.

Tamara enjoyed helping other people:

> I did my National Service at a hospital, where I was a translator for people from the Ethiopian the community—I helped the elderly, people with disabilities, anyone who needed help. It was very satisfying. I did it for one year. It was a very good year. I met nice people and I felt I am doing something significant. If I had to choose again, I would certainly do it.

David, however, completed the military service knowing that it is part of the route every Israeli young person must walk through. He gave up on doing something challenging and meaningful and "used" the service to support his survival journey as a lone immigrant. Still he indicates that "it was a good experience..."

The general positive effect that military service has on the transition to adulthood of young Israelis (Mayseless 2004) offers care leavers a "second chance" to integrate into the community. It provides an opportunity to build new social networks that are free from the stigma of care and sometimes a remedy for earlier distress.

Summary

Residential care in Israel is divided between two systems: the welfare (coercive) system that is responsible for children that most typically need to be removed because of maltreatment; and the educational system that hosts children from disadvantaged families who voluntarily send their children to youth villages. As mentioned earlier, sending children to residential facilities in Israel is deeply rooted in its history and culture, hence less stigmatized (Dolev, Ben-Rabi and Zemach-Marom 2009). Consequently, residential care is provided to a broader range of children compared with other countries. Moreover, research show that children in residential care have a relatively stable placement (Dinisman and Zeira 2011) and that their quality of life is significantly better than that of a comparison group of children who remained at home (Davidson-Arad 2005). The voices of the young people provide support to the important role of residential group care—whether coercive or voluntary—for children and adolescents whose biological families cannot support them.

Future empirical research

The findings reported in this chapter suggest some directions for future empirical studies. First, it seems that group residential care serves a broad range of children and adolescents—not only those with severe behavioral problems, but also adolescents who cannot get sufficient support from their birth parents. Consequently, more studies are needed to investigate the short- and long-term outcomes of this group. Second, the reported study was based on qualitative interviews with a small number of young people alumni of care. Meticulous sampling from this population is a major challenge faced by most studies on care leavers. This is because, once they have left the care system, some of these young people are very hard to track. Moreover, even when contact information is available, it's very difficult to engage them in the interview. Future studies—whether qualitative or quantitative—should aim at rigorous sampling procedures in order to have a better representation of alumni of the different types of residential care facilities. Lastly, the different types of residential care described in this chapter offer very different interventions. While strong emphasis is given to completing secondary education while in care, it is imperative to further investigate the long-term educational outcomes of the alumni. Such findings are necessary in order to improve the interventions while in care for a better future.

Listening to Young Alumni of Care in Israel: A Brief Note from Research about Successful Transitions to Adulthood

ANAT ZEIRA

This well-written chapter is for many reasons of great importance to the reader of this volume on TRC.

First, it provides some insight into the child welfare system in Israel. Here, an interesting cultural difference can be noticed with regard to the status residential care has and the numbers of children and young people placed in residential settings. While in many Western and non-Western countries the de-institutionalization of the child welfare system is continuing, numbers of children and young people in institutions decrease and placing children in a "natural" family is considered to serve their best interests, residential placement remains common practice in Israel. It has a good "reputation," is less controversial and seems to be far from a "last resort." Further, residential placement is not restricted to the child welfare system. In addition to coercive removal into remedial settings, voluntary placement by the Ministry of Education to youth villages is offered to a substantial number of young people. The existence of a softer form of residential care seems to have a de-stigmatizing effect.

Second, the organization of the system and the way residential care facilities are embedded in the system sheds a new light on the transition from care. Although research on outcomes shows contradictory findings, it may not be surprising that transition from care in Israel differs from transition in other countries. In many respects, "the Israeli case" may be called unique, compared with other countries in Europe, the United States and Australia. Young adults leaving care in Israel probably suffer less from the label of having grown up in a group and not in a family; military service following right after leaving care may be helpful for some youngsters, for instance to build up a social network.

Third, this chapter reports on the experiences of young people leaving residential care. Nowadays, young people's perspectives receive a lot of attention by researchers. The author gives a central place to the accounts ("voices") of young care leavers. This is what, in my opinion, makes this chapter strong. Young people's experiences of care are often very complex. Is researching them not synonymous with researching multilayered, meaning-making processes? Integrating in the same chapter young people's experiences with other outcome data may overshadow their voices. The author reports the voices of young care leavers with great respect. The many quotes illustrate well the complexity of their experiences.

In conclusion, this chapter shows the importance of including cultural and historical contexts when evaluating care systems and making cross-national comparisons of trends and evolutions in child welfare. In our search for evidence-based interventions, however, we too often ignore these cultural and historical contexts (Grietens 2013).

Critically Examining the Current Research Base for Therapeutic Residential Care

Uncovering What is Inside the "Black Box" of Effective Therapeutic Residential Youth Care

Annemiek T. Harder and Erik J. Knorth

Introduction

Young people in residential care often show a high degree of psychopathology and problem behavior, more so than young people in other types of care (Cornsweet 1990; Handwerk *et al.* 1998; McDermott *et al.* 2002; Van der Ploeg and Scholte 2003). Lyman and Campbell (1996) describe this as follows:

> The contemporary population of youths being admitted into residential treatment is characterized by chronic, multiple problem behaviors that have not responded well to previous treatment attempts... The youngsters appear to have significant skills deficits, such as in academic achievement and social competency. Their families appear to be significant dysfunctional and unstable. (Lyman and Campbell 1996, p.30)

Residential youth care programs aim to reduce the serious behavioral and developmental problems, and to improve the quality of life of these young people. However, up until now there is hardly any empirical evidence showing how residential care programs actually work to achieve these goals (Knorth *et al.* 2008b). For example, in studying 110 outcome studies on residential care that were conducted between 1990 and mid-2005, we found that a majority of 91 studies (83%) neither sufficiently described the contents of care nor focused on the association between contents of care and outcomes (Harder, Knorth and Zandberg 2006; Knorth *et al.* 2008b).

In much of the research, the residential intervention package remains too much of a "black box" (Axford *et al.* 2005; Knorth 2003; Libby *et al.* 2005; Sinclair 2010).

The aim of this chapter is to offer an overview of the current knowledge on the effectiveness of residential youth care. In describing this knowledge, we will try to uncover what is inside the "black box" of effective residential care. Therefore, we focus on the factors that are currently considered to be important in effective, residential treatment for youth with serious behavioral problems. More specifically, we will examine client and care process factors that are associated with outcomes of residential care.

Effectiveness of residential care

The effectiveness of residential care can be viewed in terms of different types of outcome. In reviewing the 110 outcome studies just mentioned (Harder *et al.* 2006; Knorth *et al.* 2008b), we found a diversity in outcome measures (see Table 15.1).

TABLE 15.1: Outcome measures applied in residential youth care studies

TYPE OF OUTCOME	N INDICATORS	%
I Functioning young people		
A *Non-behavioral*	*40*	*14*
Personality	17	6
Thoughts/attitudes	10	3
Cognitive/affective functioning	13	4
B *Behavioral*	*211*	*72*
Behavioral problems/symptoms	61	21
Recidivism/delinquent behavior	32	11
Readmission	8	3
Behavioral functioning (general/subdimensions)	46	16
Knowledge/skills	20	7
Behavior during treatment	10	3
Situation after departure	34	12
Subtotal I	*251*	*85*
II Functioning parents/family	9	3
III Goal realization	6	2
IV Treatment satisfaction	22	7
V Other	6	2
Subtotal II t/m V	*43*	*15*
Total	294	100

Note: The differences between subtotals and totals are a result of percentages being rounded up.

On average, 2.7 outcome measures were applied in each study. Outcome measures often refer to the young people's behavior, such as externalizing and/or internalizing behavioral problems during care and delinquent behavior after care (Knorth *et al.* 2008b). Family functioning is rarely applied as an outcome measure, despite the fact that family problems often seem to contribute to the admission of youth to residential care (Harder *et al.* 2006).

We additionally examined the outcomes of the 110 studies in terms of premature departure or drop-out of young people from residential care. For seven studies (6%), this outcome measure was not applicable due to the (retrospective) design. In five studies (5%) it was unclear whether youth dropped out, because it was not clearly mentioned or because the study only included program completers. In 58 studies (53%) there were no drop-outs. In the remaining 40 studies (36%) there were young people who dropped out, but seven of these studies did not include these youth in their study sample. Drop-out rates from residential care reported in 34 studies (for six studies exact information was missing) varied between 3 and 64 percent, with a mean of 26 percent young people per study (SD = 17.3). A majority of the 40 studies (64%) did not examine the drop-outs' characteristics (Harder *et al.* 2006).

Review studies on outcomes

Several review studies have been conducted on the outcomes of residential youth care in the past 30 years. In 1991, for example, Curry summarized the results of several studies on residential care from the 1970s and 1980s. He concluded, among other things, that:

> Most youngsters appear to improve within [residential] treatment. Some do not or else appear to get worse. Subject variables, including at least the severity or type of dysfunction and the reactive or process nature of its onset, appear to set limits on what can be achieved with such treatment. Adjustment within a program does not predict adjustment at a subsequent follow-up period. (Curry 1991, p.352)

Curry also concluded that there is a need:

1. for extensive aftercare treatment

2. to work with the child and family for extensive periods of time, only some of it within residential treatment

3. to include in treatment programs as many opportunities as possible for learning that can be generalized to the non-residential environment.

Two somewhat more recently published international review studies reached similar conclusions. Both a selective review on effectiveness of residential and inpatient treatment by Lyman and Campbell (1996) and a review by Frensch and Cameron (2002) on the effectiveness of residential group homes and residential treatment centers showed that the longer the follow-up period, the less convincing the findings of effectiveness. In accordance with Curry (1991), they highlight the importance of aftercare and working with the child and his/her family to improve the effectiveness of residential care.

More recently, Lee *et al.* (2011) reviewed evidence in the United States of residential *group care* effects. They included 19 studies that compared group care with other types of care, including family foster care, treatment foster care, residential group care models and non-residential care, such as family-based, intensive, in-home services and day treatment. Some studies used random assignment of participants to groups or matched participants on demographic characteristics or by statistical methods to improve equivalence between groups. Overall, family and treatment foster care was favored over group care with mainly small to moderate effect sizes (ranging from 0.05 to 0.69) for a variety of outcomes, such as residential placement in the year following departure and self-reported delinquency. There was a small effect (0.12) for family-based, intensive, in-home services to show better outcomes than residential group care in terms of family stability, legal trouble, educational progress and out-of-home placement in the year following departure, but no effect for day treatment compared with group care. The comparison of newer versus traditional group care models showed mixed results. Based on these results, the authors concluded that outcomes of group care are often less positive compared with alternative interventions and that some residential group care models seem more promising than others (Lee *et al.* 2011).

Meta-analysis on outcomes

A more systematic approach to understanding the results of outcome studies is conducted in meta-analyses (Lipsey and Wilson 2001). Several meta-analyses have been conducted on the outcomes of residential youth care during the past 30 years (De Swart *et al.* 2012; Garrett 1985; Grietens 2002; Knorth *et al.* 2008b; Scherrer 1994).

Almost 30 years ago, Garrett (1985) published a meta-analysis of 111 studies conducted since 1960 on treatment of juvenile delinquents, including 90 studies (81%) on institutional treatment. He found an overall average moderate positive effect size (0.37) for youth who received treatment over and above residential care compared with youth who received only regular or no residential care. The most frequently studied treatment approach was contingency management (22%), followed by group techniques (17%) and cognitive-behavioral approaches (16%). There was a medium effect (0.52) for psychological adjustment of youth who received residential treatment compared with youth who received regular or no residential treatment, a small to medium effect (0.41) for institutional adjustment and a small effect (0.13) for recidivism. A rather large effect (0.78) was found for academic improvement of young people who received treatment versus those who received no or regular treatment. With regard to treatment approach, life skills training and behavioral approaches seemed to show slightly higher effect sizes (0.32 and 0.30 respectively) than psychodynamic approaches (0.17).

Scherrer (1994) carried out his meta-analysis on the basis of 42 studies with a (quasi) experimental design, which represented only 4 percent of the 1030 originally included studies. His most important findings are listed here.

- Youth in a residential treatment program show approximately 14 percent more improvement in emotional problems compared with youth in control or comparison groups (e.g. untreated control groups, no treatment groups and a hospital maintenance group).

- Intervention components such as behavioral modification, (psychodynamic) milieu-therapy and family treatment have the best potential for achieving positive outcomes.

- Studies concerning short-term effects show more positive results than studies measuring long-term effects. Positive outcomes in the long run (one year after discharge) are mainly achieved through cognitive-behaviorally oriented programs.

In a review of meta-analyses by Grietens (2002), the effectiveness of residential treatment for juvenile offenders was based on effect sizes from five previously conducted meta-analyses. He included a selection of more than 300 studies from these meta-analyses with recidivism as an outcome measure. Residential treatment of delinquent youth appeared to generate an average recidivism reduction of about 9 percent. Based on these findings,

Grietens (2002) concluded that delinquent behavior is more difficult to treat compared with other problems.

More recently, in our meta-analysis we found a medium to large effect (0.60) for a decrease in general and externalizing behavior problems and a medium effect (0.45) for a decrease in internalizing behavior problems of youth during residential care (Knorth *et al.* 2008b). We also found that behavior-modification components, family-focused components and specific training aimed at social-cognitive and social-emotional skills of young people during residential care are significantly associated with reductions in problem behavior during care. Only Multi-Dimensional Therapeutic Foster Care (MTFC) seemed to be able to accomplish more behavioral progress than residential care, which was also found by Lee *et al.* (2011), who used partly the same studies. Characteristics of a treatment approach such as MTFC—i.e. small-scale; continuity and professionalism of foster parents; complementary individual therapy and family therapy for respectively the child and the biological family; co-operation with school, the justice department and the healthcare department; co-ordination of services through case-management (cf. Chamberlain and Smith 2005)—can be a source of inspiration for further improvements in residential care (cf. Knorth, *et al.* 2008a; McCurdy and McIntyre 2004; Underwood *et al.* 2004).

De Swart *et al.* (2012) examined the effectiveness of residential youth care over the past three decades by focusing on 27 quasi-experimental studies published in peer-reviewed journals. They compared residential evidence-based treatment (EBT; i.e. a structured, manual-guided treatment based on empirical evidence) with residential care as usual (CAU; i.e. regular group care) and with non-residential EBT, residential with non-residential CAU (i.e. foster family care), and residential CAU with non-institutional EBT (i.e. Multi-Systemic Treatment (MST) or MTFC). They found a significant small to medium effect (0.36) in favor of residential EBT over residential CAU. Only cognitive behavior therapy showed a significant medium effect (0.50), whereas (social) skills training and care as usual showed no effect. They concluded that residential care can be equally effective as non-residential care but that it seems more effective to provide youth with EBT (De Swart *et al.* 2012).

Based on the findings in both the four review studies and the five meta-analyses we can conclude that on average, children and young people improve in their psychosocial functioning during residential care. However, the longer the follow-up period of outcomes measured after residential care, the less convincing the findings of effectiveness. Therefore, several studies highlight the importance of aftercare services and working with the child's family to improve effectiveness of residential care. Some studies show that treatment foster care has somewhat better outcomes than residential treatment. On the other hand, residential treatment might be equally effective as other types of treatment if evidence-based treatments are applied to youth during residential care.

What works for whom

To be able to improve the quality and effectiveness of residential youth care, it is essential for research to gain more insight into *how* results are achieved instead of merely investigating the results that are achieved (cf. Libby *et al.* 2005). Despite the scarce information about which ingredients are important for a good quality of residential youth care, research has yielded several guidelines that are often referred to as "what works" principles. In recent years, considerable research attention has been given to the outcomes of care for children and young people, as well as to the ingredients that proved effective in such treatment (Barrett and Ollendick 2005; Carr 2009; Fonagy *et al.* 2002; McAuley, Pecora and Rose 2006). There are two lines of research relevant to residential youth care, namely, studies focusing on what works for youth with externalizing behavioral problems, because that group is often represented in residential care (Harder *et al.* 2006), and studies focusing on what works in (residential) youth care.

What works for youth with externalizing behavior

Important "what works" aspects for youth with externalizing behavior are principles of effective programs for reducing recidivism. Based on the findings of a meta-analysis by Andrews and colleagues (1990) and several review studies on outcomes of interventions with juvenile delinquents, MacGuire (1999) identified the following principles of effective programs.

- The *risk principle*, referring to matching between the offender's risk level and the degree of service intervention: higher-risk individuals receive more intensive services, whereas low-risk individuals receive less intensive services.

- The *needs principle*, which states that it is essential to distinguish between criminogenic and non-criminogenic needs. Interventions should focus on those client factors that are the foundations of the problem behavior.

- The *responsivity principle* means that there should be an appropriate matching between styles of workers and styles of clients.

- The *treatment modality principle* refers to the finding that interventions should be aimed at different aspects of the clients' problems (multimodal) and therefore should apply different methods. Skills-oriented programs and programs using behavioral, cognitive or cognitive-behavioral methods were found to be the most effective.

- The *program integrity principle*, which means that effective programs are those in which the stated aims are linked to the methods being used, including the availability of adequate resources to achieve these aims, appropriate training and support of staff, and an agreed-upon plan for program monitoring and evaluation.

The first three principles constitute the body of the so-called Risk-Need-Responsivity (RNR) model, a framework that is regarded nowadays as the premier model for guiding assessment and treatment of (young) delinquents (cf. Andrews *et al.* 2011).

A recent meta-analytical review of interventions for juvenile offenders by Lipsey (2009) shows that the context of the intervention (i.e. residential or non-residential) does not make a difference regarding the outcomes. He found three important factors that contributed to program effectiveness, namely:

- a "therapeutic" intervention philosophy

- specific interventions focusing on high-risk offenders with aggressive/violent histories

- interventions that were implemented with a high quality (Lipsey 2009).

What works in (residential) youth care

Studies focusing on "what works" in (residential) youth care often refer to the so-called non-specific and specific treatment factors (Van Yperen *et al.* 2010). *Non-specific* treatment factors are those factors that affect the services offered, regardless of the target group or the type of services. *Specific* treatment factors are only operating with regard to certain types of intervention and certain target groups (e.g. Duncan *et al.* 2010).

Non-specific factors are, for example, client factors and relationship factors between the client and therapist. Client factors consist of the factors that are part of the client, such as the severity of the problems, the client's strengths and motivation for treatment and factors that are part of the environment, such as supportive elements in their environment. The relationship factors refer to the therapeutic relationship, which is most commonly defined as an emotional/affective connection and/or a cognitive connection in terms of agreement on the tasks and goals of therapy (Karver *et al.* 2005) and encompasses variables that are found in a variety of therapies regardless of the therapist's theoretical orientation (Daniël and Harder 2010; Duncan *et al.* 2010). Important therapist factors related to the client–therapist relationship are, for example, a client-centered attitude, communication and listening skills and self-reflection (Ackerman and Hilsenroth 2003; Van Erve, Poiesz, and Veerman 2005).

Client and relationship factors are considered to be the most important predictors of positive outcomes in child and youth care (Carr 2009; Karver *et al.* 2006). Moreover, especially for young people with externalizing problems, there seems to be a strong association between the quality of the client–therapist relationship and treatment outcomes (Shirk and Karver 2003).

Specific treatment factors that are considered to be important for successful outcomes in residential youth care include a supportive, safe environment during care, specific treatment focusing on the individual needs of the young people during care and aftercare services (Clough, Bullock and Ward 2006; Harder *et al.* 2006; Knorth *et al.* 2008b). Family-focused interventions are also considered as important for improving residential care outcomes (e.g. Geurts *et al.* 2012), although Clough, Bullock and Ward (2006) emphasize that whether and how families can be involved in the care process should be assessed for every individual child, because for some children the involvement of family might have mainly negative consequences. In addition, Stein (2008), in reference to young people leaving out-of-home care, mentions that "family relationship are often a major dilemma for many of these young people. They need and want to have a sense of family...yet many of these young people have been damaged by their family experiences" (p.38).

Messages from research

Based on the current existing knowledge, we can give several recommendations for future research and practice in the field of residential youth care. Since an important intention of residential care is to meet the needs of young people, it is in the interest of these young people and their parents to increase the knowledge concerning factors that are associated with a successful course of treatment. It is also of public interest to gain a clear understanding of these success factors, given the seriousness of the adolescents' problems and the lack of knowledge about the (quality of) care that is offered in these settings. In addition, the high amount of costs that is associated with both the adolescents' externalizing behavior and this type of care, and the negative image of residential care, stresses the need for better insight into aspects of residential care that are important for success.

Recommendations for research

A first recommendation for researchers conducting outcome studies is to carry out more in-depth research on the *process of change* between professionals and young people in residential youth care, because many studies on residential care lack a specific description of the intervention program (Knorth *et al.* 2008b). Aspects that should receive more attention in this respect are building good relationships between young people, care workers and teachers, and between parents and staff, and the specific treatment skills of care workers and teachers that are necessary for building such relationships in the context of residential youth care (Harder, Kalverboer and Knorth 2013).

Second, *professional and organizational aspects* of residential care need more attention in research, such as the skills of group care workers that are necessary to attain and preserve a positive group climate (cf. Kamphof-Evink and Harder 2011; Van Dam *et al.* 2010; Van der Helm *et al.* 2009), the optimal type and number of adolescents for a residential group to be effective (cf. Chipenda-Dansokho and The Centre for Social Policy 2003; Harder and Knorth 2007), and good-quality education within the residential care context (cf. Harder *et al.* 2013; Houchins *et al.* 2009). By paying attention to these aspects within the process of residential care, explanations for why programs work can be generated and used to make improvements.

A third recommendation that is in line with the previous is that more good-quality research of *aftercare or follow-up services* should be carried out to make clear which adolescents are the most likely candidates for follow-up services and which services are successful for whom after leaving residential care. There is a need for research studies to compare groups of adolescents that do and do not receive services following residential youth care, while controlling for adolescents' problem characteristics at the moment of departure from residential care. Moreover, when (it is expected that) young people (will) return home to their parents after residential care, studies should include parents or families of the young people as respondents to gain an insight into their perspectives. If researchers are looking at follow-up services, they should also pay attention to the living conditions of the young people after leaving care, because studies consistently show that young people leaving out-of-home care and transitioning into adulthood are at high risk for poor outcomes, especially in terms of education, health and well-being (Harder, Knorth, and Kalverboer 2011; Harder *et al.* 2011; Munro and Stein 2008).

A fourth recommendation is that more research of *specific interventions* applied in residential care is desirable. These interventions should be aimed at the individual problems of the young people. Although research suggest that the non-specific factors have a relatively strong effect in comparison to specific treatment factors, the role of specific methods has not been sufficiently addressed in youth care studies until now (Van Yperen *et al.* 2010). For instance, our meta-analysis showed that behavior-modification and family-focused components of interventions seem to achieve positive results, as well as specific training aimed at social-cognitive and social-emotional skills of youths.

Recommendations for practice

A first recommendation for practice, which corresponds with the previously mentioned fourth recommendation for research, is that the basic therapeutic milieu (Scholte and Van der Ploeg 2000) in residential care should be completed with *specific treatment* that is aimed at the specific needs of every individual child (cf. Boendermaker, Van Rooijen and Berg 2010; Harder *et al.* 2006; Thomson *et al.* 2005).

Second, for some youth there is also an explicit need to *involve parents* during the care process. This seems to be especially important for those who (are expected to) return home with their parents after residential care. Since young people are regularly living with their parents after their departure from residential care, parents or family seem to be an important social support network for young people (cf. Courtney and Dworsky 2006). Although parental involvement in residential treatment can play an important role in improving the outcomes of residential care (Geurts 2010), several researchers also point to the need for caution when returning young people to their families (e.g. Biehal 2007; Clough *et al.* 2006).

A third implication is the need for *support of residential staff* in their contact with clients. This support should be especially focused on group care workers and teachers, since they make a relatively large contribution to the process of residential care as they provide day-to-day guidance to the young people (Knorth *et al.* 2010). The support may consist of training, coaching, supervision and working with treatment protocols (cf. Van Yperen *et al.* 2010), and needs to be focused on specific situations, such as interactions with "difficult" young people that show oppositional behavior or do not react to attempts by staff to establish contact during care. A specialization in residential youth care would also be a desirable addition to the vocational training program of care workers and teachers, so that they will be better prepared for working in this specific type of care.

Residential youth care settings should be organized in such a way that care workers, individual therapists and teachers experience sufficient support in their work so that they are able to maintain good program quality. Aspects or preconditions promoting program quality that might be especially important within the context of residential care are, for example, a positive organizational climate (Glisson 2002; Glisson and Hemmelgarn 1998), a clear vision of leaders or the management on how changes should be achieved with the young people (Berridge and Brodie 1998; Sinclair and Gibbs 1998) and involvement of staff in decisions about changes in the care process (Stals *et al.* 2008). In this respect, the quality of the primary care process in residential youth care can be improved by making improvements on *all levels* within the organization (cf. Anglin 2002; Whittaker 2006).

COMMENTARY BY BETHANY R. LEE ON:

Uncovering What is Inside the "Black Box" of Effective Therapeutic Residential Youth Care

ANNEMIEK T. HARDER AND ERIK J. KNORTH

Harder and Knorth take a close look inside the "black box" in their chapter. They summarize studies that explore the broad question of the effectiveness of residential youth care and the more nuanced explorations of what works for whom. The role of common factors (e.g. therapeutic alliance, client strengths and motivation) is considered along with specific treatment factors that are unique to the care environment (e.g. treatment model, milieu and aftercare services). The debate between the value of common factors and unique factors is well known within outpatient clinical care, but only a few research endeavors (led primarily by researchers from the Netherlands) have explored these components in the field of residential youth care.

TRC is not just a setting, but also an intervention. The actual intervention components included in the residential care program are part of the black box that needs further study. Harder and Knorth propose inclusion of interventions that are individualized to youth needs and motivate youth for treatment. Although not explicitly mentioned, manualized evidence-based treatments like Motivational Interviewing could be delivered in residential care settings, which is one method for infusing evidence-based treatment into the setting. Alternately, rigorous research trials could be designed to demonstrate that a therapeutic residential care program model is evidence-based in its entirety and can produce outcomes that rival less expensive interventions.

Several other recommendations are put forward for both additional research and practice. Among the research recommendations, a focus on aftercare studies is certainly needed. Harder and Knorth propose a study design that would compare youth who received aftercare services with those who did not. A more balanced and perhaps interesting comparison could be between youth who remained in placement for a standard length of stay with youth who experienced the same length of treatment but with the setting split between residential care and intensive aftercare services. In financially strapped systems, aftercare is valued because of the potential promise of shorter lengths of stay in placement paired with less costly community based services. Gaining knowledge about when a young person is ready for aftercare services and the needed constellation of services (with consideration to educational and vocational services as well as mental health care) will be critical to optimizing the positive effects of TRC and the post-discharge environment.

In reflecting upon the resources available to continue to build knowledge about TRC, as well as the workforce of practitioners who provide services in residential care settings, the role of formal certificate and degree programs cannot be overstated. Examples include Child and Youth Worker advanced diploma programs in Canada and the Glasgow School of Social Work's MSc in Advanced Residential Childcare. These programs, which advance the professional identity for the field, further hold the promise of developing a cadre of residential child and youth care scholars and advanced practitioners who can further unpack the black box of TRC.

CHAPTER 16

Improving the Research Base for Therapeutic Residential Care
Logistical and Analytic Challenges meet Methodological Innovations

Bethany R. Lee and Richard P. Barth

Background

At the start of the 21st century, several residential care scholars (e.g. Lieberman 2004; Teather 2001; Whittaker 2000b) provided thoughtful commentary on the state of empirical support for this field and future research priorities. They identified several factors that had stymied growth in knowledge building, including hurdles in funding for research, ideological challenges and a need to define residential care in a universally understood way. In suggesting future directions, they emphasized outcomes research measuring program effectiveness as well as understanding who benefits and the critical active ingredients for success. Although some of these challenges remain, new analytic methods and practice knowledge have created opportunities to enhance evidence for what works and infuse science into practice.

In this chapter, we review logistical and analytical challenges that researchers encounter in building empirical evidence that supports residential care. We also describe several methodological innovations to overcome these challenges. Finally, we suggest next steps in building the evidence base.

Logistical and analytical challenges

Several key challenges have limited the development of the research base for Therapeutic Residential Care (TRC). These challenges include the difficulty of randomizing assignment to treatment, generalizability of findings due to modest sample sizes and heterogeneity of youth served, use of standardized measures and the changing nature of services and client populations. In this section, we will describe these challenges and review their presence in the literature.

Research design

Although the gold standard in research design is a randomized controlled trial (RCT), many stakeholders (including judges, case managers, youth and families) are reluctant to rely on random assignment for decisions such as whether to place a child in a therapeutic residential setting. Hence, RCTs in residential care are almost non-existent. The most notable exceptions are studies of delinquent youth randomized to group care settings or Multi-Dimensional Treatment Foster Care (MTFC) (e.g. Chamberlain and Reid 1998; Leve, Chamberlain and Reid 2005).

In the absence of evidence from RCTs, the research base for TRC settings is built on two-group, non-randomized studies (which limit internal validity) or single-group, pre-post designs in a single program (which limit external validity). Although there is increased interest in building capacity for research within therapeutic residential programs (Boyd *et al.* 2007) and research is being produced from increasingly diverse countries including Italy (Palareti and Berti 2009a, 2009b), Sweden (Johansson, Andersson and Hwang 2008), Israel (Schiff, Nebe and Gilman 2011) and Botswana (Morantz and Heymann 2010), research design limits causality and generalizability.

Aggregating knowledge about TRC's effectiveness across studies is also hampered by ambiguity around what constitutes a TRC setting. Leichtman (2007) noted that "problems in defining the concept [of residential care] with which pioneers in the field struggled fifty years ago are no less present today" (p.176). To overcome the lack of a clear definition for residential care (Lee 2008), group care reporting standards have been developed to provide guidelines of descriptive content that should be included in any empirical study of a group care program (Lee and Barth 2011). Authors are encouraged to make transparent the program's goals, size, population served, setting and location, program model, practice elements, staff details, systems influences and restrictiveness (Weems 2011). Broader adoption of these standards could enhance opportunities for knowledge aggregation.

Outcome measurement

The existing research base is also stymied by inconsistency in *how* outcomes are measured (Butler, Little and Grimard 2009). Empirical evidence supporting TRC cannot be based only on improvement during the program but post-placement success must also be demonstrated. How to measure success and whether there is a "statute of limitations" for when a residential program is no longer responsible for youth outcomes are persistent challenges (Whittaker and Pfeiffer 1994, p.596). In children's services outcomes, to earn the highest rating, continued impact must be evident at one-year follow-up for the highest rating and six months or a sustained effect for the second highest rating (California Evidence-Based Clearinghouse 2013); however, similar standards are not established for residential programs.

Real-world outcomes, especially post-placement, are critical for assessing the success of TRC. Collecting data in a systematic way post-discharge is challenging. In a study of 293 residential programs in the US, 67 percent report tracking outcomes after discharge, although the tracking generally lasted six months or fewer (Brown *et al.* 2011). For longer-term follow-up studies, response rates can be low. In a five-year and 16-year follow-up study, response rates were just above 50 percent (Ringle *et al.* 2010). High rates of attrition may no longer validly represent the original population. Shorter-term outcome studies have improved response rates, including 84 percent in a one-year follow-up (Ringle *et al.* 2012) and 75 percent in a two-year follow-up (Cuthbert *et al.* 2011).

Changing context

Although TRC programs have a long history, the context of care is constantly evolving. In the US, a growth of and emphasis on community-based care has funneled youth with less serious needs into non-residential services, leaving a more challenging population for residential programs. For example, one state's admissions to residential treatment decreased each year from 2002 to 2007, but the severity of youth behavioral and emotional needs, risk behaviors and functioning impairments increased incrementally each year (Lyons *et al.* 2009). In a study comparing youth admitted to their residential program in 1995–1996 with a cohort admitted between 2004–2005, Hurley *et al.* (2009) found that the later cohort was almost twice as likely to have multiple DSM diagnoses and multiple psychiatric medications compared with the earlier cohort and a greater proportion of the later cohort were transitioning from a more or equally restrictive program.

Building the research base often requires funding for empirical studies. Large-scale federal funding for residential care research has been scarce for years in US (Whittaker and Pfeifer 1994). The dominant comparative effectiveness framework favors the least expensive approach that achieves equivalent outcomes. As such, residential programs that often have expensive capital and overhead costs are at a disadvantage in fiscally driven decisions.

The changing nature of developmental transitions to adulthood has also created changes in the US child welfare services program, where care can now be extended to age 21. Foster family placements have responded to these changes by continuing to house youth and sometimes even their offspring as well. Youth can even be adopted through age 21 and youth who leave care can, in many states, ask to be readmitted back into foster care. In contrast, the traditional nature of American residential treatment is involuntary and short-term, ending at age 18 and not allowing for much flexibility about readmission or residing with one's own children. Residential programs have struggled with developing policies and practices that are responsive to the changing needs of transition-age youth.

Methodological innovations

The challenges described above are daunting, but innovations in statistical methods and ways of knowing provide resources to surmount these obstacles. This section will describe several emerging technologies and innovations that can be engaged to improve the knowledge base for TRC. We will begin with advances in national and program-level infrastructure that enhance the availability of and systematization of data; then we will introduce new approaches to build and infuse evidence in practice settings; finally, we will provide a brief overview of statistical techniques that allow researchers to explore new questions.

Research capacity

An increased capacity for research is made possible through the growth of administrative data on a national and program level. Administrative data systems have been increasing in capacity to accurately track and analyze experiences of youth in public child welfare (Drake and Jonson-Reid 1999), as well as across public systems (Jonson-Reid and Drake 2008; Millett *et al.* 2013). Technical and technological advances have made it possible to create large databases to answer longitudinal and systems-level research questions to inform policy and practice. For example, in the US, the Adoption and Foster Care Reporting System is a depository for data on all youth in out-of-home care through the public child welfare system. Additionally, large nationally representative datasets of youth in the child welfare system are becoming increasingly available. The US National Survey of Child and Adolescent Well-being (NSCAW) collected several thousand variables from families, youth and workers investigated by child welfare or in out-of-home care; a similar study is being conducted in New South Wales, Australia. In addition, the National Data Archive for Child Abuse and Neglect (NDACAN) warehouses datasets that can be requisitioned for secondary analysis. These large data sources offer the potential to answer new inquiries related to national or widespread trends, as well as local variation in service use and need.

At a program level, accreditors (US or international) such as the Joint Commission require the engagement of outcome measurement and tracking for continuous quality improvement to earn accreditation. State licensing or regulatory bodies may also promote outcomes measurement; a study of almost 300 residential programs found that licensed programs were more than twice as likely to conduct post-discharge outcomes monitoring (Brown *et al.* 2011). Building and sustaining the capacity for systematic outcomes collection can contribute to the broader field of knowledge.

On a smaller scale, the value of a program's capacity to systematically collect knowledge about clients should improve client care directly rather than just facilitate research at the program level. A measurement feedback system (MFS) provides feedback in real time for clinicians to adjust their approach to increase effectiveness (Bickman 2008). By routinely collecting data from clients about service processes and outcomes (e.g. satisfaction, changes in functioning or symptom severity) using brief instruments, clinicians can use this feedback to drive treatment planning.

Although advances have been made in developing short, psychometrically valid instruments as well as technological solutions for data management, barriers to widespread adoption of measurement feedback systems remain (Bickman 2008). In a survey of child mental health clinicians mandated to use standardized outcome measurement, 92 percent of respondents reported never using this information in treatment planning or monitoring (Garland *et al.* 2003). These respondents also reported some skepticism about whether improvement could be quantified with standardized measures. One respondent compared using standardized measures to assess abstract constructs to "picking up jello with a fork"

(Garland, Kruse and Aarons 2003, p.398). Resistance to MFS would need to be addressed to ensure a positive impact of this effort.

The challenge is not just to collect more data but also to use it consistently to drive practice. Efforts from the common factors and common elements approaches emphasize the value of monitoring progress towards outcomes. Available tools to integrate this feedback include a clinical dashboard to track intervention components and client improvement (Chorpita *et al.* 2008) or the four-item self-report Outcome Rating Scale (ORS) and Session Rating Scale (SRS). Anecdotal evidence suggests that the use of these tools could help to better engage youth, family and providers around decision making (Sparks and Muro 2009).

Evidence of MFS in US child welfare has focused on the length of stay and other processes of care, rather than the client's care experience. In some jurisdictions, supervisors receive daily reports on cases that exceed expected timelines. Sometimes, these performance feedback systems also indicate whether referrals to ancillary services are needed. Overall, these management information systems operate in real time to enhance quality and responsiveness of services.

In considering the field of TRC, a measurement feedback system has obvious applicability. Questions related to measuring improvement during care and assessing the optimal length of stay for youth in residential care could be explored. Additionally, MFS could promote greater individualization of services within care and guide data-driven treatment modifications. Integrating the MFS of the residential program with a larger service system could allow tracking and monitoring of youth outcomes across individual providers.

Integration of evidence

Meta-analyses and systematic reviews aggregate knowledge about empirical evidence, often from RCTs or similarly strong research methodologies. The Campbell Collaboration, an international network that evaluates social service interventions through rigorous systematic reviews, has one completed systematic review related to TRC. Armelius and Andreassen (2007) reviewed the effectiveness of cognitive behavioral treatment for antisocial behavior in youth in residential treatment, using 12 RCT and quasi-experimental studies. However, these residential programs included correctional and justice programs rather than the mental health or child welfare-oriented programs more typically considered in TRC.

Despite the lack of RCTs in the field of TRC, several sophisticated reviews have been conducted recently that bolster what is known about what works. First, Knorth and colleagues (2008a) reviewed 27 pre-experimental and quasi-experimental studies on outcomes of residential child and youth care. They were able to calculate weighted mean effect sizes to conclude that residential care had a medium effect on internalizing and externalizing behaviors. Next, Lee *et al.* (2010) reviewed 19 two-group studies that compared residential care with another placement setting or compared two models of residential care. Individual effect sizes were calculated for each study outcome, with most effects ranging from small to moderate. Using similar inclusion criteria of two-group studies, De Swart and colleagues (2012) published a meta-analysis of 27 studies of institutional care. They not only calculated an overall effect size, but also found significant effects for several characteristics including the gender mix of the sample, criminal justice involvement, the treatment provided by the comparison group and the theoretical approach of the intervention. Finally, further attention to models of care was given in James's (2011b) structured review of five residential care models that both described the features of each model and summarized empirical evidence for each. She then applied the rating criteria from the California Evidence-Based Clearinghouse for Child Welfare (www.cebc4cw.com) to rate the level of scientific evidence for each treatment model. These examples demonstrate that existing studies can be employed to further knowledge development.

Meta-analysis and systematic reviews evaluate the effects of the intervention as a whole; a more recent innovation is to consider the building blocks of the intervention. Known as the "distillation and matching model", Chorpita and Daleiden (2009) designed a methodology that identifies *common practice elements* (i.e. discrete clinical techniques or strategies) from manualized interventions. This approach identifies the building blocks of the intervention for flexible implementation by clinicians. Early evidence has found that the modular common elements approach was associated with greater therapist likeability (Borntrager *et al.* 2009) and better youth outcomes (Weisz *et al.* 2012), compared with both usual care and the standard manualized treatment approaches to service delivery. Lee and colleagues (under review) used this approach to detect the common elements associated with effective programs intended to prevent out-of-home placements. This method also has the potential to identify the key ingredients for effective residential programs. In addition, this modular approach offers an opportunity to infuse components from evidence-based interventions without training residential care staff in manualized evidence-supported treatments.

Statistical innovations

The increased capacity of computing has allowed researchers to explore more complex questions. Recently, several new methods have been developed and made accessible through data analytic software packages. This section will describe the types of research questions relevant to RCTs that can now be asked and answered as a result of these innovations.

As described earlier, the paucity of RCTs has limited the attribution of causality in demonstrating the effects of TRC placement. In the last few decades, several innovations in establishing causal inference have been developed, including propensity score matching, instrumental variables and regression discontinuity models. For a full explanation of these methods, see Stone and Rose (2011). With these approaches, quasi-experimental studies (i.e. two groups that have not been randomly assigned to two different treatments) can be used to model causality.

Of these methods, only propensity score matching (PSM) has been applied in the TRC literature. Barth and colleagues (2007) applied PSM to compare youth treated in a residential program with youth who were provided intensive in-home services. They found a statistical trend that favored positive outcomes for in-home youth at one-year post-discharge. When Lee and Thompson (2008) compared youth placed in treatment foster care and residential group care on outcomes, they found that youth served in the residential program had higher rates of favorable exit, return home and avoiding subsequent placement in next six months. The PSM studies in residential care have primarily been limited to a single program or small geographic region. A notable exception is McCrae and colleagues' (2010) study using data from a nationally representative dataset comparing group care and foster care youth; they found no significant differences in academic, affective and behavioral outcomes over three years. The mixed findings and diverse samples suggest that further study is needed to more comprehensively understand the causal effects of residential care placement.

The contextual factors of a residential program are considered an important component of treatment. The "milieu" including the caregivers, environment and peers, is theorized to greatly impact care. However, large studies that include data from multiple programs often ignore within-program variation (and sometimes even between-program variation). A significant advance of the last two decades has been the growth and accessibility of techniques for measuring both individual-level variables and shared group-level characteristics for individuals nested within groups or shared environments such as cottages on campuses, or even, classrooms in residential schools. Estimating the contribution of both individual factors as well as factors that are shared within cottages or within programs can be efficiently conducted using hierarchical or multi-level modeling (MLM) regression techniques. For example, Huefner and Ringle (2012) modeled within-cottage variation of the proportion of conduct-disordered peers in the home each week, as well as the differences between cottages (tenure of residential care staff and youth length of stay). They found that the density of conduct-disordered peers in the home was not significantly associated with the number of behavioral problems within the home, which defied assumptions of negative peer contagion.

Future research endeavors should use MLM techniques to assess the extent to which unit-level or agency-level factors predict individual-level outcomes for youth. The role of unit-level factors such as adult-to-youth ratio, family engagement efforts and participation in specific enrichment activities as well as program-level characteristics such as motivation system (e.g. token economy), organizational culture and climate, and theoretical orientation could be estimated in relation to their contribution to specific youth outcomes. These findings would enhance program structure and administration.

Some of the within-program or within-unit differences are known and easy to measure, such as the examples described in the previous paragraph. However, other populations or trends that we consider as monolithic may actually reflect distinct subgroups. For example, the overall trend of behavior change can be estimated for all youth in a program using simple longitudinal modeling, but the overall trend may not accurately describe any individual participants. Although approaches such as MLM can estimate the average treatment progress for known subgroups (e.g. boys vs. girls, older youth vs. younger youth), there may be shared patterns in treatment progress that cannot be easily identified. These underlying groups that emerge from the data can now be identified through latent group modeling (Muthen 2006; Nagin 2005). Latent group models can explore subgroups at a single point in time (e.g. variations in educational ability and functioning at intake to placement) as well as over time (e.g. patterns in the trajectory of behavior change during time in care).

This technique was applied in Lee and Thompson's (2009) study of peer contagion in a residential group care program. Using a count of the number of serious behavior incidents of each youth for their first 12 months in care, they estimated five latent trajectories of behavior incidents. Most youth were categorized in the No Problem (40%) or Low-level Problem (38%) trajectories; the remaining youth showed gradual decreases in problem behaviors (11%), gradual increases (7%)

or consistently high problem behaviors (4%). This analysis uncovered distinct groups of youth who had differential benefit from the residential program; the characteristics of each group and the connection between their trajectory during care and placement outcomes (Lee, Chmelka and Thompson 2010) offered further insights. Additional applications of this method could include individualizing care planning based on intake characteristics, establishing optimal durations of care and other experiences where identifying underlying patterns or subgroups can improve decision making.

Next steps

This chapter has summarized the limitations of research on residential care and described several innovative methodologies that offer promise in furthering the scientific knowledge base for this field. In this final section, we will identify key questions for future empirical research and how new methods and technologies can carve a pathway for their exploration.

Who benefits from TRC, for how long and with integration of what other family-centered methods?

In a changing service context where in-home care is emphasized whenever possible, a clear roadmap is needed to assess when a referral to residential care would be optimal rather than requiring a youth or family to fail all less restrictive services. The length of stay in residential settings has decreased significantly on average, but the duration of time to optimally accomplish placement goals is still unknown. The importance of involving family in residential programs is well established (Hair 2005; Lee *et al.* 2010), and models of care that explicitly engage families should be pursued. However, little empirical evidence guides the blending of family care and residential stays.

Answering these questions is possible with progress in systematic data collection and the statistical advances described in the prior section. Latent class models and latent trajectory models can identify the presence of subgroups of youth who experience the greatest benefit from residential care and the patterns and plateaus in treatment progress over time to identify points of diminishing returns. To evaluate new models of residential care, statistical advances such as PSM can compare traditional and family-centered approaches.

What are the active ingredients of high-quality TRC programs?

The common elements can be applied to identify practices associated with effective interventions in care settings. Initial efforts to identify the critical elements of group care treatment models (James 2011b) along with meta-analyses (De Swart *et al.* 2012; Knorth *et al.* 2008a) have taken steps toward this goal. Further research should consider a more rigorous common elements style coding process of empirical literature and program models specific to group care as well as dismantling studies that compare programs with and without specific components. The findings from this work could direct program development and refinement and enhance the quality of care provided in the field.

How can TRC programs be included among evidence-supported interventions?

For systems committed to providing only evidence-based care to youth and families, options for out-of-home placement include only MTFC (Chamberlain and Reid 1998), which is not widely available. Rigorous efforts to establish the evidence base for residential care are needed. We suggest several steps that could contribute towards this goal.

1. Creating a Campbell Collaboration protocol for a review of TRC programs could credibly demonstrate the evidence supporting the field.

2. Less rigorously assessed program models can be reviewed and listed in resources such as the California Evidence-Based Clearinghouse for Child Welfare. Currently, only six TRC models are reviewed on the site.

3. Residential programs can join forces and develop a learning collaborative with uniform and systematic data collection efforts to create a multi-program outcomes database.

4. Individual programs can develop measurement feedback systems to enhance practice at the level of individual clients and families and promote ongoing quality improvement efforts. These strategies can escalate the knowledge base rapidly.

These efforts could be driven by productive collaborations between university researchers and residential programs or associations of residential programs. For example, Boys Town has developed a partnership with a local university, which has created rigorous and independent evaluations of their work that has merited funding from national sources. Combining the intellectual capital of academic researchers with residential programs who are receptive to research engagement can create an effective duo for accessing resources and furthering science.

Advancements in methods and knowledge building provide new opportunities to develop the research base in TRC. Many of the new tools and techniques to address these obstacles are accessible to both program administrators and researchers. Based on the resources available and the heightened understanding of the importance of these research questions, accelerated progress in the knowledge base should emerge in the coming years.

Improving the Research Base for Therapeutic Residential Care: Logistical and Analytic Challenges meet Methodological Innovation

BETHANY R. LEE AND RICHARD P. BARTH

Driven by an engaged academic curiosity Lee and Barth offer a stimulating overview of methodological innovations that might contribute to answering the key question "What works in residential care?" These innovations are very much welcomed, especially in evaluating a type of care with so many factors as potential determinants of efficacy.

The research designs to prove care efficacy and effectiveness can be hierarchically ordered: at the top, the most "powerful" but hardly applied "randomized controlled trial" (RCT), followed by the "non-randomized two groups study" and the "single-group pre-post design." Lee and Barth also include designs at the lower steps in the *stairway model* of Veerman and Van Yperen (2007): descriptive studies and theoretical studies. We will take a closer look at these two types of research that form a *conditio sine qua non* for the more sophisticated evaluation designs.

Descriptive studies intend to explore the core elements of an intervention, namely:

1. the client group

2. the care process (including personnel and organizational conditions)

3. the outcomes.

Research into client characteristics can reveal subgroups with different behavioral and emotional profiles, resulting in a need for differentiated treatment approaches. Lee and Barth refer to their own research that identified, using latent class analysis, five groups of juveniles with different trajectories of behavioral incidents in residential care. In one of our own studies we discovered, using hierarchical cluster analysis, four subgroups of youth in secure residential care with different risk profiles (Harder, Knorth and Kalverboer 2014).

Next to assessing client characteristics there is a strong need, as Lee and Barth argue, for describing the contents of care. The care process often stays a "black box," resulting in the impossibility to link outcomes to the main intervention components. Residential care is an outstanding example of an intervention that is built up by many components. The authors rightly refer in this context to the work of Chorpita, Weisz and colleagues who developed a "matching" method to detect common practice elements in interventions. At the University of Groningen we also invest in this type of research (see, for instance, Evenboer *et al.* 2012).

Concerning the description of outcomes, the authors inform us about the growing number of informative datasets in the US regarding youth in out-of-home care. They also stress the importance of routine measurements with clients, which results in data becomeing available not only for scientific purposes (accumulation of knowledge) but also for clinical, organizational or policy purposes (generating feedback at micro, meso and macro levels). At this point, the development in Europe seems to be behind. In the Netherlands, for example, there is no legal framework insisting on routine outcome measurements in child care; initiatives are a matter of private concern.

Theoretical studies—the second pillar—intended to answer the question "Why?": why is it that a care process leads to certain outcomes, considering the clients' characteristics? Lee and Barth refer here to the relevance of systematic reviews, meta-analyses and the "matching" approach. In addition, we would like to mention *qualitative* studies that can make an important contribution to our evidence by gathering data on the perspectives of clients, professionals and others involved in care.

Finally, the next steps that are proposed by Lee and Barth to improve the research base for residential care are very worthy of consideration and need straightforward implementation.

Calculating Costs for Therapeutic Residential Care

CHAPTER 17

Estimating Unit Costs for Therapeutic Residential Care

Lisa Holmes

Introduction

This volume has outlined a range of key issues for the role and use of Therapeutic Residential Care (TRC) within child welfare systems, and has provided some examples of innovative practices in therapeutic care.

Within this chapter, the focus now shifts to an exploration of the costs of providing TRC and outlines a method for estimating unit costs of placing children away from home. Examples are provided of how the method has been used to carry out cost comparisons between placement types including those that are likely to require a therapeutic placement. Furthermore, the method reported in this chapter provides an approach to linking the costs of providing placements and services with children and young people's needs and circumstances to the outcomes achieved. The chapter also uses an illustrative example of a newly trialled Social Learning Theory training programme for residential children's homes in England (RESuLT) (Connolly *et al.* 2012). The illustrative example is provided to demonstrate how the unit-cost approach could be used to provide evidence to inform costs and outcomes debates for the placement of children in therapeutic residential provision.

Children in residential care in England

In England, child welfare services favour the use of family-based care for children placed away from home; as such the latest national statistics indicate that only 9 per cent (5930) of children placed in out-of-home care were in residential provision, including secure accommodation and hostels. Of these, 4890 were placed in children's homes (Department for Education 2012). Although this figure accounts for only a small number of the total population of children in out-of-home care, there has been a renewed national policy focus on residential provision following the conclusion of a high-profile child exploitation trial and an associated inquiry on child exploitation in groups of young people who go missing from care (APPG 2012).

A recent analysis of the use and market of children's homes in England has identified that children placed in residential homes in England are predominantly teenagers, with three-quarters of children being aged between 14 and 17. Boys account for 63 per cent of the children placed in residential homes (Department for Education 2013a). The duration of residential placements in England is not dissimilar to those with foster carers, although the placements are less likely to last for more than one year. Although some children are placed in residential homes as their first placement, more than a quarter of the children and young people have had at least five previous placements (Department for Education 2013a). Furthermore, a recent research study (Berridge, Biehal and Henry 2012) has highlighted the high levels of emotional and behavioural difficulties of the children placed in residential homes in England.

Expenditure in England on children's homes placements was estimated to be in the region of £1.05 billion for the 2011–12 financial year (Department for Education 2013b). The expenditure on children's homes placements varies between local authority areas, and similarly the range of costs per week is large, with reported figures of between £1000 and £5000 per week for homes managed by local authorities and between £2000 and £5000 per week for homes provided by the non-local authority sector (independent and voluntary placement providers) (Department for Education 2013b). Some of these variations in costs can be attributed to regional differences in salary and property costs and to the commissioning strategies within local authorities. Furthermore, as highlighted by Beecham (2006), cost estimations carried out within local authority settings are based on interpretation, and on some occasions may only include controllable costs within specific departments rather than accounting for overall organisational overhead costs.

Development of a unit-costing approach

Child welfare services operate and provide support and services with finite resources. These resources need to be used to provide the best possible services and support to ensure that children are adequately safeguarded and to improve outcomes. In England in the late 1990s there were concerns at national and local government level about the delivery of good and effective services at an appropriate cost (Department of Health 2001a); these concerns, along with unexplained variations in the costs of providing services, led to the Department of Health commissioning a national research initiative (Costs and Effectiveness of Services for Children in Need), comprising 13 research studies (Department of Health 2001a; Beecham and Sinclair 2007). The focus of this chapter is on the methods developed and the findings from one of these 13 studies: *Costs and Consequences of Placing Children in Care* (Ward, Holmes and Soper 2008).

The approach adopted across the Costs and Effectiveness research initiative was a move away from 'top-down' estimations (as those outlined above) of costs of providing care that only focus on the fees or allowances paid based on total expenditure and do not capture the complexities associated with differences in children's needs and circumstances.

The conceptual framework outlined in this chapter (Holmes and McDermid 2012; Ward *et al.* 2008), is instead based on a 'bottom-up' approach to unit-cost estimations (Beecham 2000). The 'bottom-up' approach identifies the constituent parts that form the delivery of a service and assigns a value to each of these parts. The sum of these values is linked with appropriate units of activity to provide the unit cost of a service (Beecham 2000). The approach facilitates the development of a detailed and transparent picture of unit costs and is particularly well suited to child welfare services as it can accommodate variations in costs incurred by an extensive range of interventions offered to children with very different levels of need (see Ward *et al.* 2008). Furthermore, the approach may be utilised to inform longer-term cost implications of expanding specific services (Beauchamp and Hicks 2004; Beecham 2000). By identifying the number and frequency of cost-related activities occurring over a specific time period, it is also possible to draw up a longitudinal picture of average costs incurred in providing a service for groups of children with similar needs or placed in similar types of provision.

The conceptual framework was initially developed by Ward, Holmes and Soper (2008) for children placed away from home and has since been extended to include child welfare services for children who are supported within their own homes – defined as 'children in need'[1] in England

---

1   The term 'in need' is defined in the Children Act (HMSO 1989) as being a child or young person who is 'unlikely to achieve or maintain, or have the opportunity of achieving or maintaining, a reasonable standard of health or development without the provision for him/her of services by a local authority' or if his/her 'development is likely to be significantly impaired, or further impaired without the provision of such services' or if he or she 'is disabled'.

(Holmes and McDermid 2012) and to children and families in receipt of services or support as part of the Common Assessment Framework (Holmes *et al.* 2012). The framework and unit-costing approach has also been utilised for services provided to disabled children (Holmes, McDermid and Sempik, 2010) and for the implementation of Multi-Dimensional Treatment Foster Care (MTFC), an evidence-based intervention developed in the US and implemented in English child welfare systems (Chamberlain *et al.* 2011; Holmes, Ward and McDermid 2012). The framework and unit-cost method has also been trialled for child welfare systems in the US (Holmes *et al.* in press).

Nationally applicable documentation was used as the basis for the development of the conceptual framework, primarily the Core Information Requirements Process model (Department of Health 2001b), which specifies the core activities that underpin the delivery of placements and services to children in out-of-home care. These activities were then broken down and organised into eight social care processes (detailed in Table 17.1) that are carried out for children placed in the care of local authorities.

TABLE 17.1: Child welfare processes for children placed in out-of-home care in England

PROCESS NUMBER	PROCESS DESCRIPTION
Process One	Decide child needs to be placed in out-of-home care and find first placement.
Process Two	Care planning (including completion and updates to the child's individual Care Plan, Personal Education Plan and Health Assessment).
Process Three	Ongoing support to the child in placement.
Process Four	Exit from out-of-home care (includes adoption, return home, transition to independent living).
Process Five	Find a subsequent placement.
Process Six	Review (statutory meeting held at prescribed intervals to review the placement and update the care plan).
Process Seven	Legal interventions.
Process Eight	Transition to leaving care services.

Data concerning the time routinely spent on each of the activities encompassed by each process (outlined in Table 17.1) by each of the personnel involved were collected from focus group discussions with frontline practitioners. Additional data were also obtained from online surveys completed by a range of practitioners involved in supporting children placed in out-of-home care. This 'time use activity' data were then combined with data on salaries and overheads, using a standardised schema outlined by Curtis (2012) to estimate unit costs for each of the eight processes.

Variations in unit costs

The use of focus groups and online surveys proved to be robust in that there was little variation between personnel concerning the amount of time they spent completing standard tasks for each of the eight processes (see Ward *et al.* 2008; Holmes *et al.* 2009). However, substantial variations in activity were identified to support children with different needs and to arrange and support different placement types. Variations in local authority policies and procedures also impacted on the level of activity and therefore the costs of completing certain tasks.

Children's needs and circumstances

Children's specific needs were found to impact on the type of placement offered and the additional support services provided by a range of different agencies, for example, mental health and education. The types and combination of needs that were identified as impacting on activity times, and therefore costs, are detailed in Box 17.1. Information from the focus groups and online surveys also highlighted different levels of activity to find placements for children with different needs, for example, the time taken to find placements for children and young people with emotional and behavioural difficulties was substantially longer than for those children without any identified additional needs. Furthermore, practitioners also identified that the time taken to find appropriate placements became incrementally longer for children and young people who had experienced previous placement instability. Practitioners also reported higher levels of activity to support children and young people in a new placement following a placement change.

Box 17.1: Child needs that impact on costs

Simple groups

- Children with no evidence of additional support needs.
- Children with emotional or behavioural difficulties (EBD).
- Young offenders (Offend).
- Unaccompanied asylum-seeking children (UASC).
- Children with disabilities (CWD).

Complex groups

- CWD + EBD
- EBD + Offend
- UASC + EBD
- CWD + Offend
- CWD + EBD
- UASC + CWD + EBD

Placement type

The cost of providing a placement, including the fees and allowances paid, along with the ongoing activity to support children or young people in their placements were included in Process Three. In addition to variations in the payments made for placements (fees and allowances) data from the focus groups and online surveys indicated different levels of ongoing support for children in different placement types, for example, lower levels of support were reported for residential placements when a child had established a relationship with their key worker within the home. Placing children out of the area of the local authority was also found to have an impact on costs. Supporting children in these placements constituted a higher cost because of the time spent travelling for statutory visits and review meetings.

Local authority factors

Local authority factors that led to variations in activity were attributed to local geography, policy and procedures, staffing, structure and the availability of resources. The geography of the local authority area was found to have an impact on the travel time to visit children and young people in their placements. Differences in procedures also impacted on levels of activity and therefore cost. For example, there were substantial variations in the level of management at which decisions for funding were made; furthermore, some authorities reported the introduction of 'panel meetings' for funding decisions.

The salaries paid to staff and the fees and allowances paid to carers were also found to vary between authorities. The structure of staffing, for example, tiers of management and the amount of administrative support, were also found to vary between authorities and therefore impact on unit costs.

Using unit costs to explore care pathways

Standard unit costs for each of the eight processes outlined in Table 17.1 were estimated, along with a series of cost variations for each of the processes (based on the variations identified above). To illustrate some of the variations in unit costs Table 17.2 outlines the costs of each of the processes for three different placement types: local authority foster care; agency foster care; and residential care. All of these are for children with emotional or behavioural difficulties who had experienced placement instability. Following the estimation of unit costs for each of the processes – both for standard cases and all identified variations – it was then possible to estimate the costs of care episodes based on the frequency with which the processes occured, the placement provided and the provision of other support services.

During the time that they are placed in out-of-home care, not all children will experience all eight of the processes, although all will go through Processes One to Four: in each case a decision has to be made to place the child and the first placement is identified (Process One); in England all children placed away from home have a Care Plan and it is also a statutory requirement for them to have a Personal Education Plan and an annual Health Assessment – these three elements constitute the activity carried out for Process Two; once the child is in placement, activities are carried out to support both the child and their placement (Process Three); a process is also undertaken at the end of a care episode when a child returns home, is adopted or makes the transition to independent living (Process Four).

TABLE 17.2: Unit costs of eight social care processes

PROCESS	FOSTER CARE IN LOCAL AUTHORITY (LA) AREA (2010–11 PRICES) UK£ [US$]	AGENCY FOSTER CARE IN LA AREA (2010–11 PRICES) UK£ [US$]	AGENCY RESIDENTIAL IN LA AREA (2010–11 PRICES) UK£ [US$]
Process One: Decision to place and finding first placement	£1118 [$1808]	£1455 [$2353]	£1408 [$2277]
Process Two: Care planning	£126 [$204]	£126 [$204]	£126 [$204]
Process Three: Maintaining the placement (per month)	£2855 [$4618]	£5251 [$8495]	£10270 [$16610]
Process Four: Leaving care/ accommodation	£275 [$445]	£275 [£445]	£275 [$445]
Process Five: Finding subsequent placement	£664 [$1074]	£1000 [$1617]	£1084 [$1753]
Process Six: Review	£598 [$967]	£598 [$967]	£598 [$967]
Process Seven: Legal interventions	£2892 [$4677]	£2892 [$4677]	£2892 [$4677]
Process Eight: Transition to leaving care services	£1218 [$4677]	£1218	£1218

Additional processes are carried out for some children in out-of-home care: many will move to new placements during a care episode (Process Five); under legislation in England, all children who remain in out-of-home care for more than one month will be subject to the review processes (Process Six); some will require legal interventions such as care orders (Process Seven); young people in England who come under the provision of the Children (Leaving Care) Act (2000) (Department of Health 2000) will also be entitled to leaving care services – these activities constitute Process Eight.

All of the processes (except Process Three) are costed as discrete, one-off events that occur on a specific date or over a limited time period. Some of the processes will be repeated, for example, as a child moves placement. Process Three is calculated as a 'per day' cost for the duration of the child being placed in out-of-home care.

Using this approach, it has been possible to estimate costs of providing out-of-home care to different groups of children, with different needs over a specified time period (Ward *et al.* 2008). Using a decision analysis model developed for the research (the Cost Calculator for Children's Services) it has been possible to build up costs over the longer term to show different care pathways for children with differing needs and also link the costs of the care pathways to the outcomes achieved. Figure 17.1 outlines the different types of data that are used by the Cost Calculator and the outputs that are produced.

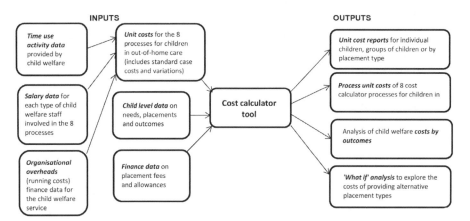

FIGURE 17.1: The cost calculator approach*
Source: reproduced from Holmes et al. (in press)

The Cost Calculator makes use of child level data, concerning needs, placements and outcomes and brings together this data with the range of unit costs outlined above. Bringing together these data items facilitates the longitudinal analysis of costs and outcomes for children placed in out-of-home care.

Analysing the care pathways of 478 children placed away from home Ward, Holmes and Soper (2008) identified that children with no evidence of additional support needs experienced fewer changes of placement. They were most likely to be placed within the area of the local authority and were also most likely to be placed either with an extended family member (kinship placement) or local authority foster carers. As such, the cost of providing out-of-home care was lower for these children. In terms of outcomes, children with no evidence of additional support needs also experienced stability in their schooling and were the most likely to achieve qualifications at the end of their statutory schooling.

As outlined above, the prevalence of emotional or behavioural difficulties was identified as a factor that impacted on the level of activity to support children in placements. Ward, Holmes and Soper (2008) found that children with evidence of emotional or behavioural difficulties were more likely to be placed in out-of-authority placements with higher fees. Furthermore, these children were also likely to have experienced shorter placements that changed frequently, both factors that have been identified as increasing costs.

The cost of providing out-of-home care was found to be highest, and the outcomes poorest, for children displaying a combination of additional needs, for example, emotional or behavioural difficulties and offending, or emotional or behavioural difficulties and a disability. In particular, those children with emotional or behavioural difficulties who had also committed a criminal offence were the most likely to experience placement instability; as such, the costs associated with finding new placements became incrementally more expensive. Children and young people with emotional or behavioural difficulties who committed criminal offences were also, on average, two years older when they started to be looked after than those children who showed no evidence of additional support needs. Furthermore, they experienced more unscheduled school changes than other children in the sample and were the most likely to leave school before the completion of their statutory education. They were also the least likely to access routine medical care, for example, dentists, and the least likely to access specialist mental health support services, often due to non-engagement with services.

The experience of this sample of children and young people reflects a complex interrelationship between: their own difficulties, the responses of professionals and the transience of their care pathway. Changes of placement were closely intertwined with changes of, or exclusions from, school and many of the young people had become alienated from services. Although as a group they accessed fewer services than children and young people without any evidence of additional support needs, the costs of placing them in out-of-home care were on average three times higher. Such care pathways are also often accompanied by a loss of self-esteem and identity (Ward, Skuse and Munro 2005).

The unit-costing approach detailed in this chapter has also been used in England to inform sustainability debates in relation to special interventions for children in out-of-home care. The approach was used to estimate the costs of providing Multi-Dimensional Treatment Foster Care in England – Adolescent programme (MTFCE-A) and compare these costs with alternative care provisions for children with similar complex needs. The research identified that the costs of MTFCE-A are comparable to other types of care and furthermore identified a reduction in overall costs when compared with placements prior to MTFCE-A (Holmes, Ward and

McDermid 2012). A summary of the costs for a sample of 22 children placed in MTFCE-A is shown in Table 17.3. This summary shows both the total cost and mean cost per child for the six month time period prior to MTFCE-A and for six months in MTFCE-A placements.

TABLE 17.3: Child welfare costs pre and during MTFCE – A placements over six-month time periods

	PRE MTFCE-A PLACEMENT (SIX-MONTH PERIOD)	DURING MTFCE-A PLACEMENT (SIX-MONTH PERIOD)
Total cost UK£ [US$]	£806,379 [$1,304,213]	£682,618 [$1,104,045]
Mean cost per child (n=22) UK£ [US$]	£36,654 [$59,283]	£31,028 [$50,184]

Being able to cost children's care pathways and link these to children's needs and the outcomes achieved makes it possible to compare the relative value, both in terms of costs and quality, of different packages of care. Using the approach outlined in this chapter, it is possible to compare the value of alternative placement options, such as providing a specialist therapeutic placement earlier in a care pathway to address specific needs and increase subsequent placement stability, or to accompany a fostering placement with extensive services from a range of agencies (see Ward *et al.* 2008 for example illustrative care pathways).

Potential application of the unit-cost method for Therapeutic Residential Care

As outlined earlier in this chapter, only a small proportion of children in out-of-home care in England are placed in children's homes, and there is evidence to indicate that placement in residential homes rather than family-based care is considered to be a last resort (Berridge *et al.* 2012; Deloitte 2007; Ward *et al.* 2008).

However, there is a recent, emerging evidence base to suggest that some local authorities are using residential care as a planned placement to meet the specific needs of a child and that the placement is viewed as an integral part of a longer care episode (Munro *et al.* 2013). There is also recognition from central government in England that children's homes offer an important placement option (Department for Education 2011).

Following the implementation of evidence-based programmes for children in out-of-home care in England, of which the focus has been placed on fostering, a number of local authorities have expressed an interest in the social learning theory underlying a number of the evidence-based programmes being extended for children's homes (Connolly *et al.* 2012). In response, a new programme has been trialled and piloted in England: an overview is provided in Box 17.2.

Box 17.2: RESuLT

RESuLT is a 12-week training programme for staff working within local authority managed children's homes using social learning theory techniques.

The main aim of the project is to develop and pilot training that focuses on how children and young people living in children's homes are helped to develop self-regulation and social skills through the methods of social learning theory. The training is based on practical examples of scenarios and situations that constitute the day-to-day working within a residential setting.

The initial trial of RESuLT in three local authorities has seen the testing of different measures to capture changes in behaviour and emotion. Data is also being collated about the number and frequency of formal sanctions, physical interventions and occurrences of children and young people going missing from placements. Furthermore, a tool has been developed to capture the experiences of staff in the children's homes. The tool comprises a number of domains including atmosphere and quality of the children's home environment and also workers experience of supervision.

The feedback to date from the local authorities involved in the trial of RESuLT has been positive (Connolly *et al.* 2012).

With this renewed impetus on the potential of residential care to be utilised as an integral part of a longer term care episode, consideration is required to ascertain whether residential care, and in particular TRC, has the potential to offer a cost-effective placement for children and young people with complex needs requiring residential provision. Furthermore, the unit-cost method outlined in this chapter could be utilised to carry out unit-cost estimations and comparisons with alternative placements for children with similar needs. These estimations would include the costs of training programme(s), the residential home running costs and ongoing support provided by child welfare workers for the children in the placements. These costs could then be linked with data on children's needs at entry to the homes and any subsequent outcomes achieved.

Conclusion

This chapter has introduced a method that has been used to estimate the unit costs of providing ongoing support and services to children in out-of-home care in England. Being able to accurately cost the ongoing support and services provided to children in out-of-home care facilitates comparisons between the relative value – both in terms of costs and quality – of different types of care and makes it easier to estimate the potential value of introducing a range of alternative packages of care. Taking a longitudinal approach and exploring how costs accrue over time, particularly when children experience placement instability, provides evidence to inform decision making in child welfare services.

Estimating Unit Costs for Therapeutic Residential Care

Lisa Holmes

This chapter by Lisa Holmes has a quiet title, but far from quiet potential to influence the conversation on both sides of the Atlantic regarding the appropriate use of TRC. From where we sit in the policy and practice context of child welfare and child mental health in the US, it is very interesting to see how Lisa Holmes and her colleagues (see also Holmes *et al.* in press) literally upend the usual approach to estimating costs of child welfare services. It is even more interesting to think about how this upended approach could change the way we understand costs *and* outcomes over time for the most complex groups of children in the system. This is a provocative piece. Let's see if we can parse it out a little.

Two generative ideas

It seems to us that there are at least two very interesting ideas within the Cost Calculator approach with particular relevance to the US context of intense scrutiny TRC. The first of these is the Core Information Requirements Process model. Lisa Holmes describes this as a kind of 'deconstruction' of out-of-home placement as a service intervention:

> The Core Information Requirements Process model…specifies the core activities that underpin the delivery of placements and services to children in out-of-home care. These activities [are] then broken down and organized into eight social care processes carried out for children placed in the care of local authorities. (p.252)

Once this is done, it is possible to look at unit service costs from a 'bottom-up' instead of essentially a snapshot approach:

> The 'bottom-up' approach identifies the constituent parts that form the delivery of a service and assigns a value to each of these parts. The sum of these values is linked with appropriate units of activity to provide the unit costs of a service. (p.251)

Beyond the clarity of measurement the Core Information Requirements Process model brings to cost, we see potential benefit in using the deconstruction approach to more sharply specify the service elements in existing as well as innovative models of TRC as we use evidence-based practices to transform TRC.

A second generative idea of the Cost Calculator as a decision analytic tool is the notion that both costs and outcomes of out-of-home placement are most usefully defined over time, just as child and family 'needs and circumstances' also vary over time. This longitudinal approach seems to us to be very beneficial to real-life practice, especially as it has the potential to inform the decidedly non-linear 'pathways of care' characterizing the experience of the highest risk young people in placement. It also enables a longer view of cost-benefit comparisons among possible helping interventions, including TRC. Lisa Holmes summarises the potential benefit of a longitudinal approach to cost-benefit comparisons this way:

> Being able to accurately cost the ongoing support and services provided to children in out-of-home care facilitates comparisons between the relative value – both in terms of cost and quality – of different types of care and makes it easier to estimate the potential value of introducing a range of alternative packages of care. Taking a longitudinal approach and exploring how costs accrue over time, particularly when children experience placement instability, provides evidence to inform decision making in child welfare services. (p.261)

Caveats and questions

The core ideas of the Cost Calculator method should be readily applicable to a range of systems of care, but there may be at least a few problems of translation to the context of TRC in the US.

The Cost Calculator as described in Lisa Holmes's chapter works least well for groups of children with multiple complex needs and circumstances, children who have experienced multiple placements and children involved with multiple helping systems beyond child welfare. In the US, insofar as there remains any place for the utilisation of therapeutic residential care, it is to serve almost exclusively this highly intensive population. We think it probable that articulating true costs (especially with multiple cost shares) and standard processes of care for this population may be easier said than done, at least for the first few iterations, as the Cost Calculator is used for cost-benefit comparisons in a very complex, multiple-service, multiple-cost environment in the US.

As noted above, we see a lot of value in establishing 'core processes of service' as a way to track costs and articulate pathways of care over time for children in placement. In addition, the eight processes of care described in this chapter seem to us to have a lot of face validity from a practice point of view. Even so, we think there may be a critical omission from the list of core processes. Actively maintaining continuity and connections between the child in care and his/her extended family and community may be as important as any other single practice and/or cost investment element in preventing multiple placements and the dire consequences of isolation in care. Successful implementation of the Cost Calculator will need to take this into account, especially as outcomes are defined in cost-benefit comparisons.

In the US, most private agencies providing TRC also provide a wide range of non-residential services to children and families. Is this an issue for the Cost Calculator, particularly regarding calculation of overhead costs? Does such potential synergy have a tendency to raise or lower rates, in general?

By acknowledging that there are groups of children for whom costs of care are both higher and highly variable, will we find ourselves expanding 'class rates', i.e. different payment rates to providers serving children with presumably highest risk at initial presentation? This seems reasonable, but might also be a slippery slope to making pathology the gateway to needed care. How does this work within the Cost Calculator approach in the UK?

Final thoughts

These questions and caveats are emphatically not meant to deter adoption of what looks to be a valuable tool. The Cost Calculator approach will require more testing to determine how broadly applicable it is to cost-benefit comparisons between and among services for the most complex groups of children, including children in TRC. It is already very interesting. Anything that makes use of child level data concerning needs, placements and outcomes, and brings these data together with rational service unit costs, should definitely get our attention as we go forward with new models of TRC built from the ground up.

ITALY: COMMENTARY BY CHIARA BERTI AND LAURA PALARETI ON:

Estimating Unit Costs for Therapeutic Residential Care

LISA HOLMES

To better cope with the task of evaluating the potential usefulness and feasibility of the costing model in Italy, we conducted a series of interviews with practitioners, policy makers and managers involved in the provision of TRC in some Italian regions. The choice of different geographical areas was justified by some general characteristics of the Italian welfare system relevant to the issue of evaluating the costs. All our interlocutors underlined the huge variability that characterises the provision of TRC in Italy, where norms are regional, welfare services can be differently organised locally and residential provisions may involve different service systems (i.e. health, justice, child and family welfare) in the management and coverage of expenses.

Before addressing the issues of utility and feasibility, we give some figures for TRC in Italy to illustrate some main differences with Anglophone countries, where residential care is used more for children with challenging behaviour or who have experienced failures in foster care.

In Italy the number of children living out of family (29,388 at 31 December 2011) is almost equally distributed between residential care and foster care, with the latter preferred for younger children. Two-thirds of those in residential services are in services identifiable as TRC (including 'family-type communities' run by adults living in), while other structures are for emergency situations or can also include adults (e.g. 'mother-child communities').

Compared with England, children in residential settings in Italy are younger (44% between 15 and 17 years old; 22.5% between 11 and 14 years old) and their permanence in the structure appears to be more stable but also very prolonged (often more than two years).

About one in three children is of foreign nationality (of which half are unaccompanied minors), while just under one in ten has some form of certified disability, mainly a mental disorder.

Fees for placements seem cheaper than in England and can vary greatly for reasons that are not always clear (certainly the geographical location and the connected logistic requests, and the specific type of service). For instance, in Emilia Romagna – where in 2009 €47 million was spent for 1804 children in residential settings – the average cost of TRC varies between €83 and €183 per day.

Feasibility

Factors favouring the transferability of the proposed methodology include the fact that the eight processes match with the constituent parts that form the delivery of residential care in Italy. More uncertainty and curiosity have been placed by some of our respondents on ease of identifying in a clear and representative way all the single activities within each process, since these will certainly be affected by the organisational configuration that the 'child welfare service' adopts in each territory and by the number and the type of services involved in the single case. In relation to this, the Cost Calculator appears easier to implement for juvenile offenders followed by the Juvenile Justice system. For them, in fact, the intervention is managed by internal operators from a specific social service that is uniform nationwide.

In general, the activities and the time devoted to them is seen as highly variable in relation to:

- type of need

- logistical conditions

- degree of collaboration

- severity of the case

- request for consultancies

- workload of the office

- individual discretion.

Beyond the technical issues, the feasibility of the method appears to be supported by the interest that our interlocutors have shown to the idea to develop the 'unit-costing approach', possibly to be experimented with by choosing carefully the child welfare services on the basis of certain elements:

1. Avoid involving services characterised by work overload and data requests also due to the presence of other initiatives.

2. Choose areas and services where projects and experimentation can then be maintained over time.

3. Choose different geographic areas.

Usefulness

First of all, usefulness of the costing model has been seen in relation to the following aims:

- To document and provide evidence of the use of the public resources.

- To develop the habit of measuring the resources used by a 'unit-costing approach' versus budget accountability.

- To enhance the awareness of the resources required for each intervention, stimulating therefore the habit to consider all the eight processes of the interventions.

- To document, analyse and explain the variability of the cost of residential projects, between and within different types of residential services.

Moreover, and specifically for the Italian system, the model can be useful to respond to some questions referring to the issues of fairness of resource allocation and criteria of social spending cuts.

In Italy, the welfare system is a public and universalistic system aimed at guaranteeing care to all citizens; it means that each request has to be accepted. Different forms of social protection historically achieved by legislation or by collective bargaining are conceived as 'rights' or entitlements, and as such are non-negotiable. Due to these features, the model could be useful to answer these questions: How fair is the allocation of resources in a universalistic system? Does the priority allocation of resources follow criteria of appropriateness?

In every country, child welfare services operate with finite resources. In Italy, due to the highest public debt of the EU members, the problem of reducing public spending is much more macroscopic and urgent than in the other EU countries, and maintaining the levels of welfare provision is a very controversial and delicate issue. Due to these circumstances, the model could be useful to cope with the questions about the criteria on which cuts in social spending are based.

To prevent and avoid the risk of using criteria imported from other fields – i.e. economic domain – or ideological criteria, without considering the relationship between need, resources and outcomes, a costing model based on the key principle of linking the costs of services with children and young people's needs and outcomes could be very useful, but with some conditions. These are related to the possibility of providing the model with informative elements for the contextual/organisational frame (see some of the sources of variability mentioned above) and for the outcomes. In relation to outcomes, for instance, the criteria of placement stability might not fit with the Italian context of residential childcare, where placements are usually more stable than in England. Otherwise, undifferentiated data on costs, irrespective of sensitive and informative elements concerning welfare policies and organisations, characteristics of the residential services, needs and outcomes, can lead to questionable conclusions and, most of all, lead to the unreasonable consequence of reducing the resources that should be devoted to good TRC.

On balance, we believe that the method of calculating unit costs presented in the chapter offers the possibility to have a clear depiction of the way in which resources are devolved, especially in cases where the cost of each intervention is not generally calculated but only the global amount of the resources allocated, and overall a stimulus to quality and equity in the allocation of human and financial resources.

SCOTLAND: COMMENTARY BY ANDREW KENDRICK ON:

Estimating Unit Costs for Therapeutic Residential Care

Lisa Holmes

The costs and expense of residential child care have been an issue for many years and have been a significant factor in the shift in emphasis away from residential care to foster care. Almost 50 years ago, Roy Parker noted that there was 'the happy coincidence that the most desirable provision was for once the most economical' (Parker 1966, p.19). As the methods of costing social work services has become more sophisticated, the more simplistic estimates of comparative costs have been revised and account has been taken of direct and indirect costs and the varying needs of children and young people, leading Davies and Knapp (1988) to conclude that comparative costs of residential and foster care are closer than previous estimates. Of course, the primary placement is only one aspect of the services that a child or young person will receive, and Lisa Holmes's chapter focuses on the development of a broader method for estimating unit costs of services in placing children away from home. This model was developed in England and the chapter provides contextual information on looked-after children and residential care in England.

One of the interesting features of the child welfare system in the UK, however, is the difference across the jurisdictions of the UK (England, Wales, Northern Ireland and Scotland), particularly with the recent focus on devolution (Mainey *et al.* 2006). The unique role of the Children's Hearings system in Scotland (Children's Hearings Scotland: www.chscotland.gov.uk), or the much higher contribution of the private sector to residential child care sector feature in England (Berridge *et al.* 2012), will impact on the unit costs of social work services and processes across the different jurisdictions. This said, however, the broad outline of processes for children placed in out-of-home care are common across the UK, and the fact that the conceptual framework outlined by Holmes involves a 'bottom-up' approach, identifying the constituent parts that form the delivery of a service and assigning a value to each of these parts, means that such differences will be taken account of in the model.

A crucial aspect of this model is its potential to link the costs of children's care pathways to their needs and outcomes. We can see that the costing models have identified the importance of taking account of children and young people's needs. The link to outcomes is also a crucial step forward because, as Holmes points out, this makes it possible to compare the relative value of children's social work services in terms of both costs and quality.

Audit Scotland (2010, p.29) highlighted that the cost of residential child care placements in Scotland is high and has been increasing over recent years. Three factors are identified as contributing to this:

1. The greater and more complex needs of children placed in the independent sector.

2. Developments in quality to meet national care standards, including improvements to accommodation and facilities.

3. Increased requirements in staff training and qualifications.

However, it also identified the lack of information about detailed costs of residential child care in Scotland, and it suggested that councils could find the Cost Calculator model useful. Audit Scotland, particularly, noted the importance of the links between costs, quality and effectiveness and the current lack of such information:

> Councils cannot be assured that they are achieving value for money as there is insufficient clarity about the quality of services and outcomes and the costs of all types of provision available. (Audit Scotland 2010, p.34)

This lack of clarity about the costs of children's services was also identified by the National Residential Child Care Initiative in Scotland, which stated that 'the development of a strategic commissioning framework will facilitate the delivery of "best value" through achieving the best outcomes while managing costs' (Bayes 2009, p.16). This work is currently being taken forward by Scottish Government and one aspect has been the development of a national framework for the provision of purchased children's residential care services. The consultation exercise on the proposed framework, however, highlighted ongoing tensions between different sectors in children's social work services as to how this would be best taken forward (Scotland Excel 2013). Given this, developing the model of calculating the cost of children's services for use in Scotland seems timely.

The ambivalence around the role of residential child care is touched on in Holmes's chapter, and this is an ongoing issue across the UK and internationally. The use of residential care as a last resort, as opposed to a planned and integrated element of a package of care services, has bedevilled the sector for many years (Kendrick 1995, 2008). An important aspect of this has concerned the varying quality of residential care services (Kendrick 2012), along with the problem of abuse in care (Kendrick 1998). The importance of the cost model is in identifying the costs and effectiveness of residential child care in the context of the full continuum of care services and the specific packages of care required to address the needs of individual children. While Holmes focuses on outlining the potential of the cost model in relation to a particular intervention in residential child care – RESuLT – one of the strengths of the model would appear to be in how it could address broader developments in TRC – those, for example, that have focused on the importance of relationships in care (Kendrick 2013). The development of social pedagogy in residential care in the UK needs further research and evaluation, as do resilience models of care (Kendrick 2012). It would seem that the model of costing of services outlined by Holmes in this chapter would be an important element in developing the evidence base for high-quality and effective residential care and positive outcomes for children and young people.

*AUSTRALIA: COMMENTARY BY FRANK AINSWORTH
AND DEIRDRE CHEERS ON:*

Estimating Unit Costs for Therapeutic Residential Care

LISA HOLMES

This chapter usefully outlines the outcomes of England's decade-long initiative in relation to the costs and effectiveness of services for children in need (Department of Health 2001a) and children in care (Beecham and Sinclair 2007). The conceptual map provided in Figure 17.1 in this chapter details the model and is highly commendable. The identification of eight child welfare processes undertaken by caseworkers in relation to children and young people in out-of-home care as shown in Table 17.1 is exhaustive. The simple and complex group characteristics of children and young people in care as reported in Box 17.1 also reflects the experience of the field.

A potential limitation of the approach used to identify the child welfare process (namely focus groups with frontline practitioners) in relation to the Australian context is that it may not reflect the actual day-to-day events that occur in a residential care placement, other than direct care staffing costs. Residential care is used less in Australia than in the UK, with limited availability of therapeutic programs, and the cost and effectiveness of TRC must account for the 24/7 nature of the service because effective TRC involves using the full range of everyday activities that occur in the residential setting to promote behaviour change (Ainsworth 2007). What therefore will be necessary is a similar data-collection process involving residential direct care practitioners to further refine Process Three – 'maintaining a placement' – and to develop a similar set of processes for use in the costing of TRC in the Australian setting.

Barriers to implementation

This costing model requires foster and residential care agencies to have well-established, comprehensive systems that collect accurate placement and outcome data, which is also able to be connected to direct costs of care. Whilst some Australian Government attempts have been made to determine unit costs for out-of-home care (Boston Consulting 2009; Ernst & Young 2010), these have generally been based on the mixed caseloads of statutory workers comprising both child-protection and out-of-home care cases and do not constitute a consistent 'bottom-up' approach such as that outlined by Holmes in this chapter. Barnardo's Australia is the only non-government out-of-home care agency known to have undertaken extensive costing work (in its permanent care programs, known as Find A Family) based on a time and motion 'bottom-up' approach (O'Neill *et al.* 2009).

In New South Wales (NSW) where the current policy direction is for outsourcing of all out-of-home care to non-government organisations, a unit price for all forms of foster and residential care is in place. Whilst, in principle the available unit cost was tested via the Ernst & Young project, concern exists that the available price was fixed based on the Government's ability to pay rather than the actual cost of these services in relation to outcomes for children in care.

The current NSW Family and Community Services placement classification system (general foster care, general foster care +1 and +2, intensive foster care, standard residential care and intensive residential care) is based on assessment of child need via application of a Child Assessment Tool (CAT) first developed by the US Annie E. Casey Foundation for Cuyahoga County in Cleveland Ohio. A file/desk-based assessment is undertaken for the child using the CAT tool to ostensibly assess behavioural indicators for placement type. The CAT assessment is then used to assign the relevant unit cost for indicated care placement. No mechanism exists to link the CAT assessment to child outcomes of care. Implementation of the CAT assessment system in NSW is a deterrent to ongoing work on accurate costing systems, since no matter how well a non-government agency can demonstrate costs greater than the fee for service using a 'bottom-up' (or any other) approach, no additional payments are easily made other than via manual override of the CAT assessment by a statutory worker. Also, the NSW unit cost for out-of-home care is not linked to any research on service effectiveness or evidence of outcomes for children and young people in care.

This is the difficulty we have in considering the use of this model in Australia. To date, we know of no agency in NSW, nor anywhere else in Australia, that has in place a cost and outcomes related data collection system. In our view, the development of such systems requires a substantial period of time and a significant input of resources, which is not currently available to out-of-home care agencies for either service delivery or research related to the costs of out-of-home care. At present there are no signs that such an initiative is under consideration anywhere in Australia.

Other issues

Beyond the outlining of the much-to-be-praised costing model, the chapter has less to offer. Table 17.2 that compares unit costs of two types of foster care placements with a residential placement reflects clearly that the costs of Process Three – 'maintaining the placement' – are considerably more for residential care than foster care; however, this is self-evident given that residential placement involves the much greater costs of rotating shift staff as compared with allowances paid to foster carers.

In addition, there is US research that points to the fact that a higher expenditure on a care placement (in this instance foster care) can lead to better outcomes for children and young people than a cheaper alternative (Kessler *et al.* 2008). Knowing the cost of care is vital information, but it does not in the end remove the need for careful judgement about which services will meet the needs of children and young people in care and most importantly produce the best life outcomes.

It is also interesting to hear of the English Government's support for a social learning theory programme RESuLT (Connolly *et al.* 2012) for residential staff. Substantial research literature exists about the teaching-parent model based on social learning theory that is in use in some notable US residential programs for children and young persons (Fixsen *et al.* 2007). This is but one residential programme model worthy of reconsideration alongside new developments that this volume will hopefully encourage.

Linking Focused Training and Critical Evaluation in Therapeutic Residential Care

A Foundation for Staff Support

Helping Staff to Connect Quality, Practice and Evaluation in Therapeutic Residential Care
The SERAR Model in Spain

Amaia Bravo, Jorge F. del Valle and Iriana Santos

Introduction

Since the middle of the 1990s, a systematic approach to residential care has been developed in Spain with the aim of helping social educators to plan the interventions (Individualised Intervention Plan) that each child may need. This includes evaluating the progression towards objectives and any resulting changes and producing monitoring reports that are the basis for decision making regarding children in residential care.

The original proposal for this system was published by del Valle (1998) to be implemented in one of Spain's 17 autonomous communities (Spain has a very decentralised administrative structure, with 17 autonomous communities or regions, each with its own parliament and government having, among other things, jurisdiction over the organisation of all social services). The significant gap that this system plugged led to its rapid application during the following decade in other communities in Spain, as well as the development of specific adaptations for children aged between 0 and 6, unaccompanied asylum seeking children and emergency children's homes.

This system was created in an attempt to link educational practice with a theoretical model that substantiated the relevance of the constructs that were to be the target of evaluation and intervention. To that end, it began with a conceptual theory based on social learning, in particular, in line with the psychological evaluation model created by Fernández-Ballesteros and Staats (1992) and with the ecology of human development (Bronfenbrenner 1979). These models permit a clear definition of the different factors that play a part in the explanation of behaviours, as well as placing them in the framework of the development contexts in which they occur. In this way, social educators (in Spain, in order to work as a residential worker one must first obtain a degree following four years of study; the qualification is called *Educador Social*, literally 'social educator') are able to have both a theoretical and practical framework for planning evaluations and interventions.

This is the origin of SERAR (Sistema de Evaluación y Registro en Acogimiento Residencial – Assessment and Recording System in Residential Child Care), the name that has been used for the system since the publication of the latest version (del Valle and Bravo 2007).

Structure of SERAR

The instruments that make up SERAR allow the systematisation of the educational intervention process. It introduces a basic intervention process (common to other social interventions), which starts with a needs assessment, followed by scheduling the individual intervention, recording the intervention, monthly evaluation of results and a monitoring report. In short, this system was created in an attempt to introduce a systematic approach to the work of social educators, facilitating the development of individual schedules and evaluations, based on the needs and strengths of the child being dealt with.

To that end, SERAR covers each of the phases in the educative intervention process.

Initial assessment

It is important to have an initial assessment of the strengths and needs of the child to begin the intervention and establish objectives. Therefore the system includes an instrument with which the social educator responsible for the case (the key social educator) summarises the information from initial admission reports and data obtained in the first month of placement in the children's home. This collection of information allows the educators to establish a starting point from which to plan the intervention.

Planning

Once the needs assessment for each child is complete and the case plan is understood, the social educators have to produce the individual intervention schedule. This schedule is reflected in the Individualised Intervention Plan (IIP), which is produced by the key social educator with the help of the rest of the social education team and with the participation of the children according to their age and level of development. This instrument details the following: high priority objectives, strategies and activities to progress, the resources needed and the method of evaluating the results. The schedule must be flexible enough to be adapted to any changes in each case. Furthermore, it must be kept current and revised monthly (by the team with the participation of the children) and be filed together with the rest of the documentation.

Intervention

The intervention itself is developed by the professionals making use of the daily routine activities and using the resources of the community. Records of strategies used are kept in the system, as are records of any changes made in each development context (this will be explained later).

Evaluation

From the moment an initial assessment is made and a subsequent intervention process carried out, it is necessary to evaluate any progress. The system recommends a monthly review starting with evaluation and registration instruments that cover the life contexts surrounding the children. These evaluations facilitate the creation of the monitoring reports, which are given to the regional child care authorities twice a year, as required by law.

The cycle of socio-educative intervention can be described as a feedback loop such that the evaluation serves to provide new data to revise the initial assessment and therefore modify the IIP. To put it briefly, it emphasises that the intervention cycle is always active, that some of the phases lead to the execution of others and that, above all, intervention in a child's life is based on consideration and planning.

In order to assist in compliance with each of the phases of the intervention process, SERAR is made up of the following three instruments: the Cumulative record, the IIP and the monitoring report.

The Cumulative record

This document is designed to record the most important information about a child, both with respect to the child's background and anything relevant that might be happening during his/her stay in the children's home. It allows all of the information about the child to be compiled in a single document so that it is more accessible, systematically organised and easy to consult, communicate and keep.

The cumulative record is, in fact, a monitoring system – an instrument for permanently collecting information that allows the reconstruction of the procedures followed in the evolution of each case. The structure of the record includes sections to record information about the child's interactions in each of the social contexts they are in, which would be microsystems according to the model of Bronfenbrenner (1979):

- The family is one of the most important contexts, as has already been shown in the scientific literature. Contact with, and links to the family are essential (unless the interests of the child suggest otherwise), both because of the affective role of these relationships and the need for family cooperation in the process, especially when the end goal is family reunification. This section is used to record basic family data and history (employment, housing, family composition, etc.) and particularly visits and contact with the child.

- The school context is relevant to every child, but in the case of those children who have been abused or neglected, there are usually numerous problems that hinder their school performance. This section is used to record academic grades and information from monitoring visits to teachers (behaviour, incidents, etc.).

- The residential context is supposed to be a context of integration, in which the child learns and puts into practice rules, the experience of shared living arrangements, affective relationships, chores and responsibilities. Similarly, the record collects whatever information is relevant (changes of educators, changes in the residential group, incidents, etc.).

- The community context is essential. One of the specific difficulties experienced by children in residential care is the establishment of a social support network that could facilitate their steps towards autonomy and social inclusion (Bravo and del Valle 2001). Therefore, it is important to observe these children's relationships with their peers and with adults outside the care context. This section records leisure or formative activities in the community and any other important incidents.

- The work context is only applicable to adolescents who are getting their first experience in this area or who are receiving specific training to join the job market within a short timeframe. This section is used to record their attainment and qualifications as well as their work experience.

In addition, a section of the cumulative record includes a place to record all of the incidents and interventions related to a child's health and development. This is a very important aspect, considering that the conditions of the previous family environment will often have provoked physical and psychological illnesses or disorders that will need treating, not forgetting preventative care and the check-ups performed on the general population during infancy and adolescence (vaccinations, developmental check-ups, etc.).

Individualised Intervention Plan

The system includes a model of an individualised plan that supports the phases of initial assessment, planning and evaluation of the educative intervention. The document is divided into three parts.

- A summary evaluation of development, adaptation and social integration. Before defining objectives, it is necessary to assess each child's specific needs and characteristics. This information comes from two sources: reports from childcare professionals and the educator's own observations during the month after the child is admitted. A summary of the results of this evaluation, referring to the individual development dimensions (cognitive, affective, social and physical) and of social adaptation and integration in each of the contexts (family, school/training, residential, community and work) is recorded in the first part of the document.

- Objective planning template. This initial evaluation results in the establishment of the objectives that are considered a priority in each case. In the second part of the IIP there is a table where the educative team notes these objectives (in an operational manner) and the resources needed and strategies that will be employed to achieve them (always in accordance with the fundamental guidelines of the Case Plan, which come from the regional child care authorities).

• List of monthly evaluation of objectives. Finally, the instrument includes a list of 114 objectives, divided by contexts (each with its own assessment areas), which must be assessed monthly by each child's group of educators (Table 18.1). The objectives are formulated in an operational manner, so that they may be assessed by the educators through observation, using a five-point Likert scale. This evaluation means a continuous check on each child's progress and allows the establishment of working objectives that support the individual plan. As the progress towards each objective is assessed monthly, the educators are able periodically to revise the plan and any strategies being used in the intervention. The following section explains the process of constructing and validating this instrument.

TABLE 18.1: Contexts and assessment areas in the list of objectives in the Individualised Intervention Plan

CONTEXTS	ASSESSMENT AREAS	
Family	Relations between child and family Family cooperation Work with the family	
School/training	Social integration Interest in learning	
Residential	Personal autonomy	Personal obligations and care Diet Homework Management of resources and independence
	Adaptation	Social integration Disposition to learn and participate
Community	Integration into the community	
Work	Pre-work Work	

Monitoring report

Finally, SERAR includes a script for the preparation of monitoring reports, which covers the evaluation of each context. This report model is one of the strong points of the system because it makes the systematisation and summarisation of relevant information related to a specific time period much easier. The social educators are required to obtain this information for the regional child care authorities and, where necessary, for other agencies such as the Fiscalía de Menores (a part of the Attorney General's department, which is responsible for safeguarding the rights of children in care in Spain), which requires periodic monitoring information about the child and the intervention process.

Construction and validation of the objective evaluation system

This evaluation system was created during the mid-1990s. It combined the work of children's homes staff and child care professionals. The goal was to reach a consensus on the constructs that would require assessment in order to deal with them operationally as observable behaviours that educators might easily assess in a child's daily life. This led to the creation of an inventory of behaviours that children should demonstrate and develop to indicate good growth and social development.

A factorial analysis was performed on the resulting initial group of items using scores obtained in the pilot study. These initial results allowed the division of the list of objectives into different sections referring to the child's social integration in family, residential-community, school and work contexts. At the same time, each of these sections was sub-divided into more specific areas, giving rise to the 14 groups of objectives or areas (Table 18.1).

This structure was revised again following the system's implementation in four autonomous communities in Spain. A new factorial validation of the list was carried out using a sample of 673 children in residential care (Bravo *et al.* 2002). At the same time, a study of the content validity was performed that analysed the relevance of each objective in evaluating the construct (suitability), the real possibility of obtaining information to evaluate the objective (feasibility) and its usefulness in carrying out the intervention process with each child (Bravo *et al.* 2004). This study was carried out by means of a jury of experts made up of 69 child care professionals.

The research performed in those years allowed the validation of the structure of the list and confirmed the adequacy of the theoretical model that lay behind its creation. In addition, some modifications were made that improved the internal consistency of the sub-lists, with alpha values between 0.83 and 0.94.

The results of this new analysis gave rise to the structure that was published in a manual (del Valle and Bravo 2007) that included a list of 114 objectives divided into 14 areas (see Table 18.1) referring to children's behaviour in five social contexts: family, residential, community, school and work. The 2007 model also included the three adaptations that had been developed in 2001 for children between the ages of 0 and 6, unaccompanied asylum seeking children and emergency children's homes.

Method and operation of SERAR

Having described the structure and construction of this system, it is important to highlight some guidelines for its use, which are key to ensuring its utility.

In the first place, there must be one instrument per child. Each child must have a SERAR in which all of the information with respect to their case is recorded, including plans and evaluations that are underway. This document will not only permit the child's history to be preserved, but will also allow communication between the different professionals who come into contact with the case.

Although the documents must be available to the entire educative team in order for them to understand the guidelines of the intervention and to be aware of the child's needs, only one educator – the child's key social educator – should be in charge of maintaining and updating the SERAR.

Another fundamental cornerstone in the development of an IIP is that the evaluation must not be carried out solely by the child's key social educator; other educators working with the child must be present during the evaluation so that the monthly assessment and revision of the plan may be performed by a team.

Finally, children have a fundamental right to participate in the decisions that concern them. In this case, the child must be involved in his/her evaluations and in the working goals that are included in the plan. This is especially important in adolescence, where this participation can encourage links with the educator and provoke the youngster's own consideration of his/her situation and the decisions that will have to be made about the future.

Implementation of SERAR

Currently, this evaluation and record system has been implemented in 9 of the 17 autonomous communities in Spain and has been translated and adapted for use in some Portuguese regions. Additionally, the system has been adapted for the foster family programme (SERAF) and is currently being implemented in two Spanish regions.

The implementation of SERAR requires an initial process of training and supervision to ensure its functionality and efficacy. The first step is to agree its implementation in the entire network of residential child care in a particular area, since it is a model of work that will influence the dynamic of the whole child care system. The next step is for all of the educative teams to receive training in the theoretical model underpinning the system, its usefulness and the method of employing each instrument. The rules of residential care are revised in these sessions, keeping in mind quality criteria, evaluation procedures, intervention techniques and considering the role these programmes play in the welfare system. The theoretical foundation of SERAR is also described, including its functions and structure, and each of the instruments is exhaustively gone through. This second part is very practical, involving exercises and exploring the possible difficulties that may crop up in each team.

Approximately six months on from the training and initial use of SERAR, follow-up visits are made to the social educator teams in each children's home. A professional who specialises in the use of SERAR meets with each team in two-hour sessions, checking how the instruments have been completed, answering any questions and solving any problems that may have surfaced. After this first follow-up visit the professionals prepare a report on the level of implementation at that time, and they give guidelines for any changes to be made and plan a second follow-up visit approximately six months later. For the second follow-up the teams are asked to send the SERAR documents they have been working with before the session itself. During the sessions these documents are used to correct deviations from proper use and answer any questions. Occasionally, depending on the regional authority responsible for initiating the system, additional follow-ups may be carried out after some months or even up to a year later.

In this way, the implementation of SERAR is overseen by specialised professionals for between one and two years. These professionals produce an evaluation at the end of the implementation based on the standard of the implementation in each children's home. In addition, from the moment when the educative teams begin working with the system, online support is available on the web to clarify questions and resolve issues related to SERAR without the need to wait for the follow-ups with the specialists.

This entire process ensures that SERAR is used in the same way in each of the facilities and regions in which it is implemented, guaranteeing its functionality and maintaining its structure, both of which have already been validated.

Utility of SERAR as a programme evaluation instrument

In addition to the acknowledged usefulness of this system in the systematisation and facilitation of educative work in residential child care, in recent years there have been various reports on outcomes assessment in residential care based on compliance with the objectives recorded in SERAR. In this way, SERAR has become established as a fundamental tool in the evaluation of these types of programmes in view of the results that have been achieved.

The systematic collection of data on children's progression towards objectives from their admission and throughout their stay has detected areas that are more and less sensitive to educative intervention.

One of the first pieces of research was carried out by Bravo and del Valle (2001), who detected significant gaps in the progression towards objectives related to family cooperation, educative strategies and care. In this research they also found low levels of success in achieving objectives related to community integration. Both of these findings have been replicated in subsequent research, reflected in unpublished reports. This hints at the difficulties that still persist in achieving family reunification and social integration in normalised contexts. At the same time, this research uncovered very good results regarding objectives related to autonomy and adaptation to the residential context. It is within the context of a child's living arrangements where the educator is best able to control the conditions that affect the child's development.

In the research carried out by Martín, Rodríguez and Torbay (2007), SERAR was used to study the progress of a sample of 175 children towards objectives during nine months. They found significant progress, although it was influenced by factors such as the reason for admission and the total time of stay in residential care.

Other research has, in a similar way, used SERAR records to evaluate the level of integration of children in the school environment (Martín, Torbay and Rodríguez *et al.* 2008), to analyse the relationship between self-perceived failure to adapt in children in care and the levels of adaptation measured by the educators in SERAR (Martín, García and Siverio 2012), and the development of links between a child and their family and the cooperation of that family with the children's home during the stay (Martín *et al.* 2008).

To put it briefly, although SERAR was developed as a support system for educative work carried out by professionals in residential care, as a monitoring system it provides an extremely useful database that strengthens research into these types of programmes. Despite the fact that in Spain, residential care, together with kinship care, is the main method used in caring for children, there is scarcely any culture of programme evaluation that examines its efficacy. SERAR allows the analysis of interventions carried out as part of these programmes and examines outcomes in very large samples, as it is a system that is used in more than half the residential facilities in the country.

COMMENTARY BY MARTHA J. HOLDEN ON:

Helping Staff to Connect Quality, Practice and Evaluation in Therapeutic Residential Care: The SERAR Model in Spain

AMAIA BRAVO, JORGE F. DEL VALLE AND IRIANA SANTOS

In this chapter, the authors, Bravo, del Valle and Santos describe a purposefully designed assessment and recording system, SERAR, as an innovative model for helping social educators connect quality, practice and evaluation in TRC in Spain. SERAR was designed to link social educators' practice to a theoretical model and provide a data system that would support a systematic approach to residential work that covers all phases of the residential intervention. The system includes an instrument that the residential worker uses to: make an initial assessment; create an individualised plan that sets objectives, strategies and identifies needed resources; track interventions and evaluate progress; and facilitate the creation of monitoring reports that allow workers to meet regulatory reporting requirements. This system was developed and validated by child care professionals and assesses and monitors children in residential care within 14 groups of objectives.

This sophisticated system raises an important workforce issue. In Spain, residential workers are required to have a four-year degree that gives them the theoretical and practical framework for assessing and planning interventions as well as evaluating progress toward meeting established goals. Without this level of education and expertise, it would be difficult to implement such a system at the direct care level. For example, in the United States, there are very few educational requirements for residential workers, and high levels of turnover result in a workforce with a deficit of theoretical information and limited practice experience.

The implementation of SERAR requires an organizational commitment and the cooperation of the entire network of residential child care in a community. By its very nature of identifying needs in all of the domains of the child's life – school, community, family, work and residence – this comprehensive data system may quickly expose limitations of basic resources and/or practice barriers needed to meet the child and family's needs. The ability of practitioners within the residential programme, as well as practitioners across programmes, to work as a team to provide necessary services could be challenging. The difficulties of introducing centralised and comprehensive systems within de-centralised child welfare systems are documented in the North American literature by Butler, Little and Grimard (2009).

In addition to its original purpose, SERAR has proven to be useful as a database to evaluate residential programmes and strengthen research efforts. This field is in great need of research that not only provides evidence of effectiveness, but also information that can point to specific areas in which additional resources and development can be targeted to improve the quality of care and services to children and families. SERAR records have been used to evaluate children's outcomes based on a standard set of objectives, identify areas that have low levels of success in achieving desired outcomes and isolate factors that contribute to successful outcomes. These types of studies can contribute to a more precise understanding of the critical components of TRC that can then be evaluated and compared with other evidence-based intervention alternatives.

CHAPTER 19

A European Perspective on the Context and Content for Social Pedagogy in Therapeutic Residential Care

Hans Grietens

Some general reflections about social pedagogy and social pedagogues

Social pedagogy is a profession and academic discipline in Continental Europe and Scandinavia. In some countries (e.g. Germany) it is part of social work, in others (e.g. the Netherlands, Spain) of pedagogy and educational sciences. Residential child care is one of the major fields of practice that social pedagogues are involved in. Social pedagogues working in residential children's homes have a Bachelor degree and are employed as group care workers. They live together with the children on a daily basis. Social pedagogues with a Master's degree are employed as staff members in children's homes. They coordinate care plans, supervise teams of group care workers and have supportive contacts with the children's families.

The work of social pedagogues may significantly contribute to the success of residential placements of children and youth. They are direct agents of change through the daily activities they do with the minor residents and the relationships they build up with them. By supervising teams of group care workers, coordinating treatment plans and providing support to parents, social pedagogues in staff positions may be indirect agents of change.

Social pedagogy is recognized in several countries in Continental Europe and Scandinavia, both as a profession and an academic discipline. It is well implemented in the practice and policy of child welfare in these countries. Social pedagogues matter. Their role is visible and adds to the roles of other professionals involved in the system (e.g. social workers, nurses, psychologists, therapists, child psychiatrists, etc.). Where social pedagogues are employed in children's homes, the discourse on residential care is positive and hopeful (Smith 2009). Social pedagogy does not exist as a discipline and profession in the Anglo-Saxon world, for instance in the United Kingdom, United States, Canada and Australia. This raises the question of whether the ideas and practice of social pedagogy need to be exported and implemented in these countries. For more than a decade, efforts have been undertaken by different research groups to "translate" social pedagogical ideas, to inform professionals and policymakers about social pedagogy being a necessary step towards a successful residential care practice and to evaluate the implementation of social pedagogy programs (see e.g. Berridge *et al.* 2011; Bird and Eichsteller 2011; Cameron and Moss 2011; Gharabaghi and Groskleg 2010).

The aim of this chapter is to critically analyze the context and content of social pedagogy in Therapeutic Residential Care (TRC) by conducting a SWOT analysis. We will discuss strengths, weaknesses, opportunities and threats of social pedagogy with regard to TRC. The analysis will be preceded by a presentation of the core elements ("building blocks") of social pedagogy in children's residential homes. We believe this chapter will help to clarify the theoretical underpinnings of our analysis and contextualize the results. At the end of the chapter, we will formulate concluding remarks about how social pedagogy may serve TRC and what its limits are.

Definitions of social pedagogy vary widely across countries and there is a wealth of literature on what should be considered the subject of the discipline. Social pedagogy has a long history in Europe, with roots going back to 18th century educational philosophy of Enlightenment. A discussion about the definitions of social pedagogy and the complexity of its subject is beyond the scope of this contribution. In this chapter we will stick to widely accepted and commonly used definitions and viewpoints that are reported in recent literature. According to Hämäläinen (2003), for instance, social pedagogy concentrates "on questions of the integration of the individual in society; both in theory and in practice," the basic idea being "to promote people's social functioning, inclusion, participation, social identity and social competence as members of society" and dealing "with the processes of human growth that tie people to the systems, institutions and communities that are important to their well-being and life management" (p.76). Social pedagogy is about the development, growth and upbringing of children and includes an education component. The word "education," however, is richer of meaning than in the Anglo-Saxon speaking countries, where its use is restricted to learning and the school setting. Social pedagogy is about education with the head, hands and heart (Stephens 2009). Moreover, education goes hand in hand with care, and both serve the child's development and well-being.

We will adopt a European perspective throughout our analysis, as social pedagogy exists in different countries on the continent (Petrie *et al.* 2006). At the same time, we are aware of the risk that taking such a perspective involves. Notwithstanding a common history and a common ethic influenced by Judeo-Christian tradition, Europe is a patchwork—a loose collection of regions, cultures and laws, without a common language (Grietens 2013). Although European institutions and bodies have formulated guidelines to standardize good child care practices and protect the rights of children in care (see e.g. Council of Europe 2006, 2009), there is no common European policy of child welfare. Child welfare systems, policies and programs across Europe differ, as do discourses and figures about children and young people in residential care (see e.g. Ainsworth and Thoburn 2013; Ezell *et al.* 2011; Gilbert, Parton and Skivenes 2011). A European perspective implies that we will use the core construct of our chapter—"social pedagogy"—in a rather abstract way and disregard the local "flavor" of the profession and discipline. Local flavor will come in, however, when we refer to studies conducted in one country or a specific region. For this reason, we invite the reader to consult comparative and critical literature on social pedagogy in Europe (e.g. Kornbeck 2009; Lorenz 1994; Petrie *et al.* 2009) in order to contextualize the studies we present in this chapter.

Building blocks of a social pedagogy in children's residential homes

Throughout the years, social pedagogues have developed a large number of theoretical models on children's functioning and well-being and these models have been applied in various ways to residential care work with children. Summarizing seminal articles and reviews on this subject (see among others Benggtson *et al.* 2008; Macdonald and Millen 2012; Petrie *et al.* 2006; Stephens 2013), the following building blocks of a social pedagogical approach with regard to high-resource using children and youth in residential homes can be identified: daily life is the most important context of change and the approach can be characterized as systemic, relational and contextual, needs-based and strengths-based.

Daily life is the most important context of change

Social pedagogy considers daily life as the primary context of change and adopts a "lifeworld orientation" (Grunwald and Thiersch 2009). In residential homes, children spend most of their time in groups. Direct work in the group takes a central place in the treatment plans. The children and the group care workers do not simply live together. The group is a gestalt—a haven where the children are looked after and learn, with each other, from each other and from their group care workers who function as models and mentors. The daily life in group is a vehicle for change and offers the children a sense of rhythm, structure, rules and discipline, but also compassion, safety, trust and belonging. Situations and activities in daily life (e.g. cooking, cleaning, playing) are used to train children and "teach" them new skills and competencies. In this sense, social pedagogy is about the "other 23 hours," supporting the ideas of milieu-therapy (Trieschman, Whittaker and Brendtro 1969).

A systemic, relational and contextual approach

Social pedagogical models can be characterized as relational. Children are seen as actors in relationships with caretakers, siblings, peers, teachers, etc. Relations are embedded in larger systems, for instance the family, classroom, group, which, in turn, are part of larger contexts (e.g. schools, services). Relationships are considered to be bidirectional and transactional with all actors influencing each other. The main aim of group care work is to increase the quality of children's relationships and to reconnect them to their environment. Modifying children's environments and their relatedness to environment is supposed to have a direct impact on their functioning and well-being. Both the stress on relationships and the idea that daily life is the most important context of change mean that relational climate in children's residential homes is considered to have a significant impact on outcomes of care, either as a moderator or a mediator, as is perceived support by staff and peers (Palareti and Berti 2009b).

A needs-based approach

Social pedagogical models are child-oriented. In the evaluation of interventions, children's development and well-being are considered to be primary outcome variables. Deficits and problems of children (e.g. developmental delay, behavioral problems) are reframed in terms of special needs (e.g. medical needs, needs to be disciplined in a non-coercive way, to be listened to). Interventions are designed to meet these needs. Needs assessment is conducted to learn what the special needs of children are and how they can be addressed in a way that makes children thrive and feel well. There is a growing interest among practitioners and researchers to include looked-after children's perspectives in needs-assessment procedures, as children are well placed when it comes to the articulation of (special) needs (Winter 2006). Needs of children living in residential homes correspond with needs of children in the general population, but they may also differ because of the adverse conditions they have been living in, the out-of-home placement and the moves in care. Children in homes may have specific needs regarding contact with the family of origin and siblings, understanding of their history, health (in case of physical and medical neglect), etc. Dealing with loss and trauma, they need to get control over their lives, to feel respected by trustful adult caregivers and to give meaning to their past (Rivard *et al.* 2004; Zelechoski *et al.* 2013).

A strengths-based approach

Social pedagogues aim to address children's strengths. Problems and deficits are not ignored and psychopathology is acknowledged, but a "truly" social pedagogical approach is focusing on the child's overall development and well-being. It is not children's problems and deficits, but their competencies and growth potential that are the starting point of intervention. Social pedagogues are deeply convicted that every child has at least one talent and one competence. Acknowledging and continuously rewarding looked-after children's talents and competencies in daily life may pave the way to success. Looked-after children with a history characterized by adversity and trauma may be disempowered, have lost belief in their talents and competencies and distrust others. Trauma-related symptoms and emotional and behavioral problems may overshadow normal development, but social pedagogues try to look behind the child's overt problems.

In addition, it may be obvious that social pedagogy is not carried out in a vacuum. Models about the functioning and well-being of children and youth evolve under the influence of theories from (related) disciplines and changing discourses in child welfare policy and practice. The mental health and in particular the "trauma lens" approach towards looked-after children, for instance, has affected the implementation of social pedagogical models. Similarly, results from affective neurosciences need to be integrated in the models (e.g. Ko *et al.* 2008; Tarren-Sweeney and Vetere 2013). Both the "trauma lens" and the neurosciences approach have been helpful to social pedagogues working in residential children's homes and increased their understanding of what needs-based and a strengths-based approaches may imply.

Can social pedagogy serve Therapeutic Residential Care? A SWOT analysis

In this volume, TRC is defined as:

> ...the planful use of a purposefully constructed, multi-dimensional living environment designed to enhance or provide treatment, education, socialization, support and protection to children and youth with identified mental health or behavioral needs in partnership with their families and in collaboration with a full spectrum of community-based formal and informal helping resources. (Whittaker, del Valle and Holmes, Chapter 1, this volume, p.24)

Can social pedagogy serve TRC? In a certain sense, this question is tautological. First, by definition, a social pedagogical approach includes a therapeutic perspective. The child's direct milieu is involved in the treatment plan to initiate and sustain change. The conceptualization of social pedagogy in residential child care comes close to what in some countries is called "milieu-therapy" (Broekaert *et al.* 2009). Second, in several countries there is a long tradition of therapeutic practice in children's residential homes, which is inspired by social pedagogy. This is, for instance, the case in the Netherlands, Belgium (Flanders), Germany and Spain (see del Valle, Sainero and Bravo, Chapter 3, this volume).

The target group of TRC—children and youth with identified mental health or behavioral needs—however, is a complex one and raises the question about whether we fully reach this group by adopting a social pedagogical approach. What is the potential and what are the limits of social pedagogy in this context? A critical analysis of social pedagogy's potential in TRC by means of a SWOT analysis may provide an answer to these questions.

Strengths

- Social pedagogues' holistic approach is non-reductionist and empowering and normalizes the lives of children and families; further, it can provide a counterbalance to one-sided models (e.g. pathology or social strain models); it may also help to confine some of the negative effects of institutionalization of children (e.g. marginalization, social exclusion).

- A child-oriented approach, in which every little stepping stone towards success is rewarded puts into practice quality standards of out-of-home care, as formulated by children themselves (see quality4children standards by SOS-Kinderdorf International 2007). A child-oriented approach may be the beginning of a voice-giving and participatory culture in residential children's homes. From a theoretical point of view, a child-oriented approach may add to our knowledge of well-being indicators in children. The strength of social pedagogy is that these well-being indicators are regarded as relational dimensions, and both the child and his/her caregivers as actors.

- The group may be experienced by children and young people with severe problems and mental health needs as a "psychosocial moratorium" where they can, at their own pace, recover from trauma and go on with their lives. It is allowed to make mistakes; the group is a safe haven. Care workers are authentic models and take different roles, for instance as coach, trainer, supporter, supervisor, counselor, guide or mentor. The "moratorium" character of the group may alleviate the mental pain of children and youth and reduce stress.

Weaknesses

- As mentioned, a number of promising practices based on social pedagogical theories have been developed and implemented in residential child care throughout the years. However, there is relatively little "hard science" testing the effectiveness and efficacy of these practices. Where is the evidence base of social pedagogy? Evaluations of outcomes of direct intervention through group care work, for instance, are scarce, as are studies on what makes group care work (Chakrabarti and Hill 2000; Fulcher and Ainsworth 2006; Grietens *et al.* 2010).

- Daily life in children's homes is very complex and for this reason it is difficult to study. In many studies, the complex reality of daily life in group is reduced to linear theoretical models. More sophisticated theoretical models and methodologies (e.g. ethnographic methods) enabling researchers to catch complex processes and dynamics in groups need to be developed. However, this will make research time-consuming and come with risks. There are some interesting studies on the processes and dynamics in groups, using more sophisticated methods (see e.g. Barter *et al.* 2004; Emond 2005), but more research on this issue needs to be conducted.

Opportunities

- It may be obvious that social pedagogy adds value to residential child care, both as a discipline and a profession. No other discipline is focusing so intensively on the "other 23 hours" in children's residential homes and the group as an agent of change. No other profession trains young adults to become specialists in group care work in such an exclusive and intensive way as the continental European Bachelor programs on social pedagogy. It is remarkable that these programs still keep on recruiting high numbers of students. In Continental Europe, as well as in other parts of the world, the deinstitutionalization of child and youth care systems is continuing and family placement is increasing. Contrary to what one would expect, social pedagogy curricula thus far have shown relatively little interest in family foster care practice and the "other 23 hours" in foster families. To become a group care worker, one has to follow a well-defined Bachelor program in social pedagogy, whereas foster care workers have diverse educational backgrounds.

- Social pedagogical models tend to be open models. Relevant findings from other disciplines can be integrated in updates of models. One example is neurosciences. Recent findings from affective and social neurosciences with regard to the impact of early trauma and adversity in the lives of children and the development and functioning of the brain can be informative to social pedagogical theory and practice. Translating results from neuroscience research into helpful interventions for children and youth suffering from the impact of maltreatment and other relational trauma, is a major challenge for the future (Perry 2009). Social pedagogues may have a bridging role in the translation processes.

- Last but not least, social pedagogues' commitment in the public debate about high-resource using children and youth is of great importance. The debate on the medicalization of child welfare practice is a typical example. Recent research in the United States demonstrates that the consumption of psychotropic medication among foster care youth has shown to be significantly higher than among general population youth (Zito *et al.* 2008). Which position do social pedagogues take in this debate?

Threats

- High-resource using children and youth in residential homes may have serious behavioral/emotional problems and mental health needs. Social pedagogues perceive an increasing complexity of problems in children and young people (e.g. severe aggression, complex trauma) (Grietens *et al.* 2010). A number of interventions address the aggression problem in groups, for instance Life Space Crisis Intervention (see Broekaert *et al.* 2009), but the number of incidents of severe aggression in residential children's homes is high and probably some of the group care workers' needs are still unmet. Relational aggression and bullying, for instance, are difficult to manage (Barter *et al.* 2004). With regard to the management of complex trauma, there still is a long way to go (Ko *et al.* 2008). In the first place, child welfare practice needs to be informed about complex trauma and the impact it may have on children and their environments. Second, professionals and policymakers have to be made aware of the trauma-inducing nature of the system. The group composition must be well thought out and placement disruptions and moves within the system need to be avoided. Finally, non-specialized group interventions are to be developed and evaluated to help children and young people recover from complex trauma.

- Being confronted day in, day out with children and young people with severe behavioral/emotional problems and mental health needs may have high impact on the health of group care workers. If unacknowledged, this may in the long-term lead to demotivation, burn out and secondary traumatization, in particular when support by colleagues and supervisors is perceived as low and caseload as high. Social pedagogues coordinating teams and monitoring treatment plans play a major role in the prevention of negative outcomes among group care workers doing direct work with children and youth.

- Making group care more trauma-informed may be expensive. Professionalizing group care workers and supervisors may be costly and time-consuming, as is designing a trauma-sensitive environment for children and youth. Little is known thus far about the benefits of these actions. Will it be worth the money spent? Uncertainty about the (long-term) effects of trauma-informed group care may have a negative impact on decisions of managers, particularly in times of economic crisis and pending budget cuts.

- Finally, it needs to be stressed that growing up in groups may produce iatrogenic effects. The dynamics of peer contagion and deviancy training are well known (see, for instance, Dishion *et al.* 1999; and Dodge and Sherill 2006). In the case of high-resource using children and youth living in TRC facilities, the risks of iatrogenic effects may be higher than in lower-end residential facilities, because of the severity and complexity of problems presented and the long trajectories of some minors in out-of-home group living arrangements.

Concluding remarks

In several countries and regions in Europe, social pedagogy has a long history as an (academic) discipline and a profession in child welfare practice. In other countries and regions, it does not exist. Social pedagogy may be attractive to policymakers and professionals from countries where it has no tradition. It has a lot to offer to child welfare, in particular to residential care. Social pedagogical models focus on the whole child, including his/her needs and strengths. In children's residential homes, social pedagogical ideas and models are put into practice through direct work with children and young people in group and direct contacts with their parents, families and social network. Children and youth are not reduced to their problems or the experiences they had in the past. A social pedagogical approach may normalize the lives of children and youth with identified mental health or behavioral needs, reconnect them with themselves, their environment and society and open a window to their futures.

The potential of social pedagogy should not be overestimated, however. Besides strengths and opportunities, several weaknesses and threats need to be acknowledged in answer to the question of whether social pedagogical models can serve practice in children's residential homes. The time may have come to start demystifying the role of social pedagogy in residential child care. Is the neighbor's grass always greener? Theoretical concepts should be deepened, models should be enriched with relevant findings from other disciplines, including affective and social neurosciences, an evidence base of interventions needs to be built up and outcomes of group care work and group processes should be analyzed in a less reductionist way. Demystification and a turn to more "hard science" will benefit social pedagogy and help social pedagogues keep making unique contributions to the care for high-resource using children and youth.

A European Perspective on the Context and Content for Social Pedagogy in Therapeutic Residential Care

HANS GRIETENS

This chapter offers an excellent presentation of social pedagogy as a model that has infused social intervention in continental Europe. In fact, a sub-discipline named "social education" has emerged in last decades in Italy and Spain (as well as in France as "specialized education") and the graduates ("social educators") have become key professionals of social services working with diverse groups at risk of social exclusion (elderly or disabled people, young offenders, children and young people in care, etc.). Currently, child care interdisciplinary teams in Spain are essentially made up of social workers, psychologists and social educators or social pedagogues, providing an interesting and complementary socio-psycho-educative perspective.

The social pedagogue or educator's contribution is based on the belief that education is a permanent and unfinished process throughout the lifecycle and that it is not constrained to formal education (school, university, etc.). In this model, informal education is presented as a powerful instrument to help people face social exclusion and develop personal competencies.

The role played by socio-pedagogues or educators has contributed significantly to dignifying the residential care job by means of achieving a high level of qualification and technical intervention. In a recent analysis (del Valle and Bravo 2013) we concluded that it is not by chance that countries with a strong tradition of socio-pedagogy have a higher proportion of residential care (compared with family foster care) and, although there is always a preference for family placements, residential care is not considered as residual or negative as in Anglophone countries (where residential staff have low qualifications and the socio-pedagogical model has not been implemented).

As the author of the chapter wisely suggests, the socio-pedagogical model has a lot of strengths and opportunities but also serious threats and weaknesses. I absolutely agree that one of the most important challenges of this model is how to implement it (see Chapter 2, this volume). The needs of young people to be addressed in these programs are primarily defined by their serious emotional and behavioral problems, so it seems to be necessary to include a stronger therapeutic component. As the chapter's author argues, the inclusion of knowledge from neuroscience (I would also add clinical psychology) could be extremely interesting and matched with the specific needs of the target group. We could say that the socio-pedagogical model is necessary but not sufficient.

I also agree that another major challenge has to do with epistemological and methodological views. Social pedagogy has been traditionally connected to qualitative and comprehensive methods (especially useful to understanding local and particular phenomena) and is often presented as antagonistic to more positivist views of science (as, for example, evidence-based programs that usually include experimental designs). High-resource programs where young people are suffering severe problems and the experiences of treatment are in serious risk of becoming ineffective (or even iatrogenic) and will require sound evaluations to guarantee both effectiveness and efficiency. It is a social, ethical and scientific duty.

CHAPTER 20

Engaging the Total Therapeutic Residential Care Program in a Process of Quality Improvement
Learning from the CARE Model

Martha J. Holden, James P. Anglin, Michael A. Nunno and Charles V. Izzo

Building a foundation for quality Therapeutic Residential Care

Recent questioning of the appropriateness of residential care has led to the need for a clearer assessment of the scope, purposes, fit, and cost of group care and its relevance and utility to a community's child welfare system (Ainsworth and Hansen 2005; Delap 2011; Noonan and Menashi 2010). As pointed out by the editors of this text, there is a need to define and build a foundation for quality child welfare services that use Therapeutic Residential Care (TRC) judiciously through a comprehensive assessment process and "for only high-need children and youth with multiple challenges in active collaboration with the full suite of empirically based family- and community-centered programs" (Whittaker, del Valle, and Holmes, Chapter 1, this volume, p.26).

We have identified three core concepts to guide quality therapeutic residential services provided by any organization or community child welfare system. These concepts include the best interests of children, organizational congruence, and an explicit program model, and their implementation depends on varying levels of professional sophistication, discipline dependent knowledge, and existing "theories in use."

1. The best interest of children has been, for some time, a widely accepted foundation in international policy and child welfare practice (Goldstein, Freud and Solnit 1979; United Nations 1989). However, assessing and working towards a particular child's best interests requires adherence to a set of explicit foundational principles that we will explore below.

2. Achieving congruence in the best interests of children demands organizational climates and interactional dynamics among staff, as well as staff and children, that reflect principles of reciprocity, consistency, and coherence to guide participatory organizational and interpersonal dynamics (Anglin 2002).

3. Quality TRC requires adherence to a system-wide program model based on the existing research and best practices that support family inclusion and cultural relevancy, appropriate developmental programing, therapeutic relationships and attachments, competence-building programs, and trauma sensitivity, within an environment that promotes caring, high expectation messages, and opportunities for contribution and participation. These practice and program principles are articulated in our Children and Residential Experiences (CARE) program model and, for most agencies, they call for substantive changes in theoretical perspective, organizational mission, data-utilization, and interactional dynamics.

What is a program model?

A program model in human services is based on a set of principles that guide policy, procedures, and practices (Lee and Barth 2011). The principles guide all interactions and interventions with families and their children. Well-articulated program models have evidence-based *theories of change* or *logic models*. These help explain and guide interventions and form the basis for both process and outcomes evaluation and research.

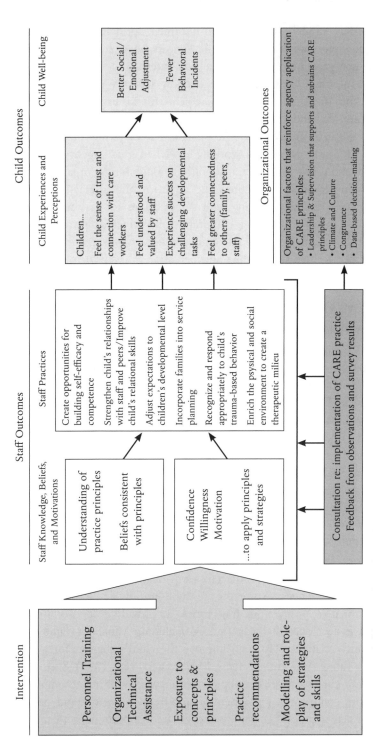

FIGURE 20.1: Children and residential experiences theory of change

The CARE model is a research-informed, principle-based, multi-component program designed to build the capacity of residential care and treatment organizations to serve the best interests of the children. The research-informed CARE principles support a theory of change (TOC) that outlines the causal pathways by which CARE is expected to improve socio-emotional and developmental outcomes for children (Holden 2009; Holden *et al.* 2010) (see Figure 20.1). This TOC lays the foundation for quality TRC and provides a working model to guide agency planning and evaluation. The principles are applied throughout the organization to inform adult-to-adult interactions and adult-to-child interactions, guide data-informed decision-making, and set priorities for serving the best interests of the children. By incorporating the principles throughout all levels of the organization and into daily practice, an organizational culture is developed to help sustain the implementation of the principles.

The CARE principles as an organizing framework to promote and assess quality

The CARE model incorporates and structures well-established findings from the social sciences literature into six basic practice principles: developmentally focused, family-involved, competency-centered, relationship-based, trauma-informed, and ecologically oriented. The aim of CARE is to bring agencies' ongoing functioning closer to well-researched best practices in residential care and to help them achieve congruence in the best interests of children within and between all organizational levels in order to improve how the agency works as a whole.

Developmentally focused

Many children who enter the out-of-home care system are on developmental trajectories that place them outside of social norms, e.g. antisocial, delinquent, or mental illness trajectories. A major task of the therapeutic residential experience is to promote the child's healthy development toward more normative, positive, life trajectories. By providing opportunities for normative developmental experiences, including enhanced family and community relations, TRC can improve the child's chances for a more fulfilling future (Hawkins-Rodgers 2007; Maier 1987, 1991). Even under the best of circumstances, development is uneven and is not accomplished by simply completing a program. Helping children grow and develop requires active support, carefully orchestrated opportunities to practice and learn psychosocial skills, and intentional interactions with caring, informed, engaged, and emotionally and culturally competent adults.

The developmental focus applies equally to staff members at all levels of the organization. The capacity of the organization to support professional development for care workers, supervisors, and administrators has a powerful impact on staff development and creativity, as well as program sophistication (Phelan 2003, 2008). At every level of the organization, staff development plans are individualized for each staff member according to their level of professional development, with strategies tailored to help them grow to the next level.

Family involvement

Family involvement and contact has been demonstrated to have positive outcomes for children in residential care (Barth 2005; Barth *et al.* 2007; Curry 1991; Frensch and Cameron 2002; Hair 2005; United States General Accounting Office 1994; Whittaker and Pfeiffer 1994) and reduced depressive symptoms for incarcerated juveniles (Monahan, Goldweber and Cauffman 2011). Separation from parents during this developmental stage is not normative and comes at a time when children are still dependent on and heavily influenced by their family. Engaging families so that they can play an important role in helping their child develop requires effort at every level of the organization. Including families provides a link to social orientation and the families' cultural environments. Effective workers are culturally competent and able to understand the family's worldview. Workers are able to adapt interventions to the unique needs of the children and families (Mohr *et al.* 2009). In order to effectively engage families, clinicians may need to work different hours, funds may need to be allocated to support travel and accommodation, biases against "inappropriate parents" have to be overcome, and staff's perception of their role may need to be redefined. When the family involvement principle is embraced and operationalized in an agency, families become part of the team.

Competency-centered

Creating a therapeutic milieu involves a balance between structure, predictable routines, and flexibility to meet individual needs and make use of teachable moments. In order for this to occur, all structures, routines, activities, and events need to have a purpose and goals. Focusing on helping children learn how to express themselves, build and maintain relationships, increase coping abilities, and develop healthy personal habits helps to put them on a more positive developmental trajectory. Engagement in activities, play, sports, and life skills routines are fundamental to developing mastery and competence in meeting life's demands. Yet many residential programs are activity poor and limit activities to children who have "earned" them (Mohr *et al.* 2009; Tompkins-Rosenblatt and VanderVen 2005) or deny them to children who demonstrate the most need for practice—the children who are not successful in the activity.

Focusing on what skills individual children need to develop, as well as what skills would enhance the development of the group, drives the structure and activities provided throughout the day. Providing normalizing experiences within the child's zone of proximal development (Vygotsky 1978) helps prepare the child for life's future challenges.

Relationship-based

Research demonstrates that environments that are consistent, safe, and nurturing are associated with positive outcomes for maltreated children (Shaffer, Egeland and Wang 2010). A person's ability to form relationships and positive attachments to others is an essential personal strength and manifestation of resiliency associated with healthy development and success in life (Benard 2004; Goleman 1998; Masten 2004). Through building alliances with caring, competent adults, children can learn to trust, feel safe, develop relationships, and obtain the assistance they need in overcoming obstacles and solving problems. Through positive attachment experiences with adult caregivers, children and adolescents can form more positive internal working models of adult–child relationships that can increase their ability to form positive secure relationships in future situations (Perry and Pollard 1998).

When staff's primary task to create attachment-building opportunities with young people is clearly defined by the organization, children and young people can and do respond. This often requires a shift from interpreting children's behavior as "attention seeking" to "attachment seeking." Staff members must be prepared to overlook inappropriate behavior at times, communicate acceptance, and encourage children to try again. Holding children accountable through continually applying consequences for "breaking rules" cannot be the primary focus if workers are to build therapeutic alliances and teach life skills. Helping children learn to be responsible and accountable by helping them be successful in their pursuits not only teaches them necessary life skills but also fosters attachments and healthy relationships. By reducing rules to safety concerns and reframing the primary focus to "expectations," more flexibility is created so that staff can be truly responsive to children's needs.

Trauma-informed

Research on trauma has resulted in new understandings of children's challenging and difficult behaviors (Aronson and Kahn 2004; Lieberman and Knorr 2007; Perry and Pollard 1998; Spinazzola *et al.* 2005). Unfortunately, simply understanding the effects of trauma on brain development and behavior does not necessarily translate into staff actually changing their practice to be more therapeutic. Staff and organizations struggle to give up punitive and coercive practices and highly regimented "reinforcement" systems. These systems are counter-productive for a trauma-sensitive population and they have the potential to be re-traumatizing (Bloom 1997; Bloom and Farragher 2013). Trauma-informed practice demands that daily activities, routines, expectations, and interactions, are designed and practiced so that children can comply without triggering overwhelming stress or trauma. Within the context of emotional regulation it is essential that an adult responds with appropriate co-regulation strategies that assist children in reframing past pain within the context of a trusting, caring relationship. CARE organizations support these relationship-based therapeutic environments by creating the capacity for safe and resilient caregiving environments (Kahn 2005) that permit both adults and children opportunities for reflection and learning (Papell and Skolnik 1992; Schon 1983, 1987). During team meetings and supervisory sessions, conversations are focused not only on what the child is experiencing but also the impact on the care workers and how they are able to use their experiences in helping the child.

Ecologically oriented

When children live in a community with caring adults who communicate their belief in each child's own strengths and abilities, children are motivated to learn and their innate drive to grow and develop is fostered (Benard 2004). The more the environment can be enhanced to motivate children to participate in increasingly complex activities and caring relationships, the more opportunities for growth and development are available.

Children are often stuck in patterns of destructive and self-defeating behaviors; residential care can provide a safe context for experimentation and intensive practice. Routines, activities, and programs are created for each individual child to facilitate new learning in all aspects of the child's environment, e.g. school, home, play, and community. Children are supported to participate in activities consistent with enriching their involvement and experience of their culture, family, and community. When children struggle to participate, the activity is adjusted or the child is given the additional support necessary to successfully engage. Children who struggle most need more opportunities to participate, not fewer.

When applied consistently and congruently the CARE principles help organizations realign and reallocate resources; set priorities; give context to assessments, services and programs; and create a culture that serves the best interest of each child.

Implementation of the CARE program model

The CARE model is implemented through research-informed strategies such as organizational and personal self-assessment, data analysis, training, and technical assistance. This strategy includes training that addresses all levels of the organization and provides guidance about how to apply CARE principles in daily practice. Organizational technical assistance helps agency leadership and supervisors build commitment to the CARE principles, develop and communicate the vision to establish congruence to the CARE principles throughout the organization, and facilitate, reinforce, and sustain that vision. Through a process of self-reflection, agencies establish structures and processes for improving collaboration, identifying barriers to integrating, and sustaining CARE principles and planning strategies for resolving those barriers, and facilitating practices to encourage data utilization.

Managing complexity and striving for continuous quality improvement

The ability to manage complexity is an essential component of organizational transformation that leads to quality services. At the managerial level, the key task is to create an extra-familial or out-of-home care environment that supports the therapeutic mission (Anglin 2002). Recent research on the implementation of the CARE program model has revealed that adapting to the complexity of a residential care setting and being able to interpret a series of principles and theoretical perspectives "in the moment" requires, in most cases, a change of mindset on the part of the staff members (Anglin 2012). Robert Kegan's work on adult mindset development has proven very applicable to the process of implementing the CARE program model within an agency context (Kegan 1994; Kegan and Lahey 2009). To achieve organizational transformation, staff members need to move beyond a *socialized mindset* characterized by technical thinking to a *self-authoring mindset* that is more adaptive and creative. The highest order, which is optimal for leaders of complex organizations, is a *self-transforming mindset* within which managers and directors can be highly creative and offer sensitive support and guidance to workers at other levels of the agency (Kegan 1994; Kegan and Lahey 2009).

In addition, complexity theory as applied to organizational development offers useful insights into the management of quality residential care. For example, one recent text, *Journey into Complexity* (De Toni and Comello 2010) proposes seven dynamics of complexity management. These seven dynamics are reflected in CARE agencies that have successfully introduced, implemented, and sustained the CARE program over three years or more.

Successful CARE agencies are able to become networked and self-regulating because people in them become better at interpreting the relatively small number of guiding principles in the complex reality of action. As competence and confidence builds at each level of the organization, the agency increasingly demonstrates shared intelligence and congruent decision-making.

In order to implement the principle-based CARE program model, a CARE organization has to introduce and sustain a certain amount of creative capacity within the organization. The creativity comes from the workers' ability and need to imagine new scenarios and responses, thus fuelling the "creative circle." Such creativity is evident across the successful CARE agencies, where many old solutions and reactions have been put aside, resulting in discontinuity and clearing the way for true creativity and responsiveness, rather than predetermined reactivity.

A theme that occurs repeatedly in CARE agencies is the increase in communication, both within and across the various programs, due to shared values and objectives. In effect, a staff member could go through any door in the agency and find relevant and informed support. The spirit of communication, collaboration, and sharing is palpable, and these dynamics lead to a shared spirit and congruence, a state of operational excellence in line with its ultimate objective—the best interests of the children.

Organizations that manage complexity expect the unexpected, tune into weak signals, and often respond in counterintuitive ways. Adopting CARE requires staff members to move away from their "natural" intuitive impulses in order to develop a new repertoire of responses in line with the CARE principles and values. Residential care requires attentiveness to small details in the behavior of the residents and other staff members in order to make necessary adjustments.

The relational network discussed in the complexity principles above becomes the early warning system that enables organizational adaptation and flexibility. Staff members need to seize the *creative moment*. Those who have implemented CARE appear able to create and take advantage of such creative moments with the residents and with each other.

When the CARE program model is implemented successfully, it resembles a village or a community with the presence of a highly interactive network of relationships. In order for workers to implement CARE, they need both the guidance of clear principles and values, and the freedom and opportunity to interpret them in action. Workers must let go of looking for formulas or technical solutions ("if A happens, do B") and become more creative and adaptive in their thinking and actions. This requires a shift from a hierarchical to a network or participatory approach. Workers share in supporting each other, but also in monitoring each other's practice to achieve the objectives and excellence for which they strive.

The CARE program model feeds "virtuous" circles rather than "vicious" ones through a culture of reciprocity, consistency, and coherence. This principle includes the famous observation of complexity theory that the flap of a butterfly's wings in South America can cause a typhoon in Asia. In other words, a small action in one moment can cause large differences in the broader system and longer term. In residential child and youth care, a significant moment in a child's experience can lead to a different life path several years down the road. We never know which moments will make the difference in helping residents to "develop a sense of normality" (Anglin 2002). The best way to proceed is to help to create as many such positive moments as possible, each and every day.

Agencies that implement the CARE program model adopt new mindsets and acknowledge and welcome errors or mistakes as important learning opportunities rather than occasions for blame. Agencies that engage in the CARE program model often have been struggling for years to discover a new way of thinking and a new set of guidelines for action that will propel them beyond their previous, largely ineffective and often rule-bound, behaviors. CARE agencies find themselves having to let go of longstanding habits of mind in order to embrace a more therapeutic mindset. After a period of two to three years, much of what CARE agencies are doing has now become the new implicit, rather than self-consciously explicit.

What changes occur among staff and children during implementation of a principle-based program?

As funders increasingly demand evidence-based practice in residential care (Mabry 2010), many agency directors and practitioners are receptive to research-informed residential care models that can guide their agency's work with families and children. Two major studies were conducted to examine CARE's impact on organizational climate, adult–child interactions, and child outcomes: a grounded theory inquiry into the organizational transformation necessary to implement the CARE program model *and* a long-term quasi-experimental study that measured a wide range of quantitative outcomes.

In 2011 Anglin examined the organizational transformation necessary to implement the CARE program model. Interviews with 70 individuals across seven CARE agencies (the initial "Pioneer" agencies) indicated that the CARE model reflects the true complexity of residential work, and therefore requires abilities on the part of all staff—line workers, supervisors, and managers—to be able to deal effectively with such complexity. A small number of workers in each agency have not been able to make the necessary transition from technical thinking to an adaptive or self-authoring mindset necessary to act in accordance with the core CARE principles. However the majority embraced the process of change and development required to implement the model (Anglin 2012). Workers in these Pioneer CARE agencies report that the environment is more calm and peaceful in the cottages, that there is less fear on the part of staff and children, and that there are fewer confrontations, power struggles and therefore fewer restraints. Further, many workers report they are happier and feel more satisfaction in their work. Agency leaders become aware of the need to review and revise their agency policies, procedures, practices, and structures, in order to be congruent with CARE. In some instances, participants indicate they now approach their own children, spouses, and other family members differently and in accordance with the CARE principles, having become more congruent as persons as well as workers. As one agency Executive Director put it, "CARE is not just what we do, it is who we are" (Anglin 2012).

The second study, funded by the Duke Endowment, examines program impact on organizational, staff, and child outcomes by comparing seven agencies receiving CARE immediately after baseline assessment in 2010 (Cohort 1) with seven similar agencies receiving CARE after two baseline assessments in 2010 and 2011 (Cohort 2). In preliminary analyses combining all 14 agencies, pre-post comparisons show improvements on some staff and child outcomes after only 12 months of program implementation (see Table 20.1) (Izzo, Anglin and Holden 2012). Independent sample *t*-tests indicated that CARE-consistent child care beliefs increased significantly from baseline to 12 months. Scores on a measure of CARE-consistent staff practices also showed an increase during the same period that approached statistical significance. Independent sample *t*-tests also showed that youth reports about the quality of their interactions with caregivers and their feelings of attachment to caregivers (Armsden and Greenberg 1987) improved significantly over the first 12 months. Data analyses are currently underway that use the quasi-experimental design to examine the one-year treatment contrast between Cohort 1 and Cohort 2 (i.e. the effect of participating in one additional year of CARE implementation) at each assessment point.

TABLE 20.1: Baseline vs. 12-month scores for staff and youth outcomes

OUTCOME MEASURE	BASELINE MEAN	12 MONTH MEAN	SIGNIFICANCE TEST (BASELINE VS. 12-MONTH)
Staff beliefs overall score			
2010 cohort	67.36	71.47	t=-5.12 (p<.01)
2011 cohort	66.83	71.92	t = 6.52 (p<.01)
Combined	67.15	71.61	t =-7.89 (p<.01)
Staff practice overall score			
2010 cohort	124.11	127.39	*NS*
2011 cohort	126.93	134.00	t = -1.76 (p=.08)
Combined	125.31	130.17	t = -1.73 (p=.09)
Youth–adult interaction quality			
2010 cohort	56.03	57.59	*NS*
2011 cohort	56.88	62.60	t = 3.06 (p<.01)
Combined	56.45	60.24	t = 2.93 (p<.01)
Youth attachment			
2010 cohort	63.54	57.59	*NS*
2011 cohort	62.34	62.60	t = 2.72 (p<.01)
Combined	63.00	60.24	t = 2.31 (p=.02)

Note: Many of the staff and most of the youth assessed at baseline were different than those assessed at 12 months, making repeated measures tests impractical. Therefore we compared scores cross-sectionally from baseline to 12 months using independent sample *t*-tests. This allowed us to use all available data rather than only analyzing the more limited samples that were present for the entire year.

In addition to showing improvements on these outcome measures, it is notable that all agencies remained actively engaged in both CARE implementation and data gathering, and those that completed three years of implementation have agreed to three additional years of sustainability activity. They have incorporated CARE in their organizational vision and maintained an effort to implement principle-based, data-informed practices to meet the current and evolving needs of children.

Conclusion

Whether any principle-based and research-informed program models like CARE can be shown to provide consistent and sustained positive outcomes for children requires further research, however findings to date from both qualitative and quantitative evaluation strategies are promising (Barth 2005; Holden *et al.* 2010; James 2011b; Sullivan *et al.* 2011). Qualitative findings show that agencies have struggled constructively to examine their mission in the service of children's best interests. Early quantitative results provide hopeful signs that the study will ultimately reveal positive impacts of CARE. It is notable that the improvements were seen in several domains critical to CARE's theory of change and that the quantitative evidence for change was reinforced by reports of improved staff–child interaction by the CARE technical consultants based on their in-home observations. The relatively small size of the increases is not surprising given that they represent changes after CARE implementation was only one third complete. This underscores the need for extended intervention periods to allow time for gradual changes to occur in mindsets, norms, and practices.

The CARE program model can be understood as a foundational platform on which residential (and perhaps other child welfare) services can be built. It seeks to offer a synthesis of relevant research findings and practice wisdom from over 70 years of child care work. CARE encompasses the five levels of an organization (including the extra-agency) and cuts across all interactional dynamics. However, it is not sufficient in that there are other bodies of knowledge and technical skill necessary for specific populations and circumstances, such as children with physical disabilities, severe psychiatric needs, and learning difficulties.

In summary, CARE presents an opportunity for rigorous research based on an articulated theory of change and a solid evidence-informed foundation of child care knowledge, skills, and attitudes. It recognizes the complexity of such work along with the challenges and opportunities addressing such complexity can bring to organizations and the young people, families, and communities they serve.

COMMENTARY BY SIGRID JAMES ON:

Engaging the Total Therapeutic Residential Care Program in a Process of Quality Improvement: Learning from the CARE Model

MARTHA J. HOLDEN, JAMES P. ANGLIN, MICHAEL
A. NUNNO AND CHARLES V. IZZO

Holden and colleagues introduce the residential care program model CARE, which is compelling in its face validity, i.e. it is based on a sound theory of change and tries to capture outcomes that are of relevance to residential care. CARE is also beginning to establish a research base that will hopefully be further strengthened through more rigorous designs. Three points are of particular importance to me.

1. *The need for a program model.* I wholeheartedly agree with the authors about the need for a well-developed and clearly explicated program model. While the specification of a program model tends to be a requirement for initial licensing, little is known to date about the dissemination or implementation of program models within residential care settings. How are staff trained in a program model? Are all staff, including residential child care staff, aware of their agency's model and able to formulate its theory of change? How does awareness of the program model affect interactions with youth? A study of residential care settings in Germany found that many staff were unable to name any therapeutic methods used in the facility, and a significant percentage could not relate utilized practices to the residential care literature (Günder 2011). I suspect that findings in other countries would be similar, pointing to the need for not only the development or identification of a program model but also its deliberate implementation.

2. *Continued debate about the "evidence" label.* The authors emphasize that "well-articulated program models have evidence-based theories of change" and introduce CARE as a research-informed program. While the validity of CARE as a theoretically sound program model is not questioned, its research evidence remains in early developmental stages, raising questions about the use of terms such as research-informed, evidence-based, empirically supported, etc. (e.g. Rycroft-Malone *et al.* 2004). Few residential care programs would claim to run a program that is not based on

research, but unfortunately few program models in the residential care arena meet the currently accepted scientific standards of evidence (e.g. James *et al.* 2013). Lack of clarity about terminology leads to considerable confusion and misunderstandings between providers and researchers. The field has to determine continuously what evidence exists, what evidence is needed to improve practice, and how to obtain it.

3. *The need for a well-trained residential child care workforce.* The CARE model embraces principles that in their implementation require critical thinking, flexibility, and a high degree of professional judgment by residential child care staff: "Staff members must be prepared to overlook inappropriate behavior at times, communicate acceptance, and encourage children to try again." It requires giving up "punitive and coercive practices and highly regimented 'reinforcement' systems." It is questionable whether these laudable objectives can be broadly implemented given notoriously low wages and consequently poor qualifications and high turnover rates among residential child care staff (e.g. Colton and Roberts 2007). In my view, the hiring, training, and retaining of qualified child care staff is a key prerequisite for improving residential care practice, especially when implementing a promising program model.

CHAPTER 21

Outcomes Management in Residential Treatment
The CANS Approach

John S. Lyons and Lauren Schmidt

Our goal in this chapter is to provide a fundamentally different way to conceptualize Therapeutic Residential Care (TRC) and, through this, offer new pathways to alter our current goals about the basic work of transforming children's lives. We propose that this is done through the use of Total Clinical Outcomes Management (TCOM). TCOM is the conceptual framework behind the use of the Child and Adolescent Needs and Strengths (CANS). In the United States, the CANS has at least one state-wide implementation in 36 states and is quickly spreading throughout the country. There are implementations on every continent except Antarctica. A substantial amount of research has proven the CANS both reliable and valid (Lyons 2009a; Lyons and Weiner 2009). Implementation of TCOM has been demonstrated to be transformative (Lyons *et al.* 1998, 2009, Lyons and Weiner 2009).

In order to be successful, a business has to manage itself. In order to manage itself, the leadership of that business must have a clear idea of its nature and purpose. This chapter presents an argument that residential treatment has been managing the wrong business. Further, we present an approach to management that is consistent with the nature of the business of residential treatment. According to Gilmore and Pine (1997), there are five types of businesses.

1. Commodities involve the sale of raw materials.

2. Products are things produced from commodities that have more direct value to customers.

3. Services are businesses, which sell the provision of a product to an interested buyer.

4. Experiences involve the sale of memories.

5. Finally, transformational offerings involve businesses in which the purpose of the enterprise is to help someone change his/her life in some important way.

Since its beginnings, residential treatment has been organized, financed, supervised, and managed as a service. It is funded on the basis of number of days spent in residence. Although there has always been a recognition that the goal of residential treatment for youth is transformational, there has only recently become an awareness that it is necessary to monitor, measure, and manage these personal change processes. This second recognition has fundamental implications for rethinking the management of residential treatment.

There are a variety of unintended consequences of our misguided approach to managing the child-serving system as a service system rather than as a transformational system. First and foremost, services pay to find someone and get him/her to show up. Transformational systems pay to find someone you can help, help them, and then find someone else. We would argue that the basic financing of residential treatment by using a per diem or daily rate is the single greatest factor in the decline of use of this intervention. By incentivizing residential treatment programs to fill their beds and keep them filled, we created a fundamental conflict of interest whereby helping youth change is actually in competition with the business model of keeping them in treatment.

Total Clinical Outcomes Management

TCOM is an approach to outcomes management designed to engineer the management of transformational offerings and is further designed to reduce the tensions in the complex service system of human services. Tensions occur at all three levels of the human service system: family and child-level tensions (e.g. parents vs. professionals), program-level tensions (e.g. business model vs. clinical model), and system-level tensions (e.g. central vs. local control).

Before understanding how TCOM works and succeeds, it may be useful to define the acronym. "Total" refers to the information about the people being served and how it is essential that this information is embedded into all areas of the human services system. "Clinical" refers to the fact that the information is about the people who are being served and not about the services that are being provided. "Outcomes" imply that the relevant factors to assessing the impacts of the treatment provided is the focus of the information about the people being served. "Management" re-enforces the philosophy that at all levels of the human services system, information about the people being served is used to make decisions about patient care (Lyons 2004, 2009a; Lyons and Weiner 2009).

TCOM is has a philosophy, a strategy, and tactics. The philosophy of TCOM is that in the human-serving system, it is necessary to make decisions based on the needs of those being served. In the child-serving system, this means that the best interests of children and families should be the driving focus of all enterprises. In the child-serving system, there are professionals of different levels and perspectives, family members with different ideas, and the person in need with his/her own outlook on the situation. All these people will have their own opinions on the best way to handle the situation. TCOM aims to help collaborate and communicate all ideas and help everyone commit to serving those in need, and places accountability between all partners at all levels of the human service system to the person(s) in need. In other words, TCOM provides a strategy for overcoming all the competing pressures that make helping children, youth, and families to change their life circumstances a challenging endeavour. Managing competing agendas requires a shared vision amongst all parties participating in the life of a family. In the child-serving system that shared vision must meet the needs and strengths of the child and family. The strategy of TCOM is to create the capacity for a system to focus on the shared vision at all levels. Thus the foundation of TCOM is the creation and communication of a shared vision—the best interests of a child and family (or children and families). That goal has led to the creation of the Child and Adolescent Needs and Strengths (CANS). The CANS comes from communication theory (i.e. a communimetric measure, Lyons 2009b), which uses an action orientation towards identifying and communicating the shared vision.

The tactic of TCOM is the strategy of the actual application of the CANS. This can be summarized in the TCOM grid (Table 21.1).

In the TCOM grid the columns represent the levels of the system and the rows represent the structured assessment. As an example, look at the TCOM grid where it begins: at the individual level as a decision support tool. By looking at the individual level, which is called "family and youth," and then looking at the first row, which is called "decision support," the plan for that level is revealed (in this case: treatment planning, effective practices, or evidence-based practices, EBPs). This method can be applied in the same way to every level of the system.

TABLE 21.1: TCOM grid of tactics

	FAMILY & YOUTH	PROGRAM	SYSTEM
Decision Support	Treatment Planning Effective practices EBPs	Eligibility, Admission & Step-down	Resource Management Right-sizing
Outcome Monitoring	Care Transitions & Celebrations	Program Evaluation	Provider Profiles Performance/ Contracting
Quality Improvement	Case Management Integrated Care Supervision	CQI/QA Accreditation Program Redesign	Transformation Business Model Design

When the philosophy, strategy, and tactics of TCOM combine, a learning environment is created in which information gained can be used to determine how to utilize the human services system to effectively and efficiently care and help the person in service through a transformative process (Lyons 2009a, 2009b).

The strategy: Child and Adolescent Needs and Strengths

The CANS multi-purpose communimetric tool is the strategy used in TCOM that allows for the shared vision to be effectively supported. It supports decision-making in the human services system in order to monitor appropriately the outcome of services and to facilitate initiatives in quality improvement. It does this by using the information gained about the person(s) in services and using it to manage the human services system at all levels. In order to do this effectively, families and all other people involved (from case workers to mental health professionals) must collaborate and be fully involved in all activities of the transformational process. Each measurement of the CANS is relevant to every decision made about the interventions that will be used.

The CANS is composed of six key principles. The first principle is that only items that might impact service planning are included. This means that every item that is included in the CANS is relevant to gaining the appropriate information required in order to make informed decisions about service planning. For example: The "fire setting" item. This item is included in the CANS because it is important to know if the child has a history of setting fires. If he/she does, it is necessary to address this to discover the cause of the need to set fires and help the child to address these problems so that he/she no longer sets fires.

The second principle is that each level translates immediately into an action level. This is illustrated through the four action levels of the CANS (Table 21.2).

TABLE 21.2: Action levels of the Child and Adolescent Needs and Strengths

FOR NEEDS	FOR STRENGTHS
0—No evidence	0—Centerpiece
1—Watch/prevent	1—Useful strength
2—Action needed	2—Potential strength
3—Immediate/intensive action needed	3—No strength identified

An example of the second principle would be: five-year-old Johnny is unable to walk and his parents are unsure why. For the "motor skills" item, Johnny would be rated a 3 on the CANS action levels scale because at five years old, Johnny should be able to walk and thus immediate action is needed to determine why he is not yet walking.

Principle three is that the CANS is about the child and not the child in service. If there is some sort of intervention in place (like medication) that is masking a need, the child would be rated on the CANS action level scale as if that intervention was not in place. For example: if a ten-year-old girl is taking medication for her ADHD and would be unable to function in class without it, she would be rated as a two or a three on the CANS action level scale due to the possibility of "impulsivity/hyperactivity," even if she is fully functional while on medication. This is because if the medication were taken away, she would go back to having problems functioning because of her ADHD.

Principle four is to consider the significance of culture and development in a child's life. This means that when rating the CANS, the child's culture and their development needs to be considered. For example: if a child who is three years old gets angry and throws a tantrum when he/she does not get what he/she wants, the child would not be rated on the "anger control" item, as such behavior is considered a normal developmental behavior at this age. If the same behavior was being seen in a 15-year-old, then the child would be rated under the "anger control" item, as such behavior is not part of the normal developmental age of a 15-year-old.

The fifth principle is that the ratings are generally "agnostic as to etiology." In other words, it is about the "what" and not the "why." This refers to the fact that the CANS is a descriptive tool. It is necessary to consider only what the behavior is and not why the behavior is occurring. The only exception to this is for trauma items and the social behavior item. For example: if a child is suicidal, the child would be identified only on the "suicide risk" item. Some people might feel inclined to also mark a suicidal child on the "depression" item. For CANS, this is not done because it is not known why the child is suicidal and we cannot assume why (whether it is because of depression, psychotic symptoms, anxiety, etc.). The only thing that can be done is to report the "what," which is the fact that the child is suicidal.

The sixth principle is that there is a 30-day window on which the ratings are based. As a general rule, the CANS is rated based only on the last 30 days unless otherwise specified in the action levels. This is to keep the ratings relevant. For example: if a child was displaying oppositional behavior three years ago and is no longer displaying any oppositional behavior, he/she would not be rated on the "oppositional" item because if that behavior is no longer displayed, incorporating treatment for an oppositional child (who has not displayed oppositional behavior in three years) would not be effective.

In summary, the six key principles of the CANS are as follows.

1. Items are included because they might impact service planning.

2. Levels of items translate immediately into action levels.

3. It is about the child, not about the service.

4. Consider culture and development.

5. It is agnostic as to etiology—it is about the "what" not about the "why."

6. The 30-day window is to remind us to keep assessments relevant and fresh.

The CANS is structured into different domains (either a needs domain or a strengths domain) and each domain has different items in it that are relevant to the version of the CANS that it is serving (mental health, autism, pre-school, educational, comprehensive, juvenile justice etc.). Each item has four actionable levels, which are different depending on whether the domain is a strengths domain or a needs domain. For the needs domain a rating of zero means that there is no reason to believe that a need exists.

This could be because there is no evidence or because it has been stated explicitly that there is no need. For example: if it is not mentioned that a child is using drugs or alcohol, and there is no reason to believe that a child is using drugs or alcohol, then the child would not be rated as having any problems with drugs or alcohol. This does not mean that the child is not having problems with drugs or alcohol, but it does mean that there is no reason to believe that there are any problems with drugs or alcohol. A needs rating of one implies watchful waiting and prevention. This could be because of a suspicion of a need or because of a history of a need. For example: if a child was suicidal two years ago, the child would still be rated as a one on the "suicide risk" item, even though there has not been any recent suicidal ideation, because the best predictor for future behavior is past behavior, and suicidal behavior could occur again under stress. A needs rating of two means that there is action needed. This means that there is a need and it needs to be addressed, as it is interfering with the functioning of the child or the child's family. For example, if a child is talking out of turn in class and keeps getting detention, then a rating of two on school behavior would be given because it is affecting the child's ability to function properly in the school environment. A needs rating of three means that immediate and/or intensive action needs to be taken. This means that there is either a dangerous or disabling behavior. For example if a child tried to commit suicide last night, a rating of three would be given to the "suicide risk" item because the behavior is recent and immediate action needs to be taken to help this child.

For the strengths domain, a rating of zero means that there is a centerpiece strength present. This means that a strength is so strong that it can be used in a strength-based plan. For example: if a child enjoys singing, takes singing lessons, and is in the school choir, that child would be rated as a zero on the "talents/interests" item. A strength rating of one means that there is a useful strength present. This means that the strength is strong enough to be included in the strength-based plan, but it would not be the centerpiece of the plan. For example: if a child enjoys going to church, the child would be rated as a one for the "spiritual/religious" item of the CANS. A strengths rating of two means that a strength is identified, but that significant efforts need to be taken in order to build this strength enough to be used as part of a strength-based plan. For example: if a child has identified family and interacts with that family, but does not yet feel comfortable approaching his/her family for advice, that child would be rated a two on the "family strengths" item. A strength rating of three means that there is no strength identified. This means that there is no evidence or no reason to believe that a strength is present. For example:

if there is no mention of whether or not the child has natural supports, the child would be rated a three on the "natural supports" item. This does not mean that the child has no natural supports, but rather that there is no evidence to believe that the child has any.

Implementation of the strategy and development of the tactics

Perhaps it is clear from the above description that measurement in TCOM is quite different than our traditional ways of thinking about the application of a measure in a research or evaluation study. The CANS is as much of a practice model approach as it is a measure per se. Probably the best way to conceptualize it is that it is a practice model that has a measurement as its output. For this reason, the CANS requires training and certification. If you are going to use a common language approach to communicating the shared vision, then it is probably reasonable to ensure that people are fluent in the common language to ensure that it is used as effectively as possible. Certification is centralized through the Praed Foundation's collaborative training website. For most jurisdictions, a reliability of 0.70 or higher using an intraclass correlation coefficient on a test case vignette is the standard for certification.

Training and certification is really just the first step and probably the easiest aspect of implementation of TCOM. The next step requires an effort to integrate the CANS into the process of care, whatever that process might be. There are two essential elements to that integration in the initial stages of implementation. First, it is important to ensure that the CANS is actually used as an individual-level decision support. In other words, it is important that over time people learn how to integrate the CANS into the plan. There are a number of approaches to treatment planning available (see www.praedfoundation.org). We are currently working with the PracticeWise group (Chorpita, Bernstein and Daleiden 2011) to integrate the CANS assessment with their approach to identifying core components of effective practice. Dollard and Rautkis (2009) have developed a quality assurance approach called the SPANS, which is designed to monitor the degree of integration of the CANS into the plan.

The second key component to the initial phase of successful implementation of TCOM is the integration of the CANS into existing supervisory structures. It is important, for example, to make sure everyone working in a supervisory capacity is trained and certified on the CANS. It is also important that supervisors review the CANS and use it in supervision. One of the interesting differences between a service system and a transformational system is the anticipated role of the supervisor. In a service system, the supervisory role often evolves into the role of a compliance officer—did the staff engage in all of the required processes and documentation requirements? This role creates a regulatory relationship with the supervisee. In a transformational system, the role of supervisor is that of mentor and teacher. Their responsibility is to ensure that the direct care staff are as effective as possible (rather than compliant). This role shift has enormous implications for an agency.

Once sufficient information is collected, feedback reports can be used to monitor change, both of individuals and groups of individuals. This is when the process becomes outcomes management. Creating and understanding outcome reports is a technical challenge for many agencies for a variety of reasons. Creating them can be accomplished by an external software engineer; understanding, however, cannot, and must be an explicit goal of the organization—teaching staff, supervisors, and program managers must monitor and use the information generated in reports.

There are two basic strategies for analyzing outcomes using the CANS—items and dimension scores. Item-level analysis is great for individual programs, as it gives information immediately relevant for program design. Table 21.1 presents an item-level analysis of behavioral/emotional needs on the CANS for a panel of 474 youth in residential treatment in Illinois. Five statistics are presented—the percentage of youth with an actionable need (two or three) at admission to residential (% Presenting); the percentage of youth with an actionable need at admission who were discharged with a zero or one (% Resolved); the percentage of youth with an actionable need at admission who had a lower level at discharge (% Improved); the percentage of youth who were admitted without an actionable need who were discharged with an actionable need (moved from zero or one at admittance to two or three at discharge, % Identified); and the percentage of youth who were a two at admittance and a three at discharge (% Worsened).

Review of Table 21.3 reveals that the greatest success of resolving actionable needs comes with "psychosis followed by "substance abuse." The lowest rates of resolution are among the most common needs— "oppositional behavior" and "attention/impulse." Further, "oppositional behavior" is the most commonly unidentified need at admittance, which is seen as actionable by discharge with nearly one quarter of youth being seen as developing this need during their residential stay. "Psychosis" and "substance abuse," on the other hand, are seldom unrecognized at admission. Interestingly, though "psychosis" and "attention/impulse" are the two needs with the highest rates of worsening —detected at admission and worse at discharge. "Attachment" and "adjustment to trauma" both have a much higher rate of "improvement" relative to "resolution," suggesting that the residential episode prepares these youth for follow-up treatment on these needs (e.g. stabilization) but does not complete treatment.

TABLE 21.3: Item level analysis of change in needs in residential treatment in Illinois

ITEM	% PRESENTING	% RESOLVED	% IMPROVED	% IDENTIFIED	% WORSENED
Psychosis	10.5	55.1	67.3	4.7	8.3
Attention/ Impulse	45.0	37.6	42.7	19.2	8.9
Depression	48.3	44.1	47.6	21.6	2.8
Anxiety	27.0	46.1	46.9	17.9	4.2
Oppositional	50.6	37.9	42.9	23.1	7.4
Conduct	27.2	47.2	51.9	14.2	4.8
Substance abuse	15.7	55.4	56.8	8.5	6.7
Attachment	40.9	43.8	51.0	16.1	5.7
Adjustment to trauma	43.0	43.3	53.1	19.3	5.0

The second strategy for monitoring outcomes using the CANS is to calculate dimensions scores (e.g. behavioral/emotional, risk, functioning, strengths). Dimension scores are generally calculated by average items within a dimension and then multiplying by ten to give uniform 30-point scales. There are two ways to use these dimension scores. First, it is possible to track these scores over time to create trajectories of recovery. Figure 21.1 presents an analysis of outcomes of residential treatment vs. other types of interventions using this approach (Lyons *et al.* 2009). Second, it is also possible to create Reliable Change Indices, in which raw change in dimension scores over residential treatment are compared with the size of change that would be reliable, given the standard deviation of the baseline dimension score and the reliability of the CANS. This approach is commonly used and several systems have reported benchmarks of between 50 percent and 60 percent of youth demonstrating reliable change on at least one dimension of the CANS over the course of residential treatment.

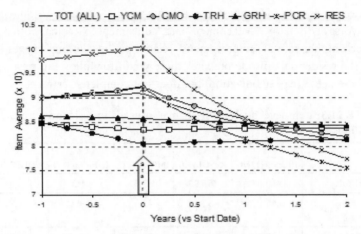

FIGURE 21.1: Hinge analysis of outcome trajectories prior to and after program initiation for Residential Treatment (RES) compared to Psychiatric Community Residence (PCR), Group Homes (GRH), Treatment Homes (TRH), wraparound (CMO) and supportive case management (YCM)

Conclusions

With the emerging awareness that most human-serving enterprises are intended to provide processes to support change, there has been growing interest in outcomes. Learning how to use outcomes to better manage residential treatment is no small task. However, we now have sufficient knowledge of the specifics of the processes to have confidence that the shift towards transformational management has the potential for profoundly positive impacts on both the business of helping and, more importantly, on the lives of the people we serve. Such success translates into the long-term success of residential treatment enterprises. The business of helping people can be designed so that everyone wins, as long as the people served are given an opportunity to change their lives in important ways.

COMMENTARY BY MARK COURTNEY ON:

Outcomes Management in Residential Treatment: The CANS Approach

JOHN S. LYONS AND LAUREN SCHMIDT

John Lyons and his colleagues have been developing the CANS system over many years. Initially used primarily to assess child and adolescent functioning in residential treatment settings, Lyons and colleagues, in collaboration with public and private child-serving agencies, have expanded the CANS into a comprehensive approach to serving children in out-of-home care. In this chapter, Lyons and Lauren Schmidt describe CANS in the context of a broader conceptual model they call Total Clinical Outcomes Management (TCOM), focusing on the use of CANS in residential treatment. The chapter highlights strengths of the TCOM approach and the use of CANS in particular, but it also raises questions about the limits of such tools given the structure of service delivery in the United States and much of the world, and our scant knowledge of the effectiveness of interventions.

Lyons and Schmidt make important observations about residential treatment and the potentially powerful role of CANS.

- Paying for services such as residential treatment on a fee-for-service basis is problematic. Purchasers of service—generally government—pay for inputs rather than outcomes. This creates the unintended consequence of incentivizing the ongoing use of residential treatment when it may no longer be appropriate.

- Residential treatment is arguably a transformational experience, and should be treated as such in assessing its place in the broader child welfare, children's mental health, and juvenile justice service realms. Residential treatment should not simply be the place that children are sent when nothing else has worked.

- CANS is ultimately a practice model and not just an assessment tool, and as such it makes lots of sense. It attempts to link the needs and strengths of children to the actions that might be expected to improve their well-being and to clarify whose actions are needed.

A major challenge in using CANS, or any other practice model for that matter, is our limited knowledge of what intervention(s) to make when confronted with particular children's needs and strengths. In most cases, no intervention has been shown to be effective in addressing an identified need. As the authors note, CANS is "agnostic as to etiology" when it comes to describing children's problems. While concern about underlying etiology should take a back seat to doing something, knowledge of the etiology of children's problems is essential to crafting effective interventions and allocating scare resources.

Another challenge to realizing the potential of TCOM and CANS is the structure of service delivery, including the decentralization of services to localities and public agency use of contracts with voluntary-sector providers for myriad services. Residential treatment exists in the context of a wide array of other out-of-home care settings and services, not to mention families and communities. Research has shown the outcomes of residential treatment to be strongly influenced by this context, particularly the child's post-discharge environment. Public agency implementation of TCOM and CANS across the entire service system is likely to have much greater impact on children's lives than when it is implemented solely within residential treatment.

Conclusion
Shaping the Future for
Therapeutic Residential Care

James K. Whittaker, Jorge F. del Valle and Lisa Holmes

As we assay the rich and varied collection of chapters and critical commentaries from our distinguished international contributors, two guiding assumptions for our collective effort are affirmed.

- The limited and declining value of any further generic discussions of "residential care" or "residential services" for high-resource using children and youth.

- The value added of cross-national discourse whether in policy initiatives, promising research directions or exemplary practices in Therapeutic Residential Care (TRC).

To say "residential care" or "residential services" communicates little beyond minimal setting information. The sheer range and variability of service components, change theories, frequency, intensity, and duration of specific intervention strategies, organizational arrangements (size of living units, lengths of stay, staffing arrangements, for example) to say nothing of protocols for staff training and development, and the integration of ongoing, systematic evaluation, all argue for increasing precision and specificity in both description and analysis. If residential services have fallen from favor as many of our contributors have noted, at least a partial reason must surely be that the term can mean so many different things in different contexts. This masking of differences in the use of umbrella terms such as "residential care" contrasts ever-more sharply with the conceptual and empirical precision that characterize many newer evidence-informed and evidence-based approaches to work with troubled youth such as Multi-Systemic Treatment (MST) and Multi-Dimensional Treatment Foster Care (MTFC) referenced in several earlier chapters. Proponents of these promising and innovative stratagems can speak with clarity and precision about intervention components, lengths of service, costs, and organizational characteristics in ways that are compelling to policymakers. In a head-to-head comparison with a largely unspecified and variable "residential" comparison, they will almost certainly win the rhetorical as well as the empirical battle.

Interestingly, this first assumption was at least partially validated by our second, that is, by our strongly felt need for serious cross-national exploration of differing patterns and processes in TRC. We chose to do this by organizing our search around a set of themes or dimensions and striving within these for cross-national insights and directions. In so doing, we limited our focus within group care to therapeutic settings that fell within the parameters of the nominal definition offered in our introductory chapter:

> Therapeutic Residential Care involves the planful use of a purposefully constructed, multi-dimensional living environment designed to enhance or provide treatment, education, socialization, support and protection to children and youth with identified mental health or behavioral needs in partnership with their families and in collaboration with a full spectrum of community-based formal and informal helping resources (Whittaker, del Valle and Holmes, this volume, p.24).

This meant that certain other uses of group residential care—such as care for AIDS orphans (Maundeni 2009; Stout 2009), provision of "places of safety" and residential academies (Little, Kohm and Thompson 2005) remain unexamined. We continue to believe this is justified in the case of more developed countries with complex social and health service systems where the case for residential placement increasingly goes beyond the need for basic care and involves a decision that high-intensity treatment services are needed for a small but challenging number of children and youth who present with multiple needs that cannot be effectively met in their family homes or communities, or even in specialized treatment foster care. Our continuing hope is that there are other pathways to effective therapeutic residential care besides that of a "last resort." Children with multiple and complex needs should not have to "fail their way" into needed services, but should receive them as a treatment of choice when indicated. To reach that point in policy and day-to-day practice, a considerable amount of research and development needs to occur—particularly in the development and testing of whole cloth models of TRC that are replicable and cost efficient as well as efficacious. This is nowhere more true than in the US where, as noted in our introduction, the most recent serious government or private foundation initiatives to actually develop innovative models of TRC are nearly a half century past. By contrast, substantial federal and private grants to alternative interventions have produced a veritable alphabet soup—e.g. MST, MTFC, FFT (Functional Family Therapy)—of promising, evidence-based and evidence-informed strategies for helping troubled youth and their families.

We believe our choice of themes, while clearly not exhaustive, offers a useful set of lenses for continuing to critically examine the multiple facets of TRC. At a minimum, the insights provided by our international contributors offers at least a tantalizing glimpse of possible future research directions.

Pathways to Therapeutic Residential Care

Our contributors here (Thoburn and Ainsworth; del Valle, Sainero and Bravo; Lyons, Obeid and Cummings; and Lausten) detail a picture of multiple needs that results in differing patterns of service arrangements in different contexts. Within them, there is some direction on who is best served in TRC. Can we further refine our analyses to identify clusters of children and youth who are most likely to benefit from placement in refined and reconstituted TRC as the treatment of first choice as opposed to last resort? Alternately, are their limits to innovative and otherwise efficacious family- and community-based programs when working with certain sub-clusters of children and youth with complex and high-resource needs?

Promising program models and innovative practices in Therapeutic Residential Care

Contributors here provide a richly detailed view of TRC including: variations within regional (Nordic) TRC (Jakobsen), a research-based, newly developed, model program (Andreassen), a data-driven model of family-style TRC with a long track record of research (Thompson and Daly), a regional initiative designed to recreate a TRC resource in an Australian state (McNamara), a careful documentation of the extent to which TRC (US) has adopted evidence-based interventions as well as an assessment of overall model development (James), and an innovative structural approach for insuring long-term familial engagement (Small, Bellonci and Ramsey).

Taken together, these contributions spur us to intensify the search for the critical or "active ingredients" in TRC: which are necessary and which are sufficient to achieve desirable outcomes?

What is the "glue" that holds these components together? Do we need more work on development of innovative whole cloth models of TRC? Alternately, to what degree will outcomes improve through the seriatim incorporation of ever-greater numbers of individual, evidence-based practices into existing TRC programs?

Preparing youth for successful transitions from Therapeutic Residential Care

Our distinguished researchers here (Okpych and Courtney; Stein; and Zeira) remind us all of the importance of anchoring our view of TRC in a timeframe and context that includes critical pre-placement factors as well as a range of supports of various kinds that will help insure post-placement maintenance of hard-won treatment and developmental gains. They also underscore the importance of raising the volume of youth and consumer voices in shaping and executing future TRC research. Their detailed references offer a glimpse of why the growing corpus of international research on transitions from care offers a rich resource in the quest for a revitalized TRC service component.

For future research, can we identify patterns of support specific to TRC and work to monetize and proceduralize these such that they can be imbedded into service contracts?

Critically examining the current research base for Therapeutic Residential Care

Working from both sides of the Atlantic, our two pairs of seasoned research contributors (Harder and Knorth; and Lee and Barth) in this area provide both a snapshot of what existing research on TRC tells us about what is "inside the black box," as well as offering solid suggestions for improving the quality of future TRC research. These include such varied stratagems as the use of latent class and latent trajectory models, meta-analyses and the use of learning collaboratives and existing scientific review processes such as the Campbell Collaboration to increase the rigor and quality of forthcoming research initiatives. They challenge us to consider: what steps will lead ultimately to the identification of an evidence-based model or models for TRC? How can research processes such as data mining help to build a research mindset and capacity within the TRC setting and thus facilitate the pathways for incorporation of specific, evidence-based practice strategies as well as efforts in the service of continuous quality improvement?

Calculating costs for Therapeutic Residential Care: regional and national perspectives

In this critical section, a singular contribution (Holmes) representing the collective efforts of the Centre for Child and Family Research Team at Loughborough University (UK) to develop an innovative, bottom-up method of calculating service costs, provided the stimulus for several thoughtful and incisive regional responses from North America (Small and Bellonci), Italy (Berti and Palareti), Scotland (Kendrick) and Australia (Ainsworth and Cheers). Viewed collectively, these contributions offer some useful pathways for future efforts to more accurately forecast TRC costs and associate these with the needs of children and expected outcomes. They raise as well some helpful directions for future research: how can the elusive search for the critical ("active") ingredients in TRC be joined effectively with the quest to determine service costs? How can research help us to monetize the multiple processes involved in TRC? Can we begin to validly and reliably compare key factors such as frequency, intensity and duration of TRC intervention to derive a better sense of dose effects and their impact on outcomes?

Linking focused training and critical evaluation in Therapeutic Residential Care: a foundation for staff support

In this final thematic section, a diverse cohort including both senior and junior researchers and scholars of the first rank, explore varied approaches for linking critical evaluation and training in existing TRC settings in such widely dispersed regional contexts as Spain (Bravo, del Valle and Santos); North America (Lyons and Schmidt) and North America, Australia and Europe (Holden, Anglin, Nunno and Izzo). The contribution from Grietens explores the distinctively European character of social pedagogy—an approach to staff preparation and program and professional development that has in recent years drawn considerable attention outside of the countries and regions of its origins. Collectively, these contributions spark a range of range of key questions for potential future research: given all that has been said about the variability of model development in TRC, what are reasonable expectations for the approaches identified here—SERAR, CANS, CARE, social pedagogy—to significantly impact and improve existing TRC programs? What are the organizational and service system requisites for adopting any of them? Are there cultural foundations, as, say, in the case of social pedagogy, that are critically important to its successful integration into new service contexts?

So it is that we conclude this brief volume on TRC with questions as opposed to definitive answers. Our efforts, and those of our distinguished contributors, yield no gilt-edged model of TRC, no panaceas, no definitive answers. What we do come away with are some workable templates and strategies for increasing our understanding of how TRC works, when it is indicated and its reasonable outcomes. We have benefitted greatly from the cross-national information provided in assembling these chapters. They illustrate for us both the commonality of issues faced by TRC and those who implement and study it, as well as the subtle nuances of culture, region and policy that shape differing responses to common problems. We continue to believe that viable answers for the future of TRC will emerge from cross-national exchange in research, policy discussion and practice. Paramount among these tasks will be the creation of a consensus-built, cross-national research agenda for TRC and concerted advocacy efforts to create the necessary government and private philanthropic resources to implement it. Leadership will be needed from our regional, national and international associations. At its core, this is a question of choice for the scores of high-resource using children and youth and their families who are the potential beneficiaries of a high-quality, revitalized TRC experience. As noted in our introduction, let us craft the best research and development we know how to do in TRC and then follow the data wherever it leads us. Let the work begin.

Contributors

Frank Ainsworth

Frank Ainsworth is Senior Principal Research Fellow (Adjunct) at James Cook University, School of Social Work and Human Services, Townsville (Queensland, Australia). He is well known nationally and internationally for his writing on child welfare issues, especially residential care services for children and youth. His first major work was: Ainsworth, F. and Fulcher, L.C. (Eds) (1981) *Group Care for Children: Concept and Issues.* London: Tavistock Publications. Frank is originally from the UK but he has lived in the US, and now for almost 30 years in Australia.

Tore Andreassen

Tore Andreassen is a psychologistwith much experience of working with children and youth. He completed a comprehensive review of residential treatment of young people with behavior problems published as a book in Norway and Sweden, which led him to develop a treatment program called MultifunC. He has also led the implementation of this model in five Norwegian units, and is leading the quality assurance team for this model in Norway. Andreassen is also the co-author of a Campbell and Cochrane review: *Cognitive-Behavioral Treatment for Antisocial Behavior in Youth in Residential Treatment*, in addition to several articles about residential treatment of juveniles. He also is a member of the Norwegian and the Danish Accreditation Panel within criminal justice.

James P. Anglin

Dr. James P. Anglin began his career as a frontline child and youth care counselor in 1970, working in a mental health center and then as coordinator of a community-based group home for adolescents before becoming involved in social policy development, children's services design and management, and education, research and training. He is a Professor and a former Director in the School of Child and Youth Care at the University of Victoria, BC (Canada), is a keen historian of the child and youth care profession and is currently researching the design and implementation of therapeutic residential care models cross-nationally. He is the author of: Anglin, J. (2002) *Pain, Normality and the Struggle for Congruence: Reinterpreting Residential Care for Children and Youth.* New York/London: Routledge; and coordinating editor of Anglin, J. (1990) *Perspectives in Professional Child and Youth Care.* New York: Haworth.

Richard P. Barth

Richard P. Barth, M.S.W., Ph.D., is Dean at the School of Social Work, University of Maryland (US). He previously held chaired professorships at the University of North Carolina and the University of California, Berkeley. His scholarship has spanned home visiting, parent training, evidence-based practice, kinship care, adoption and residential care. He was the 1998 recipient of the Presidential Award for Excellence in Research from the National Association of Social Workers, the Flynn Prize for Research in 2005, the Peter Forsythe Award for Child Welfare Leadership from the American Public Human Services Association in 2006, the Distinguished Achievement Award of the Society for Social Work and Research in 2010, and the Friends of Adoption Award from the North American Council on Adoptable children in 2012. He is currently the President of the American Academy of Social Work and Social Welfare.

Christopher Bellonci

Dr. Christopher Bellonci is a Board-certified child/adolescent and adult psychiatrist and Associate Professor at Tufts University School of Medicine (Boston, US). He has served on the Mental Health Advisory Board of the Child Welfare League for over a decade and is the President of the American Association of Children's Residential Centers. Dr. Bellonci has worked as Medical Director at Walker for 18 years, a multiservice agency that provides residential treatment. Dr. Bellonci co-authored the Practice Parameter on the Prevention and Management of Aggressive Behavior in Child and Adolescent Psychiatric Institutions with Special Reference to Seclusion and Restraint for the American Academy of Child and Adolescent Psychiatry (AACAP). Dr. Bellonci is a member of AACAP's Workgroup on Quality Issues, which is responsible for writing the practice parameters that define the standards of care for the field of child psychiatry. In 2008 Dr. Bellonci provided testimony to the US House of Representatives Committee on Education and Labor regarding unlicensed and unregulated boot camps and wilderness programs as well as the House Ways and Means Subcommittee on Income Security and Family Support regarding the increasing use of psychotropic medications for children in the child welfare system.

Chiara Berti

Chiara Berti is Professor of Social Psychology and Juridical Psychology of the University of Chieti-Pescara (Italy). She is an elected member of the Italian University Council (C.U.N.). After Graduate Studies of Medicine and Surgery at the University of Bologna, Italy, she followed postgraduate studies of Psychology at the University of Bologna and of Psychiatry at the University of Ancona, Italy. Her most recent research fields include, among others, social representation, social psychology of justice, juridical psychology and community psychology. She is a member of IAOBER, the International Association for Outcome-Based Evaluation and Research on Family and Children's Services.

Turf Böcker Jakobsen

Turf Böcker Jakobsen is Senior Researcher and Programme Director for research on child protection social work at SFI—The Danish National Centre for Social Research (Copenhagen, Denmark). He graduated in Anthropology and has a Ph.D., in Sociology. His main research interests are children and young people in public care, the changing knowledge base of social work and the meeting between clients and professionals within the welfare state. He has done extensive fieldwork in residential care settings for children and young people in Denmark, and conducted a number of mainly qualitative studies about child welfare services, including a comparative study of residential care in the Nordic countries, a study of breakdown in care for young people and research on kinship care.

Amaia Bravo

Amaia Bravo is Lecturer at the Department of Psychology in the University of Oviedo (Spain) and Assistant Director of the Child and Family Research Group devoted to program evaluation in child and youth care. As a researcher her main interests have been focused on outcomes assessment in residential child care, creating and validating instruments to support the monitoring and evaluation process of these programs. She has also researched the field of adult transitions for care leavers, outcomes assessment of interventions with young offenders and needs assessment of asylum-seeking children. Currently she is leading a national project to assess the mental health problems of children in residential care and the coverage and effectiveness of the therapies they receive. As a lecturer she teaches students of Psychology and Criminology in the field of psychosocial intervention.

Deirdre Cheers

Deirdre Cheers has been Executive Director of CatholicCare in the Catholic Diocese of Broken Bay (NSW, Australia) since 2007, and holds postgraduate qualifications in Social Work and Public Administration. She has over 30 years' experience in the specialist area of child and family practice including policy development and advice as well as extensive management expertise. She is internationally recognized as a strong advocate for innovative service improvement and quality of care outcomes for vulnerable children and families, and has worked closely with government and non-government organizations in Australia, the UK and Canada during her career. Deirdre is a member of the Australian Association of Social Workers, Chair of ACWA, the NSW Association of Children's Welfare Agencies, sits on the Ministerial Advisory Group for NSW Out-of-Home Care Transition from government to the non-government sector and is active in the NSW Catholic Education Commission.

Mark E. Courtney

Dr. Mark E. Courtney is a Professor in the School of Social Service Administration at the University of Chicago (US). His fields of special interest are child welfare policy and services, the transition to adulthood for vulnerable populations, the connection between child welfare services and other institutions serving families living in poverty, and the professionalization of social work. He is a faculty affiliate of Chapin Hall at the University of Chicago, which he served as Director from 2001 to 2006. He is an elected Fellow of the American Academy of Social Work and Social Welfare. He received the 2010 Peter W. Forsythe Award for leadership in public child welfare from the National Association of Public Child Welfare Administrators. Before moving into academia, Dr. Courtney worked for several years in various capacities providing group home care to abused and neglected adolescents.

Meagan Cummings

Meagan Cummings is a student in Psychology at the University of Ottawa, Canada.

Daniel L. Daly

Dr. Daniel L. Daly has been one of the principal architects of Boys Town's science-based youth care and education programs. He directs the Youth Care Department at Boys Town (Nebraska, US), one of the largest providers of services for at-risk children in the US. Dr. Daly has a Ph.D. in Clinical Psychology from West Virginia University and served as a US Army psychologist working with service personnel returning from Vietnam. He joined Boys Town in 1975 where he has held numerous leadership positions in such areas as clinical work, training, research and program dissemination. Dr. Daly has presented over 150 papers at scientific and service conferences, and authored or co-authored over 80 articles, book chapters and training manuals. He was on faculty at Kansas University for over 15 years. His areas of expertise are juvenile delinquency, adolescent mental health and dissemination of evidence-based programs.

Jorge F. del Valle (Co-Editor)

Jorge Fernández del Valle is the Director of the Child and Family Research Group (GIFI) and Professor of Psychology at the University of Oviedo, Spain. His research interests are in program evaluation in child care, particularly in residential and foster care. Dr. Jorge del Valle began his career as a social educator in therapeutic residential child care where he later worked as a psychologist. Since 1989 he has served on the Faculty of Psychology of the University of Oviedo where his principal areas of teaching have included psychosocial intervention, program evaluation and child and family social services. He is author/co-author/editor of 13 books and more than 80 peer-reviewed articles and book chapters in national and international journals and publications. He is Associate Director of *Psicothema*, one of the most important journals of psychology in Spain, and a member of the editorial board of numerous national and international journals. He is also member of International Foster Care (Siegen, Germany), EUSARF (European Scientific Association for Residential and Family Care for Children and Adolescents (Groningen, Netherlands) and INTRAC (International Research Network on Transitions to Adulthood from Care (Loughborough, UK).

Robbie Gilligan

Robbie Gilligan is Professor of Social Work and Social Policy at Trinity College Dublin, where he is also Associate Director (and co-founder) of the Children's Research Centre, and coordinator of the MSc in Child Protection and Welfare. He is also an (honorary) Research Fellow at SFI— The Danish National Centre for Social Research (Copenhagen, Denmark). He has been a youth worker, social worker, foster carer and board member of, and consultant to, residential children's services. His primary research interest relates to children and young people in public care (and in other challenging circumstances) and in effective responses to their needs. He has served as President of Childwatch International Research Network (2009–13). He is also a member of the Editorial Board of the journals *Child Abuse and Neglect*, *Child and Family Social Work*, *Child Indicators Research* and the *European Journal of Social Work*, and of the Advisory Boards of the journals *Adoption and Fostering* and *Children and Society*.

Hans Grietens

Hans Grietens is Full Professor in the Centre for Special Needs Education and Youth Care of the University of Groningen (Netherlands) and seconded as Professor to the Regional Centre for Child and Youth Mental Health and Child Welfare of the University of Trondheim (Norway). He is conducting research on child welfare, in particular in foster care. His core interests are the foster care experience through the eyes of (alumni) foster children, caring for foster children with a history of sexual abuse and trauma, matching foster children with foster families, mental health needs of looked-after children and historical child (sexual) abuse in care. He is President of EUSARF, the European Scientific Association on Residential and Family Care for Children and Adolescents and a member of IAOBER, the International Association for Outcome-Based Evaluation and Research on Family and Children's Services.

Annemiek T. Harder

Annemiek T. Harder, Ph.D., is Assistant Professor at the Department of Special Needs Education and Youth Care, University of Groningen (Netherlands). Her research interests include young people with serious behavioral problems, treatment approaches for reducing delinquency, interaction processes between young people and professionals during (residential) care, Motivational Interviewing and "what works" in (residential) youth care. In 2011 she finished her Ph.D. study cum laude, which was focused on the outcomes of secure residential youth care. She was the recipient of the 2009 national article prize by the Institute for the Study of Education and Human Development (ISED) and received an honorable mention (2nd prize) at the 2011 ISED dissertation prize. Currently, she is an active member of the International Research Network on Transitions to Adulthood from Care (INTRAC) and Editor of the *International Journal of Child and Family Welfare*.

Martha J. Holden

Martha J. Holden is a Senior Extension Associate with the Bronfenbrenner Center for Translational Research, the Director of the Residential Child Care Project at Cornell University and the author of the book *Children and Residential Experiences: Creating Conditions for Change*. Arlington, VA: CWLA. She provides technical assistance and training to residential child caring agencies, schools, juvenile justice programs and child welfare organizations throughout the US, Canada, the UK, Ireland, Australia and Israel. Previously she served as an administrator overseeing the day-to-day operations of a residential treatment agency for adolescents, including its education resources. Throughout her career she has been studying and working to improve the quality of care and prevent the occurrence of institutional abuse for children in out-of-home placements through her writing, curriculum development, training, technical assistance and influencing organizational culture.

Lisa Holmes (Co-Editor)

Lisa Holmes is Assistant Director of the Centre for Child and Family Research (CCFR), Loughborough University (UK). Over the past 14 years Lisa has undertaken a body of research funded by government departments, non-government organizations and children's charities to inform child welfare policy and practice. Lisa has managed CCFR's Costs and Outcomes research programme since 2007, and is responsible for the strategic development of the programme, which aims to explore the relationship between needs, costs and outcomes of services provided to vulnerable children and families. Publications include academic journal articles and books, as well as government reports and practice guides to inform policy and practice. Lisa also carries out responsive studies for various government departments in England; these include the Department of Health, Department for Education and Ministry of Justice.

The responsive studies are carried out to address specific policy issues. Lisa first started her career in child welfare as an outreach worker in 1991, working with vulnerable families, followed by two years working as a residential social worker in an adolescent children's home.

Charles V. Izzo

Dr. Charles V. Izzo is a Researcher in the Bronfenbrenner Center for Translational Research at Cornell University (US), and currently leads a multi-site evaluation of the CARE program. He is trained in Community and Clinical Psychology and has expertise in program development and evaluation, prevention science and community research methods. Dr. Izzo's research and writing focus on factors that influence caregiving, relationships between caregiving and child functioning, and methods to improve service quality. He has also provided training and consultation to human service professionals focused on local program evaluation, the utilization of data for program planning and skill development for direct service providers.

Sigrid James

Sigrid James, Ph.D., M.S.W., is a professor in the Department of Social Work and Social Ecology at Loma Linda University, California (US), and currently serves as guest professor in the Institute for Social Work and Social Welfare at the University of Kassel, Germany. She completed her graduate studies at the University of California, Los Angeles (M.S.W., 1990) and the University of Southern California (Ph.D., 2003). Her research, which has in part been funded by the National Institute of Mental Health, lies at the intersection of child welfare and mental health, and she has published numerous articles about the needs of young people in the child welfare system. She is particularly interested in effective interventions for this population, and her work in recent years has focused increasingly on effective treatments for youth in residential care settings.

Andrew Kendrick

Andrew Kendrick gained his Ph.D. in Social Anthropology at the London School of Economics before moving to the Department of Social Work at the University of Dundee. In 2001, he joined the Scottish Institute for Residential Child Care at the University of Strathclyde as Professor of Residential Child Care. He is currently Head of the School of Social Work and Social Policy, and closely involved in the work of CELCIS, the Centre For Excellence for Looked After Children in Scotland. He has carried out a wide range of research on children in care, and has been involved in a number of government inquiries addressing issues of safeguarding children in care. His current research focuses on the historic abuse of children in care and the measures required to address the needs of adults who experienced abuse as children in care.

Erik J. Knorth

Erik J. Knorth is Full Professor at the Department of Special Needs Education and Youth Care, University of Groningen (Netherlands). His research is focused on service characteristics that impact treatment outcomes for young people with serious emotional and behavioral problems, with a special interest in children and young people (at risk of) being placed out of home. He is project leader of the Collaborative Centre on Care for Children and Youth (C4Youth) and co-principal investigator of TakeCare, an extensive longitudinal study on service use and outcomes of children in care in the northern part of the Netherlands. He is an active member of international research networks including EUSARF, the European Scientific Association on Residential and Family Care for Children and Adolescents, where he serves as Vice-President. He has published widely in the field. In 2011 he received the Ubbo Emmius Award for international proliferation of northern child studies.

Mette Lausten

Mette Lausten is Senior Researcher at SFI—The Danish National Centre for Social Research (Copenhagen, Denmark). Mette has a Ph.D. in Economics from Aarhus School of Business (Denmark). Her research interests span from balancing family and work over child well-being to vulnerable children and children in out-of-home care using longitudinal data. Mette has 20 years' experience in working quantitatively on survey and register data, publishing articles and books on children in out-of-home care, children in preventive care and child well-being in general. Recent publications include: Egelund, T. and Lausten, M. (2009) 'Prevalence of mental health problems among children placed in out-of-home care in Denmark.' *Child and Family Social Work 2*, 14, 156–165; and Datta Gupta, N., Deding, M. and Lausten, M. (2010) *Medium-Term Consequences of Low Birth Weight: Is There a Catch-Up Effect?* Working Paper No.10–3. Aarhus: Department of Economics, Aarhus University.

Bethany R. Lee

Bethany R. Lee, M.S.W., Ph.D., is Associate Professor and Associate Dean for Research at the University of Maryland School of Social Work (US). Prior to her research career, Dr. Lee worked in residential programs as a frontline worker, social worker and administrator. Her current research interests explore the quality of services provided to young people at the intersection of child welfare and mental health services.

John S. Lyons

John S. Lyons, Ph.D., is the inaugural Endowed Chair of Child and Youth Mental Health Research at the University of Ottawa (Canada) and the Children's Hospital of Eastern Ontario and a Professor in the School of Psychology. He is the Editor of *Residential Treatment for Children and Youth*. He has published more than 200 peer-reviewed articles and six books.

Patricia M. McNamara

Patricia M. McNamara, Ph.D., teaches and conducts research in the Department of Social Work and Social Policy at La Trobe University in Melbourne (Australia). She is qualified in teaching, social work and family therapy, and practiced for many years as a clinician in residential psychiatric units. Her doctoral and postdoctoral research is Australia's first longitudinal follow-up with former residents in an adolescent psychiatric milieu. This study was conducted over a 15-year period. Dr. McNamara's current research interests include therapeutic foster and residential care, respite care, rural and remote social work and the expert practice of social work. She also undertakes cross-national research with colleagues in IAOBER, the International Association of Outcome-Based Evaluation and Research on Children's Family and Services; she is a Foundation Board member of this group which is based in Padua, Italy.

Michael A. Nunno

Michael A. Nunno, D.S.W., is a Senior Extension Associate with the Bronfenbrenner Center for Translational Research, the College of Human Ecology, Cornell University (US). He has examined how children die in restraints, the dynamics of adolescent female restraints episodes, investigating institutional abuse, the impact of training on organizational climates and measuring the effectiveness of the crisis prevention and monitoring system. He has published in *The American Journal of*

Orthopsychiatry, *Journal of Child and Family Studies, Child Abuse and Neglect: An International Journal, Children and Society Children and Youth Services Review, Applied Developmental Sciences,* and *Children and Youth Service Forum.* He edited the *Journal of Child and Youth Care*'s issue on institutional maltreatment and co-edited: Nuuno, M.A., Day, D.M. and Bullard L.B. (2008) *For Our Own Safety: Examining the Safety of High-Risk Interventions for Children and Young People.* Atlanta, GA: Child Welfare League of America.

Nicole Obeid

Nicole Obeid, Ph.D., is a Research Scientist at the Children's Hospital of Eastern Ontario (Canada). She recently completed her doctorate in Experimental Psychology at the University of Ottawa. She has worked with young people with eating disorders for the past 15 years.

Nathanael J. Okpych

Nathanael J. Okpych is a student at the University of Chicago (US) where he is pursuing a doctoral degree at the School of Social Service Administration and a Master's degree in Biostatistics and Epidemiology through the Department of Health Studies. His primary research interests focus on mental health and education outcomes and services for older youth in foster care. Prior to entering the Ph.D. program, he has worked in residential treatment, school and community settings with adolescents and their families. He also has several years' experience of working in college residential life.

Laura Palareti

Laura Palareti is a Researcher in Social Psychology at the Department of Education Studies of the University of Bologna (Italy). Since 2000 her studies have addressed the topic of quality evaluation of residential care, with a national research study aimed at identifying the critical ingredients related to effective programs. She also cooperated in Albania to reduce the institutionalization of children. Her research interests concern the study of risk and protective mechanisms regulating growth processes under normal and atypical conditions, with studies on multi-problematic families, chronically ill children and children in residential care. She teaches "Models and techniques of intervention in community services" and conducts workshops on programs' evaluation for a second cycle degree. She is a member of IAOBER, the International Association of Outcome-Based Evaluation and Research on Family and Children's Services, and of CESAF, the Centre for Studies and Higher Education on addiction, for which she is currently leading the evaluation of a school-based prevention program.

Susan Ramsey

Susan Ramsey, M.P.A., is a parent and children's mental health advocate. During her professional career Susan Ramsey has held senior management positions in human services and government. In 2007 she joined the staff of Walker, a multiservice agency that transforms the lives of children and youth who are dealing with complex emotional, behavioral and learning challenges, as its first Parent Liaison. As a member of Walker's Senior Leadership Team, she lends a parent's perspective to discussions and advises the agency on family engagement matters. During her tenure she has advanced family involvement in all aspects of the organization. Susan is a member of the Family Advisory Network for the Building Bridges Initiative and has been a contributor to: BBI (2012) *Engage Us! A Guide Written by Families for Residential Providers*. BBI; and Massachusetts Department of Mental Health (2012) *Creating Positive Cultures of Care Resource Guide*. Boston, MA: Massachusetts Department of Mental Health.

Ana Sainero

Ana Sainero graduated in Psychology at the University of Oviedo (Spain), and has been a member of the Child and Family Research Group since 2008. She has participated in various projects concerning several areas such as residential and foster care, as well as behavioral and mental health issues. Her main research topic is the assessment of mental health in out-of-home child care, carrying out the first study in Spain concerning the assessment of mental health of children in residential care in the autonomous community of Extremadura. In 2009 she obtained a grant for a Ph.D. program called Severo Ochoa in order to perform a longitudinal study of the assessment of development, welfare and mental health in children and youth in care. She is now concluding her doctoral dissertation on this topic.

Iriana Santos

Iriana Santos is an Associate Professor in the Education Department of the University of Cantabria (Spain) and also a member of the Child and Family Research Group in the University of Oviedo (Spain). As a researcher, her primary interests have been focused on the evaluation of both process and results in residential child care, adult transition for care leavers, needs assessment of asylum-seeking children and decision-making in child protection. Nowadays, she is taking part in the research team of a national project to assess the mental health problems of children in residential care, including treatment coverage as well as the effectiveness of the therapies they receive. She teaches students of a teaching degree in the field of Child Development Psychology and students of Criminology in the branch of Legal Psychology and Psychological Assessment.

Lauren Schmidt
Lauren Schmidt is a Project Director at the Children's Hospital of Eastern Ontario's Research Institute (Canada). She manages a project on youth suicide and oversees the Praed Foundation's collaborative training website for training and certification in the Child and Adolescent Needs and Strengths (CANS) and the Family Advocacy and Support Tool (FAST). She completed her Bachelor of Arts in Psychology from the University of Ottawa.

Richard W. Small
Dr. Richard W. Small, Ed.M., Ph.D., L.C.S.W., began his career working with troubled children while an undergraduate. After graduating from Boston College and receiving a Master's degree in education from Harvard University, Dr. Small worked for four years as a Clinical Co-ordinator at the Walker School, an experience that changed his life. In 1979, Dr. Small completed his Doctorate at the University of Washington School of Social Work in Seattle. He subsequently served for two years as the Staff Director of the Massachusetts Governor's Advisory Committee on Children and the Family. In 1981, he became an Assistant Professor at the State University of New York at Albany School of Social Welfare. Following the death of his mentor and former Walker founder, Albert E. Trieschman, Dr. Small returned to Walker in 1985 to become its second Executive Director. After stepping down as Walker C.E.O. in 2012, Dr. Small continues to work with Walker Partnerships, and serves as a part-time consultant to public and private agencies working on behalf of the most vulnerable children and families.

Mike Stein

Mike Stein is Research Professor in the Social Policy Research Unit at the University of York (UK). A qualified social worker, he has worked as a probation officer, a senior child care officer and an area manager. From 1975, at the University of Leeds, and from 1995, at the University of York, he has been researching the problems and challenges faced by vulnerable young people, including care leavers, young people running away from home and care, and neglected and maltreated adolescents. He is a joint coordinator of the Transitions from Care to Adulthood International Research Group (INTRAC). He has been involved in the preparation of Guidance for Leaving Care legislation in the UK, and been consulted on the development of leaving care services both in the UK and internationally. His most recent book is: Stein, M. (2012) *Young People Leaving Care, Supporting Pathways to Adulthood*. London: Jessica Kingsley Publishers.

June Thoburn

June Thoburn, C.B.E., Litt.D., M.S.W., is an Emeritus Professor of Social Work and member of the Centre For Research on Children and Families at the University of East Anglia (UEA) (Norwich, England). She worked in local authority social work in England and Canada before joining UEA in 1979. Her teaching and research have encompassed family support and child protection services for families in the community and services for children in care or placed for adoption. She was awarded a Leverhulme fellowship for a study of children in care in 28 jurisdictions and continues to work with academic colleagues across national boundaries to explore alternative permanence options. She is a Trustee of Break Charity, which provides longer-term group care and a transition to adulthood services for children for whom family care is not appropriate or has been tried and failed.

Ronald W. Thompson

Ronald W. Thompson is the Director and Founder of the Boys Town National Research Institute for Child and Family Studies (Nebraska, US). He has a Ph.D. in Psychological and Cultural Studies from the University of Nebraska. He has held a number of professional positions at Boys Town for the past 30 years and has a total of 40 years' experience as a clinician, program administrator, consultant, applied researcher and research administrator. Dr. Thompson has held faculty positions at the University of Nebraska Department of Special Education, Creighton University School of Medicine and the University of Kansas Department of Human Development. He has published more than 75 papers and book chapters and made more than 100 professional and scientific presentations related to residential care and treatment, parent training, childhood behavior and emotional problems, prevention and program evaluation and implementation.

James K. Whittaker (Co-Editor)

James K. Whittaker is The Charles O. Cressey Endowed Professor of Social Work Emeritus at the University of Washington, Seattle (US) where he has served as a member of senior faculty since 1970. His research and teaching interests encompass child and family policy and services, and the integration of evidence-based practices into contemporary child and family services. A frequent contributor to professional literature, Dr. Whittaker is author/co-author/editor of nine books and nearly 100 peer-reviewed papers and book chapters. In all, Dr. Whittaker's works have been translated into eight languages and he presently serves on the editorial review boards of a number of social service journals including: *Social Service Review* (US); *Journal of Public Child Welfare* (US); *The British Journal of Social Work* (UK); *Child and Family Social Work* (UK) and *International Journal of Child and Family Welfare* (Groningen, Netherlands); and *Child and Youth Care Forum* (US). He is a founding member of IAOBER, the International Association for Outcome-Based Evaluation and Research on Family and Children's Services (Padova, Italy) and an Associated Board member of EUSARF, the European Scientific Association for Residential and Foster Care for Children and Adolescents (Groningen, Netherlands).

Anat Zeira

Professor Anat Zeira is a faculty member at the School of Social Work and Social Welfare at the Hebrew University of Jerusalem (Israel), where she had served as head of the BSW program from 2004–08. She was a member of the Israeli National Council of Social Work and a member of the National Registration Committee at the Israeli Ministry of Welfare and Social Services. Currently she is Head of Research and Evaluation at the Haruv Institute. She is also a founding member of the Italian-based network IAOBER, the International Association for Outcome-Based Evaluation and Research on Family and Children's Services. Professor

Zeira has been long committed to research on the evidence base of social work practice with at-risk children and their families. Through her studies, numerous publications and international presentations, she emphasizes the importance of systematic monitoring and evaluation by practitioners and its dissemination in the field. Her recent research focuses on care leavers' transition to independent living.

References

AACRC (American Association of Children's Residential Centers) (2009a) 'Redefining residential: integrating evidence-based practices.' *Residential Treatment for Children and Youth 26*, 246–251.

AACRC (2006) *Redefining Residential: Becoming family driven.* Milwaukee, WI: AACRC (www.aacrc-dc.org).

AACRC (2009b) *Family-driven Care in Residential Treatment: Family members speak.* Milwaukee, WI: AACRC (www.aacrc-dc.org).

Abramovitz, R. and Bloom, S. (2003) 'Creating sanctuary in residential treatment for youth: from the "well-ordered asylum" to a "living-learning environment".' *Psychiatric Quarterly 74*, 2, 119–113.

Achenbach, T.M. and Rescorla, L. (2001) *Manual for the ASEBA School-age Forms and Profiles.* Burlington, VT: University of Vermont, Research Center for Children, Youths and Families.

Ackerman, S.J. and Hilsenroth, M.J. (2003) 'A review of therapist characteristics and techniques positively impacting the therapeutic alliance.' *Clinical Psychology Review 23*, 1, 1–33.

Ainsworth, F. (1985) 'Residential programs for children and youth. An exercise in reframing.' *British Journal of Social Work 15*, 2, 145–154.

Ainsworth, F. (1999) 'Social justice for "at risk" adolescents and their families.' *Children Australia 24*, 1, 14–18.

Ainsworth, F. (2007) 'Residential programs for children and young people: what we need and what we don't need.' *Children Australia 32*, 1, 32–36.

Ainsworth, F. (2012) 'Therapeutic residential care for children and young people. An attachment and trauma-informed model for practice.' Book review. *Children Australia 37*, 2, 80.

Ainsworth, F. and Hansen, P. (2005) 'A dream come true – no more residential care. A corrective note.' *International Journal of Social Welfare 14*, 3, 195–199.

Ainsworth, F. and Hansen, P. (2009) 'Residential Programs for Children and Youth: Their Current Status and Usage in Australia'. In M.A. Courtney and D. Iwaniec (eds) *Residential Care of Children: Comparative Perspectives.* New York: Oxford University Press.

Ainsworth, F. and Thoburn, J. (2013) 'An exploration of the differential usage of residential child care across national boundaries.' *International Journal of Social Welfare.* Published online 4 March 2013..

Ajzen, I. (1985) 'From Intentions to Actions: A Theory of Planned Behavior.' In J. Kuhl and J. Beckman (eds) *Action-Control: From Cognition to Behavior.* Heidelberg: Springer.

Alpert, L.T. and Meezan, W. (2012) 'Moving away from congregate care: one state's path to reform and lessons for the field.' *Children and Youth Services Review 34*, 8, 1519–1532.

Altschuler, D.M. (2008) 'Rehabilitating and reintegrating youth offenders: are residential and community aftercare colliding worlds and what can be done about it?' *Justice Policy Journal 5*, 1, 1–26.

Alwon, F.J., Cunningham, B.A., Phills, J., Reitz, A.L., Small, R.W. and Waldron, V.M. (2000) 'The Carolinas Project: A comprehensive intervention to support family-centered group care practice.' *Residential Treatment for Children and Youth 17*, 3, 47–62.

Anderson, R.L., Lyons, J.S., Giles, D.M., Price, J.A. and Estes, G. (2002) 'Reliability of the Child and Adolescent Needs and Strengths-Mental Health (CANS-MH) scale.' *Journal of Child and Family Studies 12*, 279–289.

Andreassen, T. (2003) *Treatment of Youth in Residential Care: Messages from Research*. Oslo: Kommuneforlaget. [Published in Norwegian with the title: *Behandling av Ungdom i Institusjoner – Hva Sier Forskningen?*]

Andreassen, T. (2004) *Manuals for MultifunC – Multifunctional Treatment in Residential and Community Settings*. Oslo: Kommuneforlaget.

Andrews, D. and Bonta, J. (2006) *The Psychology of Criminal Conduct* (4th edition). Newark, NJ: Anderson Publishing.

Andrews, D. and Dowden, C. (2004) 'The importance of staff practice in delivering effective correctional treatment: a meta-analytic review of core correctional practice.' *International Journal of Offender Therapy and Comparative Criminology 48*, 2, 203–214.

Andrews, D., Bonta, J. and Wormith, J.S. (2006) 'The recent past and near future of risk and/or need assessment.' *Crime and Delinquency 52*, 1, 7–27.

Andrews, D.A., Bonta, J. and Wormith, J.S. (2011) 'The Risk-Need-Responsivity (RNR) model. Does adding the good lives model contribute to effective crime prevention?' *Criminal Justice and Behavior 38*, 7, 735–755.

Andrews, D.A., Zinger, I., Hoge, R.D., Bonta, J., Gendreau, P. and Cullen, F.T. (1990) 'Does correctional treatment work? A clinically relevant and psychologically informed metaanalysis.' *Criminology 28*, 3, 369–404.

Anglin, J.P. (2002) *Pain, Normality, and the Struggle for Congruence: Reinterpreting Residential Care for Children and Youth*. Binghamton, NY: Haworth Press.

Anglin, J. (2003) *Pain, Normality and the Struggle for Congruence: Reinterpreting Residential Care for Children and Youth*. London: Haworth Press.

Anglin, J.P. (2012) 'The process of implementation of the care program model.' Paper presented at: EUSARF/CELCIS Looking After Children conference, Glasgow, Scotland.

Annie E. Casey Foundation (2010) *Rightsizing Congregate Care*. Baltimore, MD: Annie E. Casey Foundation. Available at aecf.org, accessed on 24 April 2014.

APPG (All Party Parliamentary Group) (2012) *The APPG for Runaway and Missing Children and Adults and the APPG for Looked After Children and Care Leavers report from the Joint Inquiry Into Children Who go Missing From Care*. London: APPG.

Armelius, B. and Andreassen, T.H. (2007) 'Cognitive-behavioral treatment for antisocial behavior in youth in residential treatment.' *Campbell Systematic Reviews 3*, 8.

Armsden, G.C. and Greenberg, M.T. (1987) 'The inventory of parent and peer attachment: relationships to well-being in adolescence.' *Journal of Youth and Adolescence 16*, 5, 427–454.

Arnett, J.J. (2000) 'Emerging adulthood: a theory of development from the late teens through the twenties.' *American Psychologist 55*, 5, 469–480.

Arnett, J.J. (2007) 'Afterword: aging out of care toward realizing the possibilities of emerging adulthood.' *New Directions for Youth Development 113*, 151–161.

Aronson, S. and Kahn, G.B. (2004) *Group Interventions for Treatment of Trauma in Adolescents Group Interventions for Treatment of Psychological Trauma* (pp. 89–114). New York: American Group Psychotherapy Association.

Ashby, L. (1997) *Endangered Children: Dependency, Neglect, and Abuse in American History*. New York: Twayne.

Atkinson, J. (2013) *Trauma-Informed Services and Trauma-Specific Care for Indigenous Australian Children*. Resource sheet 21. Canberra: Australian Institute of Health and Welfare and Melbourne: Australian Institute of Family Studies. Available at www.aihw.gov.au/uploadedFiles/ClosingTheGap/Content/Publications/2013/ctg-rs21.pdf, accessed on 24 April 2014.

Attar-Schwartz, S. (2008) 'Emotional, behavioral and social problems among Israeli children in residential care: a multi-level analysis.' *Children and Youth Services Review 30*, 2, 229–248.

Audit Scotland (2010) *Getting it Right for Children in Residential Care*. Edinburgh: Audit Scotland.

Australian Institute for Health and Welfare (2013) *Child Protection Australia 2011–2012*. Available at www.aihw.gov.au/publication-detail/?id=60129542755, accessed on 24 June 2014.

Axford, N., Little, M., Morpeth, L. and Weyts, A. (2005) 'Evaluating children's services: recent conceptual and methodological developments.' *The British Journal of Social Work 35*, 1, 73–88.

Baker, A.J., Archer, M. and Curtis, P.A. (2005) 'Age and gender differences in emotional and behavioural problems during the transition to residential treatment: the Odyssey Project.' *International Journal of Social Welfare 14*, 3, 184–194.

Baker, C. (2007) 'Disabled children's experience of permanency in the looked after system.' *British Journal of Social Work 37*, 7, 1173–1188.

Baker, C. (2011) *Permanence and Stability for Disabled Looked After Children (Insights 11)*. Glasgow: IRISS.

Bandura, A. (1977) *Social Learning Theory*. New York: General Learning Press.

Banks, J. and Vargas, L. (2009) *Sanctuary at the Andrus Children's Centre*. New York: ACLI. Available at www.sanctuaryweb.com/PDFs, accessed on 24 April 2014.

Barkley, R.A., Edwards, G.H. and Robin, A.L. (1999) *Defiant Teens: A Clinician's Manual for Assessment and Family Intervention*. New York: Guilford Press.

Barn, R. and Mantovani, N. (2007) 'Young mothers and the care system: contextualising risk and vulnerability.' *British Journal of Social Work 37*, 2, 225–243.

Barn, R., Andrew, L. and Mantovani, N. (2005) *Life After Care: The Experiences of Young People from Different Ethnic Groups*. York: Joseph Rowntree Foundation.

Barrett, P. M. and Ollendick, T. H. (2005) *Handbook of Interventions that Work with Children and Adolescents: Prevention and Treatment*. Chichester: John Wiley & Sons.

Barter, C.A., Renold, D., Berridge, D. and Cawson, P. (2004) *Peer Violence in Children's Residential Care*. London: Palgrave Macmillan.

Barth, R.P. (1990) 'On their own: the experience of youth after foster care.' *Child and Adolescent Social Work Journal 7*, 5, 419–440.

Barth, R.P. (2002) *Institutions vs. Foster Homes: The Empirical Base for the Second Century of Debate*. Chapel Hill, NC: University of North Carolina, School of Social Work, Jordan Institute for Families.

Barth, R.P. (2005) 'Residential care: from here to eternity.' *International Journal of Social Welfare 14*, 3, 158–162.

Barth, R.P., Greeson, J., Zlotnik, S. and Chintapalli, L. (2009) 'Evidence based practice for youth in supervised out-of-home care: a framework for development, definition and evaluation.' *Journal of Evidence-based Social Work 6*, 2, 147–175.

Barth, R.P., Greeson, J.K.P., Guo, S., Green, R.L., Hurley, S. and Sisson, J. (2007) 'Outcomes for youth receiving intensive in-home therapy or residential care: a comparison using propensity scores.' *American Journal of Orthopsychiatry 77*, 4, 497–505.

Barton, S., Gonzalez, R. and Tomlinson, P. (2012) *Therapeutic Residential Care for Children and Young People: An Attachment and Trauma-Informed Model for Practice*. London: Jessica Kingsley Publishers.

Bath, H. (2009) 'The changing role of residential care in Australia.' *Social Work Now: The Practice Journal of Child, Youth and Family 43*, 21–31.

Bayes, K. (2009) *Higher Aspirations, Brighter Futures: Overview of the Residential Child Care Initiative*. Glasgow: Scottish Institute for Residential Child Care.

BBI (Building Bridges Initiative) (2009) *Performance Indicators and Matrix*. Washington, DC: Building Bridges Initiative. Available at www.buildingbridges4youth.org/products/tools, accessed on 25 April 2014.

BBI (2010) *Self-Assessment Tool*. Washington, DC: Building Bridges Initiative. Available at www.buildingbridges4youth.org/sites/default/files/BB-SAT%20for%20youth%20%26%20families.pdf, accessed on 25 April 2014.

Beauchamp, S. and Hicks, C. (2004) 'Financial management and effectiveness in public service organisations: the CIPFA FM model.' *Public Money and Management 24*, 3, 185–191.

Becker-Weidman, A. and Shell, D. (ed.) (2010) *Attachment Parenting*. Lanham, MD: Jason Aronson.

Bedlington, M.M. (1983) 'The relationship between staff teaching and measures of youth delinquency and satisfaction: a correlational component analysis.' *Dissertation Abstracts International 44*, 4-B, 1227.

Beecham, J. (2000) *Unit Costs – Not Exactly Child's Play: A Guide to Estimating Unit Costs for Children's Social Care*. Canterbury: University of Kent: Department of Health, Dartington Social Research Unit and the Personal Social Services Research Unit.

Beecham, J. (2006) 'Why costs vary in children's care services.' *Journal of Children's Services 1*, 3, 50–62.

Beecham, J. and Sinclair, I. (2007) *Costs and Outcomes in Children's Social Care: Messages From Research.* London: Jessica Kingsley Publishers.

Benard, B. (2004) *Resiliency: What We Have Learned.* San Francisco, CA: WestEd.

Benbenishty, R. (2008) 'Israel.' In M. Stein and E. R. Munro (eds) *Young People's Transitions from Care to Adulthood: International Research and Practice* (pp.103–114). London: Jessica Kingsley Publishers.

Bengtsson, E., Chamberlain, C., Crimmens, D. and Stanley, J. (2008) *Introducing Social Pedagogy into Residential Child Care in England.* London: NCERCC/SET.

Bengtsson, T.T. and Jakobsen, T.B. (2009) *Institutionsanbringelser i Norden [Residential Care in the Nordic Countries].* Report 09:12. Copenhagen: SFI (The Danish National Centre for Social Research).

Berlin, B., Vinnerljung, B. and Hjern, A. (2011) 'School performance in primary school and psychosocial problems in young adulthood among care leavers from long term foster care.' *Children and Youth Services Review 33,* 12, 2489–2497.

Berridge, D. and Brodie, I. (1998) *Children's Homes Revisited.* London: Jessica Kingsley Publishers.

Berridge, D., Biehal, N. and Henry, L. (2011) *Living in Children's Residential Homes.* Research Report RR201. London: Department for Education. Available at http://php.york.ac.uk/inst/spru/pubs/2173, accessed on 24 April 2014.

Berridge, D., Biehal, N. and Henry, L. (2012) *Living in Children's Residential Homes.* London: Department for Education.

Berridge, D., Dance, C., Beecham, J. and Field, S. (2008) *Educating Difficult Adolescents.* London: Jessica Kingsley Publishers.

Berridge, D., Biehal, N., Lutman, E., Henry, L. and Palomares, M. (2011) *Raising the Bar? Evaluation of the Social Pedagogy Pilot Programme in Residential Children's Homes.* London: Department for Education.

Berridge, D., Beecham, J., Brodie, I., Cole, T., Daniels, H., Knapp, M. and MacNeill, V. (2003) 'Services for troubled adolescents: exploring user variation.' *Child and Family Social Work 8,* 4, 269–279.

Bettelheim, B. (1974) *A Home for the Heart.* New York: Knopf.

Bickman, L. (2008) 'Measurement Feedback System (MFS) is necessary to improve mental health outcomes.' *Journal of the American Academy of Child and Adolescent Psychiatry 47,* 10, 1114–1119.

Biehal, N. (2007) 'Reuniting children with their families: reconsidering the evidence on timing, contact and outcomes.' *The British Journal of Social Work 37,* 5, 807–823.

Biehal, N. and Wade, J. (1996) 'Looking back, looking forward: care leavers, families and change.' *Children and Youth Services Review 18,* 4/4, 425–446.

Biehal, N., Clayden, J., Stein, M. and Wade, J. (1994) 'Leaving care in England: a research perspective.' *Children and Youth Services Review 16,* 3–4, 231–254.

Biehal, N., Clayden, J., Stein, M. and Wade, J. (1995) *Moving On: Young People and Leaving Care Schemes.* London: HMSO.

Biehal, N., Dixon, J., Parry, E., Sinclair, I. *et al.* (2012) *The Care Placements Evaluation (CaPE) Evaluation of Multi-dimensional Treatment Foster Care for Adolescents (MTFC-A).* Research Brief, DFE-RB 194. London: Department for Education.

Bilson, A., Price, P. and Stanley, N. (2011) 'Developing employment opportunities for care leavers.' *Children and Society 25,* 5, 382–393.

Bird, V. and Eichsteller, G. (2011) 'The relevance of social pedagogy in working with young people in residential care.' *GoodEnoughCaring Journal 9.*

Blome, W.W. (1997) 'What happens to foster kids: educational experiences of a random sample of foster care youth and a matched group of non-foster care youth.' *Child and Adolescent Social Work Journal 14,* 1, 41–53.

Bloom, S. (1997) *Creating Sanctuary: Toward the Evolution of Sane Societies.* London: Routledge.

Bloom, S. (2005) 'The Sanctuary Model of organisational change for children's residential treatment, therapeutic community.' *The International Journal for Therapeutic and Supportive Organisations 26,* 1, 65–81.

Bloom, S. and Farragher, B. (2013) *Restoring Sanctuary: A New Operating System for Trauma-Informed Systems of Care.* New York: Oxford University Press.

Boendermaker, L., Van Rooijen, K. and Berg, T. (2010) *Residentiële Jeugdzorg: Wat Werkt? [Residential Youth Care: What Works?].* Utrecht: Netherlands Youth Institute.

Borduin, C.B., Mann, L., Cone, S., Henggeler, B., Fucci, D.B. and Williams, R. (1995) 'Multi-systemic treatment of serious juvenile offenders: long-term prevention of criminality and violence.' *Journal of Consulting and Clinical Psychology 63*, 4, 569–578.

Borntrager, C.F., Chorpita, B.F., Higa-McMillan, C. and Weisz, J.R. (2009) 'Provider attitudes toward evidence-based practices: are the concerns with the evidence or with the manuals?' *Psychiatric Services 60*, 5, 677–681.

Boston Consulting (2009) *Out of Home Care Review: Comparative and Historical Analysis.* Sydney: Boston Consulting.

Boswell, J. (1988) *The Kindness of Strangers: The Abandonment of Children in Western Europe from Late Antiquity to the Renaissance.* New York: Pantheon Books.

Bowlby, J. (1980) *Attachment and Loss (Volume 3).* New York: Basic Books.

Boyd, A.S., Einbinder, S.D., Rauktis, M.E. and Portwood, S.G. (2007) 'Building research capacity in residential treatment centers: an approach for empirical studies.' *Child and Youth Care Forum 36*, 1, 43–58.

Brack, A.B., Huefner, J.C. and Handwerk, M.L. (2012) 'The impact of abuse and gender on psychopathology, behavioral disturbance, and psychotropic medication count for youth in residential treatment.' *American Journal of Orthopsychiatry 82*, 4, 562–572.

Bravo, A. and del Valle, J.F. (2001) 'Evaluación de la integración social en acogimiento residencial.' *Psicothema 13*, 2, 197–204.

Bravo, A. and del Valle, J.F. (2009) 'Crisis and review of child residential care: its role in child protection.' *Papeles del Psicólogo 30*, 1, 42–52.

Bravo, A., del Valle, J.F., Chacón, S. and Pérez-Gil, J.A. (2002) 'Validez de constructo de un instrumento de evaluación en residencias de protección a la infancia [Content validity of an evaluation and recording system in residential child care].' *Metodología de las Ciencias del Comportamiento (vol. especial)* (95–98).

Bravo, A., del Valle, J.F., Chacón, S. and Pérez-Gil, J.A. (2004) 'La validez de contenido en un sistema de evaluación y registro en residencias de protección a la infancia [Construct validity of an evaluation instrument for residential child care].' *Metodología de las Ciencias del Comportamiento (vol. especial)* 105–112.

Bright, C.L., Raghavan, R., Kliethermes, M.D., Juedemann, D. and Dunn, J. (2010) 'Collaborative implementation of a sequenced trauma-focused intervention for youth in residential care.' *Residential Treatment for Children and Youth 27*, 2, 69–79.

Broad, B., Hayes, R. and Rushforth, C. (2001) *Kith and Kin: Kinship Care for Vulnerable Young People.* London: National Children's Bureau.

Brodie, I. and Morris, M. (2011) *Improving the Educational Outcomes for Looked After Children and Young People (Vulnerable Children Knowledge Review 1).* London: C4EO.

Broekaert, E., Soenen, B., Goethals, I., D'Oosterlinck, F. and Vandevelde, S. (2009) 'Life space crisis intervention as a modern manifestation of milieu therapy and orthopedagogy.' *International Journal of Therapeutic Communities 30*, 2, 122–145.

Bronfenbrenner, U. (1979) *The Ecology of Human Development: Experiments by Nature and Design.* Cambridge, MA: Harvard University Press.

Bronsard, G., Lançon, C., Loundou, A., Auquier, P., Rufo, M. and Siméoni, M. (2011) 'Prevalence rate of DSM mental disorders among adolescents living in residential group homes of the French Child Welfare System.' *Children and Youth Services Review 33*, 1886–1890.

Brown, J.D., Barrett, K., Ireys, H.T., Allen, K. and Blau, G. (2011) 'Outcomes monitoring after discharge from residential treatment facilities for children and youth.' *Residential Treatment for Children and Youth 28*, 4, 303–310.

Brown, J.D., Barrett, K., Ireys, H.T., Allen, K., Pires, S.A. and Blau, G. (2010) 'Family-driven, youth guided principles in residential treatment: findings from a national survey of residential treatment facilities.' *Residential Treatment for Children and Youth 27*, 3, 149–159.

Browne, K., Hamilton-Giachritsis, C., Johnson, R. and Osterbren, M. (2006) 'Overuse of institutional care of children in Europe.' *British Medical Journal 332*, 485–487.

Brunner, C. and O'Neill, C. (2009) 'Mirror families: creating extended families for life.' *Children Australia 34*, 4, 6–12.

Bruns, E.J. (2008) 'The Evidence Base and Wraparound.' In E.J. Bruns and J.S. Walker (eds) *The Resource Guide to Wraparound. Portland; or: National Wraparound Initiative.* Portland, OR: Research and Training Center for Family Support and Children's Mental Health.

Bryderup, I.M. (2005) *Børnelove og Socialpædagogik Gennem Hundrede år [Child Act and Social Pedagogy Through One Hundred Years]*. Århus: Forlaget Klim.

Buehler, C., Orme, J.G., Post, J. and Patterson, D.A. (2000) 'The long-term correlates of family foster care.' *Children and Youth Services Review 22*, 8, 595–625.

Bullock, R., Little, M. and Milham, S. (1993) *Residential Care of Children: A Review of the Research.* London: HMSO.

Burns, B.J. and Hoagwood, K. (2002) *Community Treatment for Youth: Evidence-Based Interventions for Severe Emotional and Behavioral Disorders.* New York: Oxford University Press.

Burns, B.J., Hoagwood, K. and Mrazek, P.J. (1999) 'Effective treatment for mental disorders in children and adolescents.' *Clinical Child and Family Psychology Review 2*, 199–254.

Burns, B.J., Phillips, S., Wagner, H.R., Barth, R., Kolko, D., Campbell, Y. and Landsverk, J. (2004) 'Mental health need and access to mental health services by youths involved with child welfare: a national survey.' *Journal of the American Academy of Child and Adolescent Psychiatry 43*, 960–970.

Butler, L.S. and McPherson, P.M. (2007) 'Is residential treatment misunderstood?' *Journal of Child and Family Studies 16*, 4, 465–472.

Butler, L.S., Little, L. and Grimard, A.R. (2009) 'Research challenges: implementing standardized outcome measures in a decentralized, community-based residential treatment program.' *Child and Youth Care Forum 38*, 75–90.

California Evidence-Based Clearinghouse (2013) *Scientific Rating Scale.* San Diego, CA. Available at www.cebc4cw.org/ratings/scientific-rating-scale, accessed on 25 April 2014.

Cameron, C. and Moss, P. (eds) (2011) *Social Pedagogy and Working with Children and Young People. Where Care and Education Meet.* London: Jessica Kingsley Publishers.

Carmody T. (2013) *Taking Responsibility: A Road Map for Queensland Child Protection.* Brisbane, Australia: Queensland Child Protection Commission of Inquiry.

Carr, A. (2009) *What Works with Children, Adolescents, and Adults? A Review of Research on the Effectiveness of Psychotherapy.* London: Routledge.

Casas, F., Boada, C., Jackson, S. and Cameron, C. (2010) *Young People from a Public Care Background: Establishing a Baseline of Attainment and Progression Beyond Compulsory Schooling in Five EU Countries.* Available at http://tcru.ioe.ac.uk/yippee/Portals/1/YiPPEE%20WP34%20FINAL%2026%20 03%2010%20(3).pdf, accessed on 25 April 2014.

Cashmore, J. and Paxman, M. (1996) *Wards Leaving Care: A Longitudinal Study.* Sydney, Australia: Department of Community Services.

Cashmore, J. and Paxman, M. (2006) 'Wards leaving care: follow up five years later.' *Children Australia 31*, 3, 18–25.

Cashmore, J. and Paxman, M. (2007) *Wards Leaving Care: Four to Five Years On.* Sydney: Social Policy Research Center, University of New South Wales.

Centre for Excellence in Child and Family Welfare Inc. (2013) *Breakfast Forum with James Anglin.* 17 May. Melbourne, Australia: Centre for Excellence in Child and Family Welfare Inc. Available at www.cfecfw.asn.au/event/2013/04/breakfast-forum-%E2%80%93-dr-james-anglin, accessed on 24 June 2014.

Chakrabarti, M. and Hill, M. (2000) *Residential Child Care: International Perspectives on Links with Families and Peers.* London: Jessica Kingsley Publishers.

Chamberlain, P. (2003) *Treating Chronic Juvenile Offenders: Advances Made Through the Oregon Multidimensional Treatment Foster Care Model.* Washington, DC: American Psychological Association.

Chamberlain, P. and Reid, J.B. (1998) 'Comparison of two community alternatives to incarceration for chronic juvenile offenders.' *Journal of Consulting and Clinical Psychology 66*, 4, 624.

Chamberlain, P. and Smith, D.K. (2005) 'Multi-dimensional Treatment Foster Care: A Community Solution for Boys and Girls Referred from Juvenile Justice.' In E.D. Hibbs and P.S. Jensen (eds) *Psychosocial Treatments for Child and Adolescent Disorders: Empirically Based Strategies for Clinical Practice* (2nd edition) (pp.557–573). Washington, DC: American Psychological Association.

Chamberlain, P., Snowden, L.R., Padgett, C., Saldana, L., *et al.* (2011) 'A strategy for assessing costs of implementing new practices in the child welfare system: adapting the English cost calculator in the United States.' *Administration and Policy in Mental Health and Mental Health Services Research 38*, 1, 24–31.

Chambless, D.L. and Hollon, S. (1998) 'Defining empirically supported therapies.' *Journal of Consulting and Clinical Psychology 66*, 1, 7–18.

Child Welfare Strategy Group (2013) *Florida Department of Children and Families: Assessment Findings and Recommendations.* Baltimore, MD: Annie E. Casey Foundation.

Chipenda-Dansokho, S. and the Centre for Social Policy (2003) 'The determinants and influence of size on residential settings for children.' *International Journal of Child and Family Welfare 6*, 3, 66–76.

Chor, B.K.H., McClelland, G.M., Weiner, D.A., Jordan, N. and Lyons, J.S. (2012) 'Predicting outcomes of children in residential treatment: a comparison of a decision support algorithm and a multidisciplinary team decision model.' *Child and Youth Services Review 34*, 11, 2345–2352.

Chor, B.K.H., McClelland, G.M., Weiner, D.A., Jordan, N. and Lyons, J.S. (2013) 'Patterns of out of home decision making.' *Child Abuse and Neglect 37*, 10, 871–882.

Chor, B.K.H., Mclelland, G.M., Weiner, D.A., Jordan, N. and Lyons, J.S. (2014) 'Out-of-home placement decision-making and clinical outcomes in child welfare: a longitudinal study.' *Child Welfare* (in press).

Chorpita, B.F and Daleidin, E.L. (2009) 'Mapping evidence-based treatments for children and adolescents: application of the distillation and matching model to 615 treatments from 322 randomized trials.' *Journal of Consulting Clinical Psychology 77*, 3, 566–579.

Chorpita, B.F., Bernstein, A.D. and Daleiden, E.L. (2011) 'Empirically guided coordination of multiple evidence-based treatments: an illustration of relevance mapping in children's mental health services.' *Journal of Consulting and Clinical Psychology 79*, 4, 470–480.

Chorpita, B.F., Bernstein, A.D., Daleiden, E.L. and the Research Network on Youth Mental Health. (2008) 'Driving with roadmaps and dashboards: using information resources to structure the decision models in service organizations.' *Administration and Policy in Mental Health and Mental Health Services Research 35*, 1–2, 114–123.

Clarke, A. (2011) 'Three therapeutic residential care models, the Sanctuary Model, Positive Peer Culture and Dyadic Developmental Psychotherapy and their application to the theory of congruence.' *Children Australia 36*, 2, 81–87.

Clarke, A. (2012) 'Why the Sanctuary model?' *Developing Practice: Child Youth and Family Work Journal 31*, 3–61.

Clarke, A. (2013) 'Sanctuary in action.' *Children Australia 38*, 3, 95–99.

Clausen, J.M., Landsverk, J., Ganger, W., Chadwick, D. and Litrownik, A. (1998) 'Mental health problems of children in foster care.' *Journal of Child and Family Studies 7*, 283–296.

Clayden, J. and Stein, M. (2005) *Mentoring Young People Leaving Care, Someone for Me.* York: Joseph Rowntree Foundation.

Clough, R., Bullock, R. and Ward, A. (2006) *What Works in Residential Child Care: A Review of Research Evidence and the Practical Considerations.* London: National Children's Bureau.

Coleman, J.C. and Hendry, L. (1999) *The Nature of Adolescence.* London: Routledge.

Coleman, M., Pfeiffer, S. and Oakland, T. (1992) 'Aggression replacement training with behaviorally disordered adolescents.' *Behavioral Disorders 18*, 1, 54–66.

Colton, M. and Roberts, S. (2007) 'Factors that contribute to high turnover among residential child care staff.' *Child and Family Social Work 12*, 2, 133–142.

Colton, M., Vanstone, M. and Walby, C. (2002) 'Victimization, care and justice: reflections on the experiences of victims/survivors involved in large-scale historical investigations of child sexual abuse in residential institutions.' *British Journal of Social Work 32*, 5, 541–551.

Connolly, C., Roberts, R., Waterman, C., Bengo, C. and Blackeby, K. (2012) *Children's Homes: What Might Work?* London: South London and Maudsley NHS Foundation Trust.

Cook, R.J. (1994) 'Are we helping foster care youth prepare for their future?' *Children and Youth Services Review 16*, 3/4, 213–229.

Cornsweet, C. (1990) 'A review of research on hospital treatment of children and adolescents.' *Bulletin of the Menninger Clinic 54*, 1, 64–77.

Cottle, C.C., Lee, R.J. and Heilburn, K. (2001) 'The prediction of criminal recidivism in juveniles: a meta-analysis.' *Criminal Justice and Behaviour 28*, 3, 367–395.

Council of Europe (2006) *Rights of Children at Risk and in Care.* Strasbourg: Council of Europe Publishing.

Council of Europe (2009) *Children and Young People in Care: Discover your Rights.* Strasbourg: Council of Europe Publishing.

Courtney, M.E. and Dworsky, A. (2006) 'Early outcomes for young adults transitioning from out-of-home care in the USA.' *Child and Family Social Work 11*, 3, 209–219.

Courtney, M.E. and Hughes-Heuring, D. (2009) 'Residential Care in the United States of America: Past, Present and Future.' In M.E. Courtney and D. Iwaniec (eds) *Residential Care of Children: Comparative Perspectives.* New York/Oxford: Oxford University Press.

Courtney, M.E. and Iwaniec, D. (eds) (2009) *Residential Care of Children: Comparative Perspectives.* New York: Oxford University Press.

Courtney, M.E., Dolev, T. and Gilligan, R. (2009) 'Looking Backward to See Forward Clearly: A Cross-National Perspective on Residential Care.' In M.E. Courtney and D. Iwaniec (eds) *Residential Care of Children: Comparative Perspectives* (pp.173–208). New York: Oxford University Press.

Courtney, M.E., Lee, J.A. and Perez, A. (2011) 'Receipt of help acquiring life skills and predictors of help receipt among current and former foster youth.' *Children and Youth Services Review 33*, 12, 2242–2451.

Courtney, M.E., Terao, S. and Bost, N. (2004) *Midwest Evaluation of Adult Functioning of Former Foster Youth: Conditions of Youth Preparing to Leave State Care.* Chicago, IL: Chapin Hall Center for Children at the University of Chicago.

Courtney, M.E., Dworsky, A., Lee, J.S. and Raap, M. (2010) *Midwest Evaluation of the Adult Functioning of Former Foster Youth: Outcomes at Age 23 and 24.* Chicago, IL: Chapin Hall Center for Children at the University of Chicago.

Courtney, M.E., Dworsky, A., Brown, A., Carey, C., Love, C. and Vorhies, V. (2012) *Midwest Evaluation of Adult Functioning of Former Foster Youth: Outcomes at Age 26.* Chicago, IL: Chapin Hall Center for Children at the University of Chicago.

Courtney, M.E., Dworsky, A., Cusick, G.R., Havlicek, J., Perez, A. and Keller, T. (2007) *Midwest Evaluation of the Adult Functioning of Former Foster Youth: Outcomes at Age 21.* Chicago, IL: Chapin Hall Center for Children at the University of Chicago.

Courtney, M.E., Dworsky, A., Ruth, G., Keller, T., Havlicek, J. and Bost, N. (2005) *Midwest Evaluation of Adult Functioning of Former Foster Youth: Outcomes at Age 19.* Chicago, IL: Chapin Hall Center for Children at the University of Chicago.

Curry, J.F. (1991) 'Outcome research on residential treatment: implications and suggested directions.' *American Journal of Orthopsychiatry 61*, 3, 348–357.

Curtis, L. (ed.) (2012) *The Unit Costs of Health and Social Care 2012.* Canterbury: Personal Social Services Research Unit, University of Kent.

Cuthbert, R., St. Pierre, J., Stewart, S.L., Cook, S., Johnson, A.M. and Leschied, A.W. (2011) 'Symptom persistence in seriously emotionally disordered children: findings of a two-year follow-up after residential treatment.' *Child and Youth Care Forum 40*, 4, 267–280.

Daining, C. and DePanfilis, D. (2007) 'Resilience of youth in transition from out of home care to adulthood.' *Children and Youth Services Review 29*, 9, 1158–1178.

Daly, D.L. and Nordlinger, B.R. (1997) 'National standards: guiding principles in outcome assessment.' *Caring 13*, 19–21.

Daniël, V. and Harder, A.T. (2010) *Relatie als de Sleutel? Ervaringen van Jongeren en Hulpverleners in de Residentiële Jeugdzorg [Relationship as the Key? Experiences of Young People and Care Workers in Residential Youth Care].* Amsterdam: SWP Publishers.

Davidson-Arad, B. (2005) 'Fifteen month follow up of children at risk: comparison of the quality of life of children removed from home and children remaining at home.' *Children and Youth Services Review 27*, 1, 1–20.

Davies, B. and Knapp, M. (1988) 'Costs and Residential Social Care.' In I. Sinclair (ed.) *Residential Care: The Research Reviewed.* London: National Institute for Social Work, HMSO.

Davies, C. and Ward, H. (2011) *Safeguarding Children Across Services: Messages from Research.* London: Jessica Kingsley Publishers.

De Swart, J.J.W., Van den Broek, H., Stams, G.J.J.M., Asscher, J.J., *et al.* (2012) 'The effectiveness of institutional youth care over the past three decades: a meta-analysis.' *Children and Youth Services Review 34,* 9, 1818–1824.

Defensor del Pueblo (2009) *Centros de Protección Menores con Trastornos de Conducta y en Situación de Dificultad Social [Residential Child Care for Children with Behavioral Diseases and Social Difficulties].* Madrid: Defensor del Pueblo.

del Valle, J.F. (1998) *Manual de Programación y Evaluación para los Centros de Protección de Menores [Manual for Planning and Assessment in Residential Child Care Services].* Salamanca: Servicio de Publicaciones de la Junta de Castilla y León.

del Valle, J.F. and Bravo, A. (2007) *SERAR. Sistema de Evaluación y Registro en Acogimiento Residencial [SERAR. Evaluation and Recording System in Residential Child Care Services].* Oviedo: Nieru.

del Valle, J.F. and Bravo, A. (2013) 'Current trends, figures and challenges in out-of-home child care: an international comparative analysis.' *Psychosocial Intervention 22,* 3, 251–257.

del Valle, J.F., Sainero, A.M. and Bravo, A. (2011) *Salud Mental de Menores en Acogimiento Residencial: Guía para la Prevención e Intervención en Hogares y Centros de Protección de la Comunidad Autónoma de Extremadura. [Mental Health of Children in Residential Care: A Guide for Prevention and Intervention in Residential Facilities of the Autonomous Community of Extremadura].* Badajoz: Servicio Extremeño de Salud.

del Valle, J.F., Bravo, A., Hernández, M. and Santos, I. (2012) *Estándares de Calidad en Acogimiento Residencial Especializado EQUAR-E. [Quality Standards for Specialised Residential Care EQUAR-E].* Madrid: Ministerio de Sanidad, Servicios Sociales e Igualdad.

del Valle, J.F., López, M., Montserrat, C. and Bravo, A. (2009) 'Twenty years of foster care in Spain: profiles, patterns and outcomes.' *Children and Youth Services Review 31,* 8, 847–853.

Delap, E. (2011) *Scaling Down: Reducing, Reshaping and Improving Residential Care around the World.* London: EveryChild.

Deloitte (2007) *Determining the Optimum Supply of Children's Residential Care.* London: Department for Children, Schools and Families.

Department for Education (2011) *Children's Homes Data Pack.* London: Department for Education.

Department for Education (2012) *Children Looked After in England.* London: Department for Education.

Department for Education (2013a) *Children's Homes Data Pack.* London: Department for Education.

Department for Education (2013b) *Section 251 Expenditure Return: Summary Level LA Outturn Data Reports (2011–12).* London: Department for Education.

Department of Health (2000) *The Children (Leaving Care) Act 2000: Regulations and Guidance.* London: Department of Health.

Department of Health (2001a) *Research Briefing One: Costs and Effectiveness of Services for Children in Need.* London: Department of Health.

Department of Health (2001b) *Children's Social Services Core Information Requirements Process Model.* London: Department or Health.

DHS (Department of Human Services-Verso) (2011) *Evaluation of the Theraputic Residential Care Pilot Programs: Final Summary and Technical Report.* Victoria: Verso Consulting Pty Ltd.

De Toni, A.F. and Comello, L. (2010) *Journey into Complexity.* Lexington, KY: Amazon.

DiGennaro Reed, F.D. and Reed, D.D. (2008) 'Towards an understanding of evidence-based practice.' *Journal of Early and Intensive Behavior Intervention 5,* 2, 20–29.

Dinisman, T. and Zeira, A. (2011) 'The contribution of individual, social support and institutional characteristics to perceived readiness to leave care in Israel: an ecological perspective.' *British Journal of Social Work 41,* 8, 1442–1458.

Dishion, T.J., McCord, J. and Poulin, F. (1999) 'When interventions harm: peer groups and problem behavior.' *American Psychologist 54,* 9, 755–764.

Dixon, J. (2008) 'Young people leaving care: health, well-being and outcomes.' *Child and Family Social Work 13,* 2, 207–217.

Dixon, J. and Stein, M. (2005) *Leaving Care, Through Care and Aftercare in Scotland.* London: Jessica Kingsley Publishers.

Dixon, J., Lee, J., Wade, J., Byford, S., Weatherley, H. and Lee, J. (2006) *Young People Leaving Care: An Evaluation of Costs and Outcomes. Final Report to the DfES.* York: Social Policy Research Unit, University of York.

Dockar-Drysdale, B. (1990) *The Provision of Primary Experience.* London: Free Association Books.

Dodge, K.A. and Sherrill, M. (2006) 'Deviant Peer-Group Effects in Youth Mental Health Interventions'. In K. Dodge, T. Dishion, and J. Lansford (eds) *Deviant by Design: Interventions that Aggregate Youth.* (pp.97–121). New York: Guilford Press.

Dodge, K.A., Dishion, T.J. and Lansford, J.E. (eds) (2006) *Deviant Peer Influences in Programs for Youth, Problems and Solutions.* New York: Guilford Press.

Dolev, T., Ben-Rabi, D. and Zemach-Marom, T. (2009) 'Residential Care for Children At-Risk in Israel.' In M. Courtney and D. Iwaniec (eds) *Residential Care of Children: Comparative Perspective* (pp.72–87). New York: Oxford University Press.

Dollard, N. and Rautkis, M. (2009) 'SPANS: Linking Assessment to Planning' In S.J. Lyons and D.A. Weiner (eds) *Strategies in Behavioral Healthcare: Total Clinical Outcomes Management.* New York: Civic Research Institute.

Dowden, C. and Andrews, D.A. (2000) 'Effective correctional treatment and violent reoffending: a meta-analysis.' *Canadian Journal of Criminology 42*, 4, 449–476.

Drake, B. and Jonson-Reid, M. (1999) 'Some thoughts on the increasing use of administrative data in child maltreatment research.' *Child Maltreatment 4*, 4, 308–315.

Duncan, B.L., Miller, S.D., Hubble, M.A. and Wampold, B.E. (eds) (2010) *The Heart and Soul of Change: Delivering What Works in Therapy* (2nd edition). Washington, DC: American Psychological Association.

Duppong Hurley, K., Lambert, M.C., Van Ryzin, M., Sullivan, J. and Stevens, A. (2013) 'Therapeutic alliance between youth and staff in residential group care: psychometrics of the Therapeutic Alliance Quality Scale.' *Children and Youth Services Review 35*, 1, 56–64.

Duppong Hurley, K., Trout, A., Griffith, A., Epstein, M., Thompson, R. and Mason, W.A. (2010) 'Creating and sustaining effective partnerships to advance research on youth with serious emotional and behavioral disorders.' *Journal of Disability Policy Studies 21*, 3, 141–151.

Egelund, T. and Hestbæk, A.D. (2007) 'Små børn anbragt uden for hjemmet: resultater fra et Dansk longitudinelt studie af anbragte børn fra 1995-kohorten [Young children in out-of-home care: results from the Danish longitudinal study of children, born in 1995, in care].' *Nordisk Sosialt Arbeid 2*, 120–133.

Egelund, T. and Jakobsen, T.B. (2009a) 'Standardized individual treatment: a contradiction in terms? Professional principles and social practices in residential care.' *Childhood 16*, 2, 265–282.

Egelund, T. and Jakobsen, T.B. (2009b) *Omsorg for Anbragte Børn og Unge: Døgninstitutionens Hverdag og Vilkår [Care for Children Placed Outside the Home: Conditions and Everyday Practices in the Residential Institution].* Copenhagen: Akademisk Forlag.

Egelund, T. and Jakobsen, T.B. (2011) *Døgninstitutionen: Modsætninger og Strategier når Børn og Unge Anbringes [Residential Care: Dilemmas and Strategies in Out-of-Home Care].* Copenhagen: Hans Reitzels Forlag.

Egelund, T. and Lausten, M. (2009) 'Prevalence of mental health problems among children placed in out-of-home care in Denmark.' *Child and Family Social Work 2*, 14, 156–165.

Ellis, R.A. (ed.) (2009) *Best Practices in Residential Treatment.* New York: Routledge.

Emond, R. (2005) 'From Planning to Practice: Doing Ethnographic Research with Children and Young People.' In S.M. Greene and D.M. Hogan (eds) *Researching Children's Experiences: Approaches and Methods.* London: Sage.

English, M.J. (2002) 'Policy Implications Relevant to Implementing Evidence-Based Treatment.' In J. Burns and K. Hoagwood *Community Treatment for Youth: Evidence-Based Interventions for Severe Emotional and Behavioral Disorders.* New York: Oxford University Press.

Ernst & Young (2010) *Out-of-home Care Caseload Review Report. Benchmark Study.* Sydney: Ernst & Young.

Esakl, N., Benamati, J., Yanosy, S., Middleton, J.S., Hopson, L.M., Hummer, V.I. and Bloom, S. (2013) 'The Sanctuary model: theoretical framework.' *Families in Society 94*, 1, 87–95.

Esping-Andersen, G. (1990) *The Three Worlds of Welfare Capitalism.* Princeton, NJ: Princeton University Press.

EUROARC (European Association for Research into Residential Child Care) (1998) *Care to Listen: A Report of Residential Child Care in Four European Countries.* Glasgow: The Center for Residential Child Care.

Eurochild (2010) *Children in Alternative Care.* Brussels: National Surveys.

Evenboer, K.E., Huyghen, A.M.N., Tuinstra, J., Knorth, E.J. and Reijneveld, S.A. (2012) 'A taxonomy of care for youth: Results of an empirical development procedure.' *Research on Social Work Practice 22*, 637–646.

Ezell, M., Spath, R., Zeira, A., Canali, C., *et al.* (2011) 'An international classification system for child welfare programs.' *Children and Youth Services Review 33*, 10, 1847–1854.

Farmer, E., Murphy, M. and Wonnum. S. (2013) 'Comparing treatment processes and outcomes between Teaching-Family and Non-Teaching-Family Group Homes.' Paper presented at Teaching-Family Association 36th Annual Conference, Salt Lake City, UT.

Farmer, E.M.Z., Burns, B.J., Chapman, M.V., Phillips, S., Angold, A. and Costello, E. (2001) 'Use of mental health services by youth in contact with social services.' *Social Services Review 75*, 605–624.

Fernández-Ballesteros, R. and Staats, A. (1992) 'Paradigmatic behavioral assessment, treatment and evaluation: answering the crisis in behavioral assessment.' *Advances in Behavior Research and Therapy 14*, 1, 1–28.

Fernandez, E. and Barth, R.P. (eds) (2010) *How Does Foster Care Work? International Evidence on Outcomes.* London: Jessica Kingsley Publishers.

Festinger, T. (1983) *No One Ever Asked Us: A Postscript to Foster Care.* NY: Columbia University Press.

Fixsen, D.L., Phillips, E.L. and Wolf, M.M. (1973) 'Achievement place: experiments in self-government with pre-delinquents.' *Journal of Applied Behavior Analysis 6*, 1, 31–47.

Fixsen, D.L., Blase, K.A., Timbers, G.D. and Wolf, M.M. (2001) 'In Search of Program Implementation: 792 Replications of the Teaching Family Model.' In G.A. Bernfeld, D.P. Farrington and A.W. Leschied (eds) *Wiley Series in Forensic Clinical Psychology. Offender Rehabilitation in Practice: Implementing and Evaluating Effective Programs* (pp.149–166). New York: John Wiley & Sons.

Fixsen, D.L., Blase, K., Timbers, G.D., and Wolf, M.M. (2007) 'In search of program implementation: 792 replications of the Teaching-Family model.' *The Behaviour Analyst Today 8*, 1, 96–104.

Fixsen, D.L., Blase, K.A., Naoom, S.F. and Wallace, F. (2009) 'Core implementation components.' *Research on Social Work Practice 19*, 5, 531–540.

Fixsen, D.L., Naoom, S.F., Blase, K.A., Friedman, R.M. and Wallace, F. (2005) *Implementation Research: A Synthesis of the Literature.* Florida, FL: University of South Florida.

Fixsen, D.L., Phillips, E.L., Baron, R.L., Coughlin, D.D., Daly, D.L. and Daly, P.B. (1978) 'The Boys Town revolution.' *Human Nature 1*, 54–61.

Flum, H. (1995) *Adolescents in Israel: Personal, Familial and Social Aspects* [Hebrew]. Even Yehuda: Reches.

Fonagy, P., Target, M., Cottrel, D., Phillips, J. and Kurtz, Z. (2002) *What Works for Whom? A Critical Review of Treatments for Children and Adolescents.* New York/London: Guilford Press.

Forbes, J. and McCartney, E. (2012) 'Changing Children's Services: A Social Capital Analysis.' In M. Hill, G. Head, A. Lockyer, B. Reid and R. Taylor (eds) *Children's Services: Working Together.* Harlow: Pearson.

Ford, T., Vostanis, P., Meltzer, H. and Goodman, R. (2007) 'Psychiatric disorder among British children looked after by local authorities: a comparison with children living in private households.' *British Journal of Psychiatry 190*, 319–325.

Foreman, D., Morton, S. and Ford, T. (2009) 'Exploring the clinical utility of the Development And Well-Being Assessment (DAWBA) in the detection of hyperkinetic disorders and associated diagnoses in clinical practice.' *The Journal of Child Psychology and Psychiatry 50*, 4, 460–470.

Fowler, P.J., Toro, P.A. and Miles, B.W. (2009) 'Pathways to and from homelessness and associated psychosocial outcomes among adolescents leaving the foster care system.' *American Journal of Public Health 99*, 8, 1453–1458.

Frensch, K.M. and Cameron, G. (2002) 'Treatment of choice or a last resort? A review of residential mental health placements for children and youth.' *Child and Youth Care Forum 31*, 5, 307–339.

Fretz, R. (2007) 'What makes a correctional treatment program effective: do the risk, need and responsivity principles (RNR) make a difference in reducing recidivism?' *Journal of Community Corrections 15*, 3, 5–20.

Friedman, A.S., Terras, A. and Glassman, K. (2002) 'Multimodel substance use intervention program for male delinquents.' *Journal of Child and Adolescent Substance Abuse 11*, 4, 43–65.

Friedman, R.M. (2003) 'A conceptual framework for developing and implementing effective policy in children's mental health.' *Journal of Emotional and Behavioral Disorders 11*, 1, 11–18.

Friman, P.C., Osgood, D.W., Smith, G.L., Shanahan, D., Thompson, R.W., Larzelere, R.E. and Daly, D.L. (1996) 'A longitudinal evaluation of prevalent negative beliefs about residential placement for troubled adolescents.' *Journal of Abnormal Child Psychology 24*, 3, 299–324.

Fulcher, L. and Ainsworth, F. (2006) *Group Care for Children and Young People Revisited.* New York: Routledge.

Garland, A.F., Landsverk, J.A. and Lau, A.S. (2003) 'Racial and ethnic disparities in mental health service use among children in foster care.' *Children and Youth Services Review 25*, 491–507.

Garland, A.F., Kruse, M. and Aarons, G.A. (2003) 'Clinicians and outcome measurement: what's the use?' *Journal of Behavioral Health Services and Research 30*, 4, 393–405.

Garland, A.F., Brookman-Frazee, L., Hurlburt, M.S., Accurso, E.C., *et al.* (2010) 'Mental health care for children with disruptive behavior problems: a view inside therapists' offices.' *Psychiatric Services 61*, 8, 788–795.

Garralda, M., Yates, P. and Higginson, I. (2000) 'Health of the Nation Scales for Children and Adolescents (HoNOSCA) Child and adolescent mental health service use: HoNOSCA as an outcome measure.' *British Journal of Psychiatry 177*, 52–58.

Garrett, C.J. (1985) 'Effects of residential treatment on adjudicated delinquents: a meta-analysis.' *Journal of Research in Crime and Delinquency 22*, 4, 287–308.

Gaudet, S. (2007) *Emerging Adulthood: A New Stage in the Life Course.* Ottawa, ON: Government of Canada. Available at http://dsp-psd.pwgsc.gc.ca/collection_2008/policyresearch/PH4-41-2007E.pdf, accessed on 25 April 2014.

Geurts, E.M.W. (2010) 'Ouders betrekken in de residentiële jeugdzorg: Een onderzoek naar inhoud en uitkomsten van contextgerichte hulpverlening [Involving parents in residential youth care: A study of contents and outcomes of context-focused care].' Doctoral dissertation. Antwerpen/Apeldoorn: Garant.

Geurts, E.M.W., Boddy, J., Noom, M.J. and Knorth, E.J. (2012) 'Family-centred residential care: the new reality?' *Child and Family Social Work 17*, 2, 170–179.

Gharabaghi, K. and Groskleg, R. (2010) 'A social pedagogy approach to residential care: balancing education and placement in the development of an innovative child welfare residential program in Ontario, Canada.' *Child Welfare 89*, 2, 97–114.

Giddens, A. (1991) *Modernity and Self-Identity: Self and Society in the Late Modern Age.* Cambridge: Polity Press.

Gilbert, N. (ed.) (1997) *Combatting Child Abuse: International Perspectives and Trends.* New York: Oxford University Press.

Gilbert, N., Parton, N. and Skivenes, M. (eds) (2011) *Child Protection Systems. International Trends and Orientations.* Oxford: Oxford University Press.

Gilligan, R. (2009) *Promoting Resilience: Supporting Children and Young People who are in Care, Adopted, or in Need.* London: BAAF.

Gilligan, R. (2012) 'Children, Social Networks and Social Support.' In M. Hill, G. Head, A. Lockyer, B. Reid and R. Taylor (eds) *Children's Services: Working Together.* Harlow: Pearson.

Gilman, R. and Handwerk, M.L. (2001) 'Changes in life satisfaction as a function of stay in a residential setting.' *Residential Treatment for Children and Youth 18*, 4, 47–65.

Gilmore, J.H. and Pine, B.J.I. (1997) 'Beyond goods and services.' *Strategy and Leadership 25*, 3, 11–17.

Glisson, C. (2002) 'The organizational context of children's mental health services.' *Clinical Child and Family Psychology Review 5*, 4, 233–253.

Glisson, C. and Hemmelgarn, A. (1998) 'The effects or organizational climate and interorganizational coordination on the quality and outcomes of children's service systems.' *Child Abuse and Neglect 22*, 5, 401–421.

Godley, M.D., Godley, S.H., Dennis, M.L., Funk, R. and Passetti, L.L. (2002) 'Preliminary outcomes from the assertive continuing care experiment for adolescents discharged from residential treatment.' *Journal of Substance Abuse Treatment 23*, 1, 21–32.

Godley, M.D., Godley, S.H., Dennis, M.L., Funk, R.R. and Passetti, L.L. (2006) 'The effect of assertive continuing care on continuing care linkage, adherence and abstinence following residential treatment for adolescents with substance use disorders.' *Addiction 102*, 1, 81–93.

Golan-Cook, P. and Sabag, C. (1992) *Absorption of Adolescent Immigrants from Ethiopia in Youth Villages.* Jerusalem: Hebrew University, School of Education.

Goldstein, A.P., Glick, B. and Gibbs, J. (1986) *Aggression Replacement Training: A Comprehensive Intervention for Aggressive Youth.* Champaign, IL: Research Press.

Goldstein, J., Freud, A. and Solnit, A.J. (1979) *Beyond the Best Interests of the Child.* New York: The Free Press.

Goleman, D. (1998) *Working with Emotional Intelligence.* New York: Bantam.

Gonzalez, R. and Tomlinson, R. (2011) Guidance Manual. Richmond, Australia: Lighthouse Foundation. Available at www.lighthousefoundation.org.au/ou-work/therapeutic-family-model-of-care.

Good Shepherd Youth and Family Service, Jesuit Social Services and MacKillop Family Services (2012) *I Just Want to go to School.* Report and DVD. Collingwood, Richmond and Melbourne: Good Shepherd Youth and Family Service, Jesuit Social Services and MacKillop Family Services. Available at www.mackillop.org.au/Assets/325/1/I_Just_Want_To_Go_To_School_Report_Digital.pdf, accessed on 25 April 2014.

Goodman, R. (1997) 'Strengths and Difficulties Questionnaire (SDQ).' *Journal of Child Psychology and Psychiatry 38*, 5, 581–586.

Goodman, R. (1999) 'Comparing the Strengths and Difficulties Questionnaire and the child behavior checklist: is small beautiful?' *Journal of Abnormal Child Psychology 27*, 1, 17–24.

Goodman, R. (2001) 'Psychometric properties of the Strengths and Difficulties Questionnaire.' *Journal of the American Academy of Child and Adolescent Psychiatry 40*, 11, 1337–1345.

Gottschalk, R., Davidson, W.S., Gensheimer L.K. and Mayer, J.P. (1987) 'Community-Based Interventions.' In C. Quay (ed.) *Handbook of Juvenile Delinquency.* New York: John Wiley & Sons.

Grietens, H. (2002) 'Evaluating the effects of residential treatment for juvenile offenders: a review of meta-analytic studies.' *International Journal of Child and Family Welfare 5*, 129–140.

Grietens, H. (2013) 'Is there a pan-European perspective on evidence-based practice in child welfare? A critical reflection.' *Journal of Children's Services 8*, 161–168.

Grietens, H., Thys, I. and Van den Bosch, H. (2010) 'Can the Group Still be a Therapeutic Milieu for Children in Residential Care?' In E.J. Knorth, M.E. Kalverboer, and J. Knot-Dockscheit (eds) *Inside Out. How Interventions in Child and Family Care Work. An International Source Book.* Antwerp: Garant.

Grunwald, K. and Thiersch, H. (2009) 'The concept of the 'lifeworld orientation' for social work and social care.' *Journal of Social Work Practice 23*, 2, 131–146.

Grupper, E. (2013) 'The youth village: a multicultural approach to residential education and care for immigrant youth in Israel.' *International Journal of Child, Youth and Family Studies 4*, 2, 224–244.

Günder, R. (2011) *Praxis und Methoden der Heimerziehung: Entwicklungen, Veränderungen und Perspektiven der stationären Erziehungshilfe [Practice and Methods of Home Education: developments, Changes and Prospects of Residential Child Care].* Lambertus Verlag.

Hair, H.J. (2005) 'Outcomes for children and adolescents after residential treatment: a review of research from 1993 to 2003.' *Journal of Child and Family Studies 14*, 4, 551–575.

Hämäläinen, J. (2003) 'The concept of social pedagogy in the field of social work.' *Journal of Social Work 33*, 1, 69–80.

Handwerk, M.L., Friman, P.C., Mott, M.A. and Stairs, J.M. (1998) 'The relationship between program restrictiveness and youth behavior problems.' *Journal of Emotional and Behavioral Disorders 6*, 3, 170–179.

Handwerk, M.L., Clopton, K., Huefner, J.C., Smith, G.L., Hoff, K.E., and Lucas, C.P. (2006) 'Gender differences in adolescents in residential treatment.' *American Journal of Orthopsychiatry 76*, 3, 312–324.

Hannon, C., Wood, C. and Bazalgette, L. (2010) *In Loco Parentis.* London: Demos.

Harder, A.T. and Knorth, E.J. (2007) 'Kleine groepen voor grote problemen [Small groups for big problems].' *Jeugd En Co Kennis 1*, 3, 22–29.

Harder, A.T., Kalverboer, M.E. and Knorth, E.J. (2013) Interaction inside the "black box": A systematic review of the association between the therapeutic relationship and outcomes in residential youth care. Manuscript in Preparation.

Harder, A.T., Knorth, E.J. and Kalverboer, M.E. (2011) 'Transition secured? A follow-up study of adolescents who have left secure residential care.' *Children and Youth Services Review 33*, 12.

Harder, A.T., Knorth, E.J. and Kalverboer, M.E. (2014) 'Risky or needy? Dynamic risk factors and delinquent behavior of adolescents in secure residential youth care.' *International Journal of Offender Therapy and Comparative Criminology 58* (in press).

Harder, A.T., Knorth, E.J. and Zandberg, T. (2006) *Residentiële Jeugdzorg in Beeld: Een Overzichtsstudie Naar de Doelgroep, Werkwijzen en Uitkomsten [Residential Youth Care in the Picture: A Review Study of its Target Group, Methods and Outcomes].* Amsterdam: SWP Publishers.

Harder, A.T., Köngeter, S., Zeller, M., Knorth, E.J. and Knot-Dickscheit, J. (2011) 'Instruments for research on transition: applied methods and approaches for exploring the transition of young care leavers to adulthood.' *Children and Youth Services Review 33*, 12, 2431–2441.

Harder, A.T., Huyghen, A.M.N., Knot-Dickscheit, J., *et al.* (2013) 'Education secured? The school performance of adolescents in secure residential youth care.' *Child and Youth Care Forum* (accepted).

Harris, J., Rabiee, P. and Priestley, M. (2002) 'Enabled by the Act? The Reframing of Aftercare Services for Young Disabled.' In A. Wheal (ed) *The RHP Companion to Leaving Care.* Lyme Regis: Russell House Publishing.

Hart, A. (1984) 'Resources for Transitions from Care.' In *Leaving Care – Where?* Conference Report. London: National Association of Young People in Care.

Hawkins-Rodgers, Y. (2007) 'Adolescents adjusting to a group home environment: a residential care model of re-organizing attachment behavior and building resiliency.' *Children and Youth Services Review 29*, 8, 1121–1141.

Heflinger, C.A., Simpkins, C.G. and Combs-Orme, T. (2000) 'Using the CBCL to determine the clinical status of children in state custody.' *Children and Youth Services Review 22*, 55–73.

Heglund, T.J. (1983) *Arbejds og Levemiljøer med Socialpædagogisk Sigte: En Systematisk Oversigt [Working and Living-Environments with a Socio-Pedagogical Agenda: A Systematic Review].* Aalborg: Forlag.

Heglund, T.J. (1988) *Socialt Støttende Bofællesskaber [Social Supportive Communes].* Aalborg: Forlag.

Heglund, T.J. (1994) *Fra de Tusind Blomster til en Målrettet Udvikling [From the Thousand Flowers to a Goaloriented Development].* Aalborg: Forlag.

Hellinckx, W., Broekaert, E., Vanden Berge, A. and Colton, M. (eds.) (1991) *Innovations in Residential Care.* Acco, Leuven: Amersfoort.

Henggeler, S.W., Schoenwald, S.K., Borduin, C.M., Rowland, M.D. and Cunningham, P.B. (2009) *Multisystemic Therapy for Antisocial Behavior in Children and Adolescents* (2nd edition). New York: Guilford Press.

Hestbaek, A.D. (2011) 'Denmark: A Child Welfare System Under Reframing.' In N. Gilbert, N. Parton, and M. Skivenes (eds) *Child Protection Systems: International Trends and Orientations.* Oxford: Oxford University Press.

HMSO (Her Majesty's Stationery Office) *Children Act* (1989) London: HMSO.

Hobbs, N. (1966) 'Helping disturbed children: psychological and ecological strategies.' *American Psychologist 21*, 1105–1115.

Hodges, S., Ferreira, K., Israel, N. and Mazza, J. (2010) 'Systems of care, featherless bipeds, and the measure of all things.' *Evaluation and Program Planning 33*, 4–10.

Hoge, R.D. and Andrews, D.A. (2002) *The Youth Level of Service/Case Management Inventory Manual and Scoring Key.* Toronto: Multi-Health Systems.

Holden, M.J. (2009) *Children and Residential Experiences: Creating Conditions for Change.* Arlington, VA: CWLA.

Holden, M.J., Izzo, C., Nunno, M., Smith, E.G., *et al.* (2010) 'Children and residential experiences: a comprehensive strategy for implementing a research-informed program model for residential care.' *Child Welfare 89*, 2, 131–149.

Hollin, C.R. (2000) *Handbook of Offender Assessment and Treatment.* New York: John Wiley & Sons.

Holmes, L. and McDermid, S. (2012) *Understanding Costs and Outcomes in Child Welfare Services.* London: Jessica Kingsley Publishers.

Holmes, L., McDermid, S. and Sempik, J. (2010) *The Costs of Short Break Provision*. London: Department for Children, Schools and Families.

Holmes, L., Ward, H. and McDermid, S. (2012) 'Calculating and comparing the costs of multi-dimensional treatment foster care in English local authorities.' *Children and Youth Services Review 34*, 11, 2141–2146.

Holmes, L., McDermid, S., Jones, A. and Ward, H. (2009) *How Social Workers Spend their Time: An Analysis of the Key Issues that Impact Upon Practice Pre and Post Implementation of the Integrated Children's System*. London: Department for Children, Schools and Families.

Holmes, L., McDermid, S., Padley, M. and Soper, J. (2012) *Exploration of the Costs and Outcomes of the Common Assessment Framework*. London: Department for Education.

Holmes, L., Landsverk, J., Ward. H., Rolls-Reutz, J., Saldana, L. and Chamberlain, P. (in press) *Workload and Cost Calculator Methods for Estimating Casework Time in Child Welfare Services: A Cross-National Comparison, Children and Youth Services Review*.

Holtan, A., Ronning, J., Handegard, B. and Sourander, A. (2005) 'A comparison of mental health problems in kinship and non kinship foster care.' *European Child and Adolescent Psychiatry 14*, 200–207.

Houchins, D.E., Puckett-Patterson, D., Crosby, S., Shippen, M.E. and Jolivette, K. (2009) 'Barriers and facilitators to providing incarcerated youth with a quality education.' *Preventing School Failure 53*, 3, 159–166.

Huefner, J.C. and Pick, R. (2013) 'Family contact for youth in residential care: distance to family, contact type, and outcomes.' Paper presented at Teaching-Family Association 36th Annual Conference, Salt Lake City, UT.

Huefner, J.C. and Ringle, J.L. (2012) 'Examination of negative peer contagion in a residential care setting.' *Journal of Child and Family Studies 21*, 5, 807–815.

Huefner, J.C., Ringle, J.L., Chmelka, M.B. and Ingram, S.D. (2007) 'Breaking the cycle of intergenerational abuse: the long-term impact of a residential care program.' *Child Abuse and Neglect 31*, 2, 187–199.

Hukkanen, R., Sourander, A., Santalahti, P. and Bergroth, L. (2005) 'Have psychiatric problems of children in children's homes increased?' *Nordic Journal of Psychiatry 59*, 6, 481–485.

Hurley, K.D., Trout, A., Chmelka, M.B., Burns, B.J., *et al.* (2009) 'The changing mental health needs of youth admitted to residential group home care: comparing mental health status at admission in 1995 and 2004.' *Journal of Emotional and Behavioral Disorders 17*, 3, 164–176.

Ingram, S.D., Cash, S.J., Oats, R.G., Simpson, A. and Thompson, R.W. (2013) 'Development of an evidence-informed in-home family services model for families and children at-risk of abuse and neglect.' *Child and Family Social Work* [online].

Izzo, C., Anglin, J. and Holden, M. (2012) *Assessing Organizational Change: Preliminary Findings from a Multi-Method and Multi-Site Evaluation of the Care Program Model*. Paper presented at EUSARF/CELCIS Looking After Children conference, Glasgow: Scotland.

Jackson, S. (1987) *The Education of Children in Care*. Bristol: School of Applied Social Studies, University of Bristol.

Jackson, S. (2002) 'Promoting Stability and Continuity of Care Away from Home.' In D. McNeish, T. Newman and H. Roberts (eds) *What Works For Children?* Buckingham: Open University Press.

Jackson, S., Cameron, C., Hollingworth, K. and Hauri, H. (2011) 'England.' In S. Jackson and C. Cameron (eds) *Final Report of the YiPPEE Project, WP12, Young People From a Public Care Background: Pathways to Further and Higher Education in Five European Countries*. London: Thomas Coram Research Unit, Institute of Education, University of London.

Jakobsen, T.B. (2010) 'What troubled children need: constructions of everyday life in residential care.' *Children and Society 24*, 3, 215–226.

James, S. (2011a) 'What works in group care? A structured review of treatment models for group homes and residential care.' *Children and Youth Services Review 33*, 301–321.

James, S. (2011b) 'Preliminary findings of a survey of California group homes.' Paper presented at Conference of the California Alliance of Child and Family Services, Napa, CA.

James, S., Alemi, Q. and Zepeda, V. (2013) 'Effectiveness and implementation of evidence-based practices in residential care settings.' *Children and Youth Services Review 35*, 4, 642–656.

Johansson, J., Andersson, B. and Hwang, C.P. (2008) 'What difference do different settings in residential care make for young people? A comparison of family-style homes and institutions in Sweden.' *International Journal of Social Welfare 17*, 1, 26–36.

Jones, R., Everson-Hock, E.S., Papaioannou, D. Guillaume, L., *et al.*. (2011) 'Factors associated with outcomes for looked after children and young people; a correlates review of the literature.' *Child: Care, Health and Development 37*, 5, 613–622.

Jonson-Reid, M. and Drake, B. (2008) 'Multi-sector longitudinal administrative databases: an indispensable tool for evidence-based policy for maltreated children and their families.' *Child Maltreatment 13*, 4, 392–399.

Joy Tong, L.S. and Farrington, D. (2006) 'How effective is the "Reasoning and Rehabilitation" programme in reducing reoffending? A meta-analysis of evaluations in four countries.' *Psychology, Crime and Law 12*, 1, 3–24.

Kadushin, A. (1980) *Child Welfare Services* (3rd edition). New York: Macmillan.

Kahn, W.A. (2005) *Holding Fast: The Struggle to Create Resilient Caregiving Organizations.* London: Brunner-Routledge.

Kamphof-Evink, L. and Harder, A.T. (2011) 'Delinquente vrienden: een risico voor jongeren in een jeugdinrichting? [Delinquent peers: a risk for young people in a secure residential care center?].' *Orthopedagogiek: Onderzoek En Praktijk 50*, 318–327.

Karver, M.S., Handelsman, J.B., Fields, S. and Bickman, L. (2005) 'A theoretical model of common process factors in youth and family therapy.' *Mental Health Services Research 7*, 1, 35–51.

Karver, M.S., Handelsman, J.B., Fields, S. and Bickman, L. (2006) 'Meta-analysis of therapeutic relationship variables in youth and family therapy: the evidence for different relationship variables in the child and adolescent treatment outcome literature.' *Clinical Psychology Review 26*, 1, 50–65.

Kashti, Y. (1986) 'Ethos and Social Realities in Israeli Institutions: Introductory Notes.' In Y. Kashti and M. Arieli (eds) *People in Institutions: The Israeli Scene.* London: Freund Publishing House.

Kashti, Y., Shlasky, S. and Arieli, M. (2000) *Communities of Youth: Studies on Israeli Boarding Schools.* Tel Aviv: Ramot.

Kazdin, A.E. (2005) *Parent Management Training: Treatment for Oppositional, Aggressive, and Antisocial Behavior in Children and Adolescents.* New York: Oxford University Press.

Kegan, R. (1994) *In Over Our Heads: The Mental Demands of Modern Life.* Cambridge, MA: Harvard University Press.

Kegan, R. and Lahey, L.L. (2009) *Immunity to Change.* Boston, MA: Harvard Business Press.

Keller, T.E., Cusick, G.R and Courtney, M.E. (2007) 'Approaching the transition to adulthood: profiles of adolescents aging out of the child welfare system.' *Social Service Review 81*, 3, 453–484.

Kendrick, A. (1995) 'The integration of child care services in Scotland.' *Children and Youth Services Review, 17*, 5/6, 619–635.

Kendrick, A. (1998) 'In their best interest? Protecting children from abuse in residential and foster care.' *International Journal of Child and Family Welfare 3*, 2, 169–185.

Kendrick, A. (2008) *Residential Child Care: Prospects and Challenges.* Research Highlights Series. London: Jessica Kingsley Publishers.

Kendrick, A. (2012) 'What Research Tells us About Residential Child Care.' In: M. Davies (ed.) *Social Work with Children and Families.* (pp.287–303). Basingstoke: Palgrave Macmillan.

Kendrick, A. (2013) 'Relations, relationships and relatedness: residential child care and the family metaphor.' *Child and Family Social Work 18*, 77–86.

Kennedy, S. (1999) 'Responsivity: the other classification principle.' *Corrections Today 61*, 1, 48–53.

Kessler, R.C., Pecora, P.I., Williams, J., Hiripi, E., *et al.* (2008) 'Effects of enhanced foster care on the long-term physical and mental health of foster care alumni.' *Archive of General Psychiatry 65*, 6, 625–633.

Kingsley, D.E. (2006) 'The Teaching-Family Model and post-treatment recidivism: a critical review of the conventional wisdom.' *International Journal of Behavioral Consultation and Therapy, 4*, 481–497.

Kingsley, D.E., Ringle, J.L., Thompson, R.W., Chmelka, M.B. and Ingram, S.D. (2008) 'Cox Proportional Hazards Regression Analysis as a modeling technique for informing program improvement: predicting recidivism in a Girls and Boys Town five-year follow-up study.' *The Journal of Behavior Analysis of Offender and Victim Treatment and Prevention 1*, 1, 82–97.

Knorth, E. J. (2003) 'De black box van de residentiële jeugdzorg geopend? [Has the black box of residential child and youth care been opened?].' *Kind En Adolescent 24*, 3, 153–155.

Knorth, E.J., Noom, M.J., Tausendfreund, T. and Kendrick, A.J. (2007b) 'Characteristics and Service Responses to Young People with Serious Antisocial and Oppositional Disorders: Outlines of a Practice-Based Model of Residential Care.' In H. Grietens (ed.) *Promoting Competence in Children and Families: Scientific Perspectives on Resilience and Vulnerability.* Leuven: Leuven University Press.

Knorth, E.J., Harder, A.T., Huyghen, A.M.N., Kalverboer, M.E. and Zandberg, T. (2010) 'Residential youth care and treatment research: care workers as key factor in outcomes?' *International Journal of Child and Family Welfare 13*, 1/2, 49–67.

Knorth, E.J., Harder, A.T., Zandberg, T. and Kendrick, A.J. (2008) 'Under one roof: a review and selective meta-analysis on the outcomes of residential child and youth care.' *Children and Youth Services Review 30*, 2, 123–140.

Ko, S.J., Ford, J.D., Kassam-Adams, N., Berkowitz, S.J., Wilson, C. and Wong, M. (2008) 'Creating trauma-informed systems: child welfare, education, first responders, health care, juvenile justice.' *Professional Psychology: Research and Practice 39*, 396–404.

Koehler, J.A., Lösel, F.A., Akoensi, T.D. and Humphreys, D.K. (2013) 'A systematic review and meta-analysis on the effects of young offender treatment programmes in Europe.' *Journal of Experimental Criminology 9*, 1, 19–43.

Kongeter, S., Schroer, W. and Zeller, M. (2008) 'Germany.' In M. Stein and E. Munro (eds) (2008) *Young People's Transitions from Care to Adulthood: International Research and Practice.* London: Jessica Kingsley Publishers.

Koob, J.J. and Love, S.M. (2010) 'The implementation of solution-focused therapy to increase foster care placement stability.' *Children and Youth Services Review 32*, 10, 1346–1350.

Kornbeck, J. (ed.) (2009) *The Diversity of Social Pedagogy in Europe.* Bremen: Europäischer Hochschulverlag.

Kornerup, H. (ed.) (2009) *Milieu-Therapy with Children.* Ringsted, Denmark: Forlaget Perikon.

Kramer, T.L. and Burns, B.J. (2008) 'Implementing cognitive behavioral therapy in the real world: a case study of two mental health centers.' *Implementation Science 3*, 14,

Kutash, K. and Robbins Rivera, V. (1996) *What Works in Children's Mental Health Services?* Baltimore, MD: Paul H. Brookes Publishing Company.

Landsverk, J., Burns, B.J., Stambaugh, L. and Rolls-Reutz, J. (2006) *Mental Health Care for Children and Adolescents in Foster Care: Review of Research Literature.* Seattle, WA: Casey Family Programs.

Larzelere, R.E., Daly, D.L., Davis, J.L., Chmelka, M.B. and Handwerk, M.L. (2004) 'Outcome evaluation of Girls and Boys Town's Family Home Program.' *Education and Treatment of Children 27*, 130–149.

Latessa, E.J. and Lowenkamp, C.T. (2006) 'What works in reducing recidivism?' *University of St. Thomas Law Journal 3*, 3, 521–535.

Lee, B.R. (2008) 'Defining residential treatment. (Editorial).' *Journal of Child and Family Studies 17*, 5, 689–692.

Lee, B.R. and Barth, R.P. (2011) 'Defining group care programs: an index of reporting standards.' *Child Youth Care Forum 40*, 4, 253–266.

Lee, B.R. and McMillen, J.C (2007) 'Measuring quality in residential treatment for children and youth.' *Residential Treatment for Children and Youth 24*, 1/2, 1–17.

Lee, B.R. and Thompson, R. (2008) 'Comparing outcomes for youth in treatment foster care and family-style group care.' *Children and Youth Services Review 30*, 7, 746–757.

Lee, B.R. and Thompson, R.W. (2009) 'Examining externalizing behavior trajectories of youth in group homes: is there evidence for peer contagion?' *Journal of Abnormal Child Psychology 37*, 1, 31–44.

Lee, B.R., Chmelka, M.B. and Thompson, R. (2010) 'Does what happens in group care stay in group care? The relationship between problem behavior trajectories during care and post-placement functioning.' *Child and Family Social Work 15*, 3, 286–296.

Lee, B.R., Fakunmoju, S., Barth, R.P, and Walters, B. (2010) *Child Welfare Group Care Literature Review.* Baltimore, MD: Annie E. Casey Foundation.

Lee, B.R., Bright, C.L., Svoboda, D.V., Fakunmoju, S. and Barth, R.P. (2011) 'Outcomes of group care for youth: a review of comparative studies.' *Research on Social Work Practice 21*, 2, 177–189.

Lee, B.R., Ebesutani, C., Kolivoski, K.M., Becker, K.D., *et al.* (under review) 'Program and practice elements for placement prevention: a review of interventions and their effectiveness in promoting home-based care.' *American Journal of Orthopsychiatry.*

Leichtman, M. (2006) 'Residential treatment of children and adolescents: past, present, and future.' *The American Journal of Orthopsychiatry 76,* 3, 285–294.

Leichtman, M. (2007) 'The essence of residential treatment: core concepts.' *Residential Treatment for Children and Youth 24,* 3, 175–196.

Leve, L.D., Chamberlain, P. and Reid, J.B. (2005) 'Intervention outcomes for girls referred from juvenile justice: effects on delinquency.' *Journal of Consulting and Clinical Psychology 73,* 6, 1181–1185.

Libby, A.M., Coen, A.S., Price, D.A., Silverman, K. and Orton, H.D. (2005) 'Inside the black box: what constitutes a day in a residential treatment centre?' *International Journal of Social Welfare 14,* 3, 176–183.

Liddle, H. and Rowe, C.L. (2001) *Adolescent Substance Abuse: Research and Clinical Advances.* New York: Cambridge University Press.

Lieberman, A.F. and Knorr, K.K. (2007) 'The impact of trauma: a developmental framework for infancy and early childhood.' *Psychiatric Annals 37,* 6, 416–422.

Lieberman, R.E. (2004) 'Future directions in residential treatment.' *Child and Adolescent Psychiatric Clinics of North America 13,* 4, 279–294.

Lipsey, M.W. (2009) 'The primary factors that characterize effective interventions with juvenile offenders: a meta-analytic overview.' *Victims and Offenders 4,* 2, 124–147.

Lipsey, M.W. and Wilson, D.B. (1998) 'Effective Intervention for Serious Juvenile Offenders: A Synthesis of Research.' In R. Loeber and D.P. Farrington (eds) *Serious and Violent Juvenile Offenders: Risk Factors and Successful Interventions.* Thousand Oaks, CA: Sage.

Lipsey, M.W. and Wilson, D.B. (2001) *Practical Meta-Analysis.* Thousand Oaks, CA: Sage.

Lipsey, M.W., Landenberger, N.A. and Wilson, S.J. (2007) *Effects of Cognitive-Behavioral Programs for Criminal Offenders.* Campbell Collaboration.

Lipsey, M.W., Howell, J.C., Kelly, M.R., Chapman, G. and Carver, D. (2010) *Improving the Effectiveness of Juvenile Justice Programs. A New Perspective on Evidence-Based Practice.* Washington, DC: Center for Juvenile Justice Reform, Georgetown University.

Little, L., Butler, L.S. and Fowler, J. (2010) 'Change from the ground up: bringing informed-dialectical behavioral therapy to residential treatment.' *Residential Treatment for Children and Youth 27,* 2, 80–91.

Little, M., Kohm, A. and Thompson, R. (2005) 'The impact of residential placement on child development: research and policy implications.' *International Journal of Social Welfare 14,* 200–209.

Loeber, R. and Farrington, D.P. (2000) 'Young children who commit crime: epidemiology, developmental origins, risk factors, early interventions, and policy implications.' *Deviant Psychopathology 12,* 4, 737–762.

López, M. and del Valle, J.F. (2013) 'The waiting children: pathways (and future) of children in long-term residential care.' *British Journal of Social Work.* Published online.

Lorenz, W. (1994) *Social Work in a Changing Europe.* London: Routledge.

Louisell, M.J. (2007) *Six Steps to Find a Family: A Practice Guide to Family Search and Engagement (FSE).* New York: National Resource Center for Family Centered Practice and Permanency Planning at the Hunter College School of Social Work. Available at www.nrcpfc.org/downloads/SixSteps.pdf, accessed on 25 April 2014.

Lovelle, C. (2005) 'Dialectical behavioral therapy and EMDR for adolescents in residential treatment: a practical and theoretical perspective.' *Residential Treatment for Children and Youth 23,* 1/2, 27–43.

Lowenkamp, C.T. and Latessa, E.J. (2004) 'Understanding the risk principle: how and why correctional interventions can harm low-risk offenders.' *Topics in Community Corrections,* 3–8.

Lowenkamp, C.T. and Latessa, E.J. (2005) 'Developing successful reentry programs: lessons learned from the "What Works" research.' *Corrections Today 62,* 7, 72–77.

Lowenkamp, C.T. and Latessa, E.J. (2008) 'The Risk Principle in action: what have we learned from 13,676 offenders and 97 correctional programs?' *Crime and Delinquency 52,* 1, 77–93.

Lowenkamp, C.T., Makarios, M.D., Latessa, E.J., Lemke, R. and Smith, P. (2010) 'Community corrections facilities for juvenile offenders in Ohio: an examination of treatment integrity and recidivism.' *Criminal Justice and Behavior 37,* 6, 695–708.

Lyman, R.D. and Campbell, N.R. (1996) *Treating Children and Adolescents in Residential and Inpatient Settings*. London: Sage Publications.

Lyons, J.S. (2004) *Redressing the Emperor: Improving the Children's Public Mental Health System*. Westport, CT: Praeger Publishing.

Lyons, J.S. (2009a) 'Knowledge creation through total clinical outcomes management: a practice-based evidence solution to address some of the challenges of knowledge translation.' *Journal of the Canadian Academy of Child and Adolescent Psychiatry 18*, 1, 39–46.

Lyons, J.S. (2009b) *Communimetrics: A Communication Theory of Measurement in Human Services*. New York: Springer.

Lyons, J.S. and Weiner, D.A. (eds) (2009) *Strategies in Behavioral Healthcare: Total Clinical Outcomes Management*. New York: Civic Research Institute.

Lyons, J.S., Mintzer, L.L., Kisiel, C.L. and Shallcross, H. (1998) 'Understanding the mental health needs of children and adolescents in residential treatment.' *Professional Psychology: Research and Practice 29*, 582–587.

Lyons, J.S., Woltman, H., Martinovich, Z. and Hancock, B. (2009) 'An outcomes perspective of the role of residential treatment in the system of care.' *Residential Treatment for Children and Youth 26*, 2, 71–91.

Lyons, J.S., Terry, P., Martinovich, Z., Peterson, J. and Bouska, B. (2001) 'Outcome trajectories for adolescents in residential treatment: a statewide evaluation.' *Journal of Child and Family Studies 10*, 3, 333–345.

Mabry, R. (2010) 'Current state of residential group care within the child welfare system.' *Child Welfare 89*, 2, 15–20.

Macdonald, G. and Millen, S. (2012) *Therapeutic Approaches to Social Work in Residential Child Care Settings: Literature Review*. London: Social Care Institute for Excellence.

MacGuire, J. (1999) *What Works: Reducing Reoffending. Guidelines from Research and Practice*. Chichester: Wiley.

Maier, H. (1987) *Developmental Group Care of Children and Youth*. New York: Haworth Press.

Maier, H. (1991) 'Developmental Foundations of Youth Care Work.' In J. Beker and Z. Eisikovits (eds) *Knowledge Utilization in Residential Child and Youth Care Practice*. Washington, DC: Child Welfare League of America.

Mainey, A., Milligan, I., Campbell, A., Colton, M., Roberts, S. and Crimmens, D. (2006) 'The Context of Residential Care in the United Kingdom.' In A. Mainey and D. Crimmens (eds) *Fit for the Future: Residential Child Care in the United Kingdom* (pp.6–22). London: National Children's Bureau.

Marsh, P. and Peel, M. (1999) *Leaving Care in Partnership: Family Involvement with Care Leavers*. London: The Stationery Office.

Martín, E., García, M.D. and Siverio, M.A. (2012) 'Inadaptación autopercibida de los menores en acogimiento residencial [Self-perceived unsuitability of juveniles in residential care.' *Anales de Psicología 28*, 2, 541–547.

Martín, E., Rodríguez, T. and Torbay, A. (2007) 'Evaluación diferencial de los programas de acogimiento residencial para menores [Differential evaluation of residential care programmes for minors.' *Psicothema 19*, 3, 406–412.

Martín, E., Torbay, A. and Rodríguez, T. (2008) 'Family cooperation and child's bonding with the family in residential care programmes.' *Anales de Psicología 24*, 1, 25–32.

Martín, E., Muñoz de Bustillo, M.C., Rodríguez, T. and Pérez, Y. (2008) 'From residence to school: social integration of children in residential care with their peer group in the school context.' *Psicothema 20*, 3, 376–382.

Mash, G. (2001) *Characteristics of Youngsters in Youth Villages: Research Report*. Tel Aviv: Ministry of Education.

Mason, W.A., Fleming, C.B., Thompson, R.W., Haggerty, K.P. and Snyder, J.J. (2013). 'A framework for testing and promoting the expanded dissemination of promising preventive interventions that are being implemented in community settings.' *Prevention Science* [online].

Masten, A. (2004) 'Regulatory processes, risk, and resilience in adolescent development.' *Annals of the New York Academy of Sciences 1021*, 310–319.

Maundeni, T. (2009) 'Residential Care for Children in Botswana: The Past, the Present and the Future.' In M.E. Courtney and D. Iwaniec (eds.) *Residential Care of Children: Comparative Perspectives* (pp.88–104). Oxford and New York: Oxford University Press.

Mayseless, O. (2004) 'Home living to military service: attachment concerns, transfer of attachment functions from parents to peers, and adjustment.' *Journal of Adolescent Research 19*, 5, 1–26.

McAuley, C., Pecora, P.J. and Rose, W. (2006) *Enhancing the Well-Being of Children and Families Through Effective Interventions: International Evidence for Practice.* London/Philadelphia, PA: Jessica Kingsley Publishers.

McCrae, J., Lee, B.R., Barth, R.P. and Rauktis, M. (2010) 'Comparing three year well-being outcomes for youth in group care and nonkinship foster care.' *Child Welfare 89*, 2, 229–249.

McCurdy, B.L. and McIntyre, E.K. (2004) '"And what about residential...?" Re-conceptualizing residential treatment as a stop-gap service for youth with emotional and behavioral disorders.' *Behavioral Interventions 19*, 3, 137–158.

McDermott, B.M., McKelvey, R., Roberts, L. and Davies, L. (2002) 'Severity of children's psychopathology and impairment and its relationship to treatment setting.' *Psychiatric Services 53*, 1, 57–62.

McLean, S., Price-Robertson, R. and Robinson, E. (2011) *Therapeutic Residential Care in Australia: Taking Stock and Looking Forward.* Melbourne: Australian Institute of Family Studies, Government of Australia.

McMurran, M. (2009) 'Motivational interviewing with offenders: a systematic review.' *Legal and Criminological Psychology 14*, 1, 83–100.

Mendes, P. (2009) 'Improving outcomes for teenage pregnancy and early parenthood for young people in out-of-home care, a review of the literature.' *Youth Studies Australia 28*, 3, 11–18.

Miller W.R. and Rollnick S. (1991) *Motivational Interviewing: Preparing People to Change Addictive Behavior.* New York: Guilford Press.

Millett, L.S., Kohl, P.L., Jonson-Reid, M., Drake, B. and Petra, M. (2013) 'Child maltreatment victimization and subsequent perpetration of young adult Intimate partner violence: an exploration of mediating factors.' *Child Maltreatment 18*, 2, 71–84..

Miranda, J., Bernal, G., Lau, A., Kohn, L., Hwang, W. and LaFromboise, T. (2005) 'State of the science on psychosocial interventions for ethnic minorities.' *Annual Review of Clinical Psychology 1*, 113–142.

Mohr, W.K., Martin, A., Olson, J.N., Pumariega, A.J. and Branca, N. (2009) 'Beyond point and level systems: moving toward child-centered programming.' *American Journal of Orthopsychiatry 79*, 1, 8–18.

Monahan, K.C., Goldweber, A. and Cauffman, E. (2011) 'The effects of visitation on incarcerated juvenile offenders: how contact with the outside impacts adjustment on the inside.' *Law and Human Behavior 35*, 2, 143–151.

Morantz, G. and Heymann, J. (2010) 'Life in institutional care: the voices of children in a residential facility in Botswana.' *AIDS Care 22*, 1, 10–16.

Morehouse, E. and Tobler, N.S. (2000) 'Preventing and reducing substance use among institutionalized adolescents.' *Adolescence 35*, 137, 1–28.

Morgan, R. and Lindsay, M. (2012) Y*oung People's Views on Care and Aftercare.* London: Office of the Children's Rights Director, Ofsted.

Morral, A.R., McCaffrey, D.F. and Ridgeway, G. (2004) 'Effectiveness of community-based treatment for substance-abusing adolescents 12-month outcomes of youth entering Phoenix Academy of alternative probation dispositions.' *Psychology of Addictive Behaviors 18*, 3, 257–268.

Munro, E.R., McDermid, S., Hollingworth, K. and Cameron, C. (2013) *Children's Homes: Understanding the Market and the Use of Out of Authority Placements.* London: Childhood Wellbeing Research Centre.

Munro, E.R., Lushey, C., National Care Advisory Service, Maskell-Graham, D. and Ward, H. and Holmes, L. (2012) *Evaluation of the Staying Put: 18+ Family Placement Programme Pilot: Final Report.* London: Department for Education.

Muthen, B. (2006) 'The potential of growth mixture modeling.' *Infant and Child Development 15*, 6, 623–625.

Nagin, D.S. (2005) *Group-Based Modeling of Development.* Cambridge, MA: Harvard University Press.

National Council for the Child (2012) *The State of the Child in Israel.* Jerusalem.

National Framework for Protecting Australia's Children (2009) *Protecting Children is Everyone's Business.* Canberra: Department of Social Services.

National Registry of Evidence-Based Programs and Practices (NREPP) (n.d.). Retrieved from: www.nrepp.gov.

National Social Appeals Board (2012) *Statistics on Out-of-home Care. Annual Statistics 2012.* Copenhagen: National Social Appeals Board.

NCAS (National Care Advisory Service) (2011) *FromCare2Work, Monitoring Summary, April-September 2011.* London: NCAS.

New Freedom Commission (2003). The President's New Freedom Commission on Mental Health: Tranforming revison. The Carter Center. Retrieved from: www.cartercenter.org/documents/1701.pdf.

Nicholas, B., Roberts, S. and Wurr, S. (2003) 'Looked after children in residential homes.' *Child and Adolescent Mental Health 8,* 78–83.

Noonan, K. and Menashi, D. (2010) *Rightsizing Congregate Care: A Powerful First Step in Transforming Child Welfare Systems.* Baltimore, MD: Annie E. Casey Foundation.

Nugent, W.R., Bruley, C. and Allen, P. (1998) 'The effects of aggression replacement training on antisocial behavior in a runaway shelter.' *Research on Social Work Practice 8,* 6, 637–656.

O'Neill C., Forbes C., Tregeagle S., Cox E. and Humphreys C. (2009) *The Cost of Support in Foster Care and Other Long Term Placements.* Sydney: Barnardo's.

Obrochta, C., Anthony, B., Kallal, J., Hust, J. and Kernan, J. (2011) *Issue Brief: Family-to-Family Peer Support: Models and Evaluation.* Atlanta, GA: ICF Macro Outcomes Roundtable for Children and Families.

Ogden, T. and Hagen, K.A. (2006) 'Multi-systemic therapy of serious behaviour problems in youth: sustainability of therapy effectiveness two years after intake.' *Journal of Child and Adolescent Mental Health 11,* 3, 142–149.

Osgood, D.W. and Smith, G.L. (1995) 'Applying hierarchical linear modeling to extended longitudinal evaluations: the Boys Town follow-up study.' *Evaluation Review 19,* 1, 3–38.

Palareti, L. and Berti, C. (2009a) 'Different ecological perspectives for evaluating residential care outcomes: which window for the black box?' *Children and Youth Services Review 31,* 10, 1080–1085.

Palareti, L. and Berti, C. (2009b) 'Relational climate and effectiveness of residential care: adolescent perspectives.' *Journal of Prevention and Intervention in the Community 38,* 1, 26–40.

Papell, C.P. and Skolnik, L. (1992) 'The reflective practitioner: a contemporary paradigm's relevance for social work education.' *Journal of Social Work Education 26,* 18–26.

Pardini, D. and Frick, P.J. (2013) 'Multiple developmental pathways to conduct disorder: current conceptualizations and clinical implications.' *Journal of Canadia Academian Child Adolescent Psychiatry 22,* 1, 1–23.

Parker, R.A. (1966) *Decisions in Child Care.* London: George Allen & Unwin.

Parliament of Victoria, Australia (2013) *Betrayal of Trust: Inquiry into Handling of Abuse in Religious and Other Non-government Institutions.* Final Report. 13 November. Family and Community Development Committee. Volume One available at www.parliament.vic.gov.au/images/stories/committees/fcdc/inquiries/57th/Child_Abuse_Inquiry/Report/Inquiry_into_Handling_of_Abuse_Volume_1_FINAL_web.pdf. Volume Two available at www.parliament.vic.gov.au/images/stories/committees/fcdc/inquiries/57th/Child_Abuse_Inquiry/Report/Inquiry_into_Handling_of_Abuse_Volume_2_FINAL_web.pdf, both accessed 24 June 2014.

Patterson, G.R. (1982) *Coercive Family Process.* Eugene, OR: Castalia Publishing Company.

Patterson, G.R., Reid, J.B. and Dishion, T.J. (1992) *A Social Learning Approach: IV. Antisocial Boys.* Eugene, OR: Castalia Publishing Company.

Pecora, P.J., Jensen, P.S., Hunter Romanelli, L.H., Jackson, L.J. and Ortiz, A. (2009a) 'Mental health services for children placed in foster care: an overview of current challenges.' *Child Welfare 88,* Jan/Feb, 1–25.

Pecora, P.J., Whittaker, J.K., Maluccio, A.N., Barth, R.P. and DePanfilis, D. (2009b) *The Child Welfare Challenge: Policy, Practice, and Research* (3rd edition). New Brunswick, NJ: Transaction Publishers.

Pecora, P.J., Williams, J., Kessler, R.J., O'Brien, K. and Emerson, J. (2006b) 'Assessing the educational achievements of adults who formerly were placed in family foster care.' *Child and Family Social Work 11*, 3, 220–231.

Pecora, P.J., Williams, J., Kessler, R.C., Downs, A.C., O'Brien, K., Hiripi, E. and Morello, S. (2003) *Assessing the Effects of Foster Care: Early Results from the Casey National Alumni Study.* Seattle, WA: Casey Family Programs.

Pecora, P.J., Williams, J., Kessler, R.C., Dowens, C.A., O'Brien, K., Hirpi, E., English, D., White, J. and Herrick, M. (2006a) 'Educational and employment outcomes of adults formerly placed in foster care: results from the Northwest Foster Care Alumni Study.' *Children and Youth Services Review 28*, 12, 1459–1481.

Perry, B. (2006) 'The Neurosequential Model of Therapeutics: Applying Principles of Neuroscience to Clinical Work with Traumatized and Maltreated Children.' In N. Boyd Webb (ed.) *Working with Traumatized Youth in Child Welfare.* New York: Guilford Press.

Perry, B. (2008) 'Child Maltreatment: The Role of Abuse and Neglect in Developmental Psychopathology.' In T.P. Beauchaine and S.P. Hinshaw (eds) *Textbook of Child and Adolescent Psychopathology.* New York: Wiley.

Perry, B.D. (2009) 'Examining child maltreatment through a neurodevelopmental lens: clinical applications of the neurosequential model of therapeutics.' *Journal of Trauma and Loss 14*, 4, 240–255.

Perry, B.D. and Pollard, R. (1998) 'Homeostasis, stress, trauma, and adaptation: a neurodevelopmental view of childhood trauma.' *Child and Adolescent Psychiatric Clinics of North America 7*, 11, 33–51.

Petrie, P., Boddy, J., Cameron, C., Simon, A. and Wigfall, V. (2006) *Working with Children in Europe.* Buckingham: Open University Press.

Petrie, P., Boddy, J., Cameron, C., Heptinstall, E., McQuail, S., Simon, A. and Wigfall, V. (2009) *Pedagogy: A Holistic, Personal Approach to Work with Children and Young People, Across Services. European Models for Practice, Training, Education and Qualification.* Briefing Paper. London: Thomas Coram Research Unit.

Phelan, J. (2003) 'The relationship boundaries that control programming.' *Relational Child and Youth Care Practice 16*, 1, 51–55.

Phelan, J. (2008) 'Building Developmental Capacities: A Developmentally Responsive Approach to Child and Youth Care Intervention.' In G. Bellefeuille and F. Ricks (eds) *Standing on the Precipice: Inquiry into the Creative Potential of Child and Youth Care Practice.* Edmonton, Canada: MacEwan Press.

Phillips, E.L. (1968) 'Achievement place: token reinforcement procedures in a home-style rehabilitation setting for "pre-delinquent" boys.' *Journal of Applied Behavior Analysis 1*, 3, 213–223.

Phillips, E.L., Phillips, E.A., Fixsen, D.L., and Wolf, M.M. (1971) 'Achievement place: modification of the behaviors of pre-delinquent boys within a token economy.' *Journal of Applied Behavior Analysis 4*, 1, 45–59.

Phillips, E.L., Phillips, E.A., Fixsen, D.L. and Wolf, M.M. (1973) 'Achievement place: behavior shaping works for delinquents.' *Psychology Today 7*, 75–79.

Phillips, E.L., Phillips, E.A., Fixsen, D.I. and Wolf, M.M. (1974) *The Teaching Family Handbook* (2nd edition). Lawrence, KS: University Press of Kansas.

Poulin, F., Dishion, T.J. and Burraston, B. (2001) '3 year iatrogenic effects associated with aggregating high-risk adolescents in cognitive-behavioral preventive interventions.' *Applied Developmental Science 5*, 4, 214–224.

Proctor, E.K., Knudsen, K.J., Fedioravicius, N., Hormand, P., Rosen, A., and Peeron, B. (2007) 'Implementation of evidence-based practice in community, behavioural health: Agency director perspectives.' *Administration and Policy in Mental Health Services Research, 34*, 479–488.

Priestley, M., Rabiee, P. and Harris, J. (2003) 'Young disabled people and the "new arrangements" for leaving care in England and Wales.' *Children and Youth Services Review 25*, 11, 863–890.

Pughe, B. and Philpot, T. (2007) *Living Alongside a Child's Recovery: Theraputic Parenting with Traumatised Children.* London: Jessica Kingsley Publishers.

Purdy, F. (2010) *The Core Competencies of Parent Support Providers.* Rockville, MD: National Federation of Families for Children's Mental Health.

Raider, M.C., Steele, W., Delillo-Storey, M., Jacobs, J. and Kuban, C. (2008) 'Structured sensory therapy (SITCAP-ART) for traumatized adjudicated adolescents in residential treatment.' *Residential Treatment for Children and Youth 25*, 2, 167–185.

Rapoport, T. and Lomsky-Feder, E. (2002) '"Intelligentsia" as an ethnic habitus: the inculcation and restructuring of intelligentsia among Russian Jews.' *British Journal of Sociology of Education 23*, 2, 233–248.

Rapoport, T., Rimor, M. and Mano, C. (1980) *Youth Villages: The Educational Activities Among Youth in Distress.* Jerusalem: The Szold Institute.

Reilly, T. (2003) 'Transition from care: status and outcomes of youth who age out of are.' *Child Welfare 82*, 6, 727–746.

Ringel, S., Ronell, N. and Getahune, S. (2005) 'Factors in the integration process of adolescent immigrant: the case of Ethiopian Jews in Israel.' *International Social Work 48*, 1, 63–76.

Ringle, J.L., Ingram, S.D. and Thompson, R.W. (2010) 'The association between length of stay in residential care and educational achievement: results from 5- and 16-year follow-up studies.' *Children and Youth Services Review 32*, 7, 974–980.

Ringle, J.L., Huefner, J.C., James, S., Pick, R. and Thompson, R.W. (2012) '12-month follow-up outcomes for youth departing an integrated residential continuum of care.' *Children and Youth Services Review 34*, 4, 675–679.

Rivard, J.C., Bloom, S.L., McCorkle, D. and Abramowitz, R. (2005) 'Preliminary results of a study examining the implementation and effects of a trauma recovery framework for youths in residential treatment.' *Therapeutic Community 26*, 1, 83–96.

Rivard, J.C., McCorkle, D., Duncan, M.E., Pasquale, L.E., Bloom, S.L. and Abramovitz, R. (2004) 'Implementing a trauma recovery framework for youths in residential treatment.' *Child and Adolescent Social Work Journal 21*, 5, 529–550.

Rosen, A. and Proctor, E. (2002) 'Standards for evidence-based social work practice.' In A.R. Roberts and G.J. Greene (eds.) *Social Workers' Desk Reference* (pp.743–747). New York: Oxford University Press.

Rutter, M. (1999) 'Resilience concepts and findings: implications for family therapy.' *Journal of Family Therapy 21*, 2, 119–144.

Rutter, M., Giller, H. and Hagell, A. (1998) *Antisocial Behaviour by Young People.* Cambridge: Cambridge University Press.

Ryan, J.P., Marshall, J.M., Herz, D. and Hernandez, P.M. (2008) 'Juvenile delinquency in child welfare: investigating group home effects.' *Children and Youth Services Review 30*, 9, 1088–1099.

Rycroft-Malone, J., Seers, K., Titchen, A., Harvey, G., Kitson, A. and McCormack, B. (2004) 'What counts as evidence in evidence-based practice?' *Journal of Advanced Nursing 47*, 1, 81–90.

Sackett, D.L., Richardson, W.S., Rosenberg, W. and Haynes, R.B. (1997) *Evidence-Based Medicine: How to Practice and Teach EBM.* New York: Churchill Livingstone.

Sainero, A., Bravo, A. and del Valle, J.F. (2014) 'Examining needs and referrals to mental health services for children in residential care in Spain: an empirical study in an autonomous community.' *Journal of Emotional and Behavioral Disorders 22*, 1, 16–26.

Sainero, A., del Valle, J. F., López, M. and Bravo, A. (2013) 'Exploring the specific needs of an understudied group: children with intellectual disability in residential child care.' *Children and Youth Services Review 35*, 9, 1393–1399.

SAMSHA (Substance Abuse and Mental Health Services Administration) (2006) *Building Bridges Between Residential and Community Based Service Delivery Providers, Families and Youth.* Position statement. Washington, DC: Center for Mental Health Services, available at www.samsha.gov.

Scharff, D. and Scharff, J. (1991) 'Using countertransference in family therapy.' *The Family Therapy Networker Sept–Oct*, 73–78.

Scherrer, J.L. (1994) *A Meta-Analysis of the Effectiveness of Residential Treatment Programs for Children and Adolescents (Doctoral Dissertation).* Chicago, IL: University of Illinois.

Schiff, M., Nebe, S. and Gilman, R. (2011) 'The contribution of individual, social support and institutional characteristics to perceived readiness to leave care in Israel: An ecological perspective.' *British Journal of Social Work 41*, 8, 1442–1458.

Schoenwald, S.K., Mehta, T.G., Frazier, S.L. and Shernoff, E.S. (2013) 'Clinical supervision in effectiveness and implementation research.' *Clinical Psychology: Science and Practice 20*, 44–59.

Schofield, G., Ward, E., Biggart, L., Scaife, V. *et al.* (2012) *Looked After Children and Offending, Reducing Risk and Promoting Resilience.* Norwich: Centre for Research on the Child and Family, UEA and TACT.

Scholte, E.M. and Van der Ploeg, J.D. (2000) 'Exploring factors governing successful residential treatment of youngsters with serious behavioural difficulties: findings from a longitudinal study in Holland.' *Childhood 7*, 2, 129–153.

Schon, D. (1983) *The Reflective Practitioner: How Professionals Think in Action.* New York: Basic Books.

Schon, D. (1987) *Educating the Reflective Practitioner: Toward a New Design for Teaching and Learning in the Professions.* San Francisco, CA: Jossey-Bass.

Scotland Excel (2013) *Development of National Framework for Children's Residential Care Services: Consultation Responses.* Paisley: Scotland Excel. Available at www.scotland-excel.org.uk/web/FILES/ConsultationFeedback.pdf, accessed on 15 April 2014.

Seginer, R. (1988) 'Adolescent facing the future: cultural and sociopolitical perspective.' *Youth and Society 19*, 3, 314–333.

Sempik, J., Ward, H. and Darker, I. (2008) 'Emotional and behavioural difficulties of children and young people at entry into care.' *Clinical Child Psychology and Psychiatry, 13*, 221–233.

SEU (Social Exclusion Unit) (2003) *A Better Education for Children in Care.* London: The Stationery Office.

Shaffer, A., Egeland, B. and Wang, K. (2010) 'Risk and Resilience Among Children Referred to Protective Services: A Longitudinal Investigation of Child Well-Being in Multiple Domains.' In M.B. Webb, K. Dowd, B.J. Harden, J. Landsverk and M. Testa (eds) *Child Welfare and Child Well-Being: New Perspectives from the National Survey of Child and Adolescent Well-Being.* Oxford: Oxford University Press.

Shafran, R., Clark, D.M., Fairburn, C.G., Arntz, A., Barlow, D.H. *et al.* (2009) 'Mind the gap: improving the dissemination of CBT.' *Behavior Research and Therapy 47*, 11, 902–909.

Sherwin, E. (2011) *A Global Perspective of Foster Care, Its Development and Contemporary Practice.* Vienna: SOS Children's Villages International.

Shirk, S.R. and Karver, M. (2003) 'Prediction of treatment outcome from relationship variables in child and adolescent therapy: a meta-analytic review.' *Journal of Consulting and Clinical Psychology 71*, 3, 452–464.

Simon, A. (2008) 'Early access and use of housing: care leavers and other young people in difficulty.' *Child and Family Social Work 13*, 1, 91–100.

Sinclair, I. (2006) 'Residential Care in the UK.' In C. McAuley, P.J. Pecora and W. Rose (eds) *Enhancing the Well-Being of Children and Families through Effective Interventions: International Evidence for Practice* (pp.203–216). London: Jessica Kingsley Publishers.

Sinclair, I. (2010) 'Inside the Black Box: What Makes for Success in care?' In E.J. Knorth, M.E. Kalverboer and J. Knot-Dickscheit (eds) *Inside Out. How Interventions in Child and Family Care Work: An International Source Book.* Antwerp: Garant Publishers.

Sinclair, I. and Gibbs, I. (1998) *Children's Homes: A Study in Diversity.* Chichester: John Wiley & Sons.

Sinclair, I., Baker, C., Lee, J. and Gibbs, I. (2007) *The Pursuit of Permanence: A Study of the English Care System.* London: Jessica Kingsley Publishers.

Sinclair, I., Baker, C., Wilson, K. and Gibbs, I. (2005) *Foster Children, Where They Go and How They Get On.* London: Jessica Kingsley Publishers.

Slesnick, N. and Prestopnik, J.L. (2009) 'Comparison of family therapy outcome with alcohol-abusing, runaway adolescents.' *Journal of Marital and Family Therapy 35*, 3, 255–277.

Sloper, P., Beecham, J., Clarke, S., Franklin, A., Moran, N. and Cusworth, L. (2011) *Transition to Adult Services for Disabled Young People and Those with Complex Health Needs.* Research Works, 2011-02. York: Social Policy Research Unit, University of York.

Smith, B.W. (2011) *Youth Leaving Foster Care: A Developmental Relationship-Based Approach to Practice.* Oxford: Oxford University Press.

Smith, M. (2009) *Rethinking Residential Child Care. Positive Perspectives.* Bristol: Policy Press.

Smith, M. (2011) 'Victim narratives of historical abuse in residential child care.' *Qualitative Social Work* 9, 3, 303–320.

Soberman, G.B., Greenwald, R. and Rule, D.L. (2002) 'A controlled study of eye movement desensitization and reprocessing (EMDR) for boys with conduct problems.' *Journal of Aggression, Maltreatment and Trauma 6*, 1, 217–236.

SOS-Kinderdorf International (2007) *Quality4Children Standards for Out-Of-Home Child Care in Europe: An Initiative by FICE, IFCO and SOS Children's Villages.* Innsbruck: SOS-Kinderdorf International.

Sowers, K.M. (2009) 'Foreword.' In R.A. Ellis (ed.) *Best Practices in Residential Treatment.* New York: Routledge.

Sparks, J.A. and Muro, M.L. (2009) 'Client-directed wraparound: the client as connector in community collaboration.' *Journal of Systemic Therapies 28*, 3, 63–76.

Spinazzola, J., Ford, J.D., Zucker, M., Kolk, B.a.V., *et al.* (2005) 'Complex trauma exposure, outcome, and intervention among children and adolescents.' *Psychiatric Annals 35*, 5, 433–440.

Stals, K., Van Yperen, T.A., Reith, W.J.M. and Stams, G.J.J.M. (2008) *Effectieve en Duurzame Implementatie in de Jeugdzorg. Een Literatuurrapportage Over Belemmerende en Bevorderende Factoren op Implementatie van Interventies in de Jeugdzorg [Effective and Enduring Implementation in Youth Care. A Literature Report of Obstructing and Promoting Factors of Implementation of Interventions in Youth Care].* Utrecht: Utrecht University.

Stockholm Declaration on Children and Residential Care (2003) Available at www.crin.org/docs/stockholm_declaration_pdf_english.pdf.

Steiker, L.H. (2005) 'Cultural considerations for residential treatment of children and/or adolescents.' *Residential Treatment for Children and Youth 23*, 1/2, 61–74.

Stein, M. (2008) 'Resilience and young people leaving care.' *Child Care in Practice 14*, 1, 35–44.

Stein, M. (2011) *Care Less Lives: the Story of the Rights Movement of Young People in Care.* London: Catch-22.

Stein, M. (2012) *Young People Leaving Care: Supporting Pathways to Adulthood.* London: Jessica Kingsley Publishers.

Stein, M. and Verweijen-Slamnescu, R. (2012) *When Care Ends, Lessons from Peer Research, Insights from Young People on Leaving Care in Albania, the Czech Republic, Finland and Poland.* Innsbruck: SOS Children's Villages International.

Stein, M. and Carey, K. (1986) *Leaving Care.* Oxford: Blackwell.

Stein, M. and Dumaret, A-C. (2011) 'The mental health of young people aging out of care and entering adulthood: exploring the evidence from England and France.' *Children and Youth Services Review 33*, 12, 2504–2511.

Stein, M. and Morris, M. (2010) *Increasing the Numbers of Care Leavers in 'Settled, Safe' Accommodation. Vulnerable Children Knowledge Review 3.* London: C4EO.

Stein, M. and Munro, E.R. (eds) (2008) *Young People's Transitions from Care to Adulthood: International Research and Practice.* London: Jessica Kingsley Publishers.

Stein, M., Ward, H. and Courtney, M. (2011) 'Editorial: International perspectives on young people's transitions from care to adulthood.' *Children and Youth Services Review 33*, 12, 2409–2411.

Stephens, P. (2009) 'The nature of social pedagogy: an excursion in Norwegian territory.' *Child and Family Social Work 14*, 3, 343–351.

Stephens, P. (2013) *Social Pedagogy: Heart and Head.* Bremen: Europaïscher Hochschulverlag GmbH and Co.

Sternberg, N., Thompson, R., Smith, G., Klee, S., *et al.* (2013) 'Outcomes in children's residential treatment centers: a national survey 2010.' *Residential Treatment for Children and Youth 30*, 2, 93–118.

Stewart, K.L. and Bramson, T. (2000) 'Incorporating EMDR in residential treatment.' *Residential Treatment for Children and Youth 17*, 4, 83–90.

Stone, S.I. and Rose, R.A. (2011) 'Social work research and endogeneity bias.' *Journal of the Society for Social Work and Research 2*, 54–75.

Stout, B. (2009) 'Residential Care in South Africa: Changing the Perspective from Social Welfare to Social Development.' In M.E. Courtney and D. Iwaniec (eds) *Residential Care of Children: Comparative Perspectives* (pp.105–119). Oxford and New York: Oxford University Press.

Stroul, B.A. and Friedman, R.M. (1986) *A System of Care for Seriously Emotionally Disturbed Children and Youth.* Washington, DC: CASSP Technical Assistance Center, Georgetown University Child Development Center.

Sullivan, M., Faircloth, D., Mcnair, J., Southern, D., *et al.* (2011) *Evaluation of the Therapeutic Residential Care Pilot Programs: Final Summary and Technical Report.* Clifton Hill, Victoria, Australia: Department of Human Services.

Sunseri, P.A. (2004) 'Preliminary outcomes on the use of dialectical behavior therapy to reduce hospitalization among adolescents in residential care.' *Residential Treatment for Children and Youth 21*, 4, 59–76.

Tarren-Sweeney, M. (2010) 'Concordance of mental health impairment and service utilization among children in care.' *Clinical Child Psychology and Psychiatry 15*, 481–495.

Tarren-Sweeney, M. and Hazell, P. (2006) 'Mental health of children in foster and kinship care in New South Wales, Australia.' *Journal of Paediatrics and Child Health 42*, 89–97.

Tarren-Sweeney, M. and Vetere, A. (eds) (2013) *Mental Health Services for Vulnerable Children and Young People: Supporting Children Who Are, or Have Been, in Foster Care.* London: Routledge.

Teather, E.C. (2001) 'A peek into the trenches: changes and challenges in residential care.' *Residential Treatment for Children and Youth 19*, 1, 1–20.

The Grove Street Adolescent Residence (2004) 'Using dialectical behavior therapy to help troubled adolescents return safely to their families and communities.' *Psychiatric Services 55*, 10, 1168–1170.

Thoburn, J. (2010) 'Achieving safety, stability and belonging for children in out-of-home care. The search for "what works" across national boundaries.' *International Journal of Child and Family Welfare 12*, 1–2, 34–48.

Thompson, R.W., Ringle, J.L., Way, M., Peterson, J. and Huefner, J.C. (2010) 'Aftercare for a cognitive-behavioral program for juvenile offenders: a pilot investigation.' *The Journal of Behavior Analysis of Offender and Victim Treatment and Prevention 2*, 198–213.

Thompson, R.W., Smith, G.L., Osgood, D.W., Dowd, T.P., Friman, P.C. and Daly, D.L. (1996) 'Residential care: a study of short- and long-term educational effects.' *Children and Youth Services Review 18*, 3, 221–242.

Thomson, L., McArthur, M., Long, R. and Camilleri, P. (2005) *What Works in Residential Care.* Watson, Australia: Institute of Child Protection Studies.

Tilbury, C. and Thoburn, J. (2009) 'Using racial disproportionality and disparity: indicators to measure child welfare concerns.' *Children and Youth Services Review 31*, 10, 1101–1106.

Tompkins-Rosenblatt, P. and VanderVen, K. (2005) 'Perspectives on point and level systems in residential care: a responsive dialogue.' *Residential Treatment for Children and Youth 22*, 3, 1–18.

Trieschman, A.E., Whittaker, J.K. and Brendtro, L.K. (1969) *The Other 23 hours: Child-Care Work with Emotionally Disturbed Children in a Therapeutic Milieu.* Chicago, IL: Aldine.

Trout, A.L., Tyler, P.M., Stewart, M.C. and Epstein, M.H. (2012) 'On the Way Home: program description and preliminary findings.' *Children and Youth Services Review 34*, 6, 1115–1120.

Trout, A.L., Casey, K., Chmelka, M.B., DeSalvo, C., Reid, R. and Epstein, M.H. (2009) 'Overlooked: children with disabilities in residential care.' *Child Welfare 88*, 2, 111–136.

Trout, A.L., Lambert, M., Epstein, M., Tyler, P., *et al.* (2013) 'Comparison of On the Way Home aftercare supports to usual care following discharge from a residential setting: an exploratory pilot randomized controlled trial.' *Child Welfare 92*, 27–45.

Trupin, E.J., Kerns, S.E.U., Walker, S.C., DeRobertis, M.T. and Stewart, D.G. (2011) 'Family integrated transitions: a promising program for juvenile offenders with co-occurring disorders.' *Journal of Child and Adolescent Substance Abuse 20*, 5, 421–436.

US Department of Health and Human Services (2013) *The AFCARS Report.* Washington, DC: US Department of Health and Human Services, Administration for Children and Families. Available at www.acf.hhs.gov/sites/default/files/cb/afcarsreport20.pdf, accessed on 25 April 2014.

Underwood, L.A., Barretti, L., Storms, T.L. and Safonte-Strumolo, N. (2004) 'A review of clinical characteristics and residential treatments for adolescent delinquents with mental health disorders.' *Trauma, Violence, and Abuse 5*, 3, 199–242.

UNICEF Regional Office for CEC/CIS (Central and Eastern Europe/Commonwealth of Independent States) (2007) *Romani Children in South East Europe: The Challenge of Overcoming Centuries of Distrust and Discrimination.* Discussion Paper 7. Geneva:

UNICEF Regional Office for CEC/CIS (2012) *TransMonEE Database* [online]. Available at www. transmonee.org, accessed on 25 April 2014.

United Nations (1989) *Convention of the Rights of the Child.* New York: United Nations.

United Nations Children's Fund Central and Eastern Europe Commonwealth of Independent states. Available at www.romachildren.com/wp-content/uploads/2011/08/Romani-Children-in-SEE. Overcoming-Centuries-of-Distrust.pdf.

United States General Accounting Office (1994) *Residential Care: Some High-Risk Youth Benefit, But More Study Needed.* Gaithursburg, MD: Government Accounting Office.

Unrau, Y.A., Font, S.A. and Rawls, G. (2012) 'Readiness for college engagement among students who have aged out of foster care.' *Children and Youth Services Review 34,* 1, 76–83.

Van Dam, C., Nijhof, K., Scholte, R. and Veerman, J.W. (2010) *Evaluatie Nieuw Zorgaanbod: Gesloten Jeugdzorg voor Jongeren met Ernstige Gedragsproblemen [Evaluation New Care Supply: Secure Youth Care for Young People with Serious Behavioral Problems].* Nijmegen: Praktikon/Radboud University Nijmegen.

Van der Helm, P., Klapwijk, M., Stams, G. and Van der Laan, P. (2009) '"What Works" for juvenile prisoners: the role of group climate in a youth prison.' *Journal of Children's Services 4,* 2, 36–48.

Van der Kolk, B., Roth, S., Pelcovitz, D., Sunday, S. and Spinazzola, J. (2005) 'Disorders of extreme stress: the empirical foundation of a complex adaptation to trauma.' *Journal of Traumatic Stress 18,* 5, 389–399.

Van der Ploeg, J.D. and Scholte, E.M. (2003) *Effecten van Behandelingsprogramma's voor Jeugdigen met Ernstige Gedragsproblemen in Residentiële Settings: Eindrapport [Outcomes of Treatment Programs for Youth with Serious Behavioral Problems in Residential Settings: Final Report].* Amsterdam: NIPPO (Nederlands Instituut voor Pedagogisch en Psychologisch Onderzoek).

Van Erve, N., Poiesz, M. and Veerman, J.W. (2005) 'Bejegening van cliënten in de jeugdzorg. een onderzoek naar relevante aspecten [Treatment of clients in youth care. a study of relevant aspects].' *Kind En Adolescent 26,* 2, 227–238.

Van Yperen, T.A., Van der Steege, M., Addink, A. and Boendermaker, L. (2010) *Algemeen en Specifiek Werkzame Factoren in de Jeugdzorg: Stand Van de Discussie [Common and Specific Therapeutic Factors in Youth Care: The State of Affairs].* Utrecht: Netherlands Youth Institute.

Vaughn, M.G., Shook, J.J. and McMillen, J.C. (2008) 'Aging out of foster care and legal involvement: toward a typology of risk.' *Social Service Review 82,* 419–449.

Veerman, J.W. and Van Yperen, T.A. (2007) 'Degrees of freedom and degrees of certainty: a developmental model for the establishment of evidence-based youth care.' *Evaluation and Program Planning 30,* 212–221.

Verso Consulting (2011) *Therapeutic Residential Care Evaluation.* Melbourne: Verso Consulting.

Victorian State Government (2005) *Child Wellbeing and Safety Act.* Melbourne: Victorian State Government.

Victorian State Government (2007/2013) *Best Interests Framework for Vulnerable Children and Youth.* Melbourne: Victorian State Government. Available at www.dhs.vic.gov.au/__data/assets/ pdf_file/0010/586081/ecec_best_interest_framework_proof.pdf, accessed on 25 April 2014.

Victorian State Government (2013) *Victoria's Vulnerable Children: Our Shared Responsibility Strategy 2013–2022.* Melbourne: Victorian State Government.

Vorrath, H. and Brendtro, L. (1985) *Positive Peer Culture* (2nd edition). New York: Aldine.

Vygotsky, L. (1978). *Mind and Society: The Development of Higher Mental Processes.* Cambridge, MA: Harvard University Press.

Wade, J. (2008) 'The ties that bind: support from birth families and substitute families for young people leaving care.' *British Journal of Social Work 38,* 1, 39–54.

Wade, J. (2011) 'Preparation and transition planning for unaccompanied asylum-seeking and refugee young people: a review of evidence in England.' *Children and Youth Services Review 33,* 12, 2424–2430.

Wade, J. and Dixon, J. (2006) 'Making a home, finding a job: investigating early housing and employment outcomes for young people leaving care.' *Child and Family Social Work 11,* 3, 199–208.

Walter, U.M. and Petr, C.G. (2008) 'Family-centered residential treatment: knowledge, research, and values converge.' *Residential Treatment for Children and Youth 25*, 1, 1–16.

Ward, H. (2011) 'Continuities and discontinuities; issues concerning the establishment of a persistent sense of self amongst care leavers.' *Children and Youth Services Review 33*, 12, 2512–2518.

Ward, H., Holmes, L. and Soper, J. (2008) *Costs and Consequences of Placing Children in Care.* London: Jessica Kingsley Publishers.

Ward, H., Skuse, T. and Munro, E.R. (2005) 'The best of times, the worst of times: young people's views of care and accommodation.' *Adoption and Fostering 29*, 1, 8–17.

Wasser, T., Tyler, R., McIlhaney, K., Taplin, R. and Henderson, L. (2008) 'Effectiveness of dialectical behavior therapy (DBT) versus standard therapeutic milieu (STM) in a cohort of adolescents receiving residential treatment.' *Best Practice in Mental Health 4*, 2, 114–125.

Weems, C.F. (2011) 'Guidelines for empirical papers on group care programs.' *Child and Youth Care Forum 40*, 4, 251–252.

Weersing, V.R., Weisz, J.R. and Donenberg, G.R. (2002) 'Development of the therapy procedures checklist: a therapist-report measure of technique use in child and adolescent treatment.' *Journal of Clinical Child Psychology 31*, 168–180

Weiss, B., Caron, A., Ball, S., Tapp, J., Johnson, M. and Weisz, J.R. (2005) 'Iatrogenic effects of group treatment for antisocial youth.' *Journal of Consulting and Clinical Psychology 73*, 6, 1036–1044.

Weisz, J.R., Chorpita, B.F., Palinkas, L.A., Schoenwald, S.K., *et al.* (2012) 'Testing standard and modular designs for psychotherapy treating depression, anxiety, and conduct problems in youth.' *Archives of General Psychiatry 69*, 3, 274–282.

White, C.R., O'Brien, K., White, J., Pecora, P.J. and Phillips, C.M. (2007) 'Alcohol and drug use among alumni of foster care: decreasing dependency through improvement of foster care experiences.' *Journal of Behavioral Health Services and Research 35*, 4, 419–434.

Whitehead, J.T. and Lab, S.P. (1989) 'A meta-analysis of juvenile correctional treatment.' *Journal of Research in Crime and Delinquency 26*, 3, 276–295.

Whittaker, J.K. (2000) 'Reinventing residential childcare: an agenda for research and practice.' *Residential Treatment for Children and Youth 17*, 1, 13–30.

Whittaker, J.K. (2004) 'The re-invention of residential treatment: an agenda for research and practice.' *Child and Adolescent Psychiatric Clinics of North America 13*, 2, 267–278.

Whittaker, J.K. (2005) 'Creating "Prosthetic Environments" for Vulnerable Children: Emergent Cross-National Challenges for Traditional Child and Family Services Practice.' In H. Grietens, W. Hellinckx and L. Vandemeulebroecke (eds) *In the Best Interests of Children and Youth: International Perspectives.* Leuven: Leuven University Press.

Whittaker, J.K. (2006) 'Residential Care in the US' In C. McAuley, P.J. Pecora and W. Rose (eds) *Enhancing the Well-Being of Children and Families Through Effective Interventions: International Evidence for Practice* (pp.217–228). London: Jessica Kingsley Publishers.

Whittaker, J.K. (2008) 'Children: Group Care'. In T. Mizrahi and L. Davis. *Encyclopedia of Social Work* (20th edition). New York and Oxford: NASW Press and Oxford University Press.

Whittaker, J.K. (2011) 'Residential treatment services: Is it time for a critical review?' *Sounding Board* [online]. Available at http://deewilson.wordpress.com/about, accessed on 25 April 2014.

Whittaker, J.K. (2012) 'What Works in Residential Treatment: Strengthening Family Connections in Residential Treatment to Create an Empirically Based Family Support Resource.' In A.P Curtis and G. Alexander (eds) (2012) *What Works in Child Welfare* (2nd edition). Washington DC: CWLA.

Whittaker, J.K. (2013) 'Children: Therapeutic Group Care.' In National Association of Social Workers, *Encyclopedia of Social Work* [online]. New York: Oxford University Press.

Whittaker, J.K. and Maluccio, A.N. (2002) 'Re-thinking "child placement": a reflective essay.' *Social Service Review 76*, 108–134.

Whittaker, J.K. and Pfeiffer, S. (1994) 'Research priorities for residential group child care.' *Child Welfare 73*, 583–601.

Whittaker, J.K., Greene, K., Schubert, D., Blum, R., *et al.* (2006) 'Integrating evidence-based practice in the child mental health agency: A template for clinical and organizational change.' *American Journal of Orthopsychiatry 76*, 2, 194–201.

Williamson, E. and Gray, A. (2011) 'New roles for families in child welfare: strategies for expanding family involvement beyond the case level.' *Children and Youth Services Review 33*, 7, 1212–1216.

Willner, A.G., Braukmann, C.J., Kirigin, K.A., Fixsen, D.L., Phillips, E.L. and Wolf, M.M. (1977) 'The training and validation of youth-preferred social behaviors of child-care personnel.' *Journal of Applied Behavior Analysis 10*, 2, 219–230.

Winter, K. (2006) 'Widening our knowledge concerning young looked after children: the case for research using sociological models of childhood.' *Child and Family Social Work 11*, 55–64.

Wolfe, M.M., Braukmann, C.J. and Ramp, K.A. (1987) 'Serious delinquent behavior as part of a significantly handicapping condition: cures and supportive environments.' *Journal of Applied Behavior Analysis 20*, 4, 347–359.

Wolins, M. and Piliavin, I. (1964) *Institution or Foster Family: A Century of Debate.* New York: Child Welfare League of America.

Zeira, A. (2004) 'New initiatives in out-of-home placements in Israel.' *Child and Family Social Work 9*, 305–307.

Zeira, A. (2009) 'Alumni of educational residential setting in Israel: a cultural perspective.' *Children and Youth Services Review 31*, 10, 1074–1079.

Zeira, A., Benbenishty, R. and Refaeli, T. (2012) *Transition to Adulthood of Vulnerable Youth in Israel: Needs, Social Services and Policy.* Jerusalem: The Hebrew University, Paul Baerwald School of Social Work and Social Welfare.

Zeira, A., Artzev, S., Benbenishty, R. and Portnoy, H. (in press) 'Children in educational residential care: a cohort study of Israeli youth'. *Australian Social Work.*

Zelechoski, A.D., Sharma, R., Beserra, K., Miguel, J., DeMarco, M. and Spinazzola, J. (2013) 'Traumatized youth in residential treatment settings: prevalence, clinical presentation, treatment, and policy implications.' *Journal of Family Violence 28*, 7, 639–652.

Zetlin, A., Weinberg, L. and Kimm, C. (2004) 'Improving education outcomes for children in foster care: intervention by an education liaison.' *Journal of Education for Students Placed at Risk 9*, 4, 421–429.

Zito, J.M., Safer, D.J., Devadatta, S., Gardner, J.F., *et al.* (2008) 'Psychotropic medication patterns among youth in foster care.' *Pediatrics 121*, 1, 157–163.

Subject Index

Author Index